The Wars We Took to Vietnam

The Wars We Took to Vietnam

Cultural Conflict and Storytelling

Milton J. Bates

UNIVERSITY OF CALIFORNIA PRESS

Berkeley · *Los Angeles* · *London*

University of California Press
Berkeley and Los Angeles, California

University of California Press, Ltd.
London, England

Part of chapter 3 of the present work appeared in
somewhat different form in *Mosaic* 27.1 (1994)
and is reprinted with permission. © by the University of Manitoba. Part of chapter 4 appeared in
somewhat different form in *America Rediscovered:
Critical Essays on Literature and Film of the Vietnam War* (1990), ed. Owen W. Gilman, Jr., and
Lorrie Smith, and is reprinted with permission. ©
by Garland Publishing, Inc.

Library of Congress Cataloging-in-Publication Data

Bates, Milton J.
    The wars we took to Vietnam : cultural con-
flict and storytelling / Milton J. Bates.
       p.   cm.
    Includes bibliographic references and index.
    ISBN 0-520-20432-8 (alk. paper).—
    ISBN 0-520-20433-6 (pbk. : alk. paper)
    1. American literature—20th century—
History and criticism.   2. Vietnamese conflict,
1961-1975—Literature and the conflict.   3. Vietnamese conflict, 1961-1975—Motion pictures
and the conflict.   4. Literature and society—
United States—History—20th century.   5. War
stories, American—History and criticism.   6. War
poetry, American—History and criticism.   I. Title.
  PS228.V5B38   1996
  810.9'358—dc 20   95-46772

Printed in the United States of America
9　8　7　6　5　4　3　2　1

for Jeremy and Elizabeth

Contents

Acknowledgments

Anyone who undertakes a full-scale study of Vietnam War literature and film needs all the help he can get. I have been particularly fortunate in the assistance I have received, whether it took the form of research support, information, constructive criticism, or encouragement. To begin with the first of these: fellowships from the John Simon Guggenheim Memorial Foundation and the American Council of Learned Societies provided periods of sustained research and writing, and summer stipends from the National Endowment for the Humanities and Marquette University kept the project on track between fellowships.

Information came from a variety of sources. John Newman and his assistants Rebecca L. Atkinson and Alice Spaulding helped me to make the most of the materials in the Vietnam War Literature Collection at Colorado State University in Fort Collins, Colorado. Thomas Holberg and Charles B. Elston alerted me to resources in the Marquette University Library, and Marquette's Interlibrary Loan Department performed its customary miracles in the pursuit of rare items. Lieutenant Colonel James G. Cole and Master Sergeant Robert A. Shelton, both of the Department of the Army, and Colonel Joseph A. Schlatter, of the Defense Intelligence Agency, graciously responded to my requests for information about American prisoners of war, deserters, and defectors. Susan Anderson and Li Zhu conducted bibliographic searches that saved me many hours of labor. Countless friends and colleagues shared their insights into the war literature and film or directed me to books and films that I would otherwise have missed. A short list of these includes Gayle Baldwin, Alan Ball, Alan Filreis, John Hellmann, C. J. Hribal, the late James Jablonowski, Glen Jeansonne, Thomas L. Jeffers, David Krause, Glen MacLeod, Phillip C. Naylor, John N. Serio, Carol Sklenicka, and James E. Swearingen.

For helpful criticism that went well beyond the call of duty I am grateful to Thomas L. Jeffers and Tim William Machan, who read and commented on the entire manuscript, and to Karen J. Ford and John Hellmann, who read parts of it. Aliki Barnstone, Philip D. Beidler, Evelyn J. Hinz, Michael Tomasek Manson, and Carol J. Singley suggested significant improvements while evaluating all or part of the study for publication. Carolyn Hill edited the manuscript meticulously, and Doris Kretschmer and Erika Büky guided it through the intricacies of book production. I could not have asked for more exacting yet sympathetic first readers.

The longer it takes to write a book—longer, in this case, than it took to fight the war in Vietnam—the more one counts on the encouragement of those who believe in its value. Some of these are named above; others whose moral support has meant a great deal to me are A. Walton Litz, Helen Vendler, and Alex Zwerdling. Finally, I am grateful to my family for the daily adjustments and allowances that have added up, over the years, to a heroic contribution. For them and for all of my benefactors, I hope that the end justifies the means.

Introduction

Wars and Rumors of Wars

And ye shall hear of wars and rumors of wars: see that ye be
not troubled: for these things must come to pass, but the
end is not yet. For nation shall rise against nation, and kingdom against kingdom: and there shall be famines, and pesti-
lences, and earthquakes, in divers places.

Matthew 24:6–7

In the gospel verses that serve as my epigraph, Jesus specifies the signs
by which the faithful will recognize the next-to-last chapter of human
history, the one immediately preceding "the end." His words anticipate
what I have to say about the function of endings and "the end" in war
stories. Here I simply want to draw attention to the inclusion of war—
not to mention rumors or stories of war—in a catalog of natural disas-
ters. Except for the earthquakes, the list is highly formulaic. War in its
metonymic form, "the sword," is repeatedly linked with famine and
pestilence in the prophecies of Jeremiah and Ezekiel. Inasmuch as all of
these phenomena are supposedly authorized by God and cause large-
scale human suffering, there is a grim logic in their association. What
Jesus' words obscure, however, is a fundamental difference between
war and the other catastrophes. As the military historian John Keegan
has observed, war is a human construction, a cultural artifact.[1] It does
not merely happen to us. We make war in much the same way that we
make policy, make cities, make works of art, make love, and make believe.

As a product of human culture, war varies markedly from nation to
nation and era to era. Its cultural specificity is most obvious, perhaps,
in the rituals and clothing by which we set warriors apart from society
and the weapons we place in their hands. But cultural values also inform the less palpable aspects of making war: why we go to war and

against whom, those we choose to do the fighting, what kinds of battlefield behavior we reward, how we determine whether we have won or lost. Such values even affect what we might take to be the irreducible essence of war, people killing people. The Plains Indian demonstrated his courage by touching the enemy with his coup stick without injuring him, whereas today's bomber pilot may kill hundreds of people without ever seeing them. History affords countless examples of military forces that were more intent on following traditional tactics than on engaging the enemy effectively. What James William Gibson has said of the Vietnam War, that the United States fought a "perfect" war on its own terms but took insufficient account of its opponent's strategy, is true to some extent of the combatants in every war.[2]

If war is a culturally specific invention, then the rumor of war, as a narrative reconstruction of constructed events, is doubly imbued with the assumptions, values, and purposes of human culture. In some cases the war story endorses the values of the dominant ideology; in other cases it calls them into question. Thus the war story, like war itself, is politics by other means. As Keegan has shown, Clausewitz's famous definition of war is itself culturally determined.[3] In one of its variations it nevertheless provides a good working definition of the war story. If the art of war can be called "a policy which fights battles instead of writing [diplomatic] notes," then the war story might be characterized, in its literary form, as a policy that writes notes instead of fighting battles.[4]

Yet there is one major difference between the war waged in diplomatic notes and the war waged in war stories. Notes are exchanged between parties officially at war with one another—between, let us say, the French and the Prussians in Clausewitz's day. In contrast, war stories are usually exchanged among people who belong, officially at least, to the same party. Long after the battlefield hostilities have concluded in an armistice or a surrender, storytellers revisit the scene of conflict to establish what happened, speculate what might have happened if things had gone differently, and assess the consequences and lessons of the war for themselves, the social groups with which they identify, and perhaps humankind in general. Some of these stories carry a staggering freight of historical documentation, footnotes, maps, and statistical tables. Others are told casually by one veteran to another over a beer at the American Legion post. Whatever the form of the war story or its narrative content, it is politics—often domestic or intracultural politics—by other means.

This insight informs much of the criticism of Vietnam War literature and film. Two studies published in 1982 seem, in retrospect, to have set the critical agenda for the books and articles published since. Philip D. Beidler's *American Literature and the Experience of Vietnam* argues that the war literature is very much in the American grain, even when—in fact, especially when—it seems most experimental. According to Beidler, "it seems almost as if our classic inheritance of native expression has prophesied much of what we now know of Vietnam."[5] Walter H. Capps's *The Unfinished War: Vietnam and the American Conscience*, though it glances only briefly at the war literature, is equally concerned to locate Vietnam in the context of American mythology. Whereas Beidler represents our war stories as shaped by the prewar tradition, Capps represents the war experience chiefly as an active shaper of postwar politics. "Virtually everything that has happened in the United States since the end of the Vietnam War," Capps maintains, "can be seen as both reaction and response to the war."[6] He gives particular attention to the rise of the religious right and the Moral Majority in the 1970s and the Reagan administration's search for a "good Vietnam" throughout the 1980s, in places like El Salvador, Grenada, and Nicaragua.

The criticism published since 1982 has tended to follow either Beidler's lead or Capps's—or to steer a course between the two. Tobey C. Herzog's *Vietnam War Stories: Innocence Lost* (1992), for example, resembles *American Literature and the Experience of Vietnam* in its approach but adds to the American tradition several classic works from other traditions, such as Wilfred Owen's poems and Remarque's *All Quiet on the Western Front*. Capps's approach has proven more attractive, to judge by the sheer number of books on the "unfinished war." Thomas Myers's *Walking Point: American Narratives of Vietnam* (1988) and Philip H. Melling's *Vietnam in American Literature* (1990) embellish Capps's narrative of conservative revisionism, and Andrew Martin's *Receptions of War: Vietnam in American Culture* (1993) updates it through the Persian Gulf War. Their studies show how popular culture, particularly film, endorsed President Reagan's attempt to make Vietnam a "noble cause" while the more thoughtful responses to the war—literary works, as a rule—resisted the conservative drift of popular myth.

Though the second group of critics is more overtly political than Beidler and Herzog, they generally subscribe to the Platonic-Aristotelian notion of politics as the science of government. So understood,

politics is the province of those individuals, groups, and institutions
that make or try to shape public policy—namely, the president, Congress, political parties, lobbyists, political action committees, big business, and the religious right. What we call American culture is presumed to reflect the attitudes and opinions of these groups, so that any
product of American culture can be assigned a place on the axis of
right- and left-wing politics. Paradoxically, those who look at the war
literature and film in this way, constantly discriminating between
hawks and doves, differ little in their mode of thought from the Cold
Warriors whom they hold responsible for the Vietnam War.

One of the simplest and most effective critiques of Cold War thinking comes from Le Ly Hayslip, whose memoir *When Heaven and Earth
Changed Places* (1989) was among the first books written in English to
represent the war from the Vietnamese point of view. Addressing American readers in the prologue, she writes,

> Most of you did not know, or fully understand, the different wars my people
> were fighting when you got here. For you, it was a simple thing: democracy
> against communism. For us, that was not our fight at all. How could it be?
> We knew little of democracy and even less about communism. For most of
> us it was a fight for independence—like the American Revolution. Many of
> us also fought for religious ideals, the way the Buddhists fought the Catho-
> lics. Behind the religious war came the battle between city people and coun-
> try people—the rich against the poor—a war fought by those who wanted
> to change Vietnam and those who wanted to leave it as it had been for a
> thousand years. Beneath all that, too, we had vendettas: between native Vi-
> etnamese and immigrants (mostly Chinese and Khmer) who had fought for
> centuries over the land. Many of these wars go on today. How could you
> hope to end them by fighting a battle so different from our own?[7]

Hayslip reminds us that what we called the Vietnam War was, from her
compatriots' point of view, a collection of domestic wars that divided
people according to ethnic group, class, religion, and sense of national
destiny. America failed to identify and therefore to engage the enemy
because it viewed Vietnam in politically simplistic terms, as merely another theater in the global war between democracy and communism.

Today's historians and cultural critics repeat this mistake when they
attempt what Michel Foucault calls "total history." Total history reduces the phenomena of an era to a "system of homogeneous relations"
organized around a single cause or principle.[8] So conceived, history is a
single plane in which modes of knowing relate laterally to a presumed

center. As an alternative to this model, Foucault recommends that we think of history (and therefore of culture) as stratified planes in which the layers—science, literature, politics, and so forth—overlap and irrupt into one another but remain autonomous. Foucault's new or "general" history is thus a kind of "archaeology" that studies the vertical relations among discontinuous and decentered forms of knowledge. In the passage just quoted, Hayslip in effect calls for a general history, a history with vertical as well as horizontal axes, to do justice to the array of conflicts that divided her people.

In the scheme of general history, politics must be construed more broadly to include not just government and public policy but what happens whenever someone becomes conscious of another person and understands how that person's needs and desires may shape or be shaped by one's own. As the president of a Washington, D.C., school board wittily put it, politics begins "when you have two people in a room . . . or when you have one person looking in a mirror."[9] Political relationships are influenced by the same factors that color all social interaction: physical and mental endowments, age, sex, kinship, race, ethnicity, religion, and social class. When a conflict of needs or desires escalates into a war between countries, that war is politics by other means. But a nation's politics, too, is politics by other means—the politics of "two people in a room" regularized in documents and procedures.

What Hayslip says about her Vietnam War also applies to ours. It was not one war but many, and some of these were remarkably familiar despite the exotic backdrop against which they were fought. "A nation's domestic problems," one veteran remarked, "travel overseas in its soldiers' rucksacks."[10] In this study I sort through the jumbled contents of those rucksacks. I attempt a general history of five of the wars we took to Vietnam and a general criticism of the stories we brought back. In order of treatment, these cultural conflicts include the war between those who subscribed to different visions of American territorial expansion, the war between black and white Americans, the war between the lower classes and the upper, the war between men and women, and the war between the younger generation and the older.

Some of these conflicts have come under sustained scrutiny elsewhere, though not in combination. John Hellmann's *American Myth and the Legacy of Vietnam* (1986) is an exemplary study of what I call in chapter one the frontier war. Readers familiar with Hellmann's work will recognize my indebtedness even as I try to break new ground. Christian G. Appy's *Working-Class War: American Combat Soldiers and Vietnam* (1993) is a historical rather than a critical study, but it draws on some of the same sources that I use in chapter three to illuminate the class war. Though I take issue with Susan Jeffords's *Remasculinization of America: Gender and the Vietnam War* (1989) in chapter four, her book is an important contribution to our understanding of the sex war and therefore to the archaeology of our knowledge.

My understanding of the politics of war stories informs my treatment of their poetics, that is, their formal arrangements and rhetorical strategies. Since mine is a "general" rather than a "total" criticism, I do not impose a single critical method on all cases. Depending on how a given book or film is constructed and addressed to an audience, I use insights drawn from disciplines such as anthropology, philosophy, psychology, and sociology as well as literary criticism. Since my borrowing is usually limited to a single insight, I make no attempt to rehearse the complete theory to which it belongs. Wherever possible, I translate the technical vocabulary into familiar language. I hope that in the process I have neither misrepresented the theories nor oversimplified them beyond the requirements of my argument.

My approach in each of the first five chapters is much the same. I begin by identifying the conflict to be addressed, then draw on history and the social sciences to describe it more or less empirically. Next I turn to war stories in which the conflict figures prominently in order to find out what kinds of meaning the storytellers ascribe to the conflict— to discover, in short, how they transform fact into something they regard as truth. What the stories mean cannot be separated from how they mean, so I consider their poetics along with their politics. I reserve a more systematic discussion of the war story as a genre for the final chapter, which addresses the issues of authority, mimetic form, rhetorical context, and—above all—purpose. This is by no means a comprehensive treatment of the war story, which would entail a survey of the genre in many languages and historical periods. But chapter six suggests how formal and ideological criticism, so often at odds with one another, can work effectively in tandem.

In choosing to focus on the wars we took to Vietnam, I realize that I have omitted not only the Vietnamese experience of the war but also most American attempts to reconstruct the Vietnamese experience. Thus I risk reinforcing the cultural narcissism that many critics have deplored in American representations of the war, a failure regretted by some of the storytellers themselves.[11] If, as Gibson has argued, we Americans lost the war because we failed to recognize and adapt to the otherness of the enemy, then we are in danger of losing it a second time by losing its lessons, unless we try to see the war as others—particularly the people of Vietnam, Laos, and Cambodia—saw it.

Though fully in sympathy with this criticism, I must respect my own limits as an archaeologist of culture. Others are better equipped to excavate the Vietnamese wars in Southeast Asia. The books and films coming out of Vietnam and the Vietnamese diaspora seem, as I read or view them, to echo Hayslip's gentle reproach: "Most of you did not know, or fully understand, the different wars my people were fighting when you got here." I did not know then, nor do I fully understand now. Yet the wars mentioned by Hayslip have obvious parallels in America's cultural conflicts of the 1960s and 1970s. Perhaps as we come to understand our own Vietnam wars better, we will also begin to understand the "different wars" fought by the people of Vietnam.

CHAPTER I

The Frontier War

I

In William Eastlake's *The Bamboo Bed* (1969), an early novel about the Vietnam War, Clancy, the protagonist, is severely wounded in an ambush. When he tries to recall the events leading up to the ambush, he is initially unable to distinguish it from an engagement that took place in Montana nearly a century earlier. "All I remember," he muses, "is that I was with Custer's Seventh Cavalry riding toward the Little Big Horn and we were struck by the Indians. After we crossed the Rosebud we made it to Ridge Red Boy and then we were hit. No. I must have my wars confused. That was another time, another place. Other Indians."[1] Clancy's confusion was epidemic during the Vietnam War, to judge from contemporary accounts. But unlike Clancy, many survivors of the war have been unable to shrug off their fugue state. Trauma, which often induces amnesia, seems in the case of Vietnam to have induced the compulsive recollection of America's frontier experience.

There are many reasons we might choose to revisit the American frontier in our war stories. The physical characteristics of Vietnam and its people obviously influenced the choice of historical analogy. A respected military historian maintains that "given the physical realities of Vietnam, the war there would have been much more understandable if Vietnam had been compared not to the United States in the 20th century but to America as it existed in the 1750s during the French and Indian Wars," when most settlers lived along the coast and relied on western outposts to protect them from attack.[2] Parts of western Vietnam, notably the jungle-covered slopes of the Annamese Cordillera, are still true wilderness, inhabited by tigers and tribes that the lowland Vietnamese consider primitive. American military units fought the jungle, and the enemy it protected, with the Rome plow (so named for the city in Georgia where it was manufactured) and chemical defoliants, latter-day equivalents of the pioneer's ax and torch.

It was not only the jungle that inspired fear and provoked devastation. As Roderick Nash points out in his classic study of the wilderness in American cultural history, "wilderness" is more a mythic than a scientific term. It has been used to describe any terrain, even part of a large city, that arouses feelings of bewilderment and dread.[3] Thus the terrain in which many military operations were conducted, a rural landscape of villages, hamlets, and intricately ordered paddies, was sufficiently unfamiliar to American soldiers to seem like wilderness, especially to those from the city. Their life in the field confirmed the impression of an actively hostile environment, with its daily trial by oppressive heat, monsoon rains, leeches, mosquitoes, malaria, and fungus infections.

In Vietnam American soldiers fought an enemy whose straight black hair signaled a racial connection to the American Indian.[4] As on the American frontier, they had to distinguish between friendly and unfriendly Indians. Since both looked the same, and since the friendlies became increasingly hostile under the burden of an occupying army, many soldiers thought it safest to regard all Vietnamese—as many settlers thought it safest to regard all Indians—as the enemy.

It is not surprising, then, that the war's linguistic currency seems often to have been minted in the seventeenth, eighteenth, and nineteenth centuries. Military operations were named "Daniel Boone," "Cochise," and "Crazy Horse." Viet Cong (VC) defectors serving with American infantry units were called Kit Carson scouts.[5] Covert teams of Americans and local mercenaries operating in Cambodia were known as Daniel Boone squads. Territory controlled by the enemy was called "Indian country." Going on patrol was "playing cowboys and Indians," and inevitably the only good gook was a dead gook.

We return to the frontier in our Vietnam war stories for another reason, one having to do with narrative structure rather than physical resemblance. As Paul Ricoeur observes, only when time is organized into narrative does it become meaningful. Narrative functions in a manner analogous to metaphor, drawing discordant elements into unity, a "discordant concordance."[6] Tellers of war stories are especially conscious of the discordance of their subject matter, its resistance to shaping and sense making. During World War I, soldiers in the trenches felt dislocated in space and time; as a result they later found it difficult to record their experiences in sequential order.[7] Similarly, Philip Caputo complains in the prologue to *A Rumor of War* that the nature of the fighting in Vietnam—long spells of tedium interrupted by random episodes of violence—made his work as a writer more difficult.[8]

Concordance, and therefore meaning, is achieved mainly through plot, the fiction at the heart of all narratives, whether they are ostensibly fiction or nonfiction.[9] Plot determines where a story begins and ends. Those who tell stories about the Vietnam War find it particularly difficult to locate a beginning. The protagonist of Susan Fromberg Schaeffer's novel *Buffalo Afternoon* suggests whimsically that "it began with the explosion that started the solar system."[10] Michael Herr agrees that the conventional methods of historiography cannot establish a definitive beginning of the war. In *Dispatches* he therefore uses the myth of the American frontier as one way to plot his story, starting with the New England Puritans of the seventeenth century and the American Indian removals of the nineteenth century:

> You couldn't find two people who agreed about when it began, how could you say when it began going off? Mission intellectuals like 1954 as the reference date; if you saw as far back as War II and the Japanese occupation you were practically a historical visionary. "Realists" said that it began for us in 1961, and the common run of Mission flack insisted on 1965, post–Tonkin Resolution, as though all the killing that had gone before wasn't really war. Anyway, you couldn't use standard methods to date the doom; might as well say that Vietnam was where the Trail of Tears was headed all along, the turnaround point where it would touch and come back to form a containing perimeter; might just as well lay it on the proto-Gringos who found the New England woods too raw and empty for their peace and filled them up with their own imported devils.[11]

Where Herr's story would end is even harder to specify, since in this brief passage he invokes three distinct versions of the frontier plot. The first is linear: the story begun by the Puritans leads inevitably to Vietnam as its terminus. The second is cyclical: the Trail of Tears passes through Georgia and Oklahoma to Vietnam, then loops back to postwar America, whence it will presumably lead to other "turnaround points." Herr implies a third kind of plot when he calls the loop a "containing perimeter." This is a peculiar metaphor, inasmuch as a military perimeter is established not to "contain" but to defend against invasion. On a perimeter one's attention is usually directed outward rather than inward. During the Vietnam era, however, a series of traumatic external events turned our thoughts inward and backward. For that reason the frontier plot of embattled, static containment, of circled wagons and Indian captivities, is also an appropriate narrative device.

In this chapter I consider these plots in sequence, beginning with the linear structure and proceeding to the cyclic and finally the contained or perimetric. I conclude by assessing how well these fictional and mythic structures have served us as we try to make sense of our historical experience.

II

Perry Miller observed four decades ago that the English Protestants who settled in New England "established Puritanism—for better or worse—as one of the continuous factors in American life and thought." Consequently, he said, there can be no understanding of America without an understanding of Puritanism.[12] By Puritanism Miller meant a coherent intellectual system, the "New England Mind" he had anatomized in two weighty volumes. Two decades later Sacvan Bercovitch ventured a more sweeping claim for the role of New England Puritanism in American culture. "The myth of America," he maintained in *The Puritan Origins of the American Self,* "is the creation of the New England Way."[13]

These are large claims for a small colony, by no means the only one in North America, located far from the centers of seventeenth-century civilization. Yet they become plausible if one adds to the Puritans' contemporary influence the preeminence conferred on them by student textbooks and a distinguished tradition of historical scholarship, a status only recently challenged in the name of multiculturalism. In every American epoch, and particularly during moments of national crisis, writers and thinkers have revisited New England Puritanism to assess the evils or achievements of their own day. One thinks of Franklin in the eighteenth century; Emerson and Hawthorne in the nineteenth; and William Carlos Williams, Arthur Miller, and Robert Lowell in the first half of the twentieth. The Vietnam War likewise prompted thoughtful Americans to search the Puritan legacy for answers to basic questions: How did we get into such a demoralizing and ultimately unsuccessful war? Why did it take us so long to get out? What did we learn from the experience?

When Francis Ford Coppola sought answers to these questions, he found himself tracing the myth of America back to its Puritan roots. His film *Apocalypse Now* (1979) testifies to the continuing influence of the New England Way even as it deplores the harmful consequences of that influence. To appreciate what is at stake in the film, we must review the pertinent features of early American Puritanism. What we have come to call the New England Way is a fabric of many threads, some theological, others political, economic, and cultural. So intricately are they interwoven that it is difficult to tease out a single thread without disturbing the others. To consider the New England Puritans' attitude toward the wilderness, for example, is also to consider their attitude toward the Indian, the community, and history. But for the sake of discussion I address these separately in the following distillation of New England frontier history.

As Roderick Nash points out, the New England Puritans were Europeans first and foremost. As such, they were steeped in a body of myth and folklore that represented the wilderness as a place of supernatural and monstrous beings. These included the Wild Man, a naked, hairy creature who devoured children and ravished young women.[14] He was an apt symbol of what the Puritans feared they might become were they to linger too long in the wilderness and succumb to its temptations.[15] Their mythology of the wilderness was further embellished by typological readings of the Bible, which figured the Old World—and particularly such centers of abomination as Rome and Canterbury—as Egypt or Babylon. The desolate landscape of the New World was the desert in which the Israelites wandered for forty years before entering the promised land of Canaan. Leaders such as Bradford and Winthrop were the equivalents of Moses, Joshua, and Nehemiah.

For the Puritans, wandering in the wilderness was the type of everyone's earthly sojourn. Thus Bunyan's *Pilgrim's Progress* opens with a reference to the "wilderness of this world," a metaphor elaborated by Roger Williams in his dictionary of the Narraganset language: "The Wildernesse is a cleere resemblance of the world, where greedie and furious men persecute and devour the harmlesse and innocent as the wilde beasts pursue and devour the Hinds and Roes."[16] If life as a whole could be figured as a wilderness, there were phases of life for which the figure seemed especially apt. As David R. Williams has shown, the Puritans regarded the wilderness as primarily a place in the human spirit, a domain of disorder and madness, a hellish "black hole of unknowing" that had to be negotiated during conversion and rebirth.[17] Since the true wilderness lay within, one could undergo a genuine "wilderness" experience without leaving London or Leyden.

Conversion was thought to be more likely, however, in physical circumstances that mirrored the inner wilderness.[18] Regarded from this point of view, the inhospitable landscape of New England was a mixed blessing. On the one hand, it was a place of spiritual trial; on the other hand, it was a place of closeness to God and sanctuary from Old World persecutors.[19] Their Canaan lay not beyond this wasteland, as it did for the Israelites, but within it. Through cultivation the "hideous and desolate wilderness" described by Bradford could be transformed into a land of milk and honey.[20]

The Puritans differed from their contemporaries in their emphasis on the wilderness aspect of the New World.[21] The Virginia and Maryland planters more often figured the landscape as a new Eden, and Thomas Morton, a non-Puritan notorious for his quarrel with the Puritans, characterized New England in his *New English Canaan* as a "paradice" and "Natures Master-peece."[22] This is not to say that the Puritans were immune to the beauty of the landscape, properly cultivated. Samuel Sewall's rhapsody on Plum Island, where his parents landed in 1634, represents for Miller the moment when an English Puritan became "an American, rooted in the American soil."[23]

Moreover, since wilderness was as much an inner as it was an outer phenomenon, a first-generation Puritan's view of the landscape was strongly colored by his or her sense of the human condition. The more orthodox, labeled "Arminians" by their opponents, saw themselves as sinners in need of the spiritual trial by wilderness; hence they were inclined to describe their physical surroundings as a wilderness. In contrast, those who were called "Antinomians" believed themselves to be spiritually in the land of Canaan and saw a correspondingly felicitous terrain wherever they looked.[24] Thanks to the labors of their parents, New Englanders of the second and third generations inherited a land that resembled Canaan more than the desert, so many assumed that a commensurate transformation of the spirit had taken place.[25] The Halfway Covenant of 1662 implicitly supported this view. Thereafter, children of converted church members could become provisional members of the congregation without testifying that they had personally traveled the inner wilderness.

Yet the old typology lingered as a spiritual ideal. In her classic frontier captivity narrative, Mary Rowlandson confesses that while she
lived in prosperity and comfort she sometimes wished for trials and af-
flictions.[26] When the Wampanoags held her for three months in 1675,
they forced her to repeat the first generation's painful but spiritually
efficacious entry into the wilderness. Rowlandson's story reflects the Puritan view not only of the wilderness but also of the community and the
American Indian. By structuring her account as a series of "removes"
from the community in Lancaster, Massachusetts, she endorses John
Winthrop's belief that the pilgrim soul's true home is a "city upon a
hill."[27] Winthrop's city was scarcely established on its hilltop, however,
when some of its citizens were lured back into the wilderness—not by
the desire for conversion, but by greed for land that could be purchased
cheaply from the natives. The Puritan clergy and "men of note" deplored such "Indianizing" but could do little to prevent it, beyond pub-
licizing the occasional instance of a "backsettler" punished by a native
attack.[28]

For Rowlandson and other New England settlers, the American Indian personified the wilderness and shared its ambiguous status in
European folklore and Puritan typology. The Indian was the Wild Man
of folklore, his ritual cannibalism an object of particular horror because
it mirrored, diabolically, the Christian Eucharist.[29] At the same time, his
conversion was one of the ostensible purposes of the Puritan errand into
the wilderness. According to one theory, American Indians were the lost
tribes of Israel; according to another, they were simply heathens.[30] In
either case their conversion had a place in salvation history, for it was
among the *miracula* or *magnalia* that were supposed to precede the Second Coming of Christ. Schooled in the teachings of apocalyptists like
Richard Mather and John Cotton, the Puritan emigrants believed that
they were living in the "last days" prefigured by Jesus' triumphant entry
into Jerusalem (Matt. 21) and the Book of Revelation.

With each American Indian who renounced native culture and kin
to live with other converts in "praying towns," the Second Coming and
the Christian millennium appeared a step closer. In the meantime, the
Indian served a useful rhetorical purpose. Preachers could contrast native converts with unregenerate English settlers and perhaps shame the
latter into mending their ways. Ultimately it was the conversion of their
own people that mattered to most Puritans, and the Indian was regarded more as a symbol of spiritual disorder than as a soul to be saved.

It was all the easier, therefore, for the image of the American Indian to be revised according to political expediency. Unlike other European colonists, the New England Puritans assumed that the land belonged to them by divine decree; the native "Canaanites" would have to convert or be exterminated.[31] King Philip's War in 1675–1676 brought a decisive shift in policy from conversion to extermination.[32] In his *Brief History* of that war, Increase Mather attributes the conflict in part to insufficient zeal for the conversion of the Indians.[33] But the treachery of some "praying Indians" suggested to some witnesses, including Mary Rowlandson, that the natives were incapable of genuine and lasting conversion. After the 1670s the American Indians were considered an evil to be purged from the body politic.[34] Warfare against the natives was regarded as an antitype of the Israelites' battles against the Canaanites and Amalekites and as a type of Armageddon, the great battle that would usher in the Christian millennium.

King Philip's War not only carried Puritan apocalypticism to a new height, but also called onto the stage of history an unlikely Puritan hero.[35] Before the war, Benjamin Church lived apart from any congregation in an unsettled part of Rhode Island. There he enjoyed a close friendship—thought by some to be a romantic liaison—with a female sachem named Awashonks.[36] During the war he used that friendship and American Indian methods of warfare to fight the natives, dismissing fears that his tactics would "Indianize" the English. Apparently motivated by a combination of compassion and pragmatic policy, he tried to halt the massacre of some six hundred Narraganset men, women, and children in the Swamp Fight of 1675, characterized by Slotkin and Folsom as a "seventeenth-century My Lai."[37] He led the company of white rangers and nonpraying American Indian allies that hunted down Philip and many of his lieutenants and warriors. When he captured Annawon, the military leader of the Wampanoags, the old warrior honored him with the symbolic gift of Philip's royal wampum belts.

Church fell from favor with Puritan authorities toward the end of his career when, in an action that reveals the ruthlessly pragmatic side of his personality, he ordered the execution of French prisoners while fighting the French and the American Indians. That he was never fully in sympathy with the New England Way is suggested not only by his deeds but also, Slotkin and Folsom contend, by his manner of recounting them in a personal narrative published in 1716. Whereas other Puritan narratives of the war play down individual achievement and attribute success to Divine Providence, *Entertaining Passages Relating to*

Philip's War betrays Church's personal pride in his accomplishments. By then, however, the fabric of the New England Way had already begun to unravel.

We are now in a position to see what is at stake in *Apocalypse Now*. In its plot and characterization, the film is most obviously indebted to *Heart of Darkness*, Joseph Conrad's novella about Belgian trade and conquest in Africa. Much as Conrad's Marlow journeys up the Congo to retrieve Kurtz, Coppola's Captain Willard (played by Martin Sheen) travels up the Nung (that is, Mekong) River into Cambodia to assassinate a Special Forces colonel (Marlon Brando) also named Kurtz. But in its treatment of wild places and wild men and in its conception of community and history, *Apocalypse Now* belongs to the tradition of American Puritanism. Apparently without conscious design, Coppola created a powerful contemporary image of the New England Way. Then, reacting to the image in much the same way that a later generation reacted to Puritanism, he devised a countermyth that also reflects American cultural history.

Though Colonel Kurtz, at the beginning of Coppola's film, has long since withdrawn from the city upon a hill, he is still fighting the same enemy, and his methods are for the most part identical to those of the "nabobs" whom he despises.[38] Like them, he uses friendly indigenous troops (Montagnards) to fight the Viet Cong and North Vietnamese Army (NVA). Like them, he employs selective assassination, wholesale slaughter, and psychological warfare to accomplish his aims. Kurtz acknowledges the kinship between his methods and those of the military command in a radio transmission captured on tape. "What do you call it," he asks, "when the assassins accuse the assassin?"

Despite these affinities, Kurtz must be eliminated because his methods are deemed "unsound" by military and civilian intelligence. Their unsoundness lies primarily in his separation from the community and communal authority, as mediated by his superiors. Whereas Willard is an assassin under orders, Kurtz is an assassin who recognizes no authority beyond himself. He has established what Philip H. Melling calls a "bad enclave," a separate base of power in a part of Indochina remote from Saigon and Nha Trang, where he exercises godlike power over his followers.[39] Though the crew of the river patrol boat (PBR) find this blasphemous—Chef (Frederic Forrest) calls it "pagan idolatry"— they are attracted to his Indianized style of life and warfare. Lance (Sam Bottoms), the surfer from Southern California, is the first to show signs of going native as the PBR leaves civilization in its wake; when they reach Cambodia he paints his face and trades his fatigues for a loincloth. Chef likewise exchanges his helmet for a hat of reeds, forgetting the lesson he learned in his encounter with a tiger: "Never get off the boat."

The tiger episode prompts Willard to reflect that Kurtz had not only gotten off the boat but had gone "all the way." As Willard travels up river, presumably retracing Kurtz's journey into the heart of darkness, he is confronted at every turn by vulgarized 1960s versions of the frontier myth. He comes upon an airmobile cavalry squadron whose commander, Colonel Kilgore (Robert Duvall), combines nostalgia for the glory days of the horse-mounted cavalry with a West Coast passion for surfing and beach parties. When the boat stops to refuel at Hau Phat, an appropriately named ("how fat") oasis of excess, Willard witnesses a USO show staged by the rock impresario Bill Graham, featuring Playboy bunnies dressed as a cowboy, an American Indian woman, and a cavalry trooper-American Indian hybrid.

These absurd conflations of past and present reflect, visually, the absurdities of American policy in Vietnam. Willard hears Kilgore threatening to bomb a village "back to the stone age" for its sympathy with Viet Cong "savages." At the USO show he ponders the contrast between American sex-for-success (the Playmates' performance is a reward for an operation named Brutal Force) and the enemy's political commitment. At the Do Lung Bridge on the Cambodian border, he witnesses one final example of official American policy gone awry. The lost souls who wander this purgatorial landscape, or who try to escape it by plunging into the river after the PBR, have neither a leader nor any clear sense of mission beyond the daily rebuilding of the bridge.

Willard becomes increasingly annoyed at the antics of the PBR crew, ranging from Lance's water skiing to Chief's (Albert Hall) insistence that they search a sampan even though the search will delay their mission. Willard's experiences thus supply the narrative link between the young, careerist Kurtz and the man who unaccountably defied authority and got off the boat. If Kurtz is a renegade and an egotist, a Benjamin Church writ large, he is also a reformer, a Puritan separatist in flight from the American equivalents of Egypt and Babylon. He deliberately chose the Cambodian wilderness, and with it the potential for madness, as the means to some unspecified personal Canaan. The more Willard sees of the fool's paradise that Kurtz rejected, the more he admires Kurtz and looks forward to meeting him.

Is Kurtz in fact a madman, as both his detractors and admirers be-

lieve? Certainly he is a man obsessed, like many of the New England
Puritans, with impending apocalypse. Shortly before Willard arrives at
Kurtz's headquarters in a decaying temple, he reads a front-page newspaper account of the Tate-LaBianca murders that took place in Bel Air
and Los Angeles in August 1969. After killing Rosemary LaBianca,
Charles Manson's "family" printed the words "Helter Skelter" in blood
on a refrigerator door. The title of a Beatles song, the phrase was the
Manson family's term for Armageddon. According to one family member, "Helter skelter was to be the last war on the face of the earth. It
would be all the wars that have ever been fought built one on top of the
other, something that no man could conceive of in his imagination."[40]
Kurtz appears bent on a similar project. The words "Apocalypse Now"
are crudely lettered on the temple steps, and the area is littered with
corpses and severed heads. Manson-like, he has surrounded himself
with devotees such as Colby (Scott Glenn), a would-be assassin who defected to his side and adopted face paint, and the photojournalist (Dennis Hopper) based on the Russian in Conrad's story.

Kurtz's apocalypticism seems motivated in part by a sense of divine
mission, with himself as both prophet and divinity. In biblical times
Jehovah ordered King Saul to exterminate the Amalekites along with all
their livestock for resisting the Israelites' incursion into the promised
land (1 Sam. 15). Kurtz is determined not to repeat Saul's mistake by
sparing any of the enemy, human or animal. On the taped radio transmission he is heard to say, "We must kill them, we must incinerate
them, pig after pig, cow after cow, village after village, army after
army." Kurtz's design may be even more comprehensive than Jehovah's,
to judge from the words scrawled in red ink on the first page of a type-
script found in his chamber: "DROP THE BOMB EXTERMINATE
THEM ALL." The phrase "them all" may refer only to the ostensible
enemy, the VC and NVA. Or, as in *Heart of Darkness*, it may include all
of the indigenous people, whom Conrad's Kurtz had come to regard as
"brutes."[41]

Kurtz has neither bombs nor bombers at his disposal, and one cannot imagine him collaborating with the American military command
even to accomplish his final solution. These practical considerations
aside, however, it is clear that Kurtz has arrived at the position of the
New England Puritans during King Philip's War, when exterminating
the American Indians began to seem more prudent than converting
them.

Yet Kurtz's desire for Armageddon springs from more than mad genocidal fantasy. It is also the death wish of a man who has lived his life like a snail crawling along the edge of a straight razor. He reads and rereads Eliot's poem *The Hollow Men*, with its ominous epigraph ("Mistah Kurtz—he dead") and its repeated "This is the way the world ends." He does not fear the end; the lyrics of the Doors song heard at the beginning of the film echo his conviction that "the end" is his "only friend." He is determined merely that his end shall come with a bang, not a whimper. He wants to die like a soldier, as Willard puts it, not like "some poor wasted rag-assed renegade."

Kurtz therefore grooms Willard, a fellow army officer, as his executioner, a role that the younger man might otherwise be too reverent to perform. He lectures Willard on the need to befriend "horror"; to illustrate his point, he tells an anecdote about the VC amputating the arms of children vaccinated by the Green Berets. Kurtz admires the courage of this ruthless deed. Willard, who showed himself capable of such ruthlessness on the river when he shot a wounded Vietnamese woman rather than jeopardize his mission, is subjected to one final test when Kurtz drops Chef's severed head in his lap. Then he is deemed ready to play the role of assassin.

Kurtz in effect orders his own execution, though Willard believes that Kurtz in turn takes his orders from the jungle. Here Coppola's Kurtz differs significantly from Conrad's. In *Heart of Darkness,* Kurtz is a guilty, ruined creature whose famous dying words—"The horror. The horror"—disclose a profound awareness of moral degeneracy. Marlon Brando, though he had not read Conrad's novella, wanted to play Kurtz as a figure of American guilt in Vietnam.[42] But Coppola emphatically rejected this interpretation, presenting instead a Kurtz who passes from horror to wonder without looking back. His protagonist chooses death in obedience to a grand eschatological necessity. What the military command regards as insanity he regards as clairvoyance and a virtuous determination not to lie. Unlike the New England Puritans, however, he has no illusions that his end will precipitate a new millennium. His apocalypse is both now and forever.

Yet there are clues that Kurtz also entertains an antiapocalyptic notion of history and personal destiny. Besides the Bible, with its linear scheme of history leading to the events predicted in the Book of Revelation, his reading includes Sir James Frazer's *Golden Bough* and Jessie L. Weston's *From Ritual to Romance*. These works inscribe biblical archetypes within a cyclical scheme of history, what Mircea Eliade has called the myth of the eternal return. According to this myth, particularly as set forth in the volume of *The Golden Bough* entitled *The Dying God*, Kurtz must die so that Willard can succeed him as the king of the Montagnards. Intercut with images of Willard slaying Kurtz with a machete are images of the Montagnards using the same implement to kill a water buffalo, perhaps as a totemic sacrifice. Thus Kurtz's death, intended by the military command to be merely a political assassination, is also the primal patricide and a potentially efficacious fertility ritual.[43]

Herein lies a contradiction that the film fails to resolve—namely, how the madman who calls for the extermination of "them all" can also be the sacrificial victim who offers himself for the well-being of the Montagnard community. The first Kurtz comes from Conrad's novella and Puritan typology, whereas the second seems to have evolved from Coppola's desperate search for a satisfactory ending to the film. In the original script written by John Milius, Kurtz and Willard engage the NVA in a climactic battle. When helicopters arrive to rescue them, Kurtz shoots them down rather than lose the opportunity for a warrior's death. Coppola disliked this ending, which he considered too "macho" and cartoonlike. As the filming dragged on and production costs vastly exceeded budget, he agonized over other conclusions.

At this juncture someone pointed out the similarity between the developing Kurtz-Willard story and the myth of the Fisher King.[44] Then Coppola's wife, Eleanor, persuaded him to witness a ritual performed by the Ifugao Indians who were playing the Montagnards in the film, and he made the connection between their ceremonial slaughter of animals and the killing of the divine king in Frazer. Toward the end of a documentary filmed mainly by Eleanor, *Hearts of Darkness* (1991), Coppola ruminates about the continuity of life, the cycle of death and rebirth, as humankind's oldest and profoundest insight. He apparently believed that he had passed beyond the impasse of apocalypticism—linear history leading to the end of earthly time—by reaching further back, to a more primitive, cyclical conception of history.

Even as Coppola expounds the cyclical thesis in *Hearts of Darkness*, the Doors' "This is the end" plays incongruously in the background, a reminder that *Apocalypse Now* begins and ends in the apocalyptic mode. To succeed Kurtz as the king of the Montagnards, Willard would have to remain among them. At first it appears that he might do so. From an elevated position at the top of the temple steps he surveys the worshiping tribe. The camera catches his face in the instant of decision, balanced between replacing Kurtz as king and returning to civilization as a mere soldier. Coppola wanted the film to end here, with Willard's return implied but not yet chosen. Following test screenings, however, he acceded to the wishes of viewers who preferred the less ambiguous ending in which Willard drops his machete and descends the steps.[45] Holding Kurtz's report in one hand and leading Lance with the other, he returns to the PBR. He is "on the boat" again, reversing Kurtz's journey. The final image of his face juxtaposed with the green stone face of the Cambodian goddess is meant to recall the moment when he might have chosen otherwise.

As this image fades from the screen in the Paramount Pictures videotape version of the film, the credits roll against a black background.[46] But in the 35 mm print distributed to most theaters the credits appear against footage of the fiery destruction of Kurtz's compound. Critics disagree about the significance of the more apocalyptic coda. Frank P. Tomasulo calls it a "prowar" ending that proves "Willard has learned Kurtz's lessons so well that he *has become him,* and allowed the colonel's last wish to be fulfilled."[47] Tomasulo therefore assumes that Willard answers the radio call from "Almighty," his connection with military headquarters, and calls in the map coordinates for an air strike. According to this scenario, he ruthlessly destroys the Montagnards along with Colby and the photojournalist.

John Hellmann argues, to the contrary, that the coda is Willard's "mental enactment" of Kurtz's desire, a consummation Willard himself rejects.[48] I find Hellmann's interpretation more persuasive, inasmuch as "Almighty's" call goes unanswered in the film. The bombing is represented outside the film's narrative and without the usual realistic markers; it takes place soundlessly in an infrared light. Coppola himself maintained that it is "fantasy."[49] As such, it serves as a symmetric frame to a film that begins with a fiery yet surreal napalm strike. In that prologue, the transition from burning palm trees and helicopter rotor blades to the ceiling fan in Willard's room suggests that the opening footage likewise belongs to the realm of dream.

For a sophisticated New England Puritan, a mentally enacted apocalypse would have been nonetheless real. As Frank Kermode remarks in *The Sense of an Ending,* apocalypse can be disconfirmed without being discredited.[50] When the end fails to arrive on schedule, the apocalyptic timetable can be revised. Or apocalypse can be reconstrued as immanent spiritual experience rather than imminent temporal end.[51] Like wilderness, apocalypse then becomes an individual spiritual experience—in this case the experience of crisis—rather than a historical event.

I doubt that Willard tries to realize Kurtz's genocidal fantasies by calling in an air strike. But neither am I persuaded that he rejects Kurtz's vision of the end. Willard is temperamentally a Puritan even before he meets Kurtz. He enters the terrifying wilderness of self in his Saigon hotel room and behaves like a man profoundly aware of inner disturbance and guilt. "What are the charges?" he asks the military police who come to take him to Nha Trang. There he accepts the mission as punishment for what he calls his "sins" and is coached to regard his errand into the physical wilderness as part of a metaphysical conflict between good and evil, rationality and irrationality. Though he no longer sees the world in terms of such dichotomies by the end of his journey, he remains sufficiently the Puritan to reject any pagan myth of eternal recurrence. Willard's mental enactment of apocalypse therefore reflects his spiritual kinship with Kurtz.

Like Marlow in Conrad's novella and other narrators of the genre Kenneth Bruffee has named elegiac romance, Willard is a sympathetic apologist for his heroic alter ego. Unlike them, however, he shows no sign of resolving his ambivalence toward Kurtz. As Bruffee has shown, the narrators of elegiac romance typically come to terms with loss by telling their stories; they are then able to get on with their lives.[52] In contrast, Willard appears to have reached a spiritual dead end. He can only savor the irony of returning bodily to the boat while remaining spiritually a castaway. "They were gonna make me a major for this," he reflected on his way to kill Kurtz, "and I wasn't even in their fuckin' army anymore." *Apocalypse Now* thus conforms more closely to the structure of tragedy, as defined by Kermode, than to romance: "Tragedy assumes the figurations of apocalypse, of death and judgment, heaven and hell; but the world goes forward in the hands of exhausted survivors."[53]

To refigure apocalypse as immanent rather than imminent event is to move it from the end of the *saeculum* or historical time to the middle. Apocalypse became "secular" in this sense of the word even before the dissolution of the New England Way in the early eighteenth century. During the late secular crisis of the Vietnam War, *Apocalypse Now* suggests, the American myth that derives from Puritanism became a form of cultural suicide. Although the Montagnard (Ifugao) ritual offers a way out of this dead end, Willard elects not to take it. But what if he were to choose otherwise? In the alternative scenario, he would accept the mantle of power from Kurtz and live for a time among the Montagnards. Then, perhaps, he would return to Saigon and eventually America imbued with an antiapocalyptic sense of history.

In *Apocalypse Now* this peripeteia or reversal of plot is ascribed to an exotic, primitive culture. Yet it also has an American genealogy dating back to the twilight of the New England Way. Richard Slotkin calls this reversal "regeneration through violence" and finds an intimation of it in Church's *Entertaining Passages*. It reaches full articulation, however, in John Filson's story of Daniel Boone, entitled *The Discovery, Settlement, and Present State of Kentucke* (1784).

III

Following successful attacks on the English colonies, American Indians sometimes took captives, usually women and children, who were then sold for ransom to their English compatriots or to the French in Canada. The victims' husbands, fathers, and brothers pursued the captors into the forest in an attempt to free the captives and take revenge. Thus the captivity narratives that resulted from these episodes offer two ways of relating to the wilderness: the way of the passive victim and the way of the bloody avenger.[54] There was, to be sure, the occasional captive or renegade who chose to live among the natives, but these "white Indians" were regarded with revulsion by the whites in the settlements. Not until Filson articulated the myth of Daniel Boone in *Kentucke* did it seem possible to give oneself wholly to the wilderness without becoming a savage.

Kentucke, which purports to be the authentic narrative of Boone himself but was actually written by Filson, appeared during the same decade in which the ideal of the "middle landscape" was memorably endorsed by Crèvecoeur and Jefferson.[55] For Crèvecoeur in 1782, the quintessential American was the farmer, happily situated between the savagery of the frontier and the potentially corruptive refinement of the city.[56] In 1785 Jefferson likewise celebrated agriculture as the calling of God's chosen people. Whereas shopkeepers are forced to consult their customers' whims, farmers are free to follow their own conscience.[57] Predictably, then, Filson regards Boone as an instrument for converting wilderness into farmland: "Thus we behold Kentucke, lately an howling wilderness, the habitation of savages and wild beasts, become a fruitful field."[58]

Yet Filson's *Kentucke* transcends the genre to which it otherwise belongs—the real estate brochure—by dwelling on Boone's initiation into

the wilderness and its savagery. Boone savors the sublime beauty of un-
cultivated nature and adapts to American Indian modes of hunting and
warfare. Twice captured by the Shawnee, he lives for a time as their
adopted son. Despite his thorough immersion in the wilderness, he remains committed to civilized Christian values. In the Boone myth, as
Slotkin argues, violence is regenerative.

The Boone myth made it possible to reconceive the dreaded white
Indian as a hero, indeed as the archetypal American hero. Though history and legend record another Boone who was notoriously wary of encroachment by other white settlers, Filson's mythic Boone became a
quintessential American type, an evolutionary link between the Puritan
era and our own.[59] Conspiring with Filson to alter the Puritan view of
wilderness were several intellectual developments in Europe: the cult of
the sublime, which discovered beauty in the wilder manifestations
of nature; Deism, which regarded nature (particularly in its unculti-
vated state) as the expression of God; and Romantic primitivism, which
gave us the noble savage. In this country nationalistic fervor fixed on
wilderness as that which distinguished the New World from the Old
and even gave it—supposing the Deists and Romantics were right—a
moral advantage.[60] Taking this line of thinking one step further,
Frederick Jackson Turner argued that American independence, individ-
ualism, and respect for common people—American democracy, in
short—was a product of the American frontier.[61]

Writing during the 1890s after the official closing of the frontier,
Turner was troubled by the possible effects of that closure on American
character and government. Would Americans still be Americans once
the last bit of wilderness was brought under the plow? In a 1902 essay
entitled "The Frontier Gone at Last," the novelist Frank Norris acknowledged the loss of domestic frontiers but argued that the desire for
conquest is an Anglo-Saxon trait, not to be satisfied even with the recent
leap across the Pacific into China. Anglo-Saxon America would re-
bound eastward and subdue Europe as well as Asia by means of com-
merce. Racial and geographic barriers would be gradually effaced until
"the whole world is our nation and simple humanity our country-
men."[62] As Norris saw it, the twentieth century would be a century of
new frontiers.

It was John F. Kennedy who announced the New Frontier of the 1960s
when he accepted his party's nomination as presidential candidate in
July 1960. Shaping Kennedy's vision, John Hellmann has argued, was
William J. Lederer and Eugene Burdick's *The Ugly American* (1958). As

a young senator from Massachusetts, Kennedy was one of four "distinguished Americans" who sent copies of the book to every member of the Senate.[63] Hellmann accurately characterizes *The Ugly American* as a jeremiad against a nation that, in the authors' judgment, had grown too soft, greedy, and immoral in the postwar years to stand up to communism.[64] The novel in effect urges those laboring on the international frontier (in this case Indochina) to renounce Old World decadence and return to American frontier virtues. Kennedy sounded the same note in his inaugural address, which challenged the nation to go forth anew and "conquer the deserts."[65] He particularly invited the younger generation to share in the adventure, and many responded by joining New Frontier organizations like the Peace Corps, VISTA, and the army's Special Forces.

The last of these reflects Kennedy's fascination with counterinsurgency as a means of protecting American interests on the global frontier. One of the few admirable characters in *The Ugly American* is Colonel Edwin B. Hillandale, based on Colonel Edward G. Lansdale, the legendary Central Intelligence Agency (CIA) operative who directed paramilitary operations against the Viet Minh in 1954 and 1955, roughly between the conclusion of the Geneva Convention and the official division of Vietnam along the seventeenth parallel. On completing his mission, Colonel Lansdale prepared a report that is one of the more colorful documents in *The Pentagon Papers*. Lansdale's boyish enthusiasm cannot be muffled in gray flannel prose, especially when he recalls playing a role out of America's past. Early in 1955, he writes, "Haiphong was reminiscent of our own pioneer days as it was swamped with people whom it couldn't shelter. Living space and food were at a premium, nervous tension grew. It was a wild time for our northern team."[66]

Like Daniel Boone, Lansdale and his fellow counterinsurgents fought the enemy on his own terms. Though the affiliation of New Frontiersmen changed over the following decade, from CIA "spooks" to Special Forces advisers to regular army soldiers, the Boone myth continued to influence American thinking, at least at a preconscious level. It should surprise no one, then, to find versions of the myth in literary and cinematic responses to the war. Along with vestiges of Puritan ideology, it appears in a film released shortly before *Apocalypse Now,* Michael Cimino's *Deer Hunter* (1978).

Michael Vronsky (played by Robert DeNiro), the deer hunter of the title, resembles Cooper's Deerslayer in several respects. He is versed in the American Indian signs that forecast a successful hunt and values the discipline of the one-shot kill, as though his rifle were a muzzle-loader rather than a semiautomatic. Like Leatherstocking, Kurtz, and Willard, he is more at home in a world without women. At a wedding reception he flirts with Linda (Meryl Streep), the fiancée of his housemate Nick (Christopher Walken), until he learns that the bride is pregnant by someone other than the groom. In puritanical protest against both her prurience and his own, Michael runs naked through the darkened streets of Clairton. Figuratively speaking, he runs all the way to Vietnam, where he shows himself capable of Kurtz and Willard's ruthlessness and ability to befriend horror. He sets an NVA soldier afire with a flamethrower and coolly plots an escape from enemy captivity while his comrades are paralyzed by terror or fatalism.

On his return from Vietnam, Michael dodges a "welcome home" party. His evasion of community suggests that he has gotten "off the boat," like the antisocial Green Beret sergeant whom he meets earlier in the American Legion hall. But he embraces the peripeteia rejected by Willard in *Apocalypse Now*. As he is assimilated by Clairton, he begins to nurture communal feeling in others. He persuades one buddy, confined to a wheelchair, to leave the veterans hospital and return to his wife and son. He tries but fails to persuade Nick to abandon his suicidal addiction to drugs and Russian roulette in Vietnam. The change in Michael's outlook is dramatized in the second of the two deer hunts, where he deliberately fires over the head of a majestic stag and cures a fellow hunter of the macho posturing in which he himself once indulged.

Like Filson's Boone, Michael returns from the wilderness and helps to rebuild the community, though his community resembles Winthrop's city upon a hill (Clairton means "bright town") rather than Filson's agrarian Eden. After Michael and his friends bury Nick, they adjourn to a tavern for breakfast, gradually shedding their awkwardness in the domestic rituals of pouring coffee and scrambling eggs. Having opened with one communal moment, a wedding, the film closes with another, as the party joins in singing "God Bless America" and toasting Nick's memory. Though sad, the song is far from being the "mournful dirge" described by one critic.[67] It affirms a social bond that has survived great loss.

The peripeteia in *The Deer Hunter*, the reversal that allies the film with the Boone myth rather than with Puritan apocalypticism, warrants closer scrutiny. Is it violence per se that triggers Michael's regeneration? Certainly his hunterly acceptance of violence is more conducive to surviving the war than Nick's sentimental appreciation of nature ("the way the trees are"). In Michael's case, however, the ruthlessness needs to be tempered by love. In Linda's company he takes his first steps toward reintegration into the community, and she gives him a reason to remain in Clairton. By itself, love might not be enough to effect regeneration. Nick, too, had been in love with Linda. But the combination of love and violence is portrayed as redemptive.

As an alternative to Puritan apocalyptism, Cimino's regenerative vision in *The Deer Hunter* has much to offer. Most criticism of the film has focused on a residue of the New England Way, the controversial scenes in which the VC appear as sadistic brutes who force their captives to play Russian roulette. Whether Cimino personally shared this view of the Vietnamese, a view that some critics consider racist, is beside the point.[68] The camera shows the enemy whom Michael hates, and he has little opportunity—perhaps also little inclination—to change his opinion of them after his regeneration. However troubling this negative stereotype may be, it is probably less insidious than another message endemic to the Boone myth, namely, that the end (regeneration) confers legitimacy on the means (violence).

Michael Herr's *Dispatches* legitimizes violence in much the same way. Herr invokes the Puritan myth of the wilderness when he traces the Vietnam War back to "the proto-Gringos who found the New England woods too raw and empty for their peace and filled them up with their own imported devils."[69] Later in the same chapter, alluding to Filson's revision of the Puritan myth, he describes a western movie (*Nevada Smith,* with Steve McQueen) in which the hero comes through a blood bath "burned clean but somehow old and empty too, like he'd lost his margin for regeneration through violence" (p. 60). Herr concedes that his own margin became perilously slim at times, yet he recalls the year fondly, asserting that "Vietnam was what we had instead of happy childhoods" (p. 244). Pushing Herr's logic to its absurd conclusion, one might argue that a nation should wage constant war. Why deprive any generation of a second chance at childhood happiness?

Herr is of two minds regarding whom to include in the Vietnam experience. On the one hand, he insists on its esoteric quality; only the fortunate few who have been "up the mountain" will get the point of the story told by the Fourth Division Lurp (long-range reconnaissance patroller) at the beginning of the book (p. 6). On the other hand, he wants to generalize the Vietnam experience to include an entire generation; according to the book's final words, "we've all been there" (p. 260). On the literal level, this is nonsense. As I will show in chapter three, few in the Vietnam generation went to Vietnam or were even likely to be drafted into the military. But one did not have to be a soldier to share in the violence of Vietnam; one did not even have to support the war. Speaking of those whom he calls liberals and "peace people," Herr observes, "They would like to pretend that they haven't got those capacities, that they are *not* violent people. But in their dreams and in their wishes and in their hearts they were in Vietnam too."[70]

In *Dispatches* Herr represents the 1960s as a period when violence suffused the youth culture, when "rock and roll turned more lurid and dangerous than bullfighting" and "rock stars started falling like second lieutenants" (p. 258). The rock stars who fell—Jimi Hendrix, Janis Joplin, Jim Morrison—personified the dark side of a generation that wanted to believe in the regenerative powers of love. "All you need is love," sang the Beatles. But they sang against a backdrop of militant demonstrations, the hazing of soldiers, environmental "monkey wrenching," self-destructive drug trips, and a knifing death at the Altamont Rock Music Festival in 1969. Apart from the Weathermen faction of Students for a Democratic Society, which took Charles Manson as its hero, most people who identified with the 1960s counterculture deplored violence as much as they deplored the war in Vietnam.[71] Yet they were able to adapt the Boone myth to their own purposes by playing down its violence and emphasizing the first half of the regenerative cycle, the Indianizing of the white pioneers. For those on the political left as well as those on the right, the wilderness and the Indian were ideologically charged symbols.

IV

During the 1950s books like *The Lonely Crowd* (1950) by David Riesman and *The Organization Man* (1956) by William H. Whyte, Jr., served notice that America was losing its frontier virtues. A democracy composed of free, self-reliant citizens was giving way to a faceless totalitarian state controlled by the corporations and policed with sophisticated technology. What passed for civilization in the 1950s was so conformist as virtually to demand a New Frontier. While Kennedy challenged this development from the top, the youth counterculture of the 1960s challenged it from the bottom. If the corporate state stood for civilization of a kind, then the counterculture stood for the shrinking patch of wilderness. When the city upon a hill became too oppressive, places like the Grand Canyon, Big Bend, Yellowstone, and the High Sierra could serve as "bases for guerrilla warfare against tyranny." These words happen to be Edward Abbey's, from *Desert Solitaire,* but the sentiment was familiar to Frederick Jackson Turner and Henry David Thoreau.[72] Assuming the same connection between politics and environment, the Puritan "men of note" frowned on those who strayed beyond the clearing and thus beyond the control of communal authority.

Charles Reich emphasized the conflict between nature and the corporate state by choosing *The Greening of America* as the title of his 1970 study of the counterculture. He could just as well have called it the Indianizing of America, considering the counterculture's interest in the American Indian as a revolutionary figure. Between 1969 and 1975, in episodes that were well publicized and supported by media personalities like Marlon Brando and Jane Fonda, contemporary American Indian activists recaptured land in California, South Dakota, Washington, and Wisconsin. Meanwhile, historical Indians were capturing the popular imagination in plays like Arthur Kopit's *Indians* (1969); films like Arthur Penn's *Little Big Man* and Ralph Nelson's *Soldier Blue* (both 1970); and books like Dee Brown's *Bury My Heart at Wounded Knee* (1971). In *The Greening of America,* Reich frequently invokes the Indian as a precursor of "Consciousness III," the sensibility he saw emerging from an exhausted liberalism. He notes that young people had adopted not only the American Indians' respect for nature but also their dress and "tribal" organization.[73] Even the counterculture's music and use of drugs could be construed as a return to a more primitive and therefore presumably healthier mode of life.

Though Reich nominates Wallace Stevens as the bard of Consciousness III, he would have found a better spokesman in Gary Snyder, whose *Earth House Hold,* published the year before *Greening,* anticipates and warrants many of Reich's observations. In the prose meditations "Passage to More than India" and "Why Tribe," Snyder celebrates the demise of industrial society and the nuclear, patriarchal family. The Indianized whites who took part in the "The Gathering of the Tribes" in San Francisco's Golden Gate Park in 1967 prefigured for Snyder a new relationship among human beings, between humans and their natural instincts, and between humans and the wilderness.[74] We are, he declared a few years later, "the first members of a civilized society since the Neolithic to wish to look clearly into the eyes of the wild and see our self-hood, our family, there."[75]

The counterculture's mystique of the wilderness and the American Indian influenced its interpretation of Vietnam as a "Puritan" war of extermination. For Reich the war was "the Corporate State's one unsalable product," a product that helped to precipitate disillusionment with liberalism.[76] For Snyder the war was an attempt to exorcise the ghost of the American Indian, which is why "we lash out with such ferocity and passion, so muddied a heart, at the black-haired young peasants and soldiers who are the 'Viet Cong.' "[77] In one poem he compares the Vietnamese people to a forest, implying that it was American policy to "clear-cut" Southeast Asia without regard for the size or even the political "species" of the individual "trees":

> Clear-cut
>
> Forestry. "How
> Many people
> Were harvested
> In Viet-Nam?"
>
> Clear-cut. "Some
> Were children,
> Some were over-ripe."[78]

Entitled "Toward Climax," Snyder's poem represents not the climax of a mature ("ripe") forest but the climax of genocide. This is a pervasive theme in the antiwar literature, where Vietnam is likened to either the Holocaust of Nazi Germany or the Indian wars of the American frontier. Like Snyder, Robert Bly invoked the latter at a poetry reading in 1969, where he said, "I think the Vietnam war has something to do with the fact that we murdered the Indians. . . . What you do first when you commit a crime is you forget it and then you repeat it. So therefore in my opinion what we're doing is repeating the crime with the Indians. The Vietnamese are our Indians. We don't want to end this war! We didn't want to quit killing the Indians but we ran out of Indians, and they were all on reservations."[79] Though Bly was capable of greater subtlety in his poetry, the message of his antiwar efforts like "Hatred of Men with Black Hair" is essentially the same: the United States is determined to eradicate not merely a political ideology, communism, but a race of people.[80]

Turning from these antiwar poets to antiwar intellectual journalists, one finds the same analogy at work, often with genocidal overtones. After Mary McCarthy visited Hanoi in March 1968 as a guest of North Vietnam, she described the North as "pioneer country," with the ethnic minorities of the mountainous west serving as Indians.[81] Altering the terms of her comparison slightly, she portrayed the Northerners' defense of their homeland as the stuff of cinema: "Seen in movie terms, it is a thriller, a cowboys-and-Indians story, in which the Indians, for once, are repelling the cowboys, instead of the other way around."[82] Susan Sontag, who followed McCarthy to Hanoi a month later, was likewise reminded of the movies when responding to a *Partisan Review* questionnaire in 1966. "American policy," she wrote, "is still powered by the fantasy of Manifest Destiny, though the limits were once set by the borders of the continent, whereas today America's destiny embraces the entire world. There are still more hordes of redskins to be mowed down before virtue triumphs; as the classic Western movies explain, the only good Red is a dead Red."[83] Once on the new frontier in Southeast Asia, Sontag was impressed by the noble simplicity and resourcefulness of her North Vietnamese hosts. Much as the Plains Indians had once found a use for every part of the buffalo, the North Vietnamese were turning American bombers into tools, machine parts, surgical instruments, sandals, and jewelry.[84]

Unlike Snyder and Bly, McCarthy and Sontag actually met the people whom they mythologized as noble Reds, and this complicated their responses. As Roderick Nash points out, it was chiefly European intellectuals and American gentry who developed the notions of the noble savage and the sublime wilderness. The pioneers were generally too busy clearing the woods, draining the swamps, and fighting natives to indulge in armchair anthropology.[85] The 1960s counterculture was likewise free to create, for polemical purposes, an image of the Indian largely sanitized of the violence that made the historical American Indian a successful warrior and hunter. The antiwar notion of the North Vietnamese and Viet Cong "Indian," though it allowed a measure of military aggressiveness, still required that he show extraordinary restraint and a sense of fair play. Consequently, neither McCarthy nor Sontag would entertain the possibility that captured American pilots were being tortured. Only McCarthy alludes to the communist massacre of civilians in Hue during the 1968 Tet Offensive, and she prefers to think that at least some of the three to five thousand victims were killed by American bombs.[86] Their North Vietnamese are long-suffering victims who repay American aggression with unflagging courtesy to captured pilots.

Neither writer, however, is entirely comfortable with the noble Red in the flesh. Sontag in particular is put off by the formulaic language of her hosts, which seems to reflect an absence of individual thought and feeling. The North Vietnamese seem to her more like children than mature adults. They appear passive, unsophisticated, and in some respects inferior to Westerners. McCarthy and Sontag, perhaps horrified to discover in themselves the same racism that they despised in the American "yahoo" majority, struggle to resist such judgments. The struggle avails, and each is at last able to celebrate the political and cultural virtues of the North Vietnamese. But the struggle is itself revealing, for it signals the gap between the North Vietnamese themselves and the North Vietnamese as projections of American mythology.

It also signals a paradox in countercultural thought of the 1960s. Writers such as Reich, Snyder, Bly, McCarthy, and Sontag sought regeneration in alien places and among alien people. They did not want to be ugly Americans, recreating America in Southeast Asia. In theory, then, they chose the path of Daniel Boone. But in practice they followed the New England Way of assimilating otherness rather than allowing themselves to be absorbed by it. For Snyder as for the Puritans, the real desert was the "wilderness within" of the subconscious mind.[87] To those who sought this route to the promised land, the psychedelic gurus Timothy Leary and Ken Kesey were Moses and Aaron. In the 1980s Bly urged men to seek a benign version of the "Wild Man" not in remote regions of the earth but in the recesses of their own psyches. The more politically minded tended likewise to avoid or minimize the real differences in alien cultures. Paul Porter, as president of Students for a Democratic Society (SDS), spoke of the Viet Cong as "a more victimized and better organized version of ourselves."[88] According to Todd Gitlin, a former president of SDS, the group's notion of a leftist utopia was none other than the New England ideal, turned on its head: "We inverted the traditional American innocence, and located the 'city upon a hill' in the jungles of the Third World."[89]

It would not be far-fetched to say that for those who opposed the war as well as for those who were responsible for fighting it, Vietnam was not a foreign war at all. It was a domestic cultural conflict of long standing, an American western displaced onto alien soil. This insight informs Norman Mailer's novel *Why Are We in Vietnam?* (1967), which is set entirely in North America.

V

Generically, *Why Are We in Vietnam?* might be described as a counterculture western. According to the preface Mailer added to the 1977 edition, the novel began as the story of a motorcycle gang based in the scrub thickets near Provincetown, one of the places where America began and also "the Wild West of the East."[90] His bikers were to have committed brutal crimes "out of the sheer boredom of an existence not nearly intense enough to satisfy their health" (p. 2). These outlaws thus recall the "white Negro" or hipster Mailer portrayed in a 1957 essay, a psychopathic blend of bohemian, black, and juvenile delinquent. The hipster is simultaneously an existentialist rebel against the conformity and fear of the American 1950s and "a frontiersman in the Wild West of American night life."[91]

The motorcycle gang does not appear in the published novel, but its social stance is retained, with modifications, in the characters of DJ and Tex. The former, an eighteen-year-old white Anglo-Saxon Protestant from Dallas, is the narrator. In the opening chapters he teases the reader with the possibility that he may actually be a crippled Harlem genius, impersonating a white boy as a way of taking revenge on white readers. Though born into wealth and privilege, DJ has adopted the hipster's subversive attitude and speech.

This raises the question of motive: what or whom does DJ want to subvert, and why? Some of his animus is directed at the reader, whom he tries to shock with obscene language and confuse with departures from narrative convention. But the reader is merely a surrogate target, presumed to be guilty of sharing the values of DJ's real target—his father, Rusty Jethroe. In the course of the novel DJ explains what his father stands for, recounts the tale of his own disaffection with those values, and tells how he and Tex finally escaped—so they think, anyway—the father's world. Since these thoughts preoccupy DJ on the night before he and Tex are to go to Vietnam, his story is implicitly an answer to the question posed in the novel's title.

Rusty Jethroe is an American organization man, "the cream of corporation corporateness" (p. 29). His executive appearance (part Dwight D. Eisenhower, part Henry Cabot Lodge) and competitive drive carried him to the top of a Dallas firm that manufactures parts for the space program and an effective though possibly carcinogenic cigarette filter. His competitiveness alienates his son, who as a child of five and again as a boy of thirteen suffers Rusty's physical aggression. DJ is morally intimidated by his father and feels a Kierkegaardian dread when looking into the vacancy of Rusty's eyes.

Rusty's competitiveness is aroused again on a hunting trip to the Brooks Range in Alaska. Rather than providing respite from the pressures of the corporate world, the hunt is an intensified exercise in corporate ladder climbing. Rusty must shoot an Alaskan bear so that his flunkies Bill and Pete can testify to his hunting prowess once they return to Dallas. Misadventures early in the hunt cause him first to question his manhood, then to lay claim to a grizzly he and DJ bag together. Disgusted with his father's behavior and a hunt that has degenerated into a war on the animals, DJ takes off with Tex into the wildest part of the Brooks Range, the Endicott Mountains.

Genetically, DJ and Tex are both part American Indian. In the course of the hunt they become Indianized morally as well. Their initiation into the wilderness begins on the first morning of the hunt, when Tex kills a wolf and both boys drink the warm blood. This ritual, administered by their native guide, Ollie Water Beaver, recalls the similar episode in Faulkner's *Go Down, Moses,* where Sam Fathers christens Ike McCaslin with the blood of a freshly killed buck. That same year, Ike is permitted his first glimpse of a great bear after he sheds the accoutrements of civilization: his gun, watch, compass, and staff. DJ and Tex likewise leave their weapons behind and are rewarded with sightings of wild animals, including a grizzly that runs down and kills a caribou calf.

During the night following these sightings, the lesson of universal predation and violence is driven home by the northern lights, which inscribe on the tablet of the polar sky the commandment of the wilderness beast-God, "Go out and kill—fulfill my will, go and kill" (p. 203).[92] Each of the young men lies suspended for a time between the impulse to dominate the other sexually and the fear of being killed in the attempt. The tension is resolved when, in response to a subtle shift in the electromagnetic force field, they become blood brothers instead. Their relationship intensifies over the two years that intervene between the Alaskan hunt and their departure for Vietnam. Their experience in Alaska moves them to seek "demonological" powers through experiments on the corpses in the mortuary owned by Tex's father. On reaching the minimum age of enlistment, they choose to "go and kill" in Vietnam, presumably in obedience to the voice of the beast-God.

As Philip D. Beidler observes, the dominant vision of *Why Are We in Vietnam?* is irony.[93] It is particularly ironic that the wilderness should urge the same course of action as its antithesis, the corporate state, even though the ethos of the two differs considerably. The Moe Henry and Obungekat Safari Group is committed to the wilderness ethic until Rusty corrupts his guide, Luke Fellinka, who is compared to Secretary of Defense Robert McNamara. Thereafter, the hunt resembles the Viet-

nam War and is often described in military terms. A helicopter is introduced to spot game from the air, success is measured by the body count,
and the participants are concerned chiefly with how the event will play
back home.

The Alaskan hunt is a bad hunt for some of the same reasons Mailer
believed that Vietnam was a bad war. He specified these a year later in
The Armies of the Night (1968), where he also professes his belief in the
possibility of a good war, as measured chiefly by its effects: "A good
war, like anything else which is good, offers the possibility that further
effort will produce a determinable effect upon chaos, evil, or waste."[94]
According to Mailer, killing in itself is morally neutral; the beast-God's
command is a law of nature. Whether this violence will have a regenerative effect depends on cultural factors. Driven by a Puritan version
of the frontier myth, Rusty Jethroe produces chaos, evil, and waste in
Alaska and by extension in Vietnam. Driven by a version more closely
allied to Daniel Boone, DJ and Tex find personal regeneration in
Alaska. They are nevertheless sure to be corrupted in Vietnam, where
the war is conducted by the corporate state and where they will find no
equivalent of their refuge in the Endicott Mountains.

Occasionally an author invokes both the Puritan and the Boone versions of frontier myth in a way that implies their essential compatibility.
Philip Caputo, for example, dismisses what he calls the "racist" and
"frontier-heritage" theories of the war in the prologue to *A Rumor of
War*.[95] Toward the end of the same prologue, however, he describes Vietnam as, in effect, a heart of darkness: "There was nothing familiar
out where we were, no churches, no police, no laws, no newspapers, or
any of the restraining influences without which the earth's population
of virtuous people would be reduced by ninety-five percent. It was the
dawn of creation in the Indochina bush, an ethical as well as a geo-
graphical wilderness. Out there, lacking restraints, sanctioned to kill,
confronted by a hostile country and a relentless enemy, we sank into a
brutish state."[96] Caputo's memoir is a Puritan tale of degeneration through
violence. Beginning as a college student inspired by Kennedy's vision of
a New Frontier, he ends as a guilty collaborator in the murder of two
Vietnamese civilians. Though Caputo accepts personal responsibility
for his deed, he also believes that the physical setting had released the
horror within: "The thing we had done was a result of what the war
had done to us."[97]

In Caputo's novel *Indian Country* (1987), in contrast, the protagonist escapes his preacher-father's system of guilt by "adopting" an

Ojibwa medicine man as his father. "He saw himself," Caputo writes in the last chapter, "as a kind of halfbreed: his hair and skin were pale, but the war had made him an outsider in the land of his birth. The war had reddened his heart."[98] Christian Starkmann finds personal regeneration, in other words, as a counterculture renegade, an Indianized white man. These two responses to the war, one autobiographical and the other fictional, suggest that Mailer was right: the establishment and the counterculture shared an allegiance to frontier myth. The domestic squabbles between Puritan and Boone, between cowboy and Indian, disguise their fundamental agreement and complicity.

VI

I mentioned at the beginning of this chapter that three plot structures dominate war stories deriving from the frontier myth: the linear plot associated with Puritan apocalypticism, the cyclical plot associated with the Boone story of regeneration through violence, and the plot of circular containment. The last of these is the chief pattern of the captivity narrative, though it often appears as a structural device within a linear or cyclical story. Thus in *Apocalypse Now* Willard is confined to a bamboo cage by Kurtz, perhaps as a metonym of his spiritual captivity to Kurtz's apocalyptic vision. In *The Deer Hunter* Michael Vronsky is briefly a captive of the Viet Cong before he destroys them on his way to regeneration. Craig Howes has shown in *Voices of the Vietnam POWs* how prisoner-of-war memoirs and histories parallel the Indian captivity narratives discussed by Slotkin. Drawing on his insights, we might consider how different versions of the POW story correspond to the three frontier plots.

Howes notes that between 1964 and 1973 the North Vietnamese captured and held soldiers and civilians from South Vietnam, the United States, and other countries. Until 1971 they held the captives in jungle camps located throughout North and South Vietnam as well as in urban prisons like Hoa Lo, the notorious "Hanoi Hilton." This diversity of character and setting is not registered, however, in the more or less "official" POW story promulgated in books like John G. Hubbell's *P.O.W.: A Definitive History of the American Prisoner-of-War Experience in Vietnam, 1964–1973* (1976). Notwithstanding its bulk and a title that implies an all-inclusive treatment, Hubbell's book focuses on a small and fairly homogeneous group, the air force and navy officer-pilots who were captured between 1965 and 1969, imprisoned in the

Hanoi Hilton, and repatriated during Operation Homecoming in February and March 1973. Especially prominent in *P.O.W.* are three senior ranking officers (SROs) who were confined at the Hanoi Hilton: Jeremiah Denton, James B. Stockdale, and Robinson Risner.

All three SROs wrote personal memoirs that recall the great spiritual autobiographies of Augustine, Boethius, and Bunyan as well as the captivity narratives of Mary Rowlandson and John Williams. Hubbell's account is a providential history on the order of Bradford's *Of Plymouth Plantation*. As such, it tells how the "men of note" among the American POWs created a city upon a hill under the very noses of their captors in North Vietnam. Conscious of how badly American POWs had acquitted themselves in Korea, they were determined to set a high standard of individual behavior and group discipline. Communicating by means of a simple tap code, they established a chain of command, issued orders, and assembled an oral history to pass their experiences on to new prisoners. Their bible was the Code of Conduct, six brief articles meant to ensure compliance with the Uniform Code of Military Justice. Over the years, the Hanoi SROs produced an elaborate commentary on the six articles, addressing in particular the circumstances under which a POW might supply information to the enemy. A prisoner who "fell back" under torture was expected to seek the forgiveness of his fellow POWs in a ritual resembling confession before a congregation, then to "bounce back" and resist until again tortured beyond his endurance.

As represented in Hubbell's providential history and the individual memoirs, the North Vietnamese enemy looks remarkably like the American Indian in New England captivity narratives. The Vietnamese are sadistically cruel to animals and human beings alike. Their inscrutable faces conceal all thought and intention. They are culturally primitive, dirty, and morally inferior.[99] Though the POWs were poles apart from Susan Sontag politically, they echo her descriptions of the Vietnamese as psychologically childlike, doctrinaire, and incapable of irony.[100] Fearing contamination by this alien and barbaric culture, the prisoners refused to learn the Vietnamese language, though it might have proven strategically useful. They held their captors at arm's length by giving them contemptuous nicknames. Some of the guards were named after animals, monsters, or children; others after figures from the frontier, such as Crazy Horse, Wild Bill, and Tonto.[101]

Like the New England Puritans, the Hanoi POWs shared an apocalyptic sense of history. They were sustained by belief in a day of judgment, when those who remained faithful to the code would be rewarded and those who strayed from it would be punished. They greeted the 1972 Christmas bombing of Hanoi as Armageddon. Though the bombing did in fact hasten the peace accords of the following month, it did not precipitate the day of reckoning envisioned by the SROs. When the American government and military declined the invidious task of separating the sheep from the goats, the faithful from the faithless, former prisoners like Stockdale and Theodore Guy tried to obtain through civil suits what they regarded as justice. Despite failure in this attempt, they were vindicated in the eyes of the public. America badly needed heroes in the aftermath of the Vietnam War, and the "first generation" POWs of 1964 to 1969 consciously assumed the heroic mantle. Consequently, their fairly strict interpretation of the code became the standard by which other POWs were judged.

Deviance from the code took many different forms. Some "soft-liners" endorsed the code but were willing to sign statements or make tapes for the enemy on the theory that these would be obviously the result of coercion and therefore worthless as propaganda. Others saw no harm in accepting "parole" from the North Vietnamese and early release to the United States. Still others deviated politically, as when a group of eight POWs formed a peace committee in opposition to American policy in Vietnam. One early captive, Special Forces Sergeant George Smith, proselytized on behalf of the North Vietnamese after his release. However, it was cultural rather than ideological nonconformity that most provoked the orthodox POWs. When Marine Pfc. Robert Garwood adopted the language and mannerisms of the Vietnamese, becoming a renegade "White Cong," he placed himself beyond the pale. The other POWs regarded him much as William Bradford regarded Thomas Morton. On his belated return to the United States in 1979, Garwood became the only American serviceman to be convicted of collaborating with the enemy during the Vietnam War.

For Garwood, unlike Benjamin Church and Daniel Boone, Indianizing did not prove regenerative. Rather than welcome the renegade home, Americans feared his contamination, much as the early colonists feared the moral viruses that were presumably carried by "redeemed" captives. When one interrogator told a POW that the communists would control his behavior even if he did return to the States, the threat seemed all too plausible.[102] Richard Condon's *Manchurian Candidate* (1959), set in the aftermath of the Korean War, provided a fictional precedent for such mind control. The official story of the Hanoi Hilton POWs therefore served a cultural and political purpose in the war's aftermath. It reinstated those values of the New England Way—community, discipline, faith in providence, anticipation of a judgment day, and refusal to assimilate enemy culture—that had yielded historically to the Boone myth. Invoking the authority that their trial by fire had conferred on them, the hard-liners argued in their writings and speeches for a return to orthodoxy. Stockdale's *Vietnam Experience: Ten Years of Reflection* (1984) is a jeremiad directed at the careerism, legalism, and managerial ethos that he blamed for the loss of the Vietnam War.

As Howes points out, the North Vietnamese used torture less to extract military intelligence from the Hanoi POWs or convert them to their cause than to obtain taped statements that could be used to garner support in the world community and weaken the resolve of other prisoners. Beyond this practical aim, torture was meant to demonstrate the captor's absolute control over the captive.[103] By reducing the prisoners to passive objects whom they could manipulate for their own purposes, the North Vietnamese believed that they were rewriting the American narrative of indomitable power. As the authors of the official POW story saw it, however, they triumphed over their captors by maintaining discipline and steadfastly serving their country, as Jeremiah Denton put it, "under difficult circumstances."[104] Lionel Chetwynd's film *The Hanoi Hilton* (1987) accepts this version of the story, even including a scene in which "Cat," Hoa Lo's notorious camp commander, confesses to an American SRO that he is being reassigned because of his failure to persuade more POWs to accept parole. "We won," the SRO responds, and the camera endorses his victory, looking up at the SRO and down at the camp commander.

However, popular films about the POWs tend to focus not on the winners in Hanoi but on the less disciplined and often demoralized captives who were held in the jungle camps. In Joseph Zito's *Missing in Action* (1984) and George P. Cosmatos's *Rambo: First Blood Part Two* (1985) the captives are represented as helpless victims who await rescue by a superhuman hero. In the latter, John Rambo (played by Sylvester Stallone) is cast in the Boone mold. Part American Indian, he returns to the jungles of Vietnam on a prisoner-of-war reconnaissance mission, armed with modern versions of the bow and knife. When his female Vietnamese companion is killed by the enemy, he wears her sash Apache-style as a headband. In the chase that follows, he emerges from the land, like its avenging genius, to kill a pursuing Russian soldier. Though the captives in these two films are all male, they play the more passive role ascribed to women in the classic frontier captivity narratives. They must patiently await redemption rather than redeeming themselves.

Mary Rowlandson's daughters likewise figure in Vietnam captivity narratives, though less frequently than her sons, perhaps because few women were actually captured. According to Defense Intelligence Agency records, the North Vietnamese and Viet Cong captured only nineteen women between 1962 and 1975. Eleven were Americans, including six who were taken during the final North Vietnamese offensive in the spring of 1975. Most were either missionaries or medical personnel sponsored by missionary organizations. None belonged to the American military. Two of the American women died in captivity, two escaped, and the remaining seven were released.[105] These figures suggest that the North Vietnamese rarely set out to capture women and saw little propaganda value in detaining them. Monika Schwinn, a German nurse and the only woman POW to be returned during Operation Homecoming, attributes this indifference to the inferior status of women in Vietnamese culture.[106]

Women captives are far more numerous in popular fiction and film treatments of the war than they were in real life. As with the popular male POW films, their stories are modeled more closely on the frontier captivity narratives than on historical fact. Among the first imaginative responses to the war were three romance novels entitled *Vietnam Nurse*, all aimed at an adolescent audience. One of these, written by Ellen Elliott and published in 1968, features an Australian nurse who is captured by the Viet Cong while searching for her father, a missionary in Vietnam.[107] Two American women—one an army nurse, the other a civilian—are captured by the VC in "The Unquiet Earth," an episode of the *China Beach* television series; they are held briefly in a tunnel complex, then released by a compassionate cadre. In both of these captivity narratives the VC are benign and the heroines' relationships with them entirely platonic.

One category of Vietnam captivity narrative featuring women was written for a more specialized readership. These are the pornographic novels about nurses, journalists, entertainers, civilian secretaries, and in one case even a group of radical lesbian feminists. Many, bearing titles like *Viet Cong Rape Compound* and *Sex Slaves of the Viet Cong*, were published anonymously by Star Distributors of Brooklyn as part of its "War Horrors" series in the late 1970s and early 1980s, well after the American withdrawal from Vietnam. A few pretend to be based on fact; thus the preface to one asserts that "[c]ountless numbers of American personnel, including nurses, are still being held as captives of the communists. They are still enduring the isolation and degradation of imprisonment by the cruel enemy."[108] The same novel is dedicated to the memory of an American nurse named Sandra Jean Davidson: "Born July 12, 1945. Died sometime between January 3, 1962 and December 31, 1963 in a Viet Cong prison camp. Her body is still in the hands of the communists."[109] Considering that Davidson would have been sixteen years old at the time of her capture, one is not surprised to learn that the Defense Intelligence Agency has no record of her existence.

"Total control over another person," one psychotherapist maintains, "is the power dynamic at the heart of pornography."[110] Much as the early captivity narratives decry American Indian savagery while appealing to the reader's fascination with the Indian, the pornographic novels piously lament the sexual humiliation of women while frankly appealing to prurient and sexist feelings. They are also unmistakably racist in their treatment of the Vietnamese, allowing the reader to project the guilt of vicarious pleasure onto scarcely human villains. Thus the publisher's foreword to one novel speaks of the "innate perversion of some Asian hordes" and likens the North Vietnamese to the Nazis, Mussolini, Stalin, and Charles Manson.[111] "Not even some tribes of American Indians," the writer of the foreword maintains, "in fighting the encroachment of the white man, can be compared with the beasts of Asia in perpetrating misery and madness on their enemies."[112]

Scott Grantland's *Bamboo Beast* (1968), one of the few pornographic captivity narratives to be published during the war, illustrates how the frontier captivities were recycled. The novel is typical of its subgenre as a whole, though more sophisticated in plot, characterization, and sense of military and political context. The heroine is Janice Murphy, a blonde divorcée and civilian secretary for a construction firm in Saigon. Abducted by the Viet Cong with the help of a disgruntled American construction worker, she endures a series of "removes" and sexual assaults before she is finally rescued by the marines. While held captive in a bomb factory in Cholon, she is approached by a group of Viet Cong women whom she fears almost as much as the men who assault her, for "[s]he knew in many primitive societies the women of the tribes were the most vicious."[113] Murphy is ostensibly abducted for ransom, which the Viet Cong can use to buy explosives, and also for information. The Viet Cong assume that she knows when a new airport runway will be dedicated, and they plan to assassinate three air force generals who will attend the ceremony.

Though Murphy is restored to the American community in Saigon, she is never the same after her captivity. She kills the construction worker who betrayed her, moves in with her boss, and turns to prostitution. Her disturbed behavior following the stress of captivity recalls that of former captives on the American frontier, although they suppressed this unhappy sequel in their narratives, perhaps in order to ingratiate themselves with the community. Returned captives, including Mary Rowlandson, were often suspected of having had sex with natives or having eaten human flesh. Rowlandson felt spiritually alienated from her family and was often unable to sleep at night; other women fell prey to guilt, violent behavior, and a pathological urge to public confession.[114] Mercy Short, who served as a key witness in the Salem witchcraft trials of 1692, had been captured as a girl of fifteen and taken to Canada after witnessing the murder of her family. Slotkin speculates that her "fits" during the trials, when she wrestled with diabolical specters in the likeness of American Indians, were actually a "second captivity."[115]

Today, thanks chiefly to the Vietnam War, we recognize Mercy Short's fits as flashbacks and the other women's distress as symptoms of post-traumatic stress disorder (PTSD). If PTSD qualifies as a second captivity, then we can enlarge the category of captivity narratives to include many veterans' stories. Unlike Mary Rowlandson and her fellow sufferers, soldiers did not go to Vietnam as passive victims, unless one considers them victims of the draft, discrimination (in the case of minorities and the poor), or prowar propaganda. Once in country, however, a few became prisoners of war while the rest became, to a greater or lesser extent, prisoners of the war. For every book or film that deals with the Hanoi or jungle camp POWs, there are dozens about Vietnam veterans' second captivity to PTSD, drug addiction, and Agent Orange. Taken together, these reflect the nation's ambivalence toward the captive, especially in the 1970s. In 1976, the year of the American Bicentennial, Hubbell lionized the Hanoi prisoners in *P.O.W.*; that same year Martin Scorsese represented a psychopathic veteran in the film *Taxi Driver.*

By the 1980s Americans had more sympathy for Vietnam veterans. This might be ascribed partly to the cooling of political passions and partly to films such as *The Deer Hunter* and *Apocalypse Now.* There may be yet another reason for the change. Beginning in 1979, Americans were treated to the spectacle of one captivity after another, as Iran, Lebanon, and various terrorist groups adopted the strategy used so effectively by the American Indians. Thanks in part to modern media coverage, the most powerful nation in the world was forced to endure the captive's sense of utter helplessness. Occasionally the United States was able to play the role of masculine avenger rather than feminine victim; thus the invasions of Grenada and Panama provided the sort of catharsis that the Puritans found in burning a Pequot village. More often, however, the country had to suffer its own impotence during the 1980s, deprived even of the consolation of believing, as its first settlers did, that weakness is an appeal to Divine Providence. Perhaps it was beyond even the power of Providence to redeem what the nation most wanted to redeem, namely, John F. Kennedy's image of the American as benign settler of the New Frontier.

VII

When Clancy comes to his senses in Eastlake's *Bamboo Bed*, he realizes that Vietnam is not the American frontier and the North Vietnamese are not Sioux or Cheyenne warriors. "No," he says. "I must have my wars confused. That was another time, another place. Other Indians." Clancy thus shows greater powers of discrimination than many who have told stories about the Vietnam War. So seductive are the likenesses between Vietnam and the American frontier that writers and filmmakers may overlook the differences. Here, by way of conclusion, we might consider the salient differences, relating first to the "Indian" adversary and then to the "frontier" setting.

Of the many historians who have written about the Vietnam War, Richard Drinnon has argued the most single-mindedly for its frontier genealogy. The thesis of *Facing West* (1980) is implicit in its subtitle, borrowed from Herman Melville: *The Metaphysics of Indian-Hating and Empire-Building*. According to Drinnon, racism is rooted in the Euro-American's repressive attitudes toward nature and the body. Regarding the Indian as a personification of sexual desire, the Euro-American violently suppresses the dark other. As a reward for this behavior, which is more or less reflexive and unconscious, the colonist receives the lands and goods that belonged to the Indian. Thus the "metaphysics" or psychology of Indian-hating drives colonial expansion, whether in North America, the Philippines, or Southeast Asia.[116]

Richard Slotkin and others have likewise remarked on the early American colonists' libidinal investment in the Indian. Unlike Drinnon, however, they allow for a range of responses other than repression. If some settlers killed the Indian in themselves and in the woods, others secretly envied the Indian whom they were supposed to hate. Still others became Indians for a lifetime or for a moment. One group of colonists assumed native dress in order to commit the lawless act of dumping tea into Boston Harbor. Thus they dramatized their difference from more compliant subjects of the Crown and defined the American as a cultural hybrid. The subsequent defeat of the American Indian was thus an occasion for regret as well as celebration, for it destroyed something that the white American genuinely valued and had partly assimilated.

Resemblances between the American Indian and the Vietnamese in our war stories are superficial, relating usually to their physical appearance and military tactics. Regarded from the standpoint of Drinnon's "metaphysics" of Indian-hating, the two peoples could hardly be more different. Like Sontag, the Hanoi POWs were struck by the social regimentation of the Vietnamese and their obsession with party procedures.[117] The enemy appeared to be petty bureaucrats rather than proud warriors. Instead of envying the Vietnamese their sexual freedom, Americans were more apt to despise them for an apparent lack of normal sexuality. GIs in South Vietnam assumed that many soldiers in the Army of the Republic of Vietnam (ARVN) were homosexual because they were physically slight and showed friendship by holding hands.[118] They lacked "normal" masculine aggression, often running from battle. North of the Demilitarized Zone, the Hanoi POWs likewise concluded that many of the guards and interrogators were gay and gave them nicknames like Sugar Plum Fairy and Peaches.[119] Sontag, despite her determination to admire the North Vietnamese, also wondered about their "almost sexless culture" and compared it unfavorably with the open eroticism of another communist country, Castro's Cuba.[120]

These judgments reveal more about the Euro-Americans who made them than they do about the Vietnamese or even about American Indians. But they do suggest that Drinnon's argument, and the frontier analogy that informs the other works discussed in this chapter, is flawed at its source. If the comparison depends on the empire builder's emotional investment in people of another culture, the "metaphysics" of Indian-hating, then the Vietnamese were not Indians at all.

For much the same reason, Vietnam fails to qualify as an analogue of the American frontier. The frontier had its share of Crown-appointed governors, soldiers, missionaries, and speculators who maintained their ties to the Old World. But the majority of farmers and tradespeople cast their lot unreservedly in the New World and came in time to regard themselves as American rather than English, French, Spanish, or Dutch. They were determined to settle down and realize what we have come to call the American Dream. Invoking that dream in the famous conclusion to *The Great Gatsby,* F. Scott Fitzgerald uses sexually charged imagery. The New World appears as a "fresh, green breast" to the Dutch sailors off Long Island, and Gatsby believes in an "orgiastic"—that is, an "orgasmic"—future.[121] Richard Slotkin and Annette Kolodny have traced this sexual motif in the utilitarian and imaginative literature of the frontier, showing how male settlers tended to regard the landscape as female. Their relation to the land might be that of son (as suggested by Fitzgerald's "fresh, green breast"), lover, or even rapist. Although there were undoubtedly settlers who played the first and last of these roles, it was the conjugal impulse that enabled many to leave father and mother in the Old World and cleave to the maiden landscape of the New.

Notwithstanding its great natural beauty, Vietnam has inspired few epithalamia from Americans who fought there. The land is usually represented as at best a femme fatale rather than a lover with whom the soldier might consummate the sacred marriage of ancient myth. The exceptions are works like Loyd Little's *Parthian Shot* (1975), which reflect the early phase of American involvement when the people were still friendly to Americans and the land still a tropical paradise, or late works like Gustav Hasford's *Phantom Blooper* (1990), which reflect a strong political identification with the North Vietnamese. A soldier in Larry Heinemann's *Close Quarters* speaks for many—perhaps the majority—of seasoned grunts when he remarks that Vietnam was not "worth the powder to blow it away with."[122] When a squad of American soldiers encounter a Viet Cong officer in Tim O'Brien's *Going after Cacciato,* they ask him why the country seems so menacing. "The soldier is but the representative of the land," Major Li Van Hgoc replies. "The land is your true enemy."[123] Unlike Fitzgerald's Dutch sailors, American soldiers generally found little in wartime Vietnam to entice them to stay. They came not to make their homes but to survive a twelve- or thirteen-month tour of duty and return to The World, whose claim to their affections remained unchallenged. Even as the POWs constructed their city upon a hill in Hanoi, they understood that it belonged spiritually in the States, which Jeremiah Denton called the promised land and Robinson Risner "the land of milk and honey."[124]

If Americans had little emotional investment in either the Vietnamese "Indian" or the Vietnam "frontier," why do these analogies pervade our war stories? I have already ventured several answers to this question: the prima facie resemblance between the two places and peoples, the sense of a comparable historical destiny being worked out on the New Frontier, the displacement onto foreign soil of a domestic conflict between two ways of regarding the environment and American Indian values. To these might be added the cultural influence of television and mass marketing. Many of the war novels and memoirs allude to childhood games of cowboys and Indians.[125] Nor was such play restricted to future soldiers. As Landon Y. Jones observes in his social history of the baby boom generation, the young people who would one day protest the Pentagon's firepower persuaded their parents to spend hundreds of millions of dollars outfitting them as gunslinger heroes like Hopalong Cassidy, Davy Crockett, Roy Rogers, Wyatt Earp, Gene Autry, and the Cisco Kid.[126] During the antiwar protests that ended in tragedy at Kent State in 1970, some of the demonstrators were dressed, ironically, as Daniel Boone and Davy Crockett.[127]

The peace activist with a toy six-shooter or long rifle is perhaps no more anomalous than the military leader who believes he must destroy a village in order to save it. Our Vietnam war stories suggest that we have yet to settle on a definitive version of the frontier myth. Though the Boone story of regeneration evolved from Puritan millennialism, it did not supplant its prototype. Together with the captivity plot of containment, both continue to supply the narrative structures to which we return as circumstance and ideology dictate. The third plot, so often an element in the other two, may well be the most inclusive of the three, inasmuch as it reflects our cultural captivity to myths of the frontier.

For better or worse, frontier mythology has remained what Michael Herr calls the "containing perimeter" of our collective experience. Knowing as much, and understanding the perils of regressive thought, are we now prepared to venture beyond the perimeter? George Santayana, who became a Harvard professor but never quite an American, understood the foibles of his adoptive country better than most, including its inclination to forget the past. What he may not have appreciated fully is the compulsive power of bad habits. Herr gives these their due in *Dispatches*, where, by way of a fatalistic postscript to Santayana, he quips, "Those who remember the past are condemned to repeat it too, that's a little history joke."[128]

CHAPTER 2

The Race War

I

For nearly two decades in the mid-nineteenth century, two all-black cavalry regiments skirmished with hostile American Indian tribes on the Great Plains. As told in William H. Leckie's *Buffalo Soldiers: A Narrative of the Negro Cavalry in the West* (1967), the story of the Ninth and Tenth Cavalries is a classic frontier narrative. The Plains Indians, though a noble adversary, had to be subdued if civilization was to continue its westward advance. The buffalo soldiers, so named for their close-napped hair, fought heroically for their white officers even though they were often denied the respect accorded their white comrades-in-arms. If they ever expressed any ambivalence toward the doctrine of Manifest Destiny that they helped to implement, it is not recorded in *The Buffalo Soldiers*. In fact the final sentences of the book imply that the black cavalrymen, like Filson's Daniel Boone, were content to be remembered for their role in clearing the ground for an agrarian Eden: "The Ninth and Tenth Cavalry were first-rate regiments and major forces in promoting peace and advancing civilization along America's last continental frontier. The thriving cities and towns, the fertile fields, and the natural beauty of that once wild land are monuments enough for any buffalo soldier."[1]

Leckie's study is both impressively researched and sympathetic. He traces his interest in the lot of the black soldier back to the end of World War II, when he was placed in charge of two hundred black airmen en route from service in the Pacific to separation centers in the States.[2] One wishes, however, that he had attended not only to the historical effects of the buffalo soldiers' service but also to the meaning they might have ascribed to it. Though it would be impossible to recover their intentions fully, it should be possible to locate this historical episode in the context of African American culture in the middle of the nineteenth century and so offer at least tentative answers to several nagging questions. During the period of the Indian Wars, for instance, fourteen soldiers from the four all-black regiments (two cavalry and two infantry) won Congressional Medals of Honor. Four of the medal winners were "black Seminoles," escaped slaves who had been removed from Florida during the Second Seminole War of 1832–1842.[3] How did they feel about fighting with their former enemy, the white man, against warriors of the same race as their former allies? How did black soldiers as a group feel about killing other nonwhites to secure the property of white settlers? Did they feel that their services were adequately rewarded once they had accomplished their mission?

These questions belong to the realm of "thick description," to use a phrase that the anthropologist Clifford Geertz borrowed from the philosopher Gilbert Ryle. Ryle staged an imaginary experiment in which two boys rapidly contracted their right eyelids. From the standpoint of mere phenomenalistic observation, the movements are identical. But from the standpoint of thick description one movement may register as an involuntary twitch, the other as a conspiratorial wink. In certain situations the movement of the eyelid might even be a parody of a conspiratorial wink. The significance of the event depends on its social context, the cultural web in which it is entangled. Geertz likens this web to a literary text and the anthropologist's task to textual criticism. In both cases, analysis consists of "sorting out the structures of signification . . . and determining their social ground and import."[4] The culture of a people is an "acted document" or, more precisely, "an ensemble of texts, themselves ensembles, which the anthropologist strains to read over the shoulders of those to whom they properly belong."[5] Thick description is consequently a form of intertextual study, where the "text" is any form of symbolic behavior, from writing poems to participating in a Balinese cockfight.

Though densely factual, Leckie's *Buffalo Soldiers* is "thin" in its description of American Indian and African American culture. Rather than taking what Geertz calls an "actor-oriented" approach to the black cavalrymen, reconstructing the symbolic world in which they moved and had their being, Leckie imposes a Euro-American myth of the frontier on the three races that met on the stage of the Great Plains. Where thick description might detect a wink or the parody of a wink, Leckie sees only a twitch or at best a wink with one kind of significance.

For a "thicker" description of the buffalo soldiers' experience—and therefore, from one point of view, better history—one might turn to John A. Williams's *Captain Blackman,* a novel published three years after Leckie's study and probably indebted to it. Williams's protagonist is a black officer who is wounded in an ambush in Vietnam. Delirious during recovery, he imagines himself taking part in the major American wars from the Revolution through the Korean War. In the episode devoted to the Indian Wars, he is a sergeant major in the Tenth Cavalry. While carrying the mail from one military outpost to another, he encounters two Comanche warriors who ask him why black men are fighting Indian tribes, when in the past the tribes had provided asylum for fugitive slaves. Contrasting American Indian resistance with black docility, one of the Comanches says, "Once we roamed this land from ocean to ocean, the old ones tell us. We'll be exterminated trying to hold on to a small part of it. You black people who have nothing, who let yourselves be dragged from far, far lands in chains, and who've believed, really believed that the white god was also your god, will survive us, multiply because you *do not fight,* will not fight the white man."[6]

The Comanche warrior thus reminds Blackman that in African American culture the myths of the "middle passage" and "slavery time" should decide his behavior, not the white man's myths of the frontier and Christian forbearance. Black people have purchased survival—"They endured" is Faulkner's tribute to the black cook Dilsey and her family—at the price of their humanity. Though Blackman protests that he is simply following orders as a good soldier must, he feels compromised. By placing these words in the mouth of an American Indian, Williams may be violating one culture, describing it "thinly," in order to do justice to another. The Comanche's voice is really Blackman's, and ultimately Williams's, by ventriloquism. It is the voice of African American culture and literature, testifying to its departures from the Euro-American tradition with which it shares so much.

It is of course misleading to speak of African American culture in the singular, as though it were a homogeneous entity. It is actually a plurality of cultures, varying from time to time, place to place, social class to social class. The peculiar texture of any of these cultures is the result of a complex negotiation between a group of African Americans, exotic cultures (African and Muslim, for example), and adjacent American cultures, themselves heterogeneous. But historically African American culture, in all its variety, has defined itself primarily in relation to mainstream white culture, the culture of the slaveholders. This has produced the "double consciousness" of which W. E. B. Du Bois speaks in *The Souls of Black Folk,* the "sense of always looking at one's self through the eyes of others, of measuring one's soul by the tape of a world that looks on in amused contempt and pity."[7] Yet even as African Americans have assimilated features of white culture and have judged themselves according to its standards, they have simultaneously separated themselves from that culture in virtually every sphere. The pattern of assimilation and separation, the "repeat-with-a-difference," is manifest in things as small as African American names, speech, and dress and in things as large as religion, politics, and art. To apply Geertz's analogy, African American culture is at once a text and an intertext.

In this chapter I describe those features of African American culture that help to make sense of black people's responses to the Vietnam War. I give particular attention to the military role of black Americans since the days of the colonial militias. Then I turn to works in which black and a few white writers and filmmakers have represented relations between the races during the Vietnam era, evaluating these responses in terms of their "texture," their success in making cultural meaning of the war experience. In trying to re-create the "thickness" of one culture, the African American, I have had to forgo treatment of Native, Latino, and Asian American responses to Vietnam.[8] For these too the 1960s was a decade of assimilation and separation; thus some features of the black experience of the war have parallels in theirs.

II

During the 1960s, while many young white people were trying to forget or repudiate their past, young black people were trying to recover theirs. This quest took them back not only to Africa but also to the earliest days of the nation that had yet to grant them full citizenship. They learned that the first man to die in the fight for independence from England was a runaway slave, Crispus Attucks. They learned that their people had served as soldiers in every American war except the war with Mexico, where they served as body servants.[9] They learned that many of the vexing issues raised by the Vietnam War had also been raised in previous wars. These could be posed as a series of questions: Is the war being fought for a worthy cause, one compatible with democratic ideals and practice? If there is more merit in the "enemy" cause, should black people withdraw their loyalty from the land of their birth? Finally, supposing the American cause is just, what should be the African American's proper role in the war?

All three questions were raised during the Revolutionary War, the first even before the American creed was formulated in a Declaration of Independence. That all men are created equal, that all have an unalienable right to life, liberty, and the pursuit of happiness, are among the truths this document holds to be self-evident. It was just as evident that these truths did not apply to free black people, much less slaves. Consequently, though African Americans had fought in the early battles of the war, Massachusetts decided in 1775 that enlisting slaves was "inconsistent with the principles that are to be supported, and reflect dishonor on this colony."[10] Rather than abolish slavery, Massachusetts abolished the inconsistency. The other colonies followed suit, and Congress endorsed General Washington's ban on further enlistment of black soldiers.

The second question—what to do if there is more merit in the enemy's cause—was raised when the British began to recruit slaves with the promise of freedom in return for service, a practice that soon forced the colonies to revise their ban on black enlistment. Nevertheless, approximately one thousand black men fought with the loyalists (versus five thousand with the patriots), and at the end of the war about twenty thousand were evacuated on British ships to the West Indies, Florida, Canada, and Nova Scotia. Though some of these were resold into slavery in the West Indies, most were freed.[11] Ironically, therefore, more black people obtained their freedom by siding with the Crown than with the colonies, despite the patriots' professed commitment to egalitarian principles.

The third question, regarding the African American's proper role in war, was also raised and answered during the Revolution. Black men who joined the colonial militias generally served as privates in integrated units. Though some were armed, most were used as laborers, drivers, and guides because slaveholders feared a possible insurrection if they were issued weapons and trained in their use. The Revolutionary pattern would obtain in subsequent wars, with the majority of black men occupying the lower ranks in noncombat roles. Thus a practice adopted in peculiar circumstances came to be regarded as the natural order of things, and black people were thought to be congenitally suited for labor duty rather than combat. Not until the end of the Korean War would they again serve in fully integrated units.

Doubts about black loyalty likewise surfaced in American wars both before and after the Revolution. Black people took both sides during the nearly three centuries of warfare between whites and American Indians. In 1657 black men joined the natives in an uprising in Hartford, Connecticut, an episode that resulted in their exclusion from the colonial militias for a time. During the French and Indian Wars black soldiers fought on the side of the colonies—the slaves in exchange for freedom, the freemen for enhanced social status. The War of 1812 followed the pattern of the Revolutionary War, with black soldiers fighting for the British as well as the new republic. Prior to the Civil War the Southern colonies enlisted slaves in their battles against the Yamassee, Chickasaw, and Natchez Indians, but when white troops attempted to recapture slaves who had escaped to the Seminoles, they encountered a united front of black and native warriors skilled in guerrilla warfare. The Filipino insurrection of 1899 to 1902 provides a transition from the Indian Wars to Vietnam, inasmuch as the insurgents appealed to black American soldiers to join them or else return home to fight the lynch mobs. Some deserted, including about five who went over to the rebels.[12]

Why were black people loyal to the colonial or American cause in one war and apparently disloyal in another? The answer to this question depends, for each war, on the answer to the first question posed above. Historically, African Americans have willingly fought to obtain or secure freedom and socioeconomic advantages. They have gone over to the enemy—or redefined the enemy—only when they have despaired of achieving these ends through loyalty to the American cause. When personal or political freedom was at stake, the decision was relatively clear-cut. Beginning with the Civil War, the issues became more clouded. With the Emancipation Proclamation, Lincoln acknowledged that the war was being fought not just to preserve the union but also to end slavery. Many in the North were unwilling to fight for that cause, and hundreds of black people were killed during the ugly draft riots that erupted in New York and other cities in 1863.[13] Obviously, racism would be more difficult to eradicate than slavery. Racism continued to flourish in military as well as civilian life, repeatedly confronting the black soldier with the contrast between his daily life and the ideals for which he was supposed to be fighting.

This discrepancy became an issue again in the Spanish-American War, when black leaders argued that it was hypocritical for the United

States to free Cuba from Spanish tyranny yet fail to ensure the rights of black people at home. That charge was repeated more forcefully when the United States appeared to be playing the role of tyrant during the Filipino insurrection.[14] Even in the "good war" of 1941 to 1945, black soldiers could not participate without feeling compromised. As with all American wars after the Revolution, it was fought by a Jim Crow army, with a majority of black men being assigned to service rather than combat units. This was a glaring instance of racism in a war fought ostensibly against proponents of racism, and the paradox was not lost on the black GI, especially when he observed German prisoners of war eating in restaurants that were closed to nonwhites.[15]

The two decades between the German surrender and the commitment of ground troops to Vietnam were a time of unprecedented advancement for African Americans in general and black soldiers in particular. During the first decade the armed services were in the vanguard of social change. Truman ordered the desegregation of the military in 1948, when "separate but equal" was still the law of the land for civilians. The banner passed to the civil sector in 1954, when the Supreme Court ordered desegregation of the schools. The following year Rosa Parks refused to give up her seat on a bus in Montgomery, Alabama, inaugurating the black-led movement that would culminate in the Civil Rights Act of 1964.

During the early years of the Vietnam War, black soldiers were more satisfied with their lot than ever before.[16] A high percentage served in elite combat units—particularly airborne and airmobile units—and they were two to three times as likely as white soldiers to reenlist.[17] To account for this level of satisfaction, one must look not only at the military but also at the black community. Despite the efforts of federal poverty programs and the civil rights movement, the rate of black unemployment remained high, making enlistment and reenlistment attractive even with a war in progress. Furthermore, pride in other areas of black accomplishment extended to military service. After centuries of being relegated to labor duty, the black soldier was now enjoying the prestige of the warrior. In fact some in the black community regarded him as a super soldier. *Ebony* magazine published an article in 1966 celebrating the airborne "Birdmen with Black Rifles," whose "ready adaptability to jungle warfare" particularly qualified them for service in Vietnam.[18]

Black warriors had to pay a price for their status. Since they were overrepresented in the elite combat units, they were correspondingly overrepresented in the early casualty figures. From 1961 to 1967, when

African Americans constituted 11–12 percent of the U. S. population and 9–11 percent of the armed forces, black combat fatalities ran to 14.1 percent, peaking at approximately 25 percent in late 1966 and early 1967.[19] When leaders in the black community expressed alarm at these numbers, the Department of Defense moved to limit the participation of black soldiers in combat.[20] As a result, black deaths were held to 13.1 percent of total fatalities for the war.[21]

Because the Vietnam War was America's first integrated war since the Revolution, it was expected to justify the great social experiment of desegregation. At first it seemed to do so. In 1966 *Time, Newsweek,* and *U. S. News and World Report* all published articles painting a rosy picture of interracial camaraderie; the few complaints were ascribed to the usual GI griping.[22] This image was still intact in 1967, when *Time* sent to Vietnam a team of reporters that included Wallace Terry, the Harlem-born, Brown University-educated journalist who would later compile *Bloods,* an oral history of black veterans of the war. Published in May, the *Time* cover story recorded the black soldiers' disapproval of black leaders who opposed the war, including Stokely Carmichael, Muhammad Ali, and even Martin Luther King, Jr. They approved of moderates like Massachusetts Senator Edward Brooke, Roy Wilkins, Thurgood Marshall, A. Philip Randolph, and Ralph Bunche. Reflecting on what he had seen while covering the story, Terry said, "I have observed here the most successfully integrated institution in America."[23]

As Terry and his colleagues hinted, however, this level of assimilation depended to some extent on voluntary separation. Off-duty black soldiers sought the company of other black soldiers in the bars of Soulsville, near the Saigon waterfront, or Soul Alley, near Tan Son Nhut Air Base. On base they were likely to live in all-black hooches and eat at all-black tables in the mess hall. Black self-segregation was partly a reaction against the hostility of some white soldiers, particularly those from the South who displayed Confederate flags and played country and western music. But it was primarily an assertion of "black is beautiful" racial pride, manifest in gestures such as the ditty-bop walk, the elaborate ritual handshake known as dapping, and—especially later—the clenched-fist black power salute. In an effort to separate themselves from the white man's army, to repeat its forms with a difference, black soldiers risked violations of the appearance and dress code with Afro haircuts, pick combs jutting from hip pockets, braided wrist bands, and "shades" (sunglasses) worn day and night.

Vietnam in the late 1960s was the perfect laboratory in which to observe the social dynamics that Thomas Kochman describes in *Black and White Styles in Conflict*. Black soldiers complained that white "chucks" or "rabbits"—less neutral terms were "crackers" and "honkies"—lacked "soul"; they were emotionally repressed and conventional to the point of being dull. White soldiers complained that black "brothers" or "spades"—the hostile terms are well known—were "showboats," loud and boastful. Though the two races shared more or less the same language, they had different rhetorical traditions. African Americans were schooled from early childhood in the arts of bragging (for which Muhammad Ali became notorious), signifying (which Geneva Smitherman defines as "the verbal art of insult in which a speaker humorously puts down, talks about, needles—that is, signifies on—the listener"), and the dirty dozens (insulting someone's mother, often in crudely sexual ways).[24] White soldiers did not understand these conventions, nor did they understand that for black people verbal aggression need not lead to physical aggression. Consequently, in confrontations between black and white soldiers, fighting words sometimes led to fistfights and fistfights to firefights.

Despite the violence that occasionally erupted from fundamental differences in style, race relations in Vietnam in 1967 were such that the *Time* reporters could plausibly predict that "whatever the outcome of the war, whatever its length and its price in suffering, the result of the Viet Nam experience should pay high dividends in reshaping white Americans' attitudes toward social justice and integration."[25] They could hardly have foreseen how polarized the races would become in the months ahead and how divided they would remain for the rest of the war, despite the Defense Department's belated efforts to promote racial understanding. The most dramatic event, the one that has attained quasi-mythical status in African American accounts of the war, was the assassination of Martin Luther King, Jr., on 4 April 1968.

Though King opposed the war, he was regarded by both black and white people as a moderate. He had in fact cultivated that image, shrewdly using militant separatist groups as his "big stick." If white America refused to deal with him, it would have to deal with them. To black soldiers learning about the murder over Armed Forces radio, it seemed that King had been killed not by a lone assassin—an escaped convict at that—but by white America, the "beast" of militant rhetoric. Riots erupted in Vietnam as they did in the United States, and some white soldiers countered with the hoisting of Confederate flags and the burning of crosses.[26] Even career noncommissioned officers (NCOs) who had long tolerated the younger black soldiers' taunt of "Uncle Tom" were now forced to reconsider their commitment to the military, the war, and their country.

Though there were few black officers and the young black GIs complained of discriminatory treatment when it came to promotions, punishments, and the more dangerous combat assignments, black career soldiers who remembered what military life had been like during World War II and the Korean War felt that Vietnam provided a satisfactory answer to the question of the African American's proper role in the armed services. But the other two questions became more troubling as the war dragged on. Eventually the negative responses to these canceled any satisfaction the black soldier might take in his combat role.

It was the black civilian community that forced the black soldier to examine the justice of the war and its claims on his loyalty, even as it had initially cultivated his military pride. The black soldier had to be loyal first to his own people, then to his country. But whom did his community include? Only the African Americans at home, or black people throughout the world? Perhaps all people of color? The more influential leaders in the black community paid less attention to the black soldier's enhanced military status than they did to the cost of that status. Prior to 1967 the war claimed the lives of proportionately more young black soldiers than white soldiers, and these belonged to the group that the black community could least afford to lose. Approximately 70 percent of black men were disqualified from service for poor health or low scores on the Armed Forces Qualifying Test (AFQT), as compared with approximately 33 percent for their age group as a whole.[27] The high rate of disqualification tended to offset the higher rate at which black men were drafted.[28] But the 30 percent who qualified for service were less likely than qualified white men to be deferred for education, hardship, or dependency; hence they were more likely to be sent to Vietnam, take part in combat, and become casualties. Vietnam thus claimed some of the more promising young African Americans of their generation, those to whom the black community might have turned for leadership in the postwar years.

From 1966 to 1971 the Department of Defense tried to reclaim the "wasted" one-third of the draft pool with Project 100,000. The project was regarded by its promoters as a way to solve one social problem with another, by its critics as a cynical device to generate cannon fodder—a total of over 320,000 soldiers—for the war. In theory the program was designed to break the cycle of poverty for the 36 percent of participants who were black. Black males would be removed from the "matrifocal" families in which they had been raised, taught pride and marketable skills in the armed forces, and restored to civilian life as productive members of society.

Project 100,000 failed to achieve these goals. Young men who would normally have scored too low on the AFQT were inducted, but few qualified for technical specialties, and 37 percent were assigned to combat-related specialties.[29] Military leaders resented having to provide a social service while fighting a war, and participants in the program were far more likely than their peers to go absent without leave (AWOL), receive judicial and nonjudicial punishment, and be discharged under less than honorable conditions. Though the men in Project 100,000 suffered proportionally fewer casualties than others who were sent to Vietnam, they were more likely to become casualties in civilian life. A follow-up study completed in 1989 reported that they were paid less and were more likely to be unemployed than low-aptitude nonveterans.[30]

The war claimed not only the black community's future in the form of its young men but also federal funding that would otherwise have gone into the Great Society's War on Poverty. Rather than jeopardize what support remained, civil rights leaders such as Carl Rowan, Whitney Young, and Roy Wilkins resisted any alliance with the largely white antiwar movement.[31] Wilkins maintained that foreign policy lay outside the purview of his organization, the National Association for the Advancement of Colored People (NAACP). To oppose the war was not only to oppose the president but also to risk divisiveness in the civil rights movement and invite red-baiting by conservative elements in white society. Martin Luther King, Jr., accepted these risks when he came out against the war in 1965, thus aligning the Southern Christian Leadership Conference with groups like the Student Non-Violent Coordinating Committee and the Congress of Racial Equality.[32]

King's opposition was based less on pragmatic concern for the black community than on transcendent moral and religious principles. In an address at the Riverside Church in New York in 1967, he deplored the dismantling of poverty programs but went on to point out the same contradiction that black leaders had observed in previous wars: black soldiers were being sent "8,000 miles away to guarantee liberties in Southeast Asia which they had not found in Southwest Georgia and East Harlem."[33] Surveying the violence wreaked upon Vietnamese enemy and ally alike, King likened American strategies to those used by Nazi

Germany. Violence hurts the perpetrator as well as the victim, King said, and called for a return to the Christian vision of universal brotherhood, "a world-wide fellowship that lifts neighborly concern beyond one's tribe, race, class and nation."[34]

If Roy Wilkins spoke for the black community's immediate self-interest, King spoke for its humanitarian aspirations. Between these extremes lay not only the more moderate antiwar black leaders such as James Farmer and Floyd B. McKissick but also militants such as Stokely Carmichael, H. Rap Brown, Huey Newton, and Eldridge Cleaver. The latter shared King's view that Vietnam was a genocidal war pitting one people of color against another to secure white military and economic advantages in Southeast Asia. Their sense of the black community embraced all peoples of African origin and, by extension, all nonwhite people. Malcolm X set the pattern of such thinking when he defected from the separatist Nation of Islam to embrace internationalism. Unlike King, however, the militants were prepared to take up arms against white America if necessary. Writing from political exile in Cuba, marine veteran Robert F. Williams had already put combat veterans on notice that their skills would be useful in the urban guerrilla warfare to come.[35]

Even before King's assassination, fewer black youths were willing to listen to his message of nonviolence. The more militant leaders had their ear, and they changed the character of black-white relations in the military after 1967. The posthumous influence of Malcolm X is most evident in the testimony of the Fort Jackson Eight, six nonwhite and two white soldiers who led antiwar protests at an army base in South Carolina in 1969. Several had been active in socialist and black liberationist groups prior to induction, and at least one, heeding Williams's advice, had joined the army to train for the revolution.[36]

Elsewhere in the States, forty-three black soldiers stationed at Fort Hood, Texas, refused to be sent as guards to the Democratic National Convention in 1968 because they feared that they would be used against their own people. Fort Benning, Georgia, was the scene of frequent racial brawls and assaults in 1969. Between January and August of the same year, over 160 violent racial episodes took place at Camp Lejeune, North Carolina, including the fatal beating of a white Vietnam veteran.[37] The year 1971 brought a four-day race riot at Travis Air Force Base and racial violence aboard three naval vessels. The nation as a whole was forced to pay attention to racial conflict in the armed services in 1973, when James Robert Essex, a black navy veteran, shot and killed six whites and wounded several others from the rooftop of a motel in New Orleans.

Racial strife in Vietnam was less publicized by the media but just as serious. The riots and cross burnings that followed the murder of Martin Luther King, Jr., were still a fresh memory in September 1968, when two hundred black prisoners rioted in the army stockade at Long Binh, killing one white inmate and injuring several others.[38] For a week in early 1971, Danang was the scene of open racial warfare, and countless incidents of violence, including fatal shootings and fraggings (assaults with explosive devices) occurred throughout the country. Wallace Terry was struck by the change in attitude when he returned to Vietnam for a two-year assignment ending in 1969. Far from disapproving of black leaders who opposed the war, black GIs were now three times as likely as whites to subscribe to the view that America had no business in Vietnam and should withdraw at once.[39] Furthermore, many were now prepared to take part in a riot or revolt (45 percent of black enlisted men) and join a militant group like the Black Panthers (31 percent of enlisted) when they returned home.[40] For black soldiers in Vietnam the enemy was now Charles, a term that could refer either to Charlie (the Viet Cong) or to Chuck (the white man).

The North Vietnamese and the National Liberation Front (NLF) in South Vietnam were quick to detect and exploit this division in the ranks. Ho Chi Minh had published articles on lynching and the Ku Klux Klan in 1924 and, later, a pamphlet on "the Negro question."[41] Throughout the war, the North and the NLF used leaflets, trailside signs, and the broadcasts of Hanoi Hannah to try to convince black GIs that they were fighting on the wrong side. Interrogators at the prisons in the North were well versed in black militant literature and used its arguments against captured black pilots.[42] One of those militants, Stokely Carmichael, traveled to Hanoi in 1967 to pledge the support of American blacks to the North Vietnamese cause. Another, Huey Newton, wrote to the NLF in 1970, offering to send Black Panthers to serve as revolutionary troops. Following the King assassination, black soldiers noticed that in firefights the Viet Cong would target white soldiers, sometimes allowing black troops to pass unscathed.[43]

What did these divisive tactics accomplish? Very little, measured in terms of black defections to the enemy. Though some black soldiers deserted and sought refuge in Soul Alley outside Saigon or the "Dogpatch" outside Danang, the one serviceman to be convicted of collaboration with the enemy during the Vietnam War was a white marine, Pfc. Robert Garwood. In 1971 the NLF delegation to the Paris Peace Talks claimed that American soldiers (their race unspecified) were fighting with Liberation Army troops. At the time, the Defense Department acknowledged that it had heard similar rumors but lacked any proof. A report prepared by the Defense Intelligence Agency in 1978 confirmed that some deserters had gone over to the enemy, though it was still unable to specify their number or identify them. Especially persistent, the report noted, were rumors of a biracial team of collaborators. Known only by their noms de guerre Salt and Pepper, this pair was said to have commanded enemy troops in an attack on an outpost near Quang Ngai City in 1974, after the American withdrawal from Vietnam.[44]

When a Vietnamese bar girl pointed to her own skin, then to that of a black GI and said "same-same," she appealed to feelings that he could not entirely suppress and whose political implications had been worked out by both the enemy and the militants at home. Some black soldiers found this Afro-Asian sympathy so attractive that they settled in Asia (usually Thailand or Japan) after completing their tours of duty. This is not to say, however, that this relationship was free of racism. Many black soldiers despised the Vietnamese and freely used epithets like "slope" and "gook."[45] Conversely, though the Vietnamese preferred American blacks to the Senegalese of the first Indochina war, they had absorbed the French prejudice in favor of lighter skin.[46] Though the younger, more nationalistic generation of Vietnamese disavowed this attitude, they could not rid themselves of prejudice against the minorities in their own country—particularly the Montagnards, Cambodians, and Chinese.

"Same-same" the black soldier and his Vietnamese companion might be in Southeast Asia. Back in the States, however, black veterans had occasion to contrast their lot with that of the boat people. During their fathers' war, black GIs had been forced to wait outside while German prisoners of war ate in segregated restaurants. After their own war, they watched Vietnamese immigrants move into the black community and succeed as shopkeepers.[47] Like white veterans, they often had to cope with post-traumatic stress or the effects of exposure to Agent Orange. But they also faced an unemployment rate eight or nine times that of their white peers in the twenty- to twenty-five-year-old age group, despite a job training program conducted on military bases by the National Urban League.[48]

Frustrated and anxious to disarm criticism for fighting in whitey's war, black veterans sometimes followed through on their threat to join militant organizations. According to one veteran, most of the Black Panthers in Washington were Vietnam veterans.[49] Another claimed that veterans made up a third of the Zulu 1200s in St. Louis.[50] Despite their bitterness and willingness to adapt their combat skills to urban guerrilla warfare, however, black veterans did not ignite the racial Armageddon so often predicted in the late 1960s and early 1970s. Why not?

The answer is necessarily speculative. One journalist suggested that veterans found themselves "playing catch-up" back in the States, and so were unable to lead either the militants or those entering the American mainstream.[51] Those who defied the system often did so in ways that landed them in prison, one by one. Some redefined their revolutionary objectives along nonracial lines; thus one of the Fort Jackson Eight was converted from advocating a black revolution to advocating a socialist revolution.[52]

Another answer can be traced to a significant revision of black millenarianism between 1963 and 1973. In the eighteenth century, the black slave-poet Jupiter Hammon described "The Day of Salvation" in terms of conventional Calvinist typology.[53] But for most black slaves the Second Coming was fraught with meanings that it did not have for the white master. They anticipated not only a general judgment that would separate the just from the unjust but also, according to Houston Baker, an "apocalyptic day that would bring their release from captivity and vengeance on the oppressors."[54] In the early 1960s writers such as James Baldwin and Amiri Baraka revived this familiar trope to represent the crisis of their times. Alluding to an old Negro spiritual, Baldwin concluded *The Fire Next Time* (1963) with the words, "If we do not now dare everything, the fulfillment of that prophecy, recreated from the Bible in song by a slave, is upon us: *God gave Noah the rainbow sign, No more water, the fire next time!*"[55]

In keeping with the tradition of the American jeremiad, Baldwin's conditional clause recognizes that timely reform might forestall retribution, and his plural pronoun embraces a community of "relatively conscious whites" as well as blacks. Baraka, in contrast, admitted neither a stay of execution nor any hope for collaboration with the white devil. His essay "Last Day of the American Empire (Including Some Instructions for Black People)" (1964) called on blacks to precipitate their own apocalypse, to usher in an autonomous black world through violent revolution.

What happened over the course of the following decade, the decade of the Vietnam War, can be inferred from Clyde Taylor's *Vietnam
and Black America: An Anthology of Protest and Resistance* (1973).
Though Taylor reprinted an essay in which Julian Bond dismisses the
threat of a black revolution, the collection as a whole anticipates some
such consummation.[56] Taylor speaks in his own contribution of black
people biding their time until American military and political power
becomes overextended in "some disastrous undertaking," when it will
be ripe for defeat.[57] However, the final three sections of the anthology,
entitled "The Black Soldier," "Radical Alternatives," and "A Third-
World Kind of Peace," suggest why the revolution would never come to
pass. They plot a narrative in which the process of separation begun in
Vietnam would sweep radicalized black soldiers and opponents of the
war beyond schemes for urban warfare to a vision of community with
their brothers and sisters in Africa, Asia, and other non-Western countries.

Apocalypse is redefined in Taylor's final phase as "the revolutionary
restructuring of the world that has already gotten underway."[58] Like the
immanent apocalypse that replaced imminent apocalypse in Puritan
ideology, this notion of the "last days" mitigates its terror and sense of
urgency. Taylor concedes as much in the introduction to *Vietnam and
Black America,* where he offers the collection not as a call to arms but
as historical evidence of African American investment in the war. Indeed, with American involvement in Vietnam winding down in 1973,
the book could be safely and profitably published by a major commercial press.

III

With the mention of Baldwin and Baraka, we have begun to move from
the politics of African American culture during the war to its poetics. In
the work of major African American writers one encounters the same
dialectic of assimilation and separation to be found in African American
culture. If the slave narrative is the "locus classicus" of African American literary discourse, as Baker maintains, then Frederick Douglass's
contribution to the genre might serve as a paradigm for the entire tradition.[59]

Douglass understood, from the moment his master forbade instruction in reading and writing, that his freedom depended on acquiring
these skills. First he learned the discourse of the "permission" or pass

he needed to escape, then he mastered the rhetorical conventions of abo-
litionist oratory and the personal narrative. When Douglass took his
surname from a poem about James of Douglas written by Sir Walter
Scott, he performed a characteristic gesture, simultaneously adopting a
European literary genealogy and separating himself from it by the dou-
bling of the final consonant. Though he appreciated the vernacular
forms of slave culture, particularly the "sorrow songs" to which he
traced his "first glimmering conception of the dehumanizing character
of slavery," he regarded the vernacular slave culture for the most part
as a sign of his people's degradation and therefore as something to be
transcended.[60] When an older slave gave him a magical root that was
supposed to protect him from harm, he felt embarrassed about yielding
to superstition, even though the root did seem to spare him one whip-
ping.[61]

The pattern of Douglass's *Narrative* is anticipated in the writings of
Phillis Wheatley and repeated in those of Richard Wright, Ralph Ellison, and James Baldwin. Though their work cannot be mistaken for
that of white American writers, it generally aspires to the condition of
human "universality" as defined by Western culture. In the 1960s black
writers undertook aesthetically as well as ideologically what Baker has
called the "journey back." Whereas the Black Power movement sought
to create a separate base of African American political action, the Black
Arts movement sought to create a distinctive African American artistic
culture. Following the lead of Baraka and Larry Neal, black authors of
the 1960s sought to write poetry and prose that served the political
revolution.

By the 1970s writers such as Toni Morrison, Ishmael Reed, Ernest
Gaines, and Alice Walker had subordinated ideology to the recovery of
African American vernacular forms. However disastrous the socioeconomic effects of segregation, it had helped to preserve a separate musical culture featuring the blues and jazz. Its literary resources included
not only jazz and the blues as formal devices but also African American
folklore, dialect, and rhetorical strategies. These writers also understood what Du Bois meant when he called the African American church
"the most characteristic expression of African character."[62] The church
and its forms—the Negro spiritual, pulpit oratory, testifying, call and
response—have a place in their work that they could not have in the
ideologically pure literature of Black Power, which regarded Christianity as the religion of the slaveholder.

If Vietnam was a reprise of the frontier for white soldiers and civilians, it was for African Americans a transformative "middle passage," reversing the direction of the slave trade. The reversal is evident not only in the more sophisticated literary responses to the war but also in a subliterary genre: oral history. The best example of the form, and easily the best-known collection of African American responses to Vietnam, is Wallace Terry's *Bloods* (1984). *Bloods* is more artful than most oral histories because Terry freely edited the interviews to achieve an effect similar to that of short fiction. He even invented a new generic label, the "oral novella," to describe these carefully plotted stories.[63] *Bloods* is consequently more engaging than its predecessors, Mark Baker's *Nam* (1981) and Al Santoli's *Everything We Had* (1981). It also communicates a stronger sense of each contributor's identity. Terry identifies each veteran, includes his photograph, and captures his distinctive manner of speaking. In Baker's book the contributors remain anonymous and unpictured; in Santoli's the contributions are very brief, sometimes taking up less than a page.

For all its virtues, *Bloods* cannot escape some of the shortcomings of the oral history genre. Each of the twenty interviewees has, on the average, fewer than fifteen pages in which to tell his story. Thus the reader still knows too little about each man to assess the significance—in some cases even the credibility—of his account. Furthermore, the narratives are "thin" in Geertz's sense of the word. Though Terry has rearranged the testimony of his contributors for maximum rhetorical effect, he does not provide any cultural context. To supply what is lacking (or taken for granted) in *Bloods*, I consider it in conjunction with other works that contextualize, complicate, and even contradict its testimony.

The narratives in *Bloods* fall into two groups according to the soldier's rank when he was in Vietnam. Those who were lower-ranking enlisted men tell stories of separation, whereas the former officers and senior NCOs tell stories of assimilation. Though both types begin as stories of assimilation, the enlisted men's stories usually include a classic plot reversal of some kind. Some of the enlisted men chose military service as the lesser of two evils, the greater evil being jail or working for the FBI as an informant.[64] But most regarded it as a way to "become somebody" or measure up to a parent's expectations. They became disaffected with the military and the war for the same reasons many white soldiers did, but also cite examples of racial discrimination in assignments and promotions. At this stage their sense of a shared cultural heritage based on music—usually soul music or the jazz of John Coltrane and Miles Davis—sometimes led to the study of African American history. One soldier became especially interested in the buffalo soldiers and had his picture taken for the book in front of a statue of a black cavalryman.

Several enlisted men mention the murder of Martin Luther King, Jr., as a turning point in their attitude toward the war. One recalls that after the murder Hanoi Hannah (he remembers the name as Hanoi Helen) singled out black GIs in a broadcast, saying, "Soul brothers, go home. Whitey raping your mothers and your daughters, burning down your homes. What you over here for? This is not your war. The war is a trick of the Capitalist empire to get rid of the blacks" (p. 39). The situation is one that Yusef Komunyakaa, an accomplished veteran-poet of the war, has dramatized in "Hanoi Hannah." In Komunyakaa's poem Hannah appeals to the black soldiers' homesickness, fear of betrayal by lovers, anger at the King murder, and doubts about their investment in the war. "Soul Brothers," she asks, "what you dying for?"[65] Whereas the veteran in *Bloods* accedes to the propaganda ("I really started believing it," he says), the black soldiers in the poem answer her appeals with progressively more furious displays of firepower. But they cannot silence Hannah because she speaks in their own hearts. Thus the poem transforms a simple act of acquiescence into a complex form of repression. To repeat Ryle's distinction, what appears to be a blink is really a wink.

Once the enlisted men of *Bloods* returned to the States, they expressed the urge to separate from mainstream America in various ways. Some joined the Black Panthers or other militant organizations, though one later wondered if such activism was not "just showing off" given the practical needs of the black community at the time (p. 12). Another veteran helped to hijack a post office truck carrying $320,000 and used some of the money for Robin Hood-style charity among poor black people in Washington. While serving time in prison he studied North African civilization, took an Egyptian name, and adopted African dress (pp. 102–7). One who had "heard the voice of God" in Vietnam became a Baptist minister (p. 63), and another dreamed of returning to Southeast Asia as a missionary (p. 86). In context, their religious commitment is as much a declaration of racial identity as membership in the Panthers or the Nation of Islam.

Among the other personal narratives and autobiographical fictions that trace the black enlisted man's progress from assimilation to separation are David Parks's *G.I. Diary* (1968), Stanley Goff and Robert Sanders's *Brothers: Black Soldiers in the Nam* (1982), and John Carn's

Shaw's Nam (1984). The ambivalence of Terry Whitmore's *Memphis-Nam-Sweden: The Autobiography of a Black American Exile* (1971) is particularly instructive. Before Whitmore was wounded in an ambush in 1967, he was politically innocent. While recovering in Japan he met a young woman who put him in touch with Beheiren, an international underground railroad for American deserters. Though Whitmore became something of a celebrity in Russia and later Sweden, where he settled and started a family, he resisted assimilation by anti-American ideologues. Much as Frederick Douglass's narrative was introduced by two white abolitionists, William Lloyd Garrison and Wendell Phillips, Whitmore's is introduced by a white activist, Richard Weber, who has his own agenda. But Whitmore's story resists Weber's effort to interpret it as a reversal of the historical migration from Europe to America. Though Whitmore separates himself from American policy, he refuses to think of himself as a deserter. He identifies himself instead as a black American in exile.

In his attempt to abstract a simple political message from the thick texture of Whitmore's story, Weber makes the same mistake as many other white writers who have tried to represent the African American experience of the Vietnam War. Writing about Faulkner's novels, Ralph Ellison remarked that the early fiction tends to stereotype black characters as either "good niggers" or "bad niggers."[66] The same pattern obtains in white representations of the black enlisted man; he is likely to appear as either an assimilationist noble savage (Uncle Tom, Super Soldier) or a separatist demon (Black Power Militant, Bad Nigger). Braiden, the quadriplegic who dreams of Africa in Larry Brown's *Dirty Work* (1989), belongs to the first category; Skeeter in John Updike's *Rabbit Redux* (1971), Jinx in Charles Durden's *No Bugles, No Drums* (1976), and Eddie Palmer in Walter Kempley's *The Invaders* (1976) belong to the second. James N. Pruitt's *Striker One Down* (1987), a pulp novel based on the Salt and Pepper legend, manages to include both types. Pruitt's Pepper, a cold-blooded killer who hates the Vietnamese as much as he does both black and white Americans, is counterbalanced with a patriotic black sergeant named Abraham Lincoln Richardson.

The contrast between black and white accounts is more pronounced when one turns from the enlisted men to the officers and career NCOs. One of the officers in *Bloods* served as an assistant to Admiral Elmo Zumwalt, Jr., and in that capacity pressed for reform of racist policies in the navy. Generally, however, the officers and career NCOs accepted the military on its own terms and tried to "prove themselves worthy."

These include the best-known contributors to the book: Captain Joseph B. Anderson, the West Point graduate whom Pierre Schoendoerffer featured in his documentary film *The Anderson Platoon* (1967); Colonel Fred V. Cherry, a pilot who spent over seven years as a prisoner of the North Vietnamese; and Captain Norman Alexander McDaniel, a crewman who was a prisoner for over six years. Though conscious of racial inequities on the home front, these officers continue to regard America as, in McDaniel's words, "the black man's best hope" (p. 138).

Both Cherry and McDaniel recount North Vietnamese torture and interrogations in detail, describing how interrogators used black militant literature and the King murder to induce prisoners to make propaganda tapes aimed at black GIs. Komunyakaa thickens the texture of the oral testimony in a prose piece entitled "The One-Legged Stool." His black POW, a sergeant first class, refuses to collaborate with the enemy. But in his delirium he becomes less certain about the identity of his true enemy. Addressing a prison guard in the closing passage, he says, "With your eyes pressed against the face-window, you're like a white moon over Stone Mountain. You're everywhere. All I have to go back to are faces just like yours at the door."[67] Back home in Georgia, among white faces, his position will be as precarious as it is in Vietnam, on a one-legged stool.

When representing black officers, white writers seem reluctant to show any but the most patriotic side of the officers' personalities. Among such paragons are Captain David Walsh in Edward Linn and Jack Pearl's *Masque of Honor* (1969) and Lieutenant Rufus Brooks in John M. Del Vecchio's *13th Valley* (1982). These portrayals have ample warrant in the testimony of the officers interviewed for *Bloods*. But the omission of black officers who are critical of their country or the war speaks volumes. It implies that poorer, less educated black people might have a legitimate quarrel with American policy, but not those who have gained access to college and other perquisites of the middle class. The thinking black man will presumably see the wisdom of assimilation.

In contrast, black writers suggest that the black officer might use his intelligence to subvert the system. In *Coming Home* (1971), George Davis tells the story of two black pilots stationed in Thailand. Childress is a streetwise soldier who asserts his manhood through sexual conquest and defiance of "the man." On his last mission over North Vietnam he hopes to shoot down an enemy plane and thus win a medal that he can thrust in the face of any white man who dares to call him "boy."

But when he actually returns to the States he kills a policeman and is thrown in jail. His hoochmate Ben is likewise critical of the white establishment. He holds white colonialism responsible for the war and reflects cynically that America is in Southeast Asia to protect the market for Bulova watches and Texaco gasoline.[68] Because of his Harvard education, however, Ben is less comfortable with his black identity than Childress is. He once hoped to reestablish his connection with his race through his wife, only to discover that she aspired to whiteness. Consequently, when he finally decides that he must desert rather than continue fighting for a cause he does not believe in, he cannot identify himself as a black American in exile, like Whitmore. He becomes a man without a country or a people.

Captain Aaron Rodgers in Blyden Jackson's *Operation Burning Candle* (1973) entertains no such doubts or misgivings. He is the kind of officer one might expect to find in a novel written by a former marine who led a militant faction of the Congress of Racial Equality in a demonstration on the Triborough Bridge in New York.[69] Having absorbed the ideas of Malcolm X and other militants, Rodgers enlists in the Special Forces to acquire combat training, then goes to Vietnam to recruit a team of black revolutionaries like himself. He grafts his black militant ideology onto Jung's theory of the collective unconscious, which he equates with black racial consciousness. Convinced that white America must undergo a collective psychological trauma before it will revise its image of African Americans, he returns to the States with his team and a plan. They infiltrate the Democratic National Convention at Madison Square Garden and assassinate the governor of Mississippi and Southern congressmen whom they regard as the remaining links to a slave-holding past. Though Rodgers dies in the attempt, he considers his mission a success because the black community has shown itself ready to support a revolution.

"Whatever meaning is made of the black experience in Vietnam," William M. King has said, "must be shaped by black people."[70] This overview of African American responses to the war, incomplete and cursory though it is, suggests that he is right. For white writers, as Ellison recognized, America's most visible minority remains the hardest to see. It would nevertheless be a mistake to think that black America can make sense of its Vietnam experience in isolation from white America. This is the point of Komunyakaa's "Tu Do Street," which may be the best single dramatization of black-white relations during the war.

Enjoying some R & R (rest and recreation) away from places where the
two races are united by enemy fire, the speaker of the poem walks down
a Saigon street with its unofficially segregated bars. Here too, however,
black and white are brought together by the Vietnamese, in this case
the prostitutes of Tu Do Street:

> There's more than a nation
> inside us, as black & white
> soldiers touch the same lovers
> minutes apart, tasting
> each other's breath,
> without knowing these rooms
> run into each other like tunnels
> leading to the underworld.[71]

This was Vietnam in the 1960s—a microcosm of multiracial America.
If it was a dangerous, even hellish place, it was also a place of unsus-
pected intimacy, where the marriage of convenience on the battlefield
was grounded in a marriage of cultures on the home front. Komunyakaa's alleys and tunnels are the texture of the race war, the network
of devious connections that underlie both the official racial assimilation
of 1960s America and the unofficial separation.

The works discussed thus far suggest the political dialectic of assimilation and separation in the African American experience of Vietnam.
Komunyakaa's poetry represents the formal equivalent of that experience in its blending of mainstream Western and vernacular African
American traditions. Komunyakaa remarked in an interview that the
poems of *Dien Cai Dau* owe less to jazz forms than those of his previous two collections; but at least one, "You and I Are Disappearing,"
was inspired by Thelonius Monk.[72] In another interview he acknowledged the influence of the oral tradition of "storytellers and sorcerers"
on his work, and one critic has identified Komunyakaa's performing
voice specifically as Louisiana Creole.[73]

In the following sections I consider three other works that draw
heavily on the formal and thematic resources of black storytelling. *Captain Blackman,* already mentioned in connection with the buffalo soldiers, is the work of John A. Williams, a navy veteran of World War II
and an established writer. *De Mojo Blues* (1985) is the first novel of
Vietnam veteran A. R. Flowers. *Ashes and Embers* (1982), a 16 mm
film, was written, directed, and produced by Haile Gerima, a native of
Ethiopia who came to the United States as a young man in the 1960s.

IV

The buffalo soldier episode typifies Williams's strategy for giving thick description to African American military history in *Captain Blackman*. Blackman's encounter with the Comanches, like his other interventions in history prior to the Korean War, is represented as a dream, an imaginative reconstruction of events that he had studied in conventional history texts and documents and taught in his black history seminar. To a greater degree than in most historical novels, the genre to which *Captain Blackman* belongs, there is a disjunction between historical resources—the letters, reports, and other primary documents that are reproduced verbatim—and the narrative in which they are embedded. This contrast of styles sets up a dialogue between the two kinds of discourses, a dialogue whose ideological implications have been worked out in the theory of the Russian formalist critic Mikhail M. Bakhtin.

According to Bakhtin, the language of a given people is not a single language but several languages in contention.[74] These are not dialects in the linguistic sense of the word, but "social speech types." One can distinguish between two basic kinds of social speech types: those conducive to sociopolitical and cultural centralization, and those conducive to decentralization. In the first or "centripetal" group are the languages of official discourse and highbrow literature. In the second or "centrifugal" group are the languages of the folk saying, the anecdote, and popular literature. What Bakhtin calls the "heteroglossia" of the culture as a whole, its medley of social discourses, is reflected in a form such as the novel and indeed in every spoken or written utterance.

For Bakhtin, the discursive tensions in the text mirror the social class conflicts of the culture in which it originated. In *Captain Blackman*, class conflict occasionally cuts across racial lines. Thus the bigotry of Blackman's nemesis, Whittman, is attributed partly to his lower-class origins, and the hostility of black soldiers to one of their own race is attributed partly to his being a "college boy."[75] By and large, however, the novel sorts the speech types along racial lines. White official rhetoric seeks to maintain the status quo while endorsing lofty egalitarian ideals. The black English vernacular of Blackman and the other African American characters works to subvert the authority of white speech, and thus white power, by disclosing its hypocrisy.

The forms of black "guerrilla discourse" become more sophisticated over the course of the novel. During the American Revolution Black-

man counters a general's disparaging remark by farting in formation (p.
40). Prior to the Battle of New Orleans a black soldier breaks out in
laughter and rolls on the ground when General Jackson speaks of the
advantages his race has enjoyed under the republic's "mild and equitable government" (p. 48). In the twentieth century, black resistance becomes more articulate. For each of the two world wars, Williams includes a barracks performance of a toast: for World War I it is "Shine"
(that is, "Shine and the Sinking of the Titanic"); for World War II,
"The Signifying Monkey."

Both the content of the toasts and their setting are significant. The
hero of the "Shine" story is a lowly black man who stokes the engines
of the Titanic, which had refused passage to the black prize fighter Jack
Johnson. Resisting the overtures of the proud white captain and his
daughter (in some versions of the story she is the captain's wife or a
millionaire's daughter) to save them, Shine swims back to Harlem. In
"The Signifying Monkey" the monkey "gets over" on the more powerful lion by egging him on to fight the elephant. Afterwards, while ex-
ulting over the beaten king of the jungle, the monkey falls from his tree.
In some versions of the story he manages to talk his way out of this
predicament and lives to signify again, but in Williams's version the
lion does not give him a second chance (p. 245).[76]

In *Captain Blackman* the two toasts are performed in similar circumstances. The black soldiers gather in a place apart from the curios-
ity and possible harassment of whites. They then prevail on the group's
official raconteur to recite a story with which they are already thoroughly familiar. The pleasure of the occasion derives partly from the
performer's virtuosity—his intonation of the words, his turning of the
rhymed couplets, his dramatic flair. It also derives from the group's participation in a ritual of racial and cultural solidarity, a solidarity that
defines itself obliquely yet aggressively against the dominant white culture. They are fortified by the exploits of Shine and the signifying monkey, trickster heroes who, like Brer Rabbit in the Uncle Remus tales, use
language and mother wit to disarm superior force.

"The Signifying Monkey" is also, especially in the shorter version, a
cautionary tale, reminding black people that they may have to pay a
price for excessive or misdirected verbal aggression. Shortly before the
"Signifying Monkey" performance, Benjy, one of Blackman's friends,
uses "joning" or the dirty dozens to distract a white guard while Blackman sneaks back onto the post. Benjy opens with a volley of abuse directed at the guard's mother, including the formulaic "Does your mom-

ma wear drawers, boy?" (p. 239). He then proceeds to question the guard's masculinity, taking care to stop before the guard starts shooting. Within the black community, as Smitherman points out, the dozens are understood to be a display of verbal ingenuity, not an accurate description of anyone's mother.[77] Since the guard does not understand this convention, Benjy wisely backs off.

Captain Blackman incorporates other forms of black vernacular culture as well. References to music, especially "jass" (jazz) and the blues, are pervasive. Voodoo and its African American form hoodoo are mentioned in passing (p. 19), and a black prayer service is treated with respect even though Christianity is regarded as the religion of the slaveholder (pp. 225–26). None of this cultural background had presumably been discussed in Blackman's seminars in black military history. As recounted in his dreams, however, it lends texture to the history and serves the same purpose, namely, to provide the younger black soldiers with a "sense of continuity" and racial identity (p. 15).

Blackman decides to offer the seminar when he learns that the younger black soldiers are being assimilated all too well in the integrated military of the Vietnam era. From white soldiers they are acquiring the racist attitudes and language that make it easier to mistreat and even murder the Vietnamese. Vietnam therefore marks the turn of the integrationist tide for Blackman. His reconstructionist history lessons and recovery of vernacular culture point the other way, toward separation. Blackman's efforts are tolerated by his commanding officer, a white man, because he underestimates its significance and prefers this milder form of separation to total disaffection. He would rather have proud African Americans in his army than Black Panthers.

Toward the end of the novel, as Blackman lies in a hospital bed with one lung gone, a leg amputated, and a bullet through his scrotum, he realizes that even this form of separation-within-assimilation does not go far enough. In a reversal of Du Boisian double consciousness, he sees himself through the eyes of a signifying black militant: "Nigger layin up there with his dick practically shot off, one leg, one lung, takin Charlie's goddamn medal. Shoulda killed the nigger" (p. 318). Even as Blackman accepts the Medal of Honor for serving courageously in the white man's army, he realizes that the real enemy of his race has always been the white man, even in Vietnam: "The blacks and the whites really wanted to kill each other, not the Vietnamese, and only the fact that there *were* Vietnamese to kill prevented them, most times, from doing so to each other" (p. 314).

Having belatedly learned the fundamental lesson of the history that he was trying to teach, Blackman devises a strategy for winning the race war. Urban guerrilla warfare will not succeed, he believes, because the black guerrilla cannot venture inconspicuously outside the ghetto. He therefore proposes to move black militants, especially veterans, to cities in Africa. There light-skinned black cadres will undergo a kind of baptism in their racial and cultural identity before infiltrating American and European military defense systems. Blackman estimates that in approximately thirty years he will be able to disarm the white man and take control of the world without having to fire a single shot. His strategy is one the signifying monkey might adopt during the Cold War, pitting the capitalist lion against the communist elephant.

In the final section of the novel Whittman, now the ranking general in the American military, realizes that he has lost the race war to Blackman. He is taken captive and flown to Africa on his own plane, piloted by Woodcock, a black "Trojan horse" who can pass for white. The novel ends with Woodcock singing "Sewanee River" in an exaggerated black dialect: "All de world am sad and dreary, ebrywhere I roam, oh darkies, how my heart grobes weary" (p. 336). In this brilliant bit of signifying, a black man with a white face puts on blackface to sing minstrel show lyrics written by a white man, Stephen Foster. Ryle's paradigm of thick description only begins to account for the multiple ironies of this gesture; it is a parody of a parody of a wink.

Unfortunately from Blackman's point of view, it is only a rhetorical victory, mere wish fulfillment rather than accomplished fact.[78] He still lies in bed, his future in doubt. Speaking to an interviewer following publication of the novel, Williams said that he personally doubted that Blackman's millennial vision could ever be realized. "No matter how bad the situation is in America," he said, "Black Americans are still Americans—I think that's what's holding us up."[79] Thus Williams acknowledged that Blackman's dream of "truly becoming one with the people" of Africa (p. 328) might be unrealistic and possibly sentimental, even though he regarded separation as the only permanent solution to the so-called "Negro problem."

In The Destruction of Black Civilization: Great Issues of a Race from 4500 B.C. to 2000 A.D., an ambitious and controversial work of black historical reconstruction published the year before Captain Blackman, Chancellor Williams similarly advised black readers to recognize that "The White man is their Bitter Enemy," and he cited the recent race riots in Vietnam as evidence that integration had failed to end the race war.[80] Also like the author of *Captain Blackman,* Chancellor Williams felt that African Americans were not fully committed to separation; this he considered their major "weakness."[81] Rather than create an all-black nation in Africa as Blackman dreams of doing, he proposed that black people in America set an example for black people around the world by setting up a separate "race organization" in the United States, with its own departments of economic development, land reclamation, health, education, and so forth, duplicating the functions of the federal government but modeled on African tribal structures.[82]

Chancellor Williams dedicated his book to black youth of the 1960s, who had precipitated what he called "the Second Great Emancipation." Yet he acknowledged that emancipation would remain incomplete until black people could overcome a weakness that had plagued them in the past and was likely to remain their fatal flaw through at least the year 2000—namely, tribalism. *Captain Blackman* dramatizes many divisions among African Americans: light-skinned versus dark, lower class versus middle class, urban versus rural, the young militants versus the older "Uncle Toms," those interested in the good of their race versus those interested in personal gain.

The most striking division in the novel separates male from female. Blackman is represented as a consummate soldier and sexual athlete in the *Superfly* Hollywood mode. Even as the novel ridicules white stereotypes of black male sexuality and white fears of miscegenation, it enacts and even exaggerates them. Blackman and his fellow black soldiers are obsessed with sexual conquest as a means of demonstrating their manhood. Though they wince at racist epithets like "slope" and "gook," they routinely reduce their nameless, faceless sexual partners to "pussy" or "leg." The women are human beings only by synecdoche. Blackman's lover Mimosa almost becomes a credible character when she is not confirming his image of himself as a superstud. During a conversation with a black army physician about her future with the captain, she is seen for once without the lens of male sexual fantasy—and immediately put in her place. The doctor assumes, we are told, a posture of "hardness" and "command" that goes "deeper and farther back" than his military authority (p. 290). It goes back, in other words, to the same tradition of male dominance that prompted Stokely Carmichael's notorious remark about women serving the revolution in the prone position.

Perhaps taking his cue from Eldridge Cleaver, who characterized the rape of white women as an "insurrectionary act" in *Soul on Ice,* Blackman regards the white woman as a means of striking back at his true

enemy, the white male.[83] In an episode set during the Civil War, Blackman determines to take revenge on Whittman for raping Mimosa. He
steals into the bedroom where Whittman is sleeping beside the daughter
of a plantation owner, knocks him unconscious, and ties him to a chair
so that when he revives he is forced to witness Blackman's rape of the
daughter. To Blackman's surprise, though he had half-anticipated such
a response, Whittman becomes aroused by the rape. Before leaving the
bedroom, Blackman lifts the unconscious young woman from the bed
and causes her to straddle Whittman's lap. On whom, one wonders, is
he really taking revenge? Even before the deed, he had imagined its consequences for the daughter in more chilling detail than for Whittman:
"He would plant black seed in her so that what she hated would always
be next to her, its heart beating time with hers for three quarters of a
year, and if she tried to rip it out and succeeded, she would still have
the memory; it would stalk her on nights like this for her entire life; she
would sleep behind barred doors, flinch at the sound of every black
voice and weep at the sight of every black face" (p. 87).

There is, then, an unmistakable strain of misogyny in *Captain Blackman.* Whether or not Williams was conscious of this element, it dimin-
ishes the rhetorical effectiveness of the novel for many readers. As the
history of the women's movement of the late 1960s demonstrates, it
would also compromise the kind of large-scale, coordinated revolution
of black people that Blackman envisions. The "prone" warrior is in no
position to help fight the race war.

V

Like *Captain Blackman,* Flowers's *De Mojo Blues* interweaves two kinds
of narration—the realistic and the visionary or dream modes. The realistic narrative is symmetrical and more or less "closed," whereas the
visionary narrative is open-ended, depending on future events and the
reader for its closure.

The novel begins and ends with a grouping of three young black
men, each of whom negotiates the assimilation-separation dilemma in
his own way. The opening scene recalls the docking of a slave trader's
ship as the three step off an airplane—for most soldiers the "Freedom
Bird"—in handcuffs. Escorted by a military policeman, they are taken
to Oakland Army Base, where they are dishonorably discharged from
the army. The discharge is punishment for fragging their white platoon
leader in Vietnam, an offense actually committed by another black sol-

dier. Flowers is apparently interested in the symbolic value of the opening scene rather than its plausibility, since a court-martial would normally punish homicides more severely. Later, the men take advantage of veterans' benefits that would be unavailable to those with dishonorable discharges.

These lapses aside, the men make a believable transition from military to civilian life. During the hours they spend in San Francisco before dispersing to different parts of the country, they try to prolong the sense of solidarity they had known as blacks in the white man's army. Then Willie Brown goes to New York City, where he lets his hair grow out into dreadlocks, marries, and engages in grassroots community activism in the Bronx and Harlem. Mike Daniels, a light-skinned black man, heads for Washington, D.C., where he marries and divorces while going through law school, then gets on the fast track in a major white corporation. He regards his assimilationist strategy cynically, referring to the firm as "Massa's plantation" and his salary as "golden handcuffs."[84]

The novel glances only occasionally at the lives of Willie and Mike while following more closely the career of the third veteran. Tucept HighJohn returns to his home in Memphis, where he undergoes the last of three "conversion" experiences. The first came when he was a student in high school and college, growing up in a solidly middle-class household. In defiance of the values of his parents and Martin Luther King, Jr., all of whom he later comes to appreciate, he adopts the dress and attitudes of a black militant. Why he drops out of school and joins the army is never made clear. But in the military he first discovers the diversity of African American cultures. Though he initially resists dapping as too showy, he undergoes a second conversion, becoming "blackinized" in the mode peculiar to black soldiers (pp. 110–111). The major influence on this phase of his life is Jethro Tree, a "bad nigger" from the Mississippi Delta. It is Jethro who initiates Tucept into Southern black culture, giving him a magical root and a small leather bag associated with hoodoo.

The root is presumably the same kind that Frederick Douglass had received from a fellow slave. Jethro tells Tucept that it is the famous mojo root of HighJohn de Conquer (or Conqueror), a "tricking man" whose spirit returns to walk the earth "whenever blackfolks' backs are pressed up against the wall" (p. 61). In Zora Neale Hurston's retelling of the High John story, this trickster returned to Africa once the slaves were freed but left the root behind so that he could be summoned whenever he was needed.[85] Like Douglass, Tucept is skeptical of such folklore, even though his surname derives from it. Nor is he ready to believe Jethro's prophecy that he, Tucept, will play a role in HighJohn's reappearance.

Jethro is subsequently killed in an ambush, and it is not until two years after Tucept's homecoming that Tucept acknowledges his true vocation as root doctor and conjurer. In the meantime he feels alienated from his family and community in ways common to many Vietnam veterans, but complicated by his black identity. Activists in both the moderate Martin Luther King, Jr., and radical, Marxist-Leninist camps accuse him of being too bourgeois to contribute to the well-being of his people. His relationships with women reflect the double bind of the early 1970s, when black women were beginning to assert themselves as women as well as blacks. When he tries to put black women in "their place," as the doctor in *Captain Blackman* does, they assert their independence. When he tries to be considerate, they despise him for his weakness.

Finally Tucept spills the contents of the mysterious mojo bag onto the floor and has the first of his dream visions. It leads him to Beale Street, the birthplace of the blues, and a hoodoo master named Spijoko. Tucept asks Spijoko about a text that Jethro mentioned, the Lost Book of Hoodoo. In the process of looking for this book, which he never finds, he recovers the text of African American vernacular culture. Hoodoo and conjuring, the blues, Bob Marley's reggae music, the folklore of slavery, Nigerian art, and the reading of historical works such as Chancellor Williams's *Destruction of Black Civilization* all contribute to Tucept's third conversion experience. He feels ambivalent about his progress, fearing that it may be merely bourgeois self-cultivation. But he sticks with it because it supplies a power with which he can minister to the weary souls of other black people.

Near the end of the novel Tucept invites Willie and Mike to Memphis for a reunion. After the obligatory exchange of war stories they discover that they are all still searching for a way to make Black Power, the slogan of the 1960s, a reality in the unpropitious years of the Reagan presidency. Mike has become active in black electoral politics, and Willie is involved in a covert pan-African movement. Though both are amused at Tucept's interest in hoodoo, which he has updated with computer technology, they are taken aback by his knowledge of their secret activities. Tucept presents each of his friends with a mojo root and implants in their minds the myth that he had been shaping during his hoodoo apprenticeship. His narrative begins with Moj, the first monkey to stand upright, recounts the past achievements of African culture in the manner of Chancellor Williams, and finally projects the struggle of black people into the future. In Tucept's millenarian vision of ultimate victory, the three veterans recover a sense of unity they had not known since Vietnam.

Tucept's calling embraces several roles. He is a warrior and revolutionary in the manner of his namesake, Toussaint L'Ouverture. He is also a black Moses, if one recalls that in black folklore Moses' father-in-law, Jethro, was "a great hoodoo man" who recognized Moses' potential as a leader and instructed him in hoodoo lore.[86] First and foremost, however, he is a mythmaker, and most of his other roles—as conjurer, soul doctor, bluesman, visionary, and trickster—converge on this one. In African culture, the spoken word is believed to create reality.[87] Tucept's power is the kind he calls "sayso," the capacity to make things happen by putting them into words (p. 102). In the larger scheme of things this kind of power is more important than economic gain or political influence (represented by Mike and Willie) because it sustains and coordinates them, countering the tribalist tendency toward fragmentation.

Yet Tucept realizes that he must work behind the scenes, like Brer Rabbit or the signifying monkey, as long as the white man controls the more mundane forms of power. The verses from the Shine story that frame the novel suggest that in the 1980s the black man must swim in an ocean full of hungry sharks. Tucept consequently identifies with Papa LaBas, the divine trickster of West African mythology (pp. 62, 186).[88] "No one knows where my truths end and my tricks begin," Tucept warns. "I got tricks in tricks in tricks. I got tricks it'll take generations to unravel" (p. 198). Tucept's fictions are his tricks, comprehensible only to those who need them.

In the next-to-last section of the novel, the narrative voice changes from third to first person, as though A. R. Flowers were taking the baton from his alter ego, Tucept. The speaker tells of climbing a mountain at sunrise to issue a call to the black people of the world to muster for a holy war. He recounts his myth, which vacillates between illusion and reality for a moment, then becomes reality as the people chant their response. In the novel's final section the transformation from oral story to written text is complete, as the author issues an uncompromising call to the reader: "Such is my myth and so it is written. Believe or be damned. That is all" (p. 216). According to the convention of call and response in the African American church, the reader is invited to say Amen to HighJohn and Flowers's vision and so bring it to pass in the world of politics and economics.

As summarized here, Tucept's spiritual pilgrimage appears fairly straightforward. In the decade and a half following his tour of duty in Vietnam he outgrows his slavery to one system and becomes the master of another. As recounted in the novel, however, each advance requires a step back. The memories of Vietnam that punctuate the narrative suggest that the war provides the impetus to change. It is in Vietnam that Tucept learns about African American solidarity on the one hand and factionalism and betrayal on the other. There he learns, like Captain Blackman, that the white man is his chief enemy and the race war his essential war. Vietnam also sends him back to the cultural and spiritual resources that he needs to fight the race war. In the vernacular culture of the slave-holding South, and particularly in hoodoo and the blues, he recovers the racial identity his family was losing through middle-class assimilation.

De Mojo Blues is the product of that recovery, and each word of its title is significant. The article "de" reflects Flowers's use of black dialect in both the mimetic passages (those reporting the characters' speech directly) and the diegetic or narrative passages. The novel is a vernacular work of art, like Twain's *Adventures of Huckleberry Finn* and Hurston's *Their Eyes Were Watching God*. The adjective "mojo" suggests the folkloric content, and the noun "blues" suggests its formal analogue. Unlike the typical blues song about lost love and loneliness, *De Mojo Blues* is a sorrow song about the losses in Vietnam, epitomized by the loss of a close friend. Like other blues songs, however, it also bears artful witness to the recuperative powers of the human spirit.

VI

Sharing many points of resemblance with Flowers's novel is Haile Gerima's *Ashes and Embers*. The central character in the film is Ned Charles (played by John Anderson), a Vietnam veteran who works as an actor in Los Angeles. Much of his story is told in a flashback when he and another black actor (Barry Wiggins) are pulled over by the police and searched. His life passes before his eyes (and ours) while a policeman holds a revolver to his head. The story covers the period from his military discharge to about 1981 and turns on the key relationships in his life: with a young widow (Kathy Flewellen) and her son; with a fiftyish television repairman who could pass for white; and with his grandmother (Evelyn A. Blackwell), who lives alone in a weathered house in the rural South.

The young woman recalls Tucept HighJohn's college girlfriend. She displays a Malcolm X poster in her apartment and belongs to a study group of middle-class intellectuals who talk in Marxist-Leninist terms of African liberation and the way white people have exploited African Americans, sending them off to Vietnam to kill babies. Though Charles is put off by their rarefied discussion and angrily confronts them, he nevertheless absorbs their insights into white colonialism; he even signifies on Colonel Kilgore's "I love the smell of napalm in the morning" speech in *Apocalypse Now*. Representing Charles's consciousness, the camera draws parallels between a white real estate agent in his automobile and American soldiers in their armored personnel carriers and between his grandmother and elderly Vietnamese women. He sees himself both as a collaborator in colonialism, like the real estate agent's black employee, and as its victim. Thinking of a Viet Cong prisoner being kicked by American soldiers, he himself doubles up and falls to the pavement. His compassion for his lover and her son grows when he learns that they too are victims of the war, having lost a husband and father in Vietnam.

Another important influence on Charles is the fatherly television repairman, who helps him with practical matters and gets him through periods of discouragement. The older man's spiritual resources—a knowledge of black history, admiration for black "warriors" such as Du Bois, Malcolm X, and Paul Robeson, and commitment to the struggle for pan-African unity—eventually become Charles's when he moves to Los Angeles. Unlike his roommate, he refuses to assimilate Hollywood values if that means portraying Africans in nonauthentic ways.

The most powerful figure in Charles's life is his elderly grandmother. She appears at first to be a frail, stereotypical mammy, sitting on her porch swing or resting in bed when she is not feeding him an elaborate Southern meal. Her strength, so important to his recovery from the war, resides in her connection to a racial consciousness that is deeper and older than any available to the intellectuals and activists. On one occasion, when Charles, his lover, and her son are helping the grandmother hoe her garden, she shows him a branch broken from the "main tree" and asserts that it will take root in whatever foreign land it is planted. This symbol recalls the folklore of *De Mojo Blues*, in which Jethro, whose surname is Tree, comes from Taproot, Mississippi, and Spijoko is described as a "barkbrown man" who smells of "ancient forests thick with sweet rottening foliage and damp pinecones, gnarled oaks and deepchested maples" (p. 66).

Charles doesn't know what to make of the branch, and his girlfriend is openly skeptical. Near the end of the film, however, the young woman is presented with the same lesson in terms she can understand. Sitting in front of the grandmother's hearth with her son, she listens to the old woman recounting the story of Nat Turner as it had been handed down to her. "Don't you forget," the grandmother says repeatedly, implying that black revolutionary activity must be informed by a lively sense of history, not just theories about the class struggle. In the ashes of the past lie the embers for the fire next time, whatever form that fire may take. Though Charles had humiliated his grandmother by bolting from the church where she had taken him to give thanks for his safe return, he is nevertheless reconciled with her in the final scene, where he embraces her and all that she stands for.

As the camera pans away from their embrace, the words "The Second Coming" appear on the screen. Whose second coming, one wonders, and when will it take place? Might the phrase refer to Ned Charles as an avatar of Nat Turner? These questions remain unanswered, a glancing allusion to the millenarian hopes spelled out in *Captain Blackman* and *De Mojo Blues*. *Ashes and Embers* is ultimately less interested in the future than in the past, as embodied in an elderly black woman. Charles's grandmother, like the "aunt" of African American folklore, is one of the "old ones" who serve as living links between slavery time and the last days.[89]

Williams's novel, we have seen, looks to the younger generation for change. *De Mojo Blues*, like Gerima's film, emphasizes the revolutionary role to be played by black elders. What Tucept cannot find among the militants of his own generation he finds in his mentor Spijoko. He appreciates his mother not only for the sophistication reflected in her college essays but also for her backwoods North Carolina grit and her family's belief in hoodoo. Living within sight of Tucept's house is another old woman who watches and waits, bearing witness to the return of the ancient spirits. *De Mojo Blues* and *Ashes and Embers* thus align themselves with Ernest Gaines's *Autobiography of Miss Jane Pittman* (1971) and Alice Walker's *Meridian* (1976) in looking to the past and its living representatives for direction in the future.

VII

When Houston Baker characterized the recovery of black vernacular culture in the 1960s as a "journey back," he used a metaphor that warrants closer scrutiny. Insofar as it suggests a return to a past like sixth-century Byzantium or twelfth-century France, when a national culture was relatively stable and permeated the lives of all the people, it is a misleading metaphor. African American culture, like other North American cultures, has always been pluralistic and local. To penetrate the soil of African American culture in search of some essential bedrock is to bypass the sedimented layers that constitute the culture itself. When the drill hits Africa, it has arrived not at the bedrock of black American culture but at its terminus a quo.

Consequently, the African American culture "recovered" in the 1960s never existed in precisely that form at any time in the past. As Henry Louis Gates, Jr., has pointed out, black Americans of that era were engaged in a process that might be called self-invention rather than self-discovery.[90] From the accumulated culture of three and a half centuries they selected elements that they found strategically useful as they turned from assimilation to separation. Though this hypostatizing of vernacular culture expressed their pride in being black, it also disclosed what Gates calls an "anxiety of identity formation."[91]

In the 1980s that anxiety played itself out in the academic arena in the debate between literary critics such as Baker, who advocated a return to black vernacular culture, and "reconstructionists" such as Gates, who sought to assimilate the theories of white academicians.[92] The episode reveals more about their emotional investment in the issue than any substantive differences, for Baker's *Blues, Ideology, and Afro-American Literature: A Vernacular Theory* (1984) and Gates's *Signifying Monkey: A Theory of African-American Literary Criticism* (1988) both demonstrate how a product of black vernacular culture can be theorized in ways that are consonant with Western poststructuralist thought.

African American critical theory belongs, then, to the texture of assimilation and separation, of repetition-with-a-difference, within which African American narratives of the Vietnam War have been and still are being written. It was purely by accident that the war coincided with the rise of the Black Power ideology and the Black Arts aesthetic, yet it was in some respects a happy accident. If the armed services ultimately failed to create a model of racial integration (the Great Society's equiva-

lent of the city upon a hill) or even to train young blacks in useful civilian skills, they did inadvertently create a school for racial consciousness-raising. The military in general and Vietnam in particular were
places where lower-class blacks were acculturated—or "blackinized,"
to use Flowers's term—in the Black Power ideology of their peers on
college campuses. Thus the American military in Vietnam modeled the
"nation within a nation" advocated by separatists such as Chancellor
Williams.

For all their "tribal" factionalism, African Americans in the military
experienced a kind of community and historical continuity that was
rare among white people, as reflected in the war literature and film. Michael Cimino's *Deer Hunter* aside, white writers and filmmakers have
usually represented the Vietnam veteran as an alienated, socially marginal figure. They treat the war either as the cul-de-sac of American
history, apocalypse now, or as an episode that takes place outside history in a house of horrors with no before or after. For artists such as
Komunyakaa, Williams, Flowers, and Gerima, Vietnam is merely one
battle in a larger—indeed, a global and millennial—war. If the black
soldier was vilified by the more militant members of his own community, he nevertheless found ways to connect with two African American
modes of heroism: the warrior and the victim-survivor.[93]

Though Vietnam was scarcely a "good" war by any standard, it was
a "better" war for black soldiers in another way. The African American
soldier has always fought two wars simultaneously—the war against
his country's ostensible enemy and the war for respect from his ostensible ally, the white American. Even when the justice of the first war was
in doubt, the justice of the second was not. After World War I, when
black veterans experienced once again the ingratitude of a grateful nation, Du Bois could still summon the optimism to write, "no matter for
what America fought and no matter for what her enemies fought, the
American Negro always fought for his own freedom and for the self-re-
spect of his race. Whatever the cause of the war, therefore, his cause
was peculiarly just."[94] By Du Bois's criterion Vietnam was likewise a
just war for the black soldier, whether he was a career NCO seeking
assimilation or a Black Power militant seeking separation.

These are a couple of the limited victories that the black soldier has
managed to snatch from defeat. But the most important battle is still
being fought—the battle against invisibility. At a conference held in
1985, Wallace Terry gloomily predicted that by the year 2000 the African American role in Vietnam would be erased from cultural memory.[95]

What Ryle might call the "blink" of black culture in Vietnam—the black power salute, dapping, and so forth—may well be forgotten by those who did not understand the ideology behind the gestures. As we have seen, however, their complete meaning resides not in politics alone but in the encompassing web of African American culture, in the warp and weft of its thick texture. This is where black storytellers come in. For black and white Americans alike, they re-create the cultural text in books and films, rendering that text visible and memorable. When they succeed, their stories are acts of recuperation. Like the blues song, the war story is then, in Komunyakaa's words, "an affirmation—the theft of possibility, words made flesh."[96]

CHAPTER 3

The Class War

I

Shortly after noon on 8 May 1970, a violent mob marched down Wall Street in New York City. The scene recalled other scenes of racial violence and antiwar protest that had marked the decade then drawing to a close. This time, however, the mob consisted of two hundred construction workers, and they were advancing on the Federal Hall National Memorial, where students were conducting a peaceful demonstration against the war in Vietnam. A police cordon around the demonstrators melted away, and the workers assaulted the students with hard hats, wrenches, pliers, wire snippers, and hammers. Between forty and sixty of the wounded were taken to a first aid station in Trinity Church on Broadway, and the church itself came under siege. By this time another three hundred workers had joined the original group, and they stormed up Broadway to City Hall. There they forced the deputy mayor to raise the flag, which was flying at half-mast in memory of the four students who had been killed by National Guard troops on the fourth at Kent State University. After singing the "Star Spangled Banner" they crossed the street to Pace College, which they entered by force, and beat any students whom they could get their hands on. It was mid-afternoon before the workers returned to Wall Street and finally dispersed.

They were back again on the eleventh, marching through Wall Street in a phalanx swollen to two thousand. This time the police, who had been chastised by Mayor Lindsay for capitulating to the marchers on the eighth, were able to prevent serious violence. Nine days later, on the twentieth, the construction workers were joined at City Hall by long-shoremen and others, a total of one hundred thousand demonstrating their support for the Nixon administration's policies in Indochina. Nixon wrote to Peter Brennan, president of the Building and Construction Trades Council of Greater New York, expressing his appreciation. He also invited Brennan and other union leaders to the White House on the twenty-sixth. On that occasion Brennan presented the president with a yellow hard hat, which had now become, along with the flag, a symbol of patriotism for some and of neo-Nazism for others. In a speech delivered at a Republican rally the following October, Vice President Agnew equated the hard hat with honesty, thrift, hard work, prudence, common decency, and self-denial. Given a choice between the hard hat and the "high hat" (elitism, radical liberalism, cynicism, egotism), Agnew said, "the American people would come down on the side of the hard hat every time."[1]

The events of the eighth—dubbed Bloody Friday in the electronic and print media—suggested that American workers, long silent on the issue of the Vietnam War, were finally and spontaneously expressing themselves with their fists. But the workers' rampage was far from spontaneous, as Fred J. Cook revealed in an account of the May demonstrations in the *Nation*.[2] Bloody Friday was orchestrated by Ralph L. Clifford, publisher of the New York *Graphic*, a right-wing periodical. It had the tacit support of the New York Police Department, which had been warned in advance of the demonstration. The much larger rally on the twentieth was also easy to account for: the unions ordered the construction workers and longshoremen to march, and the contractors paid them for the time they were absent from their jobs.

Though the workers' demonstrations of May 1970 were highly unusual, their manipulation was not. In this chapter I consider how the working class was used for other people's purposes during the Vietnam War and how it is still being exploited in our war stories.

II

To say that the workers were used by politicians and others in May 1970 is not to say that their anger against Mayor Lindsay and the student protesters had to be artificially contrived. But it proceeded less from prowar sentiment than from class antipathy, the kind of feeling Spiro Agnew turned into a political career. "We wanted to tell off those kids," said the wife of a worker arrested during the May 11 demonstration. "They have too much."[3] The workers did not oppose the students' privileges as such; on the contrary, they sought them for their own children. "I want my kids to go to college," said a construction worker who took part in the skirmish on Wall Street. "There won't be no schools for them to go to if these here kids ruin them all."[4] If the workers regarded the students as pampered snobs who trampled on the flag and gave comfort to the communists, the students often regarded the police as "pigs" and other workers either as the humorous figures of television situation comedies like *The Honeymooners* and *The Life of Riley* or as the homicidal maniacs of films like *Joe, Straw Dogs,* and *Easy Rider.*[5]

Many people assumed that because the construction workers disrupted a demonstration against the Vietnam War they supported the war themselves. Yet one of the workers arrested on the eleventh went on record as saying that he did not like the war either. "But when they try to ruin the country and desecrate the flag, I can't stand it."[6] Jimmy Breslin challenged the hawkish stereotype of the construction worker in a postmortem report on Bloody Friday published in *New York* magazine. Vietnam originated, he observed, not in a working-class bar in Queens but in the libraries of Cambridge and New Haven.[7] When members of the middle class turned against the war, they neglected to recruit support outside their own class. "From the start," Breslin wrote, " . . . the great failure of the anti-war movement has been its arrogance toward people who work with their hands for a living and its willingness not only to ignore them, but to go even further and alienate them completely."[8]

Rather too optimistically, Breslin predicted that the war would end the same day workers marched in opposition to Nixon's policies. But he was prophetic in saying that if antiwar politicians continued to ignore the working class the field would be left to the George Wallaces and Spiro Agnews. In the election of 1972 Wallace and Nixon received strong support from the traditionally Democratic working class. There were, to be sure, attempts at building an antiwar coalition of students and workers. In February 1971, for instance, a group of labor leaders, professors, and students formed a Labor-University Alliance in Cambridge, Massachusetts. By and large, however, class bias prevented the antiwar middle class from recognizing kindred sentiments in the working class, much less building on those sentiments.

Yet evidence collected at the time suggests that antiwar sentiment was stronger in the working class than in the middle class.[9] In 1964 two national surveys showed that support for escalation of the war came from persons who were college-educated, in the professional or managerial occupations, and earning more than $10,000 per year. Support for withdrawal came from those who had not finished high school, were employed in blue-collar occupations, and earned less than $5,000 per year.[10] The same pattern obtained in Gallup polls conducted in 1968 and 1969. Local referendums held in five communities between 1966 and 1968 disclosed even stronger working-class opposition to the war.[11]

The labor unions remained somewhat more hawkish than the rank and file. The AFL-CIO, a federation embracing 120 of the 185 unions and headed by George Meany, consistently supported the president's policy in Vietnam and departed from tradition in 1972 by not endorsing the Democratic candidate, the antiwar George McGovern. But twenty-five AFL-CIO unions endorsed McGovern anyway, and throughout the war individual member unions—the clothing workers, meat cutters, woodworkers, public workers—and union locals dissociated themselves from the federation's position. The United Auto Workers (UAW) strenuously opposed the war, and its president, Leonard Woodcock, denounced Nixon for seeming to condone the Wall Street violence of May 1970. In 1968 and again in 1972 the UAW and other unions sponsored antiwar conferences. At the 1972 conference delegates representing the auto workers, longshoremen, public workers, teamsters, and farmworkers formed a national Labor for Peace organization.[12]

Such is the power of symbolism and personality, however, that middle-class America tended to regard all workers as reactionary hard hats and all labor leaders as hawks in the George Meany mold. The workers themselves were not always conscious of their liberalism and would not have worn it as a badge of honor. A truck driver interviewed by Studs Terkel alluded to the conservatism of most truck drivers, then qualified his remark: "But underneath the veneer they're really very democratic and softhearted and liberal. But they don't *realize* it. You tell 'em they're liberal and you're liable to get your head knocked off. But when you start talking about things, the war, kids, when you really get down to it, they're for everything that's liberal. But they want a conservative label on it."[13]

Americans tend to support the president on issues that are remote from their personal experience, such as foreign policy. But in the case of the Vietnam War foreign policy impinged directly on their lives, particularly if they belonged to the working class. Though the war produced new jobs—more than a million between 1965 and 1967—it also brought higher taxes, a trade deficit, a recession in 1970 and 1971, wage controls, and inflation.[14] A dollar worth one hundred cents in 1967 was worth only seventy-five cents in 1973.[15] As Richard F. Hamilton has observed, workers benefit less from military spending than they do from other forms of federal spending.[16] But it was the "blood tax" that working-class families resented most. They suspected that their sons were doing a disproportionate share of the fighting in Vietnam, and they were right.

Their suspicions were shared, either guiltily or arrogantly, by those who benefited from the arrangement. In an essay with the provocative title "What Did You Do in the Class War, Daddy?" James Fallows recalls the morning he and a group of other young men from Cambridge, most of them students at Harvard or MIT, took their preinduction physical examination at the Boston Navy Yard. They had prepared carefully for the event by studying the army's code of physical regulations and attending seminars run by medical students. They reported with letters from their doctors and a repertoire of chants and disruptive behavior meant to convince examiners that they were not military material. Fallows was disqualified for service, along with "perhaps four out of five" of his classmates from Harvard.[17] Shortly before they left the Navy Yard they saw the buses bringing in those who would take their places in Vietnam, "the boys from Chelsea, thick, dark-haired young men, the white proles of Boston." In contrast to the Cambridge group, those from Chelsea "walked through the examination lines like so many cattle off to slaughter."

Why such fatalism? The "proles" were no more eager to be drafted than the students from Harvard and MIT, though they were certainly younger and less educated, being just out of high school. Interviewing Vietnam veterans from Dorchester, another working-class suburb of Boston, Christian G. Appy learned that in the 1960s many of them regarded military service as a normative rite of passage.[18] Usually, however, they were simply making the best of a situation that seemed beyond their control. They felt helpless in the grip of the Selective Service System, which seemed to offer no choices besides jail, Canada, and Vietnam.

The American way of choosing military conscripts has always been selective, and in this respect it mirrors the country's socioeconomic order as a whole.[19] In theory all are created equal and all are treated equally under law. But in practice some are more equal than others; some earn more money, pay less in taxes, and enjoy a greater share of what Max Weber called "life chances." In the traditional stratification of American society into upper, middle, working, and lower classes, the upper and middle classes live better and less dangerously than the working and lower classes, particularly in time of war. Precise data are difficult to come by, since neither the local draft boards nor the army recorded the socioeconomic status of draftees. Such status is in any case hard to define. Should it include occupation only, or occupation, income, and education? If occupation is the chief criterion of social class, which occupations belong in the working-class category?[20] What about style of life or even one's subjective placement in society?[21] Should the draftee just out of high school, who generally has no occupation or income, be assigned to his parents' social class or the class to which he aspires?

Conceding the difficulties in collecting and interpreting useful data about social class and the Vietnam-era draft, researchers nonetheless conclude that class, even more than race, shaped a young man's chances of being drafted, being sent to Vietnam, and being killed or wounded in combat.[22] A study of 380 Wisconsin servicemen killed in Vietnam through 1967 shows that a disproportionate number of the dead came from poor (27.2 percent) and working-class (60.3 percent) families; by comparison, their high school cohort was 14.9 percent poor and 51.9 percent working class.[23] A study of 101 communities in Cook County, Illinois, likewise disclosed a significantly higher rate of Vietnam casualties in communities of lower socioeconomic status (as defined by income, occupation, and education), even after variables such as race, the number of eligible males, and rate of military participation were taken into account.[24] A study conducted at the University of Notre Dame and based on a survey of 1,586 men in South Bend, Indiana; Ann Arbor, Michigan; and Washington, D.C., concluded that men from disadvantaged (low income, poorly educated) backgrounds "were about twice as likely as their better-off peers to serve in the military, go to Vietnam, and see combat."[25]

Such class discrimination was not inadvertent. Had fairness been the main objective of the Selective Service System, universal conscription or a draft lottery would have served that purpose better, but a lottery was not implemented until the end of 1969, and it still provided for deferments. According to Lewis B. Hershey, the director of the system, long-range social planning or "channeling" was an important objective. In theory the threat of being drafted would force a young man to enter a program of study that would benefit the nation. Alternatively, he might go to work in an occupation or industry that the National Security Council (NSC) deemed essential to the national interest. But in practice local boards rarely considered the social value of programs of study, and channeling served further to crowd already congested fields like teaching and engineering. A presidential commission found that about half of the occupational deferments went to men who were not in critical occupations or industries, and the NSC suspended its list of critical occupations early in 1968.[26] Deferments for marriage and fatherhood were available one year and not the next.

As these caprices suggest, Selective Service was primarily a device to expand and contract the pool of eligible males according to the needs of the military. Since Vietnam was a "limited" war and the baby boom generation began to reach draftable age in 1964, only about 6 percent of draft-age young men were needed to fight the war.[27] It was up to local draft boards to decide who would serve at a time when the vast majority did not serve. In an authoritative study of Wisconsin draft boards, James W. Davis, Jr., and Kenneth M. Dolbeare have shown that the boards were a solidly middle-class institution. The typical board member was an older, well-educated white male in one of the professional or proprietor-managerial occupations.[28] Board members were not elected, and they recruited replacements among others of their kind. Though often veterans, they supported student deferments at a much higher rate than the general population (pp. 92–93). When deciding on borderline deferment cases they tended to rely on factors such as the young man's personal appearance or word choice in a letter (p. 81). Particularly in rural areas, they sometimes used the draft as a form of social control, to punish those who violated community norms (p. 72).

Though intended to secure the support and acquiescence of the people, the system of local draft boards had the opposite effect. Many felt that a centralized national system would have been more equitable and consistent in its policies than a network of semiautonomous local boards. Blue-collar workers, who made up only 9 percent of the nation's draft boards, were, along with homemakers, most opposed to the local board concept (pp. 59, 178). Because board areas were defined along socioeconomic lines, those located in lower-class communities, where many registrants failed to meet the physical and mental standards, had to dip more deeply into the pool of qualified registrants to meet their quotas than boards located in more affluent areas (p. 149). Davis and Dolbeare conclude that the system placed the greatest burden of military service on "rural, white, lower-income, non-college youths and physically and mentally acceptable Negroes" (p. 129). Another scholar concurs, observing that "exclusions at the bottom [for failing to meet physical and mental standards] precluded the creation of a poor man's army. The exclusions at the top guaranteed that it would look more like a working-class army."[29]

In some urban lower-class neighborhoods a young man could evade the draft simply by not registering. This became progressively more difficult as one moved up the social scale. A man from a working-class family could apply for an occupational deferment if he worked in a defense-related industry or his employer enjoyed good rapport with the local draft board. In a Kansas town aptly named Protection, Calvin Trillin came across a manufacturer of concertina wire whose employees were mostly draft-age young men, deferred to work in this "essential industry."[30] For the middle- and upper-class young man who could afford to go to college, the deferment of choice was the II-S student deferment. The II-S provided immunity for four years plus (until 1968 in most fields of study) several more years for graduate school. This was usually sufficient to get the student beyond his twenty-sixth birthday and vulnerability to the draft.[31] If not, he could seek to convert his student deferment into an occupational deferment.

Since the student deferment was obviously linked to socioeconomic status, it caused particular rancor in the lower and working classes. Even at state universities, where the tuition was usually modest, the student or his family had to pay for room and board, books, and transportation. Often the family could not afford to pay these expenses, and if the student reduced his course load in order to work part-time he was no longer eligible for a deferment. According to Veterans Administration statistics compiled through June 1971, soldiers who served in Vietnam were more likely to have started college than those who served in World War II. But many dropped out; only 2.6 percent had completed four years by the age of twenty-four, as compared with 8.5 percent of GIs in World War II.[32]

Families that could afford to keep their sons in college purchased more than a four-year respite from the draft. They also gained access to the most sophisticated draft counseling services in the country. Most draft counseling was conducted on or near college campuses, where it provided a safety net for those whose II-S deferment was about to expire. Along with courses in English literature and calculus the student could receive instruction in how to fail the preinduction physical or write a persuasive application for conscientious objector status. Such counseling proved highly effective; it was unusual for a counselor to enjoy a rate of success under 90 percent.[33] A student who required more help might be referred to a draft lawyer, who for a fee of $200 to $1,000 could virtually assure that the young man would not be drafted.[34] If for some reason a college graduate wanted to fulfill his military obligation but wished to avoid Vietnam, he had a range of options available to few whose education ended with high school: the Army Reserves or National Guard; the Navy, Air Force, or Coast Guard.

Ironically, many draft counselors set out to help the disadvantaged obtain the deferments to which they were entitled. When only the advantaged sought their help, they sometimes rationalized such counseling on the grounds that their success would force the government to rescind all deferments and exemptions. As Lawrence M. Baskir and William A. Strauss observe, however, their efforts had the opposite effect of reinforcing a class bias already built into the Selective Service System.[35] Draft counselors became in effect agents of government pacification, disarming the antagonism of the more vocal and influential middle and upper classes by keeping their young men out of harm's way.

According to conventional wisdom, these were the people whom President Johnson hoped to keep on his side when he declined to send the Reserves to Vietnam. But when his authority to draft came up for renewal in 1967, Johnson endorsed some of the recommendations submitted by his National Advisory Commission and called for further discussion of others. Calculated to reduce class bias in the system, these included eliminating all but hardship deferments, employing random selection (a lottery), closing the Reserves and National Guard to those without prior service (unless they enlisted before being classified I-A), and centralizing the Selective Service System. This time it was Congress that rejected any change in the status quo—an arrangement that happened also to favor the sons and grandsons of senators and representatives.[36]

As a result of this systematic, structural discrimination, the social classes most in favor of sending American troops to Vietnam lost the fewest sons to the war and so remained insulated from its human costs. Writing on "The American Class System" in *Newsweek* in 1970, Stewart Alsop noted that just over 10 percent of the previous year's draftees had been college men, and that Yale, Harvard, and Princeton had graduated only two students (one from Yale, one from Harvard) who had been drafted and killed in Vietnam.[37] The author and university professor Leslie Fiedler, writing in the *Saturday Review* in 1972, admitted that he had never known a single family with a son killed, wounded, missing, or held prisoner in Vietnam.[38] Vietnam, he remarked, was turning into "the first war of which it can be said unequivocally that it is being fought for us by our servants."

The master-servant analogy is apt, given the arrogance of some who avoided the draft. In its milder variation this took the form of the "I have more important things to do" argument used by the conservative newspaper columnist Cal Thomas. Not wanting to be sidetracked from "a budding career in journalism," Thomas enlisted in the army to qualify for an opening in the New York office of the Armed Forces Radio and Television Service.[39] "Taking a chance with the draft and possibly winding up in Vietnam (probably as a broadcaster)," he recalled, "seemed to me a foolish and unnecessary risk." In its more offensive form the arrogance became contempt for the "nobodies" and "suckers" who allowed themselves to be drafted.[40] Even those children of the middle class who rebelled against the values of their parents and identified with the poor and racial minorities, often adopting their style of dress, were unwilling to surrender the chief perquisite of social caste during the Vietnam years—exemption from the draft.

III

What the working-class conscripts found when they arrived in Vietnam was—work. War has been compared to work, and work to war, at least since Marx characterized laborers as "privates of the industrial army . . . placed under the command of a perfect hierarchy of officers and sergeants."[41] Reversing the analogy, Eric J. Leed has described the ways in which war was "proletarianized" during World War I. Men who were raised and trained in the image of the soldier as heroic aggressor found themselves digging defensive trenches. Meanwhile the artillery, machines serviced by men, fought their battles in a manner reminiscent of modern industry. War was not play, as they had thought, but work; not a liberation from material conditions, but total subjection to them.[42] If this lesson was to some extent forgotten during World War II, it was relearned in Vietnam, the working man's war.

For a detailed picture of the worker's life in America during the Vietnam War, and therefore a practical sense of its kinship with the soldier's life, one might turn to Studs Terkel's encyclopedic oral history on the subject. *Working* (1974) includes testimony from people in all classes of American society, some of whom find fulfillment in their occupations.

More often than not, however, those in blue-collar jobs describe their work as tedious, exhausting, and unfulfilling. They complain that they are treated not as human beings but as machines or animals. They resent the owners and managers who profit from their labor, also the supervisors who constantly look over their shoulder and decide when they can take a break or use the rest room. Occasionally they sabotage the product or service, lacking any other way to place the stamp of personal identity on it. The voices in *Working* testify, in short, to what Marx called "alienation"—the separation of workers from the product and processes of production, from ownership of the tools of production, and ultimately from their own humanity.[43]

Working opens with the sentence, "This book, being about work, is, by its very nature, about violence—to the spirit as well as to the body."[44] The violence to the spirit has already been suggested. The violence to the body can be hinted at statistically and anecdotally. From 1961 to 1969 approximately 46,000 Americans were killed in Vietnam; during the same period 126,000 American workers were killed in industrial accidents.[45] This figure does not include the enormous number of injuries due to accidents—perhaps twenty-five million a year, according to one estimate—or the permanent impairment of health due to toxic chemicals, airborne particles, and excessive noise.[46] Contrasting his working conditions with those of an office worker, a steel worker told Terkel, "Where you have to eat all that dust and smoke, you can't work hard and live a long life."[47]

The work of war is most obviously like factory or construction work in its physical danger. Besides the threat posed by enemy fire, mines, and booby traps, there is the danger inherent in using weapons, explosives, sophisticated machinery (planes, helicopters, tanks, armored personnel carriers), and toxic chemicals such as the defoliant Agent Orange. In Vietnam the engines of war were operated by very young men (nineteen was the average age, though the pilots of fixed-wing aircraft were older) after minimal training and often in a state of physical exhaustion and inattention. The work was hard and afforded little sense of accomplishment. Larry Heinemann, whose writings are discussed later in this chapter, manned the .50-caliber machine gun on an armored personnel carrier. "If you think of the Army as work," he told an interviewer, "it's some of the most grueling, backbreaking drudgery imaginable. . . . One reason people work is because they want to do a good job. But in the infantry, nothing you do produces good feelings, unless you are a medic. Nobody but an insane person could get satisfaction from killing people."[48]

The product of the soldier's work in Vietnam was a body count, the number of enemy killed. If there is little satisfaction in killing people, the foot soldier rarely had even this satisfaction. Revered in military circles as the "Queen of Battle," the infantry in Vietnam became its handmaiden. Most of the killing was done by the so-called support arms—aircraft and artillery. The role of the foot soldier on a search and destroy mission was to draw fire so the enemy could be located and— providing contact lasted long enough—destroyed by bombs, napalm, and artillery shells. Though infantry operations were given names to distinguish one from another, they were mostly variations on a single operation that James Webb calls "Dangling the Bait." He describes it as follows in his novel *Fields of Fire:* "Drifting from village to village, every other night digging deep new fighting holes, every day patrolling through other villes, along raw ridges. Inviting an enemy attack much as a worm seeks to attract a fish: mindlessly, at someone else's urging, for someone else's reason."[49]

The war literature and film offer ample evidence that the average grunt understood how he was being used and deeply resented it. Like the worker on the assembly line, he felt that he was less important and more expendable than the weapons and machines he used. The machines remained in Vietnam, whereas a succession of soldiers manned them—if they were lucky enough not to be killed or seriously wounded—for twelve- or thirteen-month shifts.

The soldier-worker had reason to resent those who were using him, the war's foremen and managers. Numerous studies have drawn attention to the failure of leadership during the Vietnam War and have blamed this failure for the ineffectiveness and demoralization of the armed services.[50] These studies suggest that enlisted morale is highest when the officer corps is relatively small but of high quality, when officers are motivated by concern for military honor and duty, when they share the sacrifices of their men, and when they are concerned for their well-being. In Vietnam there was one officer for every 6.5 enlisted men, as compared with one officer per 11.9 enlisted in World War II.[51] Since the size of the officer corps increased at the same time as the number of college graduates decreased, to the extent that quality can be correlated with level of education and maturity, officer quality declined.

Even more detrimental to morale in Vietnam was a significant change in the style of leadership. In previous wars senior officers (the rank of major and above) shared the dangers of combat with their men and suffered a corresponding number of casualties. In Vietnam the senior officer thought of himself less as a warrior than as a manager. Since he worked for a "corporation" whose product was a body count, he was judged for promotion and awards on the size of the body count and was occasionally even assigned quotas. In some units his efficiency rating was expressed in terms of a "kill ratio," reflecting the number of losses in relation to the number of kills. In other units American losses were not even taken into account, which further encouraged "dangling the bait." The helicopter replaced the bunker as a command post, reducing the senior officer's risk while qualifying him for Air Medals and an occasional Distinguished Flying Cross.

Faced with a surplus of officers wanting combat commands, the Pentagon typically reassigned them from combat to staff positions in six months or less. Though this policy benefited officers who looked upon Vietnam as an opportunity to "punch their tickets," it increased the cynicism of the soldiers in their command, who were continually having to break in inexperienced officers at considerable risk to their own lives. The structure of the Vietnam War further eroded the loyalty of the troops. In a war with definite battle fronts, the command staff (personnel, intelligence, operations, logistics) remains well behind the lines, out of sight of the infantrymen. In Vietnam enormous, relatively secure bases were surrounded by progressively smaller and more vulnerable satellite bases. When field soldiers returned to the larger bases for periodic "stand-downs," they could not help noticing the comfort in which rear echelon officers and enlisted men lived. Clearly, the dangers and hardships of war were not being shared equally.

The hostility that followed this recognition divided soldiers along several lines of conflict. Soldiers in the field, regardless of their rank or social class, resented soldiers in the rear, regardless of their rank or social class. Thus William Broyles, Jr., who served as a marine platoon leader in Vietnam, recalls that he and his men felt a stronger bond of kinship with enemy soldiers than with Americans on the large bases: "The NVA soldiers, after all, were out in the jungle too. They were wet and tired and scared, just like us. They were grunts, just like us. The Americans back in Da Nang, however, were the handiest of the other enemies—everyone who wasn't out there with us. *We* were here because *they* had sent us."[52] Another line of conflict followed conventional categories of social class, pitting enlisted men (usually from the lower or working class) against officers (usually from the middle class). As Charles C. Moskos has shown, during the period between World War II and Vietnam this form of class warfare underwent some modification, becoming primarily a conflict between single-term soldiers and the career officers and NCOs known as "lifers."[53]

Particularly after 1968 the single-term soldier, like the alienated workers of his generation back home, expressed his disaffection with the war by absenteeism (AWOL and desertion), sabotage, use of drugs, work stoppages (mutiny in the field), and occasional violence against the supervisors and managers (lifers).[54] From 1969 to 1972 alone, 1,016 fraggings were reported in Vietnam. These were aimed mostly at officers and NCOs, and resulted in eighty-six deaths. The figure, which does not include shootings, is thought to represent less than a tenth of the actual number of assaults.[55] Moskos estimates that only about one in five fraggings was committed by an individual soldier pursuing a personal vendetta; most were the work of a group and reflected group solidarity.[56] A navy SEAL suggested the intensity of this war-within-a-war when he said, "I was more at war with the officers there than I was with the Viet Cong."[57]

Marx predicted that the growth of industry would help to unite the proletariat against the bourgeoisie because factories bring together workers who would otherwise remain isolated, competing against one another for wage-labor.[58] We have seen that military service, and particularly a tour of duty in Vietnam, had an analogous effect on black soldiers, who often became more militant while serving with others of their race in the white man's army. John Helmer's *Bringing the War Home* (1974) shows that this was likewise true of at least a minority of working-class whites. Helmer's study of ninety white working-class veterans from the Boston area allows us, in effect, to follow the progress of Fallows's Chelsea "proles" from induction through their Vietnam tours and return home.

Helmer chose thirty subjects from each of three categories: the "straights," who were members of the Veterans of Foreign Wars (VFW) at the time of the study; the "addicts," who were then undergoing rehabilitation for drug use; and the "radicals," who were members of Vietnam Veterans Against the War (VVAW). Helmer does not pretend that any of these groups represents a third of the population of working-class veterans; in fact, he conjectures that the addicts and radicals may constitute no more than a "sizable minority."[59] He found that the straights conformed most closely to the stereotype of the anti-ideological soldier.[60] They tended to accept the military command's view of the war in Vietnam, and on their return to the States they felt alienated from their nonveteran peers, who by this time had come to oppose the war. They moved closer to their families and the older generation, turning to the VFW for friends their own age with similar values.

Like the straights, the addicts and radicals were "juicers" (consumers of alcoholic beverages) before going to Vietnam. On arriving in country, they had no strong predisposition toward either alcohol or drugs, but within a month they identified themselves as "heads," users of marijuana and one or more hard drugs like opium, heroin, and morphine. Whether they became juicers or heads seemed to depend on which squads or hooches they were assigned to. Once identified as heads, however, they adopted a distinctive ideological stance. They turned against the war and began to regard the military command, and by extension the juicers, as their enemy. They approved of the antiwar movement back home, listened regularly and with interest to the broadcasts of Hanoi Hannah, and made a greater effort to relate to blacks and the Vietnamese. On their return to the States they felt more at ease with nonveterans their own age than with their families. The radical heads joined the antiwar movement, though they retained their veteran identity as members of the VVAW. They felt that they had earned their opposition to the war in a way their nonveteran peers had not.

To the large number of lower- and working-class soldiers who became combat casualties in Vietnam can be added the walking wounded, the veteran drug addicts who, Helmer believes, would not have become addicted had they not served in the military and gone to Vietnam.[61] Even those who managed to escape death, disablement, and addiction faced a diminished quality of life on their return to the States. Unemployment is a problem faced at least temporarily by veterans after most wars. In November 1945 13.6 percent of the seven million veterans in the civilian labor force were unemployed. But a strong economy quickly absorbed the new workers; by the following November their unemployment had declined to 5.5 percent, and a year later it was down to 3.8 percent.[62] The smaller, more gradual demobilization of the latter years of the Vietnam War coincided with an economic recession caused, some maintain, by the war itself. Only a million veterans were discharged during the year ending in June 1971, yet their unemployment rate reached 10.8 percent in the first quarter of 1971, as compared with 8.4 percent for nonveterans in the same age group and a general rate of 6 percent.[63] The gap between veteran and nonveteran annual unemployment rates did not close until 1973.[64] At the same time, Vietnam veterans were making less use of the GI Bill than veterans of World War II had done, partly because it no longer covered as large a share of the costs of college education or technical training.[65]

As Richard Severo and Lewis Milford demonstrate in *The Wages of War* (1989), the treatment accorded veterans after Vietnam was closer to the historical norm than that enjoyed by veterans of World War II. America has a long tradition of treating its former soldiers shabbily. Fallows predicted in "What Did You Do in the Class War, Daddy?" that such treatment would have long-term repercussions. He believed that class conflict would intensify in America after the mid-1970s because Vietnam, unlike World War II, afforded little opportunity for a mingling of the classes. Lacking firsthand experience of their working-class peers, middle-class writers and intellectuals of the Vietnam generation would revert to the social postures of the 1930s, either despising workers or romanticizing them in the manner of Clifford Odets's *Waiting for Lefty*. As an embarrassing reminder of class privilege, the Vietnam veteran would be either ignored or demonized as a junkie and pathological killer.[66]

Fortunately, the kind of thoroughgoing repression Fallows describes was only a temporary phase of America's recovery from Vietnam, a phase whose symptoms included Travis Bickle in Martin Scorsese's *Taxi Driver* (1976) and the homicidal vets of the *Kojak* and *Hawaii Five-O* television series. This was followed by the equally fulsome and short-lived phase Myra MacPherson has called "Viet Guilt Chic," during which those who were spared military service indulged in an orgy of confession.[67] Yet the class war continues, as suggested by public controversy in the late 1980s over the wartime conduct of Vice President Dan Quayle and in the 1990s over that of President Bill Clinton. By an exercise of class privilege, Quayle, who supported the war, secured an assignment to the National Guard to avoid going to Vietnam. Clinton, though he opposed the war, worried that evading the draft might jeopardize his political career. While running for the presidency, he shrewdly disarmed criticism by choosing Al Gore, a Vietnam veteran, as his running mate. Once in office he forged alliances with military leaders whenever confronted with issues of defense or restoring diplomatic and trade relations with Vietnam. Even so, his administration—and therefore American policy—was shaped by decisions he made in the 1960s.

The class war rages not only in the spheres of public and personal politics but also in literary and cinematic responses to the war. I consider several of these below, proceeding from stories that illustrate the upper- or middle-class perspective on the working-class soldier to stories that represent the soldier's view of those who sent him to Vietnam.

IV

Responding to a *Partisan Review* questionnaire in 1966, Susan Sontag writes that America was settled by the "surplus poor of Europe," who then proceeded to inflict their tawdry taste on the landscape.[68] With just a trace of irony, she concedes that her portrait of the country's benighted population may seem incredible to "those who live in the special and more finely modulated atmosphere of New York and its environs" (p. 196). So she invites her New York readers to cross the Hudson and see Yahooland for themselves, with all its racism, bigotry, and militarism. Since her mythology requires angels as well as demons, Sontag goes on to romanticize the New Left. Though she avoids identifying them as students, instead using class-neutral terms like "young people" and "the kids," she is clearly referring to a privileged group with the leisure to debate the merits of Freud, Marx, and Dadaist art.

Sontag was apparently unconscious of her own provincialism and class bias until she traveled to Hanoi, where her revolutionary enthusiasm collided with the cultural and intellectual limitations of flesh-and-blood revolutionaries. "Maybe," she wistfully speculates early in "Trip to Hanoi," "I'm only . . . one more volunteer in the armchair army of bourgeois intellectuals with radical sympathies in the head" (p. 224). Such humility is ingratiating but short-lived. As she warms to the simplicity of her North Vietnamese hosts, she reverts to her disdain for the American masses. Soldiers are not human beings with ideas of their own but "partly unemployable proletarian conscripts" (p. 255). When a Vietnamese describes her as "the very picture of the genuine American," she flinches because she had come to think of "flag-waving Legionnaires and Irish cops and small-town car salesmen who will vote for George Wallace" as the true Americans (pp. 266–67). Though she resolves not to slip back into "the old posture of alienation" on her return to America (p. 269), she actually cultivates that stance—never suspecting, it would appear, how she and others who felt superior to the cops and the car salesmen had helped to drive them into the Wallace camp.

Like Sontag, Mary McCarthy finds that when it comes to people's revolutions, her sympathy for revolution exceeds her sympathy for people. In her memoir of Hanoi the Vietnamese soldiers come off much better than the Americans. Whereas the North Vietnamese troops attend poetry readings for entertainment, their American counterparts presumably go to see a belly dancer.[69] McCarthy's account of her meeting with two captured American pilots, by 1968 a standard feature of the visitor's itinerary, differs tellingly from Staughton Lynd and Tom Hayden's experience with another POW three years earlier. Lynd and Hayden were acutely sensitive to the prisoner's discomfort and strove to minimize it, even persuading the North Vietnamese to treat him less like a criminal.[70] McCarthy, in contrast, takes pains to distance herself from the POWs, characterizing American pilots generally as "beings from a protozoic world" and her specimens in particular—one is Robinson Risner—as "somewhat pathetic cases of mental malnutrition" (pp. 111, 122). She much prefers the company of her North Vietnamese hosts, with whom she can converse in French about philosophy and medicine. Yet McCarthy is shrewd enough to realize that this inversion of the usual sympathies is based as much on class bias as it is on politics or conscience. "To be against the Vietnamese war," she reflects, "was an economic privilege enjoyed chiefly by the middle and professional classes" (p. 112).

The narratives of both Sontag and McCarthy are suffused with what Leo Marx calls "revolutionary pastoralism."[71] Sophisticated products of a complex society, these writers hanker for the presumed virtues of simpler—in this case communist—societies. Simple societies appear attractive and virtuous, however, only as long as they are exotic. When comparable manifestations of "simplicity" are encountered closer to home in the American working class, they are regarded with contempt.

The reverse of this attitude, what one might call blue-collar pastoralism, can be seen in Mailer's *Armies of the Night* (1968). Halfway through book two Mailer abandons his "historical" account of the October 1967 march on the Pentagon for a "novelistic" treatment of the event. Since he was not personally present at the confrontation between demonstrators and army troops deployed around the Pentagon, having been arrested earlier, he must reconstruct the event from newspaper accounts. Like a novelist, he relies on imagination to supply the social and psychological dimensions of the scene, particularly where it narrows to the six inches of "no man's land" between the soldiers and their civilian peers. What he discovers there is a class war: "They looked across the gulf of the classes, the middle classes and the working classes. It would take the rebirth of Marx for Marxism to explain definitively this middle class condemnation of an imperialist war in the last Capitalist nation, this working class affirmation."[72]

Like Sontag and McCarthy, Mailer mistakenly assumes that the working class is solidly behind the war in Vietnam. He is nevertheless right to observe that classic Marxist theory does not account for middle-class condemnation of the war. According to *The Communist Manifesto,* the bourgeois owners of capital perpetually seek new markets for their goods overseas and exploit the labor of the proletariat in the process.[73] Vietnam was regarded by many on the left as a war of economic expansion. Why, then, would the middle-class beneficiaries of the war object to it? The most generous explanation would allow for motives other than economic self-interest, motives that have no place in Marxism. Assuming the role of a reborn Marx, Mailer takes a different tack. He argues that in twentieth-century America it is the middle class rather than the working class that is alienated—from America, from real power, from a firm sense of identity.

Mailer's revision of Marxist alienation offers one way to account for the malaise of the Sontags and McCarthys. They feel powerless to stop a war that they ascribe to working-class militarism and patriotism (most of the soldiers are from the working class, aren't they?). In a curious inversion of Marx, they shift the burden of political responsibility to the proletariat, which they regard as the class of reaction rather than revolution. According to Mailer the younger, more disaffected generation of bourgeoisie further compounds this legacy of alienation:

> The sons and daughters of that urban middle class, forever alienated in childhood from all the good simple funky nitty-gritty American joys of the working class like winning a truly dangerous fist fight at the age of eight or getting sex before fourteen, dead drunk by sixteen, whipped half to death by your father, making it in rumbles with a proud street gang, living at war with the educational system, knowing how to snicker at the employer from one side of the mouth, riding a bike with no hands, entering the Golden Gloves, doing a hitch in the Navy, or a stretch in the stockade, and with it all, their sense of élan, of morale, for buddies are the manna of the working class: there is a God-given cynical indifference to school, morality, and job. (p. 287)

Here, following a perceptive analysis of the class war within the Vietnam War, Mailer lapses into the sentimental working-class pastoralism of television beer commercials. Taken one by one, the "good simple funky nitty-gritty American joys of the working class" might be occasions of regret to those who actually experience them. Mailer shows elsewhere in *Armies* that he knows better. Having served in the melt-ing-pot army of World War II, he came to know not only the urban worker but also his rural counterpart, whom he calls later in the same paragraph "the true American son of the small town and the farm" (p. 288). In the faces of the federal marshals at the Pentagon, he sees what has happened to many of those young men in the twenty-odd years since the war: their capacity for goodness and generosity has been crushed by the conditions of their lives, leaving only greed and hatred (p. 174).

Mailer feels genuine sympathy for these small-town Southerners, and it is manifest when he is detained overnight in the minimum security prison in Occoquan, Virginia. There another detainee, a member of Students for a Democratic Society, gleefully confides that he papered a cell wall with political stickers. "These middle-class kids," Mailer muses, anticipating the effect this will have on the prison guard detailed to clean the cell, "no matter the depth of their commitment, were also having a game with the campus cop" (pp. 221–22).

Mailer, too, is playing a game, though a much deeper one. His occa-sional identification with the working class, like his earlier identifica-tion with the hipster, is calculated mainly *pour épater le bourgeois*. Speaking extempore at the Ambassador Theater on the Thursday eve-ning preceding the march, he deliberately uses the word "shit" to of-fend his middle-class audience. Though the audience is opposed to the war and therefore ostensibly on his side, Mailer intuits the connection between their love of technology and the technowar in Vietnam. His scatological language is, to his mind, a blow struck for democracy, like the obscenity an enlisted man might use against an officer (p. 61). It is also the language Mailer uses so artfully in *Why Are We in Vietnam?*, to the consternation of the "brass" in the literary establishment.

Anxious as he is to escape his social class and its proprieties, Mailer is not for a moment seduced by his own rhapsody on the joys of the working class. Rather, he—or at least the comic character he calls "Mailer"—aspires to the patrician status of men like the poet Robert Lowell of Boston and U.S. Commissioner Scaife of Virginia. He takes great satisfaction in reflecting that he and Lowell are, "in private, *grands conservateurs,* and if the truth be told, poor damn émigré princes" (p. 29). His self-deprecating humor cannot conceal his hankering for upward mobility, though political expediency demands that he ally himself temporarily with the despised "middle-class cancer pushers and drug-gutted flower children" (p. 47). In this respect as in so many others, book one does exactly what Mailer says it is supposed to do: it acquaints us with the idiosyncratic, flawed instrument called "Norman Mailer" through which we view the landscape of book two (p. 245).

Few indeed are the works of Vietnam War literature and film that represent the lower and working classes without condescension of either the Sontag-McCarthy or Mailer variety. Though Michael Cimino's *Deer Hunter* succeeds as an endorsement of the Daniel Boone myth, it betrays discomfort with its working-class materials. As seen through the lens of Cimino's camera, Clairton is a place of ethereal beauty rather than grime, and the main character, Michael, is not the average steelworker. He is Leatherstocking in overalls and a hard hat. Tom Molloy's *Green Line* (1982) and Jimmy Breslin's *Table Money* (1986) portray working-class Vietnam veterans similar to those in John Helmer's study. But neither novel makes much of its protagonist's war experiences. Both focus instead on the working-class Irish male's attempts to cope with the new assertiveness of blacks and women.

For sustained and illuminating treatments of the Vietnam War and social class, we might turn instead to Oliver Stone and Larry Heinemann. As chance would have it, these two storytellers are veterans not only of the same war but also of the same battle. Both were in battalions attached to the 25th Infantry Division when it engaged a North Vietnamese Army regiment along the Cambodian border on New Year's Day, 1968.[74]

V

Following its premiere in December 1986, *Platoon* was widely praised for its realism. *Time* magazine ran a cover story entitled "*Platoon:* Viet Nam As It Really Was," in which viewers as different as David Halberstam and Steven Spielberg acclaimed the film's authenticity.[75] Unlike epic adventures such as *The Deer Hunter* and *Apocalypse Now, Platoon* appeared to forgo sweeping cultural statement in favor of close-up, tightly cropped images of mud, insects, leeches, elephant grass, heat, fear, and frayed nerves. The result, Stone observed in an address to the National Press Club, was cinema that dispensed with "ideology" to get at "the six inches in front of [his] face."[76]

Stone's rendering of that six inches was praised not only by many critics but also by his most exacting audience, veterans of the two platoons—one in the 25th Infantry, the other in the 1st Air Cavalry—with which he had served in Vietnam. At a reunion organized by Vietnam

Veterans of America (VVA) in the summer of 1987, platoon members tried to identify themselves in the parts played by various actors. Speaking of the last battle, in which NVA troops overrun an American position, one testified, "My God it was just like that. I swear." Another agreed: "Really, that's what it was like. Oliver caught it all."[77] In a letter to the *VVA Veteran,* a veteran who had served as the 25th Infantry's counterintelligence officer wrote, "I saw nothing in this movie, from the opening credits on, that didn't ring true to my own Vietnam experiences."[78]

Further bolstering *Platoon*'s claim to authenticity, Stone let it be known in interviews and a memoir he wrote for *American Film* magazine that the story of Chris Taylor (played by Charlie Sheen) is in many respects his own. As an adolescent Stone felt that he was "being groomed for financial-commercial America."[79] So he dropped out of Yale during his first year to take a job teaching Chinese students in Saigon, a place he considered free of the "neuroticism and slackness of Western living."[80] Following a stint as a merchant seaman, he turned at the age of twenty to writing, producing a fourteen-hundred-page autobiographical novel entitled *Child's Night Dream.*[81] Up to this point Stone's career roughly parallels Herman Melville's and might be explained in terms of the "primitivist" paradigm that James Baird has applied to Melville. According to Baird, primitivism originates in cultural failure. Primitivists turn to a time or a place, usually Asia or Oceania, in the belief that it will supply the religious symbolism and authority they cannot find in their own culture.[82]

If one takes Baird's account a step further and supposes that Melville sought the primitive not only in Polynesian culture but also in a social class, the common sailors celebrated as knights and squires in *Moby-Dick,* then one sees yet another way in which he anticipated Stone. When Stone's novel failed to find a publisher, he felt compelled to do penance for his authorial hubris by joining the army. "I went into this feeling I had to be anonymous," he recalls. "I had to atone for the act of individuality. So I had to become like a common soldier. I had to have my hair cut, I had to be a number."[83] By enlisting in the army Stone simultaneously repudiated bourgeois self-assertion and asserted his manhood to his father, a Wall Street stockbroker.[84] Determined not to be the kind of man Louis Stone had become after serving as a colonel in World War II, he sought what he called "a more visceral manhood" less preoccupied with making money.[85]

When Stone returned to Southeast Asia as a soldier in 1967 he sought renewal not only in identification with the working-class men who filled the enlisted ranks but also in the experience of combat. "I felt teaching was good," he said, recalling his first adventure in Vietnam. "But now I wanted to see another level, a deeper level, a darker side. What is war? How do people kill each other? How will I handle it? What is the lowest level I can descend to to find the truth, where I can come back from and say, *I've seen it?*"[86] In Vietnam Stone apparently hoped to find Richard Slotkin's "regeneration through violence." What he actually found was the disillusionment he would later represent in *Platoon* and *Born on the Fourth of July* (1989).

In *Platoon* Taylor is a sheltered young man who is gradually initiated into the esoteric knowledge of combat, of killing and nearly being killed. Most of the film is devoted, however, to re-creating the social context of his initiation. Taylor is disillusioned even before he arrives in Vietnam. His parents had expected him to graduate from college, earn a comfortable income, buy a home, and raise a family. Instead, like Stone, he dropped out of college, enlisted in the army, and volunteered for the infantry and Vietnam. His motives are complex, involving elements of rebellion, class guilt, and puritan self-abnegation. He enlists to protest a system of class discrimination that sent the poor and uneducated to war while exempting the sons of the middle class. Taylor's rebellion is manifest not only in his rejection of his parents' notion of success but also in his choice of his grandmother as confidante. She is presumably a neutral party, one who stands outside the conflict of generations yet can still mediate between them.

Taylor is further disillusioned to learn that the same system of class privilege obtains in the military, where the warrior ethos has given way to the ethos of the corporate manager. Managerial calculation dictates that Taylor's battalion be positioned near the Cambodian border, within striking distance of an NVA regiment. As Taylor says, "We knew we were going to be the bait to lure them out." The battle is won not by the battalion, which suffers heavy losses, but by Phantom jets that bomb both the "bait" and the "fish." The screenplay represents Lieutenant Wolfe (Mark Moses), the platoon leader, as initially an eager participant in the corporate game, a junior manager with "an intense get-ahead look."[87] But Wolfe is despised because he lacks the manager's competence as well as the warrior's courage. The platoon suffers several casualties because of his mistakes in map reading. In the rear the managerial ethos fostered corruption and what Stone in his National Press Club address called a "corporate Miami Beach/Las Vegas mentality."[88]

Taylor's friend King (Keith David) feels justified in stealing beer from the "lifer" first sergeant because the first sergeant had stolen it from the grunts. Already alienated from his parents and their bourgeois values, like Mailer's Pentagon marchers, Taylor experiences in Vietnam the classic Marxist alienation of the worker from the work and the products thereof.

The theme of class discrimination cannot be overlooked in *Platoon,* and Stone underscored it in his address to the National Press Club. Of all the evils spawned by the Vietnam War, he said, "The ultimate corruption was, of course, President Johnson sending only the poor and uneducated to the war—in fact, practicing class warfare wherein the middle and upper classes could avoid the war by going to college or paying a psychiatrist. I am sure to this day that if the middle and upper classes had gone to Vietnam, their mothers and fathers—the politicians and businessmen—would have ended that war a hell of a lot sooner."[89]

Considering Stone's emphatic stand on the question of class conflict, it is hard to understand why critics, chiefly in the academy, have faulted him for avoiding hard political questions. By focusing only on the six inches in front of his face, they contend, he allowed his personal antiwar views to be subverted by those who sought to win the war after the fact. Since popular culture abhors an ideological vacuum, the "neutral" artifact will sooner or later be co-opted by the dominant ideology. Consequently they argue that *Platoon,* no less than revisionist fantasies like Joseph Zito's *Missing in Action* (1984) and George Cosmatos's *Rambo: First Blood Part Two* (1985), ends up denying the painful lessons America should have learned in Vietnam.[90]

As an example of such co-optation, several of these critics cite the Chrysler Corporation commercial that precedes *Platoon* on the Home Box Office videotape.[91] In the commercial, Chrysler chairman Lee Iacocca conflates Vietnam with World War II and the Korean War as theaters in which the American soldier served as honorably and unquestioningly as the jeep. In the process of selling Chrysler products Iacocca also sells Vietnam as a "good" war, and *Platoon* presumably lets him get away with it.

I believe, on the contrary, that the supposed "absence" of ideology in *Platoon* is really an absence in the spectrum of political issues to which these critics are willing to respond. In their minds the justice of the war qualifies as a political issue, but not the justice of the military draft. Their response illustrates what Fallows said in 1975 about a post-Vietnam rift between the academy and the working class. In a maladroit attempt to bridge that gap, the editors of one collection of essays show how wide it is. After echoing what their contributors say about the absence of ideology in *Platoon* and other Vietnam War films, they go on to "note with considerable distress that the thinking gathered here will not reach more than a few of those for whom the issues it raises are most immediate: working-class men and women whose material circumstances make them most susceptible to the military's promises of opportunities for training, travel, and a better future."[92] It does not bode well for the future of class relations in America when those who miss or dismiss the social message of *Platoon* offer themselves as the salvation of the working class.

Yet the fault does not lie entirely with the critics and editors who define politics too narrowly. *Platoon,* for all its attention to class conflict as an important social and political context of the Vietnam War, is by no means a univocal cultural text. Though it does not romanticize the worker in the manner of *Waiting for Lefty,* it does represent Taylor's encounter with the working class as a romance. Ideologically speaking, the effect is much the same, as we can see when we consider the film's departures from realism. These are glaringly obvious in the screenplay published by Random House in 1987. Described as the "complete original screenplay," this is apparently what Stone committed to paper during the bicentennial summer of 1976. As urtext the screenplay discloses generic intentions that are not always manifest in the finished film.

Not everyone was impressed by *Platoon*'s realism when it first appeared. A few critics, including Pauline Kael, William Adams, and Bert Cardullo, pointed to the confrontation of pure good and pure evil in the film—personified by Sergeants Elias (Willem Dafoe) and Barnes (Tom Berenger)—as evidence that its realism is more rhetorical than structural, a thin veneer over a substrate of melodrama. The binary opposition of good and evil is a feature not only of the melodrama but also, as Fredric Jameson has observed, of the romance.[93]

Stone himself cited epic as well as romantic antecedents for Barnes and Elias. On coming to Vietnam, he told an interviewer, he felt that suddenly everything he had read in Homer was coming true: "I was literally with warriors. Barnes was Achilles, a truly great warrior, Elias was Hector, and I was with them in another world."[94] The screenplay describes Barnes as "Achilles, towering in his rage" when he realizes that the lieutenant has called in the wrong coordinates for an artillery barrage (p. 90). In his *American Film* memoir Stone recalled the thrill of fighting beside the original Barnes, "actually hauling his radio, the equivalent, I suppose, of driving his chariot."[95] Barnes had a worthy opponent in Elias, "the conscience-stricken Hector fighting for a lost cause on the dusty plains of Troy." Men such as these initially fostered the illusion that Vietnam was a world of "warrior kings" rather than managers and workers. As their understudy, Oliver Stone learned to "accept the evil the Homeric gods had thrown out into the world. To be both good and evil."

If Stone's heroes have one foot in the world of the epic, the other is planted in the more permissive realm of romance. As Northrop Frye explains in his classic account of the major literary modes, the romance hero moves in a world in which the "ordinary laws of nature are slightly suspended," enabling him to perform "prodigies of courage and endurance."[96] Thus Elias absorbs dozens of bullets and runs hundreds of yards before succumbing to death, and the scar on Barnes's face is a reminder that he had been shot seven times yet is still miraculously alive. Stone recalled that the original Barnes had taken a bullet above his left eye. "The resulting scar ran the whole left side of his face in a large, sickle-shaped pattern layered with grafted skin from the indentation above his eye to his lower jaw. It was a *massive* job, indicative of equally massive damage to the nerves and possibly the brain."[97]

Barnes's scar associates him with another prodigy of romance, Melville's Ahab. The connection is drawn explicitly when the platoon marches on a Vietnamese village, determined to avenge the death of a soldier found trussed to a tree. "Barnes was at the eye of our rage," Taylor recalls in a voice-over, "and through him, our Captain Ahab, we would set things right again." Stone elaborates the analogy in his *American Film* memoir, remarking that Barnes had evil in his heart yet also epitomized Ahab's line, "O this lovely light that shineth not on me."[98] Barnes is evil and Elias good; Barnes is darkness and Elias light. Elias plays Starbuck to Barnes's Ahab, though with more steel in his spine. Taylor is Ishmael, to whom Stone compares his younger self in the memoir—an observer who is eventually compelled to act.[99]

Like the crew of the *Pequod*, members of the platoon are fascinated onlookers at the confrontation between two of their leaders. The screenplay includes a scene in which platoon members discuss the background of Barnes and Elias in much the same way that Melville's sailors trade stories about Ahab's past. In the following snatches of dialogue, Rhah (Francesco Quinn) supplies the mythic answer to Taylor's questions, while Lerner (Johnny Depp) adheres to the facts, insofar as they are known:

CHRIS: Where's he from?
RHAH: Barnes comes from Hell.
LERNER: Tennessee someplace. Hill country.

. . . .

CHRIS: Where's Elias come from?
RHAH: 'Lias come naturally.
LERNER: . . . don't know. Done some time. Heard he worked the oil wells
            in Oklahoma, made some bread and washed up in El Lay. (pp.
            76–77)

King adds some details to Lerner's account of Elias, saying that in Los Angeles he had been busted for drugs and given the choice between jail and Vietnam. Like Barnes, he had reenlisted and remained in Vietnam for several consecutive tours of duty.

Platoon is a romance not only in its characterization but also in its narrative structure or mythos. According to Frye, romance is concerned with adventure, particularly the quest.[100] Occupying the opposite pole from realism, it is allied with dreams and wish fulfillment.[101] If we regard Taylor rather than Barnes or Elias as the questing protagonist of *Platoon* (a proposition to which I shall return in a moment) what Frye says about the relation between dream and reality in romance could have been written with Taylor in mind: "Translated into dream terms, the quest-romance is the search of the libido or desiring self for a fulfilment that will deliver it from the anxieties of reality but will still contain that reality. The antagonists of the quest are often sinister figures, giants, ogres, witches and magicians, that clearly have a parental origin; and yet redeemed and emancipated paternal figures are involved too, as they are in the psychological quests of both Freud and Jung."[102] This passage recalls Barnes's "I am reality" speech and Taylor's reflection, at the end of the film, that he is the child of two fathers. One is a sinister antagonist, the other a means of redemption and emancipation.

If the quest for fulfillment is the essence of romance, we might ask what Taylor seeks in Vietnam with the help of the good father and despite the bad. What he seeks is nothing less than the "born again" self of the gospels and evangelical religion. Here one detects the biblical origin of Western literary genres, as suggested by Frye. The Christian mythos of death and rebirth is invoked in the film's opening image of replacements arriving in Vietnam, where the rear hatch of a C-130 slowly drops to reveal a group of untested soldiers in brand-new fatigues. They appear stunned and uncertain, like newborn infants. Their innocence is immediately contrasted with two forms of experience—that of the dead soldiers in body bags and that of the survivors boarding the plane. One calls out to the replacements, "365 and a wake-up—O Lawd!"

We then shift to the platoon, hacking, climbing, and wading its way through the jungle. Conspicuous among the troops on this *via dolorosa* is Elias, who walks with both arms draped over an M-60 machine gun carried across both shoulders, behind the neck. This is the only time we see him with the M-60, since it is normally Tex (David Neidorf) who carries the weapon, until Tex is wounded and replaced by King. When Elias protests his squad's assignment to a night ambush, O'Neill (John C. McGinley), another squad leader, says, "Guy's in three years, he thinks he's Jesus fucking Christ or something." In death Elias is again made to resemble Jesus, with his arms raised to heaven near a ruined church; "Elias crucified" reads the laconic note in the screenplay (p. 97). When Barnes subsequently dismisses Elias as a "waterwalker," Chris openly defies Barnes for the first time. His very name—short for Christopher or Christian—reflects his discipleship.

Yet Elias's mythic genealogy antedates the gospels. He is also a pagan vegetation god of the kind described by Frazer in *The Golden Bough*. Whereas Barnes is identified with the machine—"when the machine breaks down, *we* break down"—Elias "come[s] naturally," as Rhah says, and is consistently identified with nature. The screenplay includes a conversation between Taylor and Elias on the subject of reincarnation. Elias calls death "a big return ticket" and says that he expects to come back as a deer (p. 81). Later, when Barnes stalks Elias in the jungle, he is described as a deer hunter and Elias as a deer. The ensuing murder is characterized in the screenplay as a "crime against nature" that prompts a bird to cry out in protest (pp. 94–95). The morning after the battalion is overrun, Taylor regains consciousness and, in both the film and the screenplay, discovers that he is being watched by a deer. The significance of this is muted in the film, which lacks the discussion about reincarnation. The screenplay, however, is explicit to the point of being heavy-handed: the deer is "a sign of grace—the grace of Elias" (p. 124). Despite all the evidence of death and destruction Taylor is represented as an American Adam, awakening in a "garden of eden."

During the fade-in to this scene the jungle vegetation changes from an overexposed gray-green, presumably the "holy light" called for in the screenplay (p. 124), to the saturated green that serves as backdrop to Taylor's revenge. By killing Barnes in cold blood he avenges Elias's murder and his own near-murder the night before. This deed ostensibly completes his personal cycle of death and rebirth and allies him with the protagonists of *Apocalypse Now* and *The Deer Hunter*, the "mythic" films that *Platoon* was meant to supplant. But what has Taylor personally done or endured to effect his apotheosis? His mere identification with Elias seems inadequate to produce this result, as does his revenge on Barnes. Reviewing Taylor's experiences, however, we discover a death-and-rebirth story that parallels Elias's but is framed in social rather than religious or anthropological terms. It is here that the romance genre of *Platoon* intersects with its political message.

A voice-over early in the film informs us that Taylor has rejected college as the haven of rich kids and cast his lot with the poor and unwanted of society. "They're the bottom of the barrel," he says, "and they know it." But he adds that they're also "the best [he's] ever seen . . . the heart and soul." Consequently, he anticipates that his descent into the working class will be redemptive: "Maybe I've finally found it, way down here in the mud. Maybe from down here I can start up again and be something I can be proud of, without having to fake it, be a fake human being." As he speaks these words the camera pans up from a mud puddle to Taylor's face. Like Oliver Stone doing penance for his first novel, Taylor seeks the anonymity of the common men who went to Vietnam. They constitute a kind of primal ooze in which he can shed the "fake" identity that he inherited from his parents. His bourgeois idealism will not allow him to wallow in the mud indefinitely, however. The panning camera anticipates his ascent to a new identity.

Moments later, due largely to the negligence of one of the men whom he had idealized as "the best," a platoon member is killed and Taylor is slightly wounded in the neck. In his panic Taylor believes that he is dying, a notion that proves to be metaphorically true. Having sloughed off his middle-class self, he assumes a working-class identity in a scene with mythic overtones. Descending into the underground bunker where Elias's squad relaxes when not in the field, he encounters a figure seated on a sandbag throne. This is Rhah, a Rhadamanthine figure (hence his name) who according to the screenplay "seems to be the lord of final judgment in this smoky underworld" (p. 44). When Rhah asks Taylor why he has come to the underworld, King answers for him, "This here ain't Taylor. Taylor been shot. This man here is Chris. He been resurrected."

Taylor's acceptance by this faction of the platoon is significant. In keeping with the pattern described by Helmer, Taylor identifies with the heads within about a month after his arrival in-country. Also following the typical pattern, he had not used drugs in the States and is unfamiliar with the term "heads." He becomes a head partly because of his unit assignment; had he been assigned to O'Neill's squad rather than Elias's, he might well have become a juicer.

How the two factions differ from one another is dramatized in a triptych strategically inserted between Taylor's wounding and the titanic fistfight between the two sergeants. The Jefferson Airplane's "White Rabbit," a drug-tripping allegory that likewise features an underworld journey, plays in the background as Taylor greets the heads and partakes of the communal pot pipe. Then he spots Elias in the back corner of the hooch, surrounded by burning candles and a poster of Ho Chi Minh. Elias reclines luxuriously on a hammock with his shirt off, munching on a banana. Noticing Taylor, he smiles and waves in a coquettish manner—behaving, in short, like the "sensual little Egyptian whore" called for in the screenplay (p. 46). The scene concludes with Elias "shotgunning" marijuana smoke into Taylor's lungs, a normally neutral act that becomes erotically charged in this context.

Merle Haggard's "Okie from Muskogee" (they don't smoke marijuana in Muskogee) marks the transition from the heads' bunker to the juicers' barracks. Here the lighting is harsh, the setting unobscured by smoke. Sensuality and communal feeling give way to masculine aggression and contentiousness. Junior (Reggie Johnson), a black soldier, makes fun of the country and western music and repeats the black militant line, ignoring a Confederate flag displayed on one wall. Bunny (Kevin Dillon), the killer, tries to impress the lieutenant by taking a bite out of an empty beer can. Another soldier sticks his sheath knife in the floor. O'Neill brags about someone he'd beaten in a fight and cracks an anti-Semitic joke. There is no sexual ambiguity here, unless one counts the lieutenant's nervous joke about being "raped" if he were to take part in Barnes's card game. As in rape, the juicers' sexuality is mixed up with violence, pain, and domination. Bunny turns to "pussy" for respite from the rigors of killing, a venereal disease warning is broadcast over the Armed Forces radio station, and a copy of *Playboy* serves as the voyeuristic subtext of the card game for a full minute before the camera shifts back to the heads for the last panel of the triptych.

The music in the heads' hooch has changed to "Tracks of My Tears," a Motown recording about lost love by Smokey Robinson and the Miracles. The scene is suffused, as the screenplay indicates, with a "yearn-ing for tenderness, for femininity." The men are "thinking of dance partners that can't be here tonight" (p. 54). Rhah hugs a carved statu-ette of a naked woman in a ludicrous pantomime of Robinson's lyrics about the "substitute" to whom he turns when rejected by his true love. Here, of course, the flesh-and-blood substitutes are all male. Elias dances with Crawford (Chris Pedersen) while the others jive independently to the music and lip-synch the lyrics. They throw arms around each other's shoulders, black and white in a fraternal embrace. This scene is the more remarkable when one considers the de facto racial segregation of most bases in the rear at this time, on the eve of the assassination of Martin Luther King, Jr. As Helmer points out, white working-class heads were more receptive to blacks than the juicers were, but were gen-erally no more successful in breaking down the barriers to social inter-action.[103]

By casting his lot with the heads, Taylor identifies with the portion of the working class that shared the antiwar sentiment, hedonism, gen-der blurring, racial tolerance, recreational drugs, and even music of middle-class student culture. Beyond this crude division into two fac-tions, the common soldiers of *Platoon* are only minimally differentiated from one another, reflecting their function as a means to Taylor's self-transcendence. Taylor's final deed is to rise above both groups. From the deck of the helicopter that whisks him away, he smiles down on Rhah's chest-thumping heroics and the slow-motion, antlike movements of those who cannot leave the war. Then, his eyes on the horizon, he con-templates his postwar destiny: "Those of us who did make it have an obligation to build again, to teach to others what we know, and to try with what's left of our lives to find a goodness and meaning to this life."

Even critics who liked the rest of the film (Vincent Canby and Ter-rence Rafferty, for example) found the final voice-over banal. William Adams judged it dangerously romantic—an endorsement of war for the special kind of insight it can provide.[104] This is nevertheless the apothe-osis toward which the film's romance plot moves from the opening scene. It is as though Taylor were saying, "Now I will become Oliver Stone and make films like *Platoon, Born on the Fourth of July,* and *Heaven and Earth.*" To become Oliver Stone, who likewise believed that he had been "saved" to write a book or make a movie about Viet-nam, Taylor must transcend both of his working-class fathers and re-claim his birthright as a solid son of the middle class.[105] This apotheosis, coupled with regret at the loss of two heroic figures, identifies *Platoon* as an elegiac romance.

Kenneth Bruffee credits Joseph Conrad with combining the romance and the elegy to create a new form, though he sees in Melville's *Moby-Dick* a precursor of the genre. In the traditional romance our attention is focused on the adventures of the knight. In the elegiac romance the "knight" is usually dead before the story begins, and our attention turns instead to the inner quest of the "squire"—Ishmael or Marlow, for example—who narrates the story. The squire has invested much of himself in the knight, and tells his tale as a way of coming to terms with his loss. As a symbolic act, his narrative succeeds to the extent that it liberates him from his displaced Oedipal feelings and allows him to mature and move on to other spheres of action. Bruffee maintains that in novels like *Heart of Darkness* and *Lord Jim* Conrad hit upon a literary form that captured the twentieth century's nostalgia for nineteenth-century heroic virtues and infallible authority. Like primitivism, it was a response to the degeneration of a culture.

Applying this paradigm to *Platoon,* one is struck not only by the structural congruence of the whole but also by the appropriateness of specific details: the ironic epigraph from the Book of Ecclesiastes ("Rejoice O young man in thy youth"); the elegiac, even lugubrious, tone of Georges Delerue's arrangement of Barber's "Adagio for Strings"; the Oedipal "child of two fathers" motif; the rewriting of Milton's *Lycidas* ("fresh Woods and Pastures new") in the final voice-over. The film nevertheless departs from convention in a couple of ways. In the elegiac romance the fictional past is represented in counterpoint with the fictional present so as to apprise the reader of both the hero's exploits and the narrator's considered response to them.[106] In film versions of literary elegiac romances, Bruffee observes, the filmmaker usually dispenses with the fictional present of narration altogether in order to exploit the more sensational story of the hero's adventures.[107] *Platoon* steers a course between the two. It retains a fictional present in the voice-overs, but these are relatively unobtrusive and formally unstable. Initially, the voice-overs represent Taylor's letters to his grandmother, written in Vietnam; by the end of the film they represent his subsequent reflections on his experience of war: "I think now, looking back."

Platoon departs from generic convention in another respect: it portrays Taylor's relationship with two heroes rather than one. With this bifurcation the film verges on melodrama but accomplishes one of the aims of contrapuntal structure, namely, disclosure of the narrator's present ambivalence toward a man he once admired unreservedly. In the screenplay Rhah directs Taylor's attention to the words "love" and "hate" tattooed on his fists (p. 77). Lerner recognizes this as an allusion to the movies—specifically Charles Laughton's *Night of the Hunter* (1955). Though the words are meant to stand for Elias and Barnes, they also express Taylor's complex attitude toward a single style of heroism. For all their differences, the two sergeants have much in common as seasoned combat veterans and leaders, and Taylor is reminded by Rhah that he had once admired Barnes as much as Elias.

Inasmuch as ambivalence and its resolution are the forces that drive elegiac romance, Stone's choice of genre tells us something about the autobiographical and political dimensions of *Platoon*. Bruffee speculates that Conrad and other practitioners of the form found it as cathartic as their fictional narrators. The elegiac romance delivered them from past attachments, allowing them to get on with their lives and artistic careers.[108] As autobiography Stone's next film, *Wall Street* (1987), realizes *Platoon*'s promise of upward mobility. Though *Wall Street* follows the "true father–false father" pattern that John Hellmann has traced in Vietnam war narratives, it reverses the configuration of *Platoon*. The young protagonist of *Wall Street* (played by Charlie Sheen) is the biological son of a blue-collar airline maintenance chief. His surrogate fathers are both stockbrokers, one greedy and unscrupulous, the other honest and conscientious. Stone's revision of the "child of two fathers" motif, together with the dedication of *Salvador* and *Wall Street* to Louis Stone, suggests reconciliation with his stockbroker father and middle-class values. In fact the prodigal son may never have strayed far from home. At the reunion organized by Vietnam Veterans of America, Stone's fellow platoon members recalled that he read the *Wall Street Journal* regularly and dispensed advice on how to play the stock market.[109]

Stone's ambivalence toward the working class, even when its heroes are viewed through Homeric and Melvillean lenses, is reflected not only in his choice of the elegiac romance as the controlling genre of *Platoon* but also in his blending of the realistic and romance modes. As Frye points out, realistic fiction often parodies the idealization of life in the romance.[110] When Taylor reveals that he came to Vietnam because he considered it unfair for rich kids to hide behind student deferments, King plays Sancho Panza to his Don Quixote, saying, "What we got here is a crusader. . . . Sheeit, you gotta be rich in the first place to think like that. Everybody know the poor always being fucked by the rich.

Always have, always will." As the voice of social realism, King exposes
Taylor's ideals to ridicule. At the same time, he gives Taylor permission
to retreat to middle-class privilege when his crusade proves futile.

According to Jameson, each literary mode or genre is an ideology in
its own right. Yet the ideology of a genre is not easy to specify because
the form is "sedimented" with all the messages it has carried in the
past.[111] For example, realism, the favored mode of Marxist narrative in
the early twentieth century, bears ideological traces of its origin in the
nineteenth-century bourgeois novel. The realism of *Platoon* serves a
bourgeois purpose though associated with working-class characters. As
for romance, before there was a true middle class the mode was associated with the aristocracy and, in its use of folklore, with the peasantry.
Later it became antibourgeois and even revolutionary. Richard Chase
maintains that American writers such as Poe, Hawthorne, Melville, and
Faulkner found the romance particularly well suited to the "radical
forms of alienation, contradiction, and disorder" inherent in American
culture.[112] Jameson even proposes that Marxist writers turn from realism to romance to escape or subvert the overly determinate realism of
late capitalism.[113]

Jameson believes that romance remains an attractive mode because
it invokes liberating "categories of Otherness" that can be redefined for
different eras. The magic of medieval romance, for instance, is metamorphosed into psychology in Stendhal's *La Chartreuse de Parme*.[114]
The primary category of otherness in *Platoon* is the working class—not
as a social reality but as an idea in both Taylor's mind and Stone's. The
ordinary soldiers in the film have scarcely more individuality than the
North Vietnamese enemy, and they are attractive for precisely that reason. They serve as the fluid medium in which Taylor can extinguish for
a time the flame of middle-class consciousness. The controlling myths
of regeneration ensure that he will be reassimilated by the middle class
and even granted a measure of authority he had not enjoyed previously.

To Stone's credit, he has used his authority as veteran-auteur to protest the systematic class discrimination of the Vietnam years. He also
hoped, he told an interviewer, to dissuade young people dazzled by Tony
Scott's *Top Gun* (1986) from making the same mistake he had made.[115]
If these messages have not come across as clearly as they might have,
the fault lies partly with viewers who would rather not hear them. As
we have seen, however, their repression is subtly encouraged by Stone
through his manipulation of the realist and romance modes. What
Jameson says about every novel might also be said about every film:

each is an attempt to harmonize narrative patterns that have separate and often contradictory ideological meanings.[116] So regarded, the work is a dialogue of genres as well as (to recall Bakhtin's theory) a dialogue of social speech types. In the generic dialogue of *Platoon* Stone suppresses the antibourgeois voice of the romance in order to tell a story of middle-class regeneration and youthful *Bildung*. Though he allows the voice of social realism to be heard, it lends authority not to the working class but to the young bourgeois who undergoes a working-class rite of passage.

Jameson believes that it is the critic's task to locate generic discontinuities in the literary or cultural text and specify their ideological significance.[117] Inasmuch as *Platoon* is a cultural text and not merely Oliver Stone's autobiography, it both criticizes and exemplifies an instrumental view of the working class in America. Workers are useful for building jeeps and fighting unpopular wars, and their utility does not end with these physical functions. The worker is also useful as an idea, in much the same way that the Oriental and the Polynesian were useful to nineteenth-century primitivists. As idea, the worker can be used to defy one's parents, criticize the dominant ideology, and reaffirm one's sense of social destiny and intellectual mission. If *Platoon* were really about the six inches in front of a soldier's face, it would touch on none of these political issues, though it might serve as a benchmark experiment in realism. What qualifies the film as an important cultural artifact, what makes it still painful to watch, is paradoxically its romance.

VI

Larry Heinemann's *Paco's Story* challenges the instrumental view of the worker that informs *Platoon*. Like Stone, Heinemann believed that money insulated many young men of his generation from the war. He minced no words in an interview for the *Chicago Tribune:* "I know there were people who opposed the war for moral and political reasons, but I also know there were many people against it because they were chicken and because their mommy and daddy had money to keep them in the streets."[118] Heinemann made it clear in the same interview that his resentment of affluent evaders is not based on prowar politics: "They told us this was a good war, a righteous war, and it wasn't. It was one of the most evil things I've ever been a party to."[119] These statements, at once antiwar and anti-war evader, are not as contradictory as they might seem, since the "they" who sent Heinemann to Vietnam belonged to the same social class as those "in the streets" and were often their parents.

Heinemann criticizes the warmongers and the draft evaders alike from a working-class perspective. The son of a bus driver who worked himself to an early death, he was born in Chicago and raised in a suburb swelled by the urban flight of the working class in the 1940s and 1950s. He tried to improve on his father's lot and avoid the draft by attending a two-year college in Evanston. Though he prolonged his stay for a third year, he was financially unable to continue his schooling and was drafted shortly after graduation in 1966. In Vietnam he served in an armored reconnaissance platoon in the 25th Infantry Division, manning the .50-caliber machine gun on an armored personnel carrier (APC). When he returned to the States he held a series of blue-collar jobs— Chicago Transit Authority (CTA) bus driver, Convenient Food Mart counterman, cab driver—while taking courses in creative writing and eventually becoming an instructor himself.

When Heinemann's first novel, *Close Quarters,* appeared in 1977, it was widely praised for its authenticity. One critic singled out in particular his feeling for the implements and labor of war.[120] His description of the soldier's work is in fact thematically central to the novel. Heinemann consciously set out to write a book that would do for the work of war what Melville had done for whaling and Twain for piloting a steamboat.[121] Philip Dosier, the narrator of the novel, is assigned to a mechanized infantry platoon (as Heinemann had been), where he develops a love-hate relationship with his "track," an APC named the Cow Catcher. The night before he leaves Vietnam, he reflects that he has "lost a good deal" during a year at war. His hands, the worker's primary tools, epitomize the damage to body and spirit:

> My hands are stiff and cold, they ache with the changing of the season. The backs are wrinkled and spliced with small scaly cuts, and the fingers shiver when I hold them out. The nails are long and hard, discolored and chipped. The palms are drawn and chapped, and calluses have grown on the insides of the knuckles and joints. There is not the slightest inkling of texture or coolness or warmth, and everything I do now has a slack baggy feel to it. All touch is the same: the small shards of wool at the edge of a blanket; the wood of my shotgun stock; the oily wooden handle of the ball peen hammer; a clean shave; the inside of a thigh.[122]

Rarely has the absence of feeling been represented with such feeling. This is the paradox at the heart of *Close Quarters* and *Paco's Story,* published nine years later.

Paco's Story was initially passed over by the New York Times Book Review, then belatedly reviewed when it seemed to be in contention for the National Book Award for fiction. When it won the award, eclipsing Toni Morrison's Beloved and Philip Roth's Counterlife, there was considerable controversy and second-guessing about the judges' motives and criteria. In a review published two months later in the New York Review of Books, Robert Towers characterized Paco's Story as "essentially a sentimental novel" in the way it exploits the reader's feelings of revulsion, pity, and guilt.[123] "That it should have been chosen as the best novel of the year," Towers concluded, "suggests that the judges, for whatever reasons, made a sentimental decision of their own." Before turning to the novel's rhetoric, the target of Towers's criticism, we first need to consider its subject matter and plot.

Like Close Quarters, Paco's Story details the work of war. Because it is set in the States rather than Vietnam, it can present the labor of war in tandem with what Studs Terkel calls the "violence" of apparently peaceful labor. The novel's structure emphasizes the similarities between the two. As Paco looks for work in the middle-American town of Boone and then settles into his job as dishwasher at the Texas Lunch, he recalls the work he and others had done in Vietnam.[124] In one section, the relationship between the two kinds of labor is developed with particular intricacy; the clause "While we're on the subject of work" serves as the segue from a detailed rendering of Paco's Saturday-night chores to an account of a soldiers' sabbath in Vietnam.[125] The grunts drink and smoke marijuana in a base camp bunker while Gallagher, the company killer and clown, tells how his father—whom Heinemann based on his own father—returned home each evening, brutalized by his work as a CTA bus driver. "My old man busted his ass all his life," Gallagher recalls, "and all's he got out of it was beat-up hands, bad eyes, and a bend in his neck" (p. 124). He is reminded of his father by the look of "pale and exhausted astonishment" on the face of a soldier whose arm had been shattered by a mortar shell two days previously.

The scene then shifts back to the Texas Lunch, where the owner, Ernest Monroe, crosses the bridge the other way. Assuming the role played by Gallagher, he sits in the dining room drinking homemade wine and telling a story about the Pacific theater in World War II. Like Gallagher, Monroe mentions a soldier whose arm was blown off; also like Gallagher, he knows that there is more violence than glory or satisfaction to be had in the soldier's labor. "Work's work," he says, "but I tell you from the bottom of my heart that Iwo Jima was a sloppy, bloody buttfuck" (p. 128). Combat, so often compared to sex in war narratives, is here de-eroticized by the comparisons to hard labor and sodomy.

In *Paco's Story* war is repeatedly seen as menial labor and menial labor as a form of sustained assault on mind and body. Though work and war are entwined with one another formally, it is nevertheless useful to trace them separately through the novel, proceeding from ordinary work to the work of war.

Paco's pilgrimage from the Texaco station to the Texas Lunch is a digest of working America, Terkel's *Working* in travelogue form. Halfway to the restaurant Paco encounters an artifact that symbolizes the work ethic at its best:

> Paco walks briskly to the spindly, spidery bridge (known in the engineering trade as a Howe-type, through-truss bridge, you understand)—the asphalt roadway better than a foot thick and oozing out the runoff gutters like frozen globs of sludge. The intricate ironwork—the tension beams and torsion beams and, overhead, trellis-looking crossbeams—is delicate and well made. The bridge is so banged up—pounded on and painted over, rusted up and painted again—that the builder's plate is indecipherable and there's no telling what year it was built. (pp. 66–67)

To a Marxist the bridge might epitomize the worker's lot under capitalism. Those who designed and built it have faded into a rusted-up, painted-over anonymity, leaving only the product of their labors. Yet the passage emphasizes the durability of the bridge (it has been standing since 1904), the pride of an old man who participated in its construction as a water boy, and its structural beauty, especially compared with the "godawful ugly" railroad bridge further downstream.

The bridge sets a standard by which most of the other workmanship in the novel is judged and found wanting. Though savvy and professional, the driver of the cross-country bus is not about to waste any of his dinner break on Paco. The young mechanic who drives him as far as Rita's Tender Tap is good-natured but a slacker. Rita's is the refuge of a group of county maintenance workers whom Paco associates with army lifers; they will never "crank a decent day's work" in a lifetime on the public dole (p. 65). After crossing the bridge he encounters other loafers and a couple of townspeople doing real work—one a barber, the other an antique dealer who thinks of war (in this case the Russian Revolution) while repairing a clock. Paco is instantly recognized as a veteran whose battering in the work of war disqualifies him for jobs that must sustain the illusion of health and civility. He is dismissed by a haberdasher, a pharmacist, and a telephone solicitor before Ernest

Monroe, himself a twice-wounded marine veteran, hires him out of fellow feeling.

Nearly half the novel is devoted to Paco's search for "work and a place to stay." Once Paco finds his niche at the back sink of the Texas Lunch, Heinemann devotes a half-dozen pages to the daily routine of busing and washing dishes, a routine built around mealtimes and the changes of shift at the foundry (pp. 110–16). It is backbreaking work, especially for someone in Paco's condition. Each night he returns to his room in the Geronimo Hotel "ass-whipped tired, his legs tingling and throbbing, wobbly even, his feet soaked and sore—that goddamned lye-soap rash on his arms as red as rope burns" (p. 168). Like Gallagher's father, he must stand in his room and "put away his work" before going to bed, sometimes, again like Gallagher's father, holding his aching head in his hands.[126] The work produces no tangible product, and the dishes and pots and pans will not stay clean. The pay is enough to buy the food, lodging, medicine, and cheap booze he needs in order to keep on working, but little more. Cleaning the grease trap each Saturday night takes him back to Fire Base Harriette and "the stench of many well-rotted human corpses" (p. 116).

There are, to be sure, moments of grace when Paco finds the labor unaccountably easy and even agreeable (p. 137). These never last because they are the immediate prelude to terrifying dreams, some of which carry him back to Vietnam and "the grueling, *grinding* shitwork of being a grunt" (p. 73). In this connection we recall what Heinemann told the *Tribune* interviewer about the absence of satisfaction in military labor. In the infantry, he said, "nothing you do produces good feelings, unless you are a medic. Nobody but an insane person could get satisfaction from killing people."[127] The novel qualifies this statement. Paco does take pride in his skill at setting booby traps, even though these kill people and are known to violate the Geneva Convention Rules of War. Conversely, the medic who finds Paco all but dead at Fire Base Harriette breaks down, has a heart attack, and abandons his plan to become a doctor. He is devastated by the realization that "no matter what he did or how much, it was never enough; no matter how hard or neat he worked—grim and earnest—the wounded always died" (p. 28).

As represented in *Paco's Story*, the labor of war is not only physically and mentally exhausting but also destructive and pointless. It includes killing ninety-two members of a company—one's own men—with "friendly fire," brutally raping and murdering a Viet Cong girl, killing an enemy soldier with a fillet knife, and harvesting thirty-nine pairs of ears with a straight razor. The military engagements, when they happen, resemble gang street fights rather than epic contests between Homeric heroes (p. 5).

In *Paco's Story* as in *Platoon* the war managers closest to the war workers are the objects of greatest scorn. Like the "see no evil" Wolfe of *Platoon*, Lieutenant Stennett, an English major from Dartmouth, studiously ignores the rape and murder of the VC girl while making himself a cup of coffee. Also like Wolfe, he calls in the artillery and air strike that reduces Alpha Company to ashes. The company commander, Captain Culpepper, though more competent, is a West Point careerist, "a real eager beaver" out to collect medals regardless of the cost to his men (p. 22). Only when Paco is far from Vietnam, recuperating in a hospital in Japan, does he meet an officer whom he respects. Though he cannot remember what the colonel whispered in his ear after pinning a Purple Heart and a Bronze Star to his pajamas, he associates the gesture with his father and keeps the medals as souvenirs of the colonel's kindness.

Given the nature of soldierly work and the managerial style of most officers, it is not surprising that the grunts' bitterness hardens into class hatred and alienation from America. Though a veteran of the "good war," Ernest Monroe refuses to fly the American flag "right side up, upside down, inside out, crosswise, ass backward, or fuck-you otherwise" (p. 126). Jesse, a Vietnam veteran and drifter who stops at the Texas Lunch for a late-night supper, still harbors resentment toward two lifers and the military police (pp. 154–55). Like Heinemann and other working-class soldiers, Jesse realizes that his manager-exploiters also include members of Congress; war profiteers of every stripe, including the news media and professional glorifiers of war; and even "those mouthy, snappy-looking girlies from some rinky-dink college" who assume that all veterans are killers and rapists (p. 156). Ernest expresses his anger by denying himself one form of symbolism; Jesse expresses his by indulging imaginatively in another. His Vietnam War monument would be a gigantic granite bowl filled with hundred-dollar bills stirred into a glutinous mixture of unspeakable wastes. All who choose to wade into this version of the Vietnam quagmire will be rewarded with those desiderata of the upwardly mobile, money and media coverage.[128]

Jesse's remark about the rinky-dink college girls strikes closer to home than he knows. Much of the second half of the novel is devoted to Paco's peculiar relationship with Cathy, the hotel owner's niece who is taking summer courses at a local teachers' college. Though Cathy feels "like a piece of meat" when men stare at her (p.201), she knows how to capitalize on—to make psychological capital of—her sexual attractiveness. She teases Paco by parading in various stages of undress past a window opposite the back door of the Texas Lunch, later by lounging at her open door when he returns in the evening. On hot summer nights when both have their windows open, she makes audible love to her boyfriend while Paco tosses restlessly on his bed. A voyeur as well as an exhibitionist, Cathy initially finds Paco attractive because of his scars. In this respect she is like Betsy Sherburne, a rich young woman from Boone who fantasizes about a night with Paco, and the other women in his past, who patiently waited for him to finish his war story "so they could get him into bed, and see and touch all those scars for themselves" (p. 72).

In Paco's first sexual encounter as a scarred man, while still in an army hospital in Vietnam, a nurse masturbated him with an almost maternal compassion; the act was meant to help restore him to manhood. Though Paco hopes to find redemption and a "livable peace" in sex (pp. 173–74), his subsequent encounters with women serve rather to reinforce his victimhood. As a sexual fetish, the scar confers power on the unviolated partner. In Paco's relationship with Cathy, the balance of power shifts temporarily when he catches her watching him from her window. Then, losing her sense of control over Paco as the object of her gaze, she ceases to think him "cute" and "good-looking" and begins to see him instead as "a dingy, dreary, smelly, shabby, *shabby* little man" (pp. 202, 205). She has a terrible nightmare in which Paco, while making love to her, peels off his scars and applies them to her body, in effect transferring his victimhood to her.

Paco learns of the change in Cathy's attitude when he sneaks into her room and reads her diary. Previously, she had not only spied on him but had also entered his room and "read" his war story in a petri dish containing the shrapnel and bone fragments removed from his body. When their roles are reversed Paco initially enjoys a sense of power in eavesdropping on her most intimate thoughts and feelings. He settles comfortably into his role as the reader of a mildly pornographic narrative in which Cathy is an object of male fantasy. But when Paco encounters himself as a character in her story, he can no longer sustain the readerly illusion of control. The diary reinstates Paco as an object in Cathy's subjectivity, this time with his full knowledge. Thus it accomplishes emotionally what the "friendly fire" at Fire Base Harriette had accomplished physically.

Paco writes a note to Ernest, thanking him for the work that had temporarily distracted him from the bleak knowledge of how he is seen and used by his "betters." Then he boards a bus headed west, clinging desperately to the hope that there is "less bullshit" in that direction (p. 210). As Jesse the drifter could tell Paco, there are no truly egalitarian communities to be found in America. The "bullshit" will be waiting for him in the next Boone down the pike and every Boonetown after that. Unlike Jesse, who never stays anywhere long enough to be assigned a role in the socioeconomic community, Paco persists in looking for "work and a place to stay." He seeks what he dreads most, social definition. If his scars identify him as a Vietnam veteran, his work and his communal standing mark him just as surely, though less visibly, as the "*shabby* little man" whom Cathy finds so repulsive.

Like *Platoon, Paco's Story* is a pastiche of several genres. On one level, it is picaresque narrative, "The Adventures of Paco Sullivan." On another, it is a western, with a showdown between Paco and Cathy (and all that she represents) at the turning point in the action. Other discursive forms embedded in the narrative include the diary, announcements on a bulletin board, menus, signs, popular songs, and newspaper headlines. The reader is lured into these genres and discourses by a chapter entitled "The First Clean Fact." That fact is the earthly annihilation of the ninety-two men who are telling Paco's story. We are therefore asked at the outset to suspend disbelief in a ghost story told by the ghosts.[129]

The reader's sense of unreality and disorientation does not end there, for the ghosts begin telling their tragic story in the wildly improbable style of a carnival spiel. For this reason they can plausibly maintain that they are not telling a war story. Though their spiel is a story about war as well as work, it elicits none of the emotions usually associated with war. Their Vietnam is a geek show with Paco appearing first as the company wise guy and then as the geek. But this gambit cannot be sustained in the chapters that follow, where Vietnam comes to resemble a butcher shop rather than a carny sideshow. So why do the ghosts even make the attempt?

Partly, no doubt, because they realize that any direct appeal to pity or guilt will strike some listeners (or readers) as sentimental. Here they anticipate Towers's review. The ghosts divide their audience into several categories according to social class. At the bottom of the social order are the "dipstick yokels" who are easily conned into shelling out their hard-earned cash. At the top are the "people with the purse strings and apron strings gripped in their hot and soft little hands" (p. 3). So rarely do the latter indulge in vulgar entertainment that they have to be told what a geek is: "A geek, James, is a carnival performer whose whole act consists of biting the head off a live chicken or a snake." The Jameses of the world are skeptical and tightfisted. They must be wheedled, bullied, or titillated into witnessing "artfully performed, urgently fascinating, grisly and gruesome carnage," whether it takes the form of a geek show or a war story (p. 4). Yet the ghosts know their darkest secret—that they will pay the price of admission in order to feel superior to the geek.

Not content to tell a story about class struggle, the ghosts of Alpha Company reenact it in the way they engage the auditor-reader whom they call "James." On one level the name is meant to recall the war novelist James Jones, who, like Heinemann's father, was unable to understand Vietnam.[130] James thus suggests the gulf separating one generation of veterans from another. As Heinemann points out in the novel's foreword, however, James is also a more formal version of the Jim, Jack, or Jake that "street folks" use when addressing strangers (p. ix). Within the story, working-class characters often address one another as "Jack." But the narrators consistently use "James" when addressing the reader, who is presumed to be of a higher social class and largely ignorant of blue-collar work and its specialized vocabulary, whether in war ("fragmentation grenades—frags we called them" [p. 10]), construction ("a Howe-type, through-truss bridge, you understand" [p. 66]), or farming ("Ask someone who knows shit from shit and shinola about farming, James" [p. 179]).

According to Towers, *Paco's Story* is sentimental because it requires the reader to make an emotional investment in excess of the facts supplied. As a character, Paco "is so rudimentarily conceived that he hardly exists apart from his wretched situation."[131] Towers is partly right: Paco is not so much the subject of the story as he is an occasion for telling it. The "story" in Heinemann's title refers to a process or a performance rather than a product. When we attend to the storytelling rather than the story told, character and plot become less important than the political drama played out between the narrators and their implied audience.

To respond only to the sentiment in *Paco's Story* (I would prefer to call it pathos, for reasons specified below) is therefore to miss half the story, the half that belongs to the ghostly narrators. Though disarmingly humorous, they are out to take posthumous revenge on those who sent them to Vietnam. They tell their story for much the same reason that Heinemann claims to write his novels: "It's more polite than a simple fuck you."[132] On the one hand, the ghosts refuse to sentimentalize Paco's role in the rape and murder of the VC girl; in fact they force him to replay that "moment of evil" in his memories and dreams (p. 184). On the other hand, they demand that the reader share some of the responsibility for Paco's deeds. To the extent that he and his fellow soldiers are instruments rather than agents, their guilt belongs to the people who use them.

This is not to say that the novel represents Paco exclusively as the passive object of middle-class manipulation or desire, though the moments when he lives for his own reasons are few and far between. One such moment occurs on the medevac helicopter that carries him, all but dead, to a base hospital in Vietnam. "*I must not die,*" he tells himself repeatedly (p. 46). Another follows his arrival at the Texas Lunch, when the phenomena of the scene coalesce in a moment of aesthetic contemplation worthy of Walter Pater. Though the moment is "not lost on Paco" (p. 100), he cannot afford the luxury of prolonging it indefinitely. Yielding to the realities of the marketplace, he must exchange the riches of subjectivity for work and a place to stay.

Paco's Story differs fundamentally from *Platoon* in several ways. First, it represents a working-class character as at least occasionally a desiring subject rather than an instrument. Second, it manifests greater confidence in the adequacy of working-class materials. Paco is not Achilles' chariot driver, nor will his immersion in the world of work lead to any apotheosis. Third, the novel does not allow the reader to identify with Paco, whatever his sentimental investment in Paco's story. The generic convention of the geek show spiel reinforces the alienation of the social classes even as it reminds the reader of the grisly contract that binds them together in time of war.

VII

Like Clifford Geertz, Fredric Jameson recommends that cultures be approached as "texts." He claims that this strategy displaces our attention from the empirical object itself—whether the "object" is an institution, an event, or an individual work—to its constitution as an object and its relationship to other objects.[133] So understood, a culture or a cultural phenomenon is not a "work" in the conventional sense, a determinate product of signification. Rather, it is a "text" in Roland Barthes's sense of the word, a field for the free play of signifiers.[134] As long as one heeds this distinction, resisting the temptation to reduce history and material culture to purely aesthetic forms, one has a useful device for linking politics and poetics.[135]

As a text, Stone's *Platoon* reflects the larger narrative of American upper- and middle-class culture during the Vietnam War. At least in fantasy, life for members of the upper classes was an adventure, a quest for the fulfillment of every desire. Like the characters in a romance, they could feel superior to men and women of the lower classes and occasionally even to the laws of nature. When social or physical reality proved overwhelming, as it inevitably did from time to time, they could shift imaginatively from the romance mode to epic or tragedy without losing caste. In their own eyes, they lived and died on a heroic scale.

Paco's Story suggests that members of the working class, whatever fantasies they entertained, often had to accept the life narratives inflicted on them by their employers, officers, and social betters. At best, they lived out their days like the characters in comic drama or realistic fiction, which means, according to Frye, that their personal suffering and loss could never rise to tragedy. Their stories could never elicit an emotion more powerful than pathos, a pathos sometimes heightened by their inability to articulate it.[136] Pathos, as Frye remarks, "is a queer ghoulish emotion." Heinemann's novel simultaneously indulges the reader's ghoulish fascination with war stories and calls attention to its ghoulishness.

The construction workers who marched in May 1970 understood these conventions and their ideological significance, even though they would not have expressed them in the language of literary criticism. When they forced the deputy mayor of New York to raise the flag from its position at half-mast they were using the language of symbols to say that the deaths of four middle-class students should not count more than the deaths of nearly fifty thousand young men and women, many of them from the working class, in Vietnam. To them, the flag at half-mast signaled high tragedy, an officially sanctioned effort to induce a catharsis of pity and fear. Fully raised, the flag stood for patriotic values that compensated, albeit inadequately, for the pathos of their losses.

The workers won the battle of Bloody Friday, but they lost the class war waged during the 1960s. Theirs was a loss that cannot be measured solely in terms of dead and wounded. It was also a loss of community.

According to Jameson, the reader of any text must identify not only its ideology but also its utopia, the specific form of collective unity that it seeks to embody.[137] During the Vietnam War institutions like the Selective Service System and higher education served to consolidate the power of the upper classes. A film such as *Platoon* validates that project on one level while criticizing it on another. Chris Taylor, like so many alienated middle-class children during the 1960s, ultimately reaffirms the utopia of his parents.

Among working-class youth the traditional ritual of military service should have fostered social solidarity. For some it did, as Helmer's "anti-ideological" veterans and Michael Vronsky in *The Deer Hunter* suggest. For others, like Helmer's alienated veterans and Heinemann's Paco and Jesse, the war located utopia literally nowhere. Unable to connect with their fellow workers, unable even to define the sort of utopia they sought, they drifted from place to place or disappeared into the déclassé underworld of the homeless. Paco might be expressing their predicament at the end of the novel, as he prepares to leave Boone. His thoughts also reveal the extent to which he has internalized the middle-class narrative of his existence, as expressed in a metaphor from Cathy's diary: "Whatever it is I want, it ain't in this town; thinking, Man, you ain't just a brick in the fucking wall, you're just a piece of meat on the slab" (p. 209).

CHAPTER 4

The Sex War

I

No retrospective on the 1960s would be complete without a token Vietnam veteran, preferably wounded in the war and strung out on drugs. So Lawrence Kasdan seems to have reasoned when he assembled his cast of characters for *The Big Chill* (1983), a film elegy for the played-out idealism of the 1960s. Kasdan's veteran Nick (played by William Hurt) isn't typical of most veterans; he is a college graduate and doctoral program dropout. Though he had been something of a ladies' man at the University of Michigan, he can no longer live up to his reputation because, like Hemingway's Jake Barnes, he has been sexually "nicked" in combat.[1] An old girlfriend learns of this deficiency when she approaches him with a delicate proposition. Meg (Mary Kay Place), now a lawyer, sees in Nick an opportunity to add motherhood to her résumé. But she is forced to look elsewhere when he tells her what happened to him in Vietnam. Nick eventually takes up with Chloe (Meg Tilly), who accepts him even though he cannot, as he puts it, "do anything." He decides to forgo his current line of work as a drug dealer in order to build a new life with Chloe in a backwoods cabin.

Why Chloe rather than Meg? The answer has as much to do with the sex wars of the 1960s as it does with the nature of Nick's wound. Meg is just about Nick's age and bent on success in a career once dominated by men. She dresses in a "power suit" and, not anticipating that a classmate's funeral will evolve into a weekend-long class reunion, arrives with an attaché case stuffed with legal briefs rather than a toothbrush or a change of clothing. In contrast, Chloe is a belated flower child of the younger generation, devoted to physical rather than mental culture and blissfully ignorant of the past. In her complacency she is a throwback to the stereotypical American helpmate of the 1940s and 1950s, perhaps even to the Asian bride favored by some veterans of World War II and Korea. With Chloe, Nick will not have to refight the sex wars of the 1960s.

The Big Chill never seriously engages any of the issues it revisits. Instead, it is calculated to mine the vein of nostalgia uncovered by a similar and better film, John Sayles's *Return of the Secaucus Seven* (1980). Yet it does raise some of the questions that I address in this chapter: What were the sources of conflict between men and women in the 1960s? How did Vietnam generally, and the experiences of soldiers in particular, contribute to this conflict? How has the conflict been represented in books and films about the war? Finally, what is the current status of the sex war? Is it a war that can be won, either in personal and political relationships or in war stories?

II

First we need to distinguish the sex war of the 1960s from the sexual revolution of the same period. The phrase "sexual revolution" is often used to designate two separate phenomena: a significant increase in nonmarital (that is, premarital or extramarital) sex; and a redefinition of masculine and feminine identity. Social historians and pollsters debate the extent of the former, and some deny that it ever happened. Few detect an increase in nonmarital sex prior to the late 1960s.[2] The Kinsey Institute found little more sexual experience among college students in 1968 than in 1948, despite the relaxation of policies restricting dormitory visitation.[3] By the end of the decade, however, surveys and opinion polls began to register the shift toward sexual permissiveness that flourished in the 1970s. One mid-1970s poll of students in eight colleges disclosed that three-fourths of both men and women had experienced intercourse by their junior year, and that the women were more active sexually than the men.[4]

Understood in the first sense, as an increase in nonmarital sex, the sexual revolution contributed to generational conflict, inasmuch as young men and women of the late 1960s and 1970s defied the sexual mores of their parents. Understood in the second sense, as a redefinition of sexual identities, the sexual revolution was largely intragenerational, often pitting male against female. This produced the sex war of the 1960s, a war fought on several fronts at once—in the courts, in the civil rights and antiwar movements, and in academic communities and intellectual salons. I propose to consider these in sequence, beginning with the women's equal rights movement.

In the years following World War II, as Betty Friedan pointed out in *The Feminine Mystique* (1963), American women became wives and mothers at a progressively younger average age, contrary to the trend in other industrialized and many underdeveloped countries.[5] The traditional dichotomy between virgin and whore was supplanted by the dichotomy between "the feminine woman, whose goodness includes the desires of the flesh, and the career woman, whose evil includes every desire of the separate self."[6] Friedan found that "feminine" women often became obsessed with sex, demanding from their husbands and lovers a kind of fulfillment they could not possibly provide.[7] She urged women to seek the cure for their malaise in the workplace. Why should they not have what men have always had, both career and family? They would in fact be better wives and mothers once they satisfied those desires of the "separate self."

As the conservative logic of that last statement suggests, *The Feminine Mystique* was a product of its time—and therefore of the feminine mystique—as well as a catalyst for change. Later, when Friedan looked back on the 1960s from the vantage point of the 1980s, she had to concede that a career is not always the solution to "the problem that has no name."[8] Many women lack the skills or freedom to pursue the more challenging careers she envisioned, and those who have the opportunity often discover that yesterday's glamorous career is today's routine job. *The Feminine Mystique* nevertheless opened new worlds to a particular group of young women—generally white, middle-class, well-educated— and set the stage for direct political action affecting many more women. Its publication was timely, coming just before the Civil Rights Act of 1964 banned discrimination in employment on the basis of sex as well as race. When the government failed to act on cases of sex discrimination, Friedan and several other women formed the National Organization for Women (NOW) as a pressure group. Partly because of their efforts, Congress passed the Equal Rights Amendment (ERA) in 1972 and sent it to the states for ratification.

That the ERA is not yet the law of the land (an extension of the usual seven-year period for ratification expired in 1982) is a result of both external opposition, particularly from pro-family and pro-life groups, and dissent within the ranks of NOW and the women's movement.[9] Dean K. Phillips, who served as special assistant to the general counsel of the Veterans Administration from 1977 to 1981, believed that veterans' groups also helped to defeat the ERA in several crucial states because NOW and other women's organizations opposed laws awarding extra points to veterans who apply for civil service positions.[10] Phillips, who tried unsuccessfully to persuade NOW to moderate its stance in the late 1970s, questioned the organization's consistency on the issue of equal rights and military service. During the Vietnam War, he pointed out, no women's group had participated in a suit for equal access to the armed services.[11] But when registration for the draft was reinstated in 1980, during a time of peace, NOW protested male-only registration as a form of discrimination against women.

In NOW's defense, it must be said that no organization was likely to demand equal access to the military during an unpopular war. When NOW delegates passed the resolution opposing preference for veterans at their 1971 national convention, they also passed a resolution calling for an immediate end to the Vietnam War. At the time, they denounced war as an expression of the "masculine mystique."[12] But with each year that has passed since Vietnam the equal rights faction of the women's movement has become more committed to the "right to fight." Betty Friedan, in particular, is troubled by the attitude of women who seek equal rights without also accepting equal responsibilities, including military service.[13]

Regarding war and the military, the equal rights faction was less single-minded than another branch of the women's movement. Even before Friedan and her associates founded NOW, a group of younger women were learning very different lessons from the civil rights movement, which led them to reject the careerism of the NOW group. Casey Hayden, Mary King, and other white women who worked with the Student Non-Violent Coordinating Committee (SNCC) during Freedom Summer of 1964 identified not with the successful journalists, lawyers, and politicians who formed the inner coterie of NOW but with the victims of the American Dream, poor black people in the rural South. In the urban centers of the North other young women, mostly college students, were simultaneously working with black people and the poor under the auspices of the Economic Research and Action Projects organized by Students for a Democratic Society.

The women of SNCC and SDS developed an ideology that they would later sum up in a slogan borrowed from C. Wright Mills, "The personal is political."[14] Politics was not merely a matter of passing laws and winning votes; politics suffused relationships with family, friends, and fellow activists in the "participatory democracy" of the movement. It was in their relationship with male activists that SNCC and SDS women noted a contradiction between theory and practice. The New Left, as one historian of the women's movement has observed, "embodied the heritage of the feminine mystique far more strongly than the older left had."[15] Men occupied the positions of leadership and expected women to do the "chickwork"—running the mimeograph machine, stamping envelopes, and dispensing peanut butter sandwiches and even sex on demand. When Hayden and King protested this treatment in a position paper presented at a SNCC staff retreat in 1964, Stokely Carmichael's reply was crude but to the point: "The only position for women in SNCC is prone."

Carmichael's remark, which provoked both outrage and laughter at the time, is the most salient of many bits of mid-1960s folklore all expressing the same truth—that young men and women who shared the same goals, worked side by side, and even dressed alike were still separated by an abyss of misunderstanding. At first the women appealed to shared ideals as a way of bridging the gap, comparing themselves to the oppressed classes and races that groups like SNCC and SDS were committed to helping.[16] If the comparison appeared ludicrous to poor blacks in the rural South and northern cities, coming as it did from college-educated whites, it nevertheless reflected the level of desperation among these women shortly before they struck off on their own to start the women's liberation movement. That movement first attracted national media attention in 1968, when a group of radical feminists protested the Miss America pageant. Over the course of the following year, women's liberation became a staple news item in the popular press.

These were also the peak months of protest against the Vietnam War, framed on one side by the Tet Offensive of January 1968 and on the other by the first draft lottery of December 1969. Surely the war was an issue that could bring the sexes back together? News footage and photographs of antiwar demonstrations, featuring women as prominently as men, suggest that it did. But the appearance is deceptive. Examining the role played by women at the March on the Pentagon in the fall of 1967, Norman Mailer implies in *The Armies of the Night* (1968) that they were merely pawns in the real contest between soldiers and male demonstrators. The real issue, according to Mailer, was the virility of the men on either side of the line. The antiwar males were in effect saying to the troops, "I will steal your élan, and your brawn, and the very animal of your charm because I am right and you are wrong and the balance of existence is such that the meat of your life is now attached to my spirit, I am stealing your balls."[17] In reply, the soldiers appeared to single out female demonstrators with their rifle butts, humiliating the male demonstrators who sat helplessly by, unable to defend their women.[18]

Even allowing for the avowedly "novelistic" latitude of these passages in *Armies*, one has to grant their kernel of truth. Young men who joined the civil rights movement or the New Left had to forgo or at least postpone a conventional mode of demonstrating manhood through success in a career. By way of compensation, some adopted the exaggerated machismo of Third-World revolutionaries or (in the case of whites) of the racial minorities among whom they worked.[19] This accounts for some of the sexism of the men in SNCC and SDS. It also helps to account for their growing impatience with nonviolence as a political strategy. Pondering the movement's turn to violence, Todd Gitlin wrote in 1968, "We are living through some profound crisis of masculinity, explained but not wholly justified by the struggle to shake off middle-class burdens of bland civility."[20] Opposing the Vietnam War deepened this crisis of masculinity, since it denied men of the New Left a rite of passage that their fathers had undergone in World War II. Some feigned homosexuality so as to be declared unfit for service, only to wonder later how much was pretense and how much truth. There was finally no way to feel morally justified without also feeling sexually compromised.

The SNCC-SDS pattern of conflict between the sexes was repeated in the antiwar movement at large. Women were not allowed to forget that they had less at stake in opposing the war, since they were exempt from the draft. They were to be, in effect, camp followers of the antiwarriors. As in the civil rights movement, their support was implicitly sexual as well as moral. The slogan emblazoned on a British propaganda poster of World War I, "Women of Britain Say—Go!," was revised to read, "Girls Say Yes to Guys Who Say No." Eventually it occurred to the "girls" of the New Left that when they said yes they reaffirmed the pattern of exploitation they were protesting in Southeast Asia. The war taught them that they were not merely a disadvantaged race or class but a politically and economically oppressed segment of the world's population. "As we analyze the position of women in capitalist society and especially in the United States," argues a paper drafted in a women's liberation workshop in 1967 and published in *New Left Notes,* "we find that women are in a colonial relationship to men and we recognize ourselves as part of the Third World. . . .Women, because of their colonial relationship to men, have to fight for their own independence."[21]

The belief that personal relationships are also political, together with the leftist ideology of the SNCC-SDS women, likewise informed the feminist writing that began to come out of the academy in the late 1960s. Kate Millett's *Sexual Politics,* originally submitted as a doctoral dissertation in 1969, became a bestseller when it was published as a book the following year. *Sexual Politics* sets out to demonstrate that "sexual dominion obtains . . . as perhaps the most pervasive ideology of our culture and provides its most fundamental concept of power. This is so because our society, like all other historical civilizations, is a patriarchy."[22] Millett supports her thesis with evidence from history, Freudian psychology, and literature. Drawing her chief literary exhibits from D. H. Lawrence, Henry Miller, Norman Mailer, and Jean Genet, she characterizes the first three as "counterrevolutionary sexual politicians" because of the way they represent men dominating and sometimes humiliating women in sexual relations.[23] Genet, as a sexual pariah, affords some perspective on the others and represents what Millett regards as a progressive tendency.

In a postscript to *Sexual Politics* Millett implicitly relates its thesis to the war in Vietnam. She singles out not only the women's movement but also the "revolt of youth against the masculine tradition of war and virility" as a sign of better things to come.[24] The voices of reaction—typified by Lawrence, Miller, and Mailer—are no longer compelling. Women, as the largest "alienated element" in society, will lead a coalition of blacks, students, and poor people toward a world without war, caste privilege, or prescribed sexual roles. Once the transformation of personal consciousness is complete, the political and economic utopia will inevitably follow.

Millett's postscript thus echoes the conclusion to Susan Sontag's "Trip to Hanoi," published the year before. Reflecting on the North Vietnamese she had met in Hanoi and the students who defied the Paris police in May 1968, Sontag likewise concluded that "the particular historical form of our human nature" was undergoing a beneficial transformation.[25] In 1966, responding to Leslie Fiedler's criticism of the counterculture's androgyny ("The New Mutants"), Sontag had defended the young people, arguing that the ills of Western white civilization, including the war in Vietnam, could be traced to its excessively "masculine" character. For Sontag, health—indeed, the very survival of the human species—lay precisely in the Oriental and feminine modes of thought that Fiedler considered inappropriate for young Western males.[26]

Both Millett and Sontag envisioned a revolution that would fundamentally alter the way sexual roles are defined and power distributed under patriarchy. Neither was so naive as to base sexual identity solely on biology. In fact Millett criticized defenders of patriarchy for conflating masculinity (a social construction) with maleness and femininity with femaleness. Like many writers of this period, however, Millett and Sontag conceived of masculinity and femininity as binary opposites. War, aggression, and violence are masculine in their scheme of things, while peace and nurturing are feminine. Therefore an end to the Vietnam War, and human progress generally, lay in cultivating the feminine. It was in keeping with this belief that NOW president Aileen Hernandez advised women in 1971 that they were "the last great hope of civilization."[27]

Jean Bethke Elshtain has shown how this kind of essentialist thinking muddies the waters whenever war and peace are discussed in connection with gender. In nineteenth-century domestic ideology a woman was expected to be the "angel in the house," nurturing moral and religious values while her husband engaged in the Darwinian struggle of the marketplace. In time of war, woman is regarded as the "Beautiful Soul" and her male counterpart as the warrior—ideally, the "Just Warrior." By arguing that women are "naturally" less inclined to war than men, radical feminist pacifists bolster this mythic dichotomy as effectively as pro-family conservatives. As Elshtain shows, the myth does not stand up to historical scrutiny, though it may be effective as a polemical device.[28]

Toril Moi demonstrates in her survey of Anglo-American feminist criticism that the essentialist categories and binary oppositions of Millett's *Sexual Politics* remained more or less intact when feminist critics turned their attention from male to female authors in the 1970s. For an alternative to essentialism, one had to look to the French feminisms deriving from existentialist and deconstructionist thought. Simone de Beauvoir's famous dictum from *The Second Sex* (1949) typifies the existentialist notion of gender: "One is not born, but rather becomes, a woman."[29] Femininity, in other words, is not an essence but an acquisition.

Deconstructionist theory, as expounded by Jacques Derrida, proved useful to feminists such as Hélène Cixous, Luce Irigaray, and Julia Kristeva. They denied that the meaning of signifiers like "masculine"

and "feminine" is present in these terms or derives from a simple opposition of the two. Rather, their meaning depends on a potentially infinite series of related but unspecified signifiers. There is no transcen-
dental signified, no masculine or feminine essence, in which this
deferral of meaning can come to rest. To believe that meaning is present
in a word or that an author is present in a text is to lapse into the
"metaphysics of presence" generally discredited by modern philosophy.

Following a thoroughgoing deconstruction of gender, one could not
define "masculine" or "feminine" at all. But as Toril Moi observes, only
Kristeva has carried her investigation to this conclusion; Cixous and
Irigaray cling to vestiges of essentialism. From a political standpoint,
their reluctance to follow through makes sense. As the Marxist critic
Raymond Williams points out, an endless deferral of meaning is possible only to a socially alienated observer. Most users of language belong
to groups that have chosen to limit deferral through social contracts.[30]
Thus someone who believes that "feminine" values have something special to contribute to the world might choose to remain practically an
essentialist while recognizing the theoretical inconsistency of that position. Sara Ruddick, for example, invokes the traditional binary oppositions in *Maternal Thinking: Toward a Politics of Peace* (1989) even
though she comments on the problem of using gendered language and
rejects the notion that war is inherently masculine and peace inherently
feminine.[31]

With this excursion into French feminism and deconstructionist
thought, we seem to have strayed far from the women's movement of
the late 1960s as a context of the sex war being fought in representations of Vietnam. We are now equipped, however, with the concepts
and vocabulary we need to evaluate the soldier's experience of basic
training, combat in Vietnam, and postwar rethinking of masculinity.
Here too the essentialist, constructionist, and pragmatic notions of sexual identity come into play.

III

In mobilizing essentialist categories of gender for political purposes, the
women's peace movement adopted a strategy long used in military training. Recruiting posters promise to "build men," presumably from material that is not manly, and recruits are sometimes attracted to military
service for this reason. Theirs is a practical rather than a philosophical
existentialism whose premise might be, "One is not born, but rather

becomes, a man." To become a soldier is to acquire masculinity, even if one happens to be biologically female. Recalling her experience of basic training with other medical personnel at Fort Sam Houston, Lynda Van Devanter says, "They weren't attempting to turn us into killers, but I began to think before the morning was out that they were trying to change our gender. Although our company was divided about evenly between men and women, with a mix of doctors, nurses, and administrative officers, the sergeants always referred to us as gentlemen."[32]

As Margaret Mead points out, in most societies the members of each sex incorporate behavior of the opposite sex as a negative ideal.[33] A girl becomes a woman not only by imitating the behavior of mature women but also by rejecting what those women regard as "mannish" behavior—playing rugby, using crude language, not shaving her legs, and so forth. A boy becomes a man in the same way, and a young man becomes a soldier by further refinement of the process. Until he completes basic training, the primary military rite of passage, he is called a "girl," a "lady," a "pussy."[34] To the outsider these derogatory terms may suggest that the military deliberately cultivates misogyny. To most drill sergeants and recruits, however, they signify characteristics that might be acceptable in civilian life but are deadly in combat. Few soldiers hypostatize these traits into actual women and begin to hate their mothers, sisters, or lovers. At least unconsciously, they understand that the "woman" they must reject is within them.

This is not to say that the boundary between "within" and "without" is never blurred. Veterans like Tim O'Brien, Philip Caputo, and Gustav Hasford have written memorable accounts of basic training that focus on its rejection of the feminine and sometimes of women. As summarized in O'Brien's *If I Die in a Combat Zone* (1973), the trainee's repertoire of marching songs inculcated the bitter lessons that New Left women were learning about their Third-World status: "There is no thing named love in the world. Women are dinks. Women are villains. They are creatures akin to Communists and yellow-skinned people and hippies."[35] Caputo recalls in *A Rumor of War* (1977) how he shunned marginal recruits and "unsats" who might carry the "virus" of weakness. He could not imagine a fate worse than having to drop out of marine basic and return home to the "emasculating" affection of his family.[36]

Even as the recruit tries to shed his "feminine" characteristics, he learns to refocus erotic desire in militarily useful ways. On the one hand, he seeks to become his rifle—hard, precise, and ready to inflict death without feeling any remorse. This obviously phallic identification is underscored in a little ditty that he is forced to recite, with appropriate gestures, whenever he fails to distinguish between the preferred term for his weapon and the slang word for penis:

> This is my rifle,
> This is my gun;
> This is for fighting,
> This is for fun.

On the other hand, his rifle serves as an object of desire. "I don't want no teenage queen," goes one marching song. "All I want is my M-14." In Hasford's *The Short-Timers* (1979), translated to the movie screen in Stanley Kubrick's *Full Metal Jacket* (1987), Sergeant Gerheim orders his marine recruits to give their rifles feminine names, saying, "This is the only pussy you people are going to get. . . .You're married to *this* piece, this weapon of iron and wood, and you *will* be faithful."[37] By the end of basic training, Hasford's recruits not only sleep with their rifles but also fantasize intimate conversations with them. Leonard Pratt, who rises from platoon goat to outstanding recruit during basic, shoots Gerheim through the heart when the sergeant tries to take "Charlene" away from him. A moment later, in a gesture that dramatizes the sexual ambiguity of the recruit's relationship with his rifle, he fatally consummates his marriage with "Charlene."

Woman is to be lusted after; woman is to be despised. Woman is Jane Fonda in Roger Vadim's *Barbarella* (1968); woman is Fonda visiting Hanoi four years later. Tim O'Brien, who recalls that *Barbarella* ran for three weeks straight at the Fort Lewis movie theater while he went through advanced infantry training, sought to defend the integrity of his imagination against these stereotypes by conjuring up muse-like figures.[38] He memorized letters from his girlfriend and imagined that she had written the Auden poem she sent him.[39] When he decided to desert to Sweden, he went first to a sorority house at the University of Washington for moral support, then abandoned his carefully researched plans when he failed to get a date. Thus he used one cultural construction of the feminine to counter another, pitting his muse against the Lilith-Eve of military typology.

Mary Ellmann has remarked on the tendency, especially in literary criticism, to "classify almost all experience by means of sexual analogy."[40] The war literature abounds with evidence that this happens in combat as well. Caputo recalls the "ache as profound as the ache of orgasm" that he felt when leading his platoon in a surprise attack on the Viet Cong.[41] More voyeuristically, Michael Herr, a journalist who claims that he was in Vietnam "to watch," compares a firefight to undressing a girl for the first time.[42] Their experiences were in keeping with the country's eroticized foreign policy. President Johnson notoriously compared escalation of the war to the seduction of a woman: it had to be sufficiently gradual that China would not slap him in the face.[43] On another occasion, resorting to more sadistic sexual metaphors, he is supposed to have bragged, "I didn't just screw Ho Chi Minh, I cut his pecker off."[44]

Instead it was America that was castrated on the sexualized battle-field of Vietnam. Johnson's secretary of state, Dean Rusk, regretted that the policy of gradually escalating the war in response to North Vietnamese initiatives meant that the American military was always on the defensive, strategically speaking.[45] Even offensive tactics like search-and-destroy had a way of becoming defensive when used against guerrilla forces. The enemy initiated about 80 percent of firefights, then disappeared into tunnels and friendly villages before artillery or air support could be called in.[46] Mine fields typified the war in the way they punished intrusion, and Bouncing Betty mines (named, perhaps, after the Bouncing Bet flower) sometimes emasculated soldiers when they exploded at waist level.

Given the sexual analogy implicit in this kind of warfare, it is not surprising that some GIs came to fear and loathe Vietnamese women. Prostitutes sympathetic to the Viet Cong were said to conceal glass or razor blades in their vaginas and entice soldiers into having sex with them. Whatever the factual basis of this obsessively recounted bit of folklore (most soldiers knew someone who had heard the story from someone else whose buddy had bled to death in just this way), it has obvious symbolic import.[47] The very landscape of Vietnam was a *vagina dentata*.

Tim O'Brien captures the conflation of land and woman in his memoir. The evening before a combat assault on Pinkville, a hostile section of the Quang Ngai Province that includes My Lai, he and his company were entertained by a Korean stripper:

> She did it to Paul Simon and Arthur Garfunkel's music. *Homeward bound, I wish I was, homeward bound*. She had big breasts, big for a gook everyone said, damn sure. Pinkville. Christ, of all the places in the world, it would be Pinkville. The mines. Sullen, twisted dinks.
> The Korean stripped suddenly, poked a tan and prime-lean thigh through

a slit in the black gown. She was the prettiest woman in the Orient. Her beastly, unnaturally large breasts quivered like Jello.[48]

The Korean stripper is Pinkville, Indochina, the Orient in all their ambiguity. She is at once seductive and repulsive. She reminds them of home, where they would rather be, yet is dangerously exotic. Tonight she can be dominated visually by the leering soldiers; tomorrow she will unman them with exploding shrapnel.

It reflects no credit on American soldiers that some sought to resolve the tension between attraction and fear through rape. By dominating Vietnamese women physically, they may have felt that they could prove that these inscrutable creatures were "just women" and "mere gooks." Rape was also a way to assert their own manhood while humiliating and demoralizing the men on the other side. In Southeast Asia rape was never the large-scale, calculated practice it would become in the Balkan wars of the 1990s. Whether it was more common in Vietnam than in previous American wars may never be known. Susan Brownmiller is properly skeptical of official court-martial records as an index of its frequency, since few rape cases were ever prosecuted.[49] But she is rather too willing to believe sources who informed her that soldiers raped Vietnamese women whenever they had the opportunity.[50] Such anecdotal evidence confirms her thesis, that "rape in war reveals the male psyche in its boldest form, without the veneer of 'chivalry' or civilization."[51]

What rape actually reveals is not the male psyche in its boldest form but the human psyche in its most degraded form. Human beings who are degraded by war or by their prewar experience will find other ways to hurt their victims if they lack the physiological means to commit rape. Marguerite Duras, for example, took part in torturing a Frenchman who informed on the Resistance during World War II.[52] Along with torture, rape is nevertheless the most common and most powerful expression of war's effect on victims and perpetrators alike, and this may have as much to do with its frequent appearance in fictional accounts of the Vietnam War as its empirical reality. When Brian De Palma made a film of Daniel Lang's *Casualties of War*, a true story of rape cited by Brownmiller, some reviewers regretted the damage it would do to the veteran's already tarnished image. "The unspoken message of *Casualties of War*," one asserted, "is that the norm in Vietnam was rape and murder—and that only a brave handful of GIs acted humanely."[53] Two veterans wrote in response to the review, both defending De Palma. Taking the symbolic interpretation to another level, one pointed out that rape and murder were not peculiar to Vietnam but are facts of American life. Rather than deny our image in the looking glass, he wrote, "we should applaud even those flawed efforts which attempt to get Americans to examine the lessons of the Vietnam War—especially the hard lessons."[54]

Among the many hard lessons of Vietnam, the American soldier learned that he was not John Wayne. Nor did he want to be, once he understood the potentially fatal consequences of identifying with the hero of films such as *The Sands of Iwo Jima* (1949) and *The Green Berets* (1968). Though Wayne was never a soldier himself, his Hollywood persona embodied a deadly kind of masculinity.[55] In March 1972, while many of their fellow soldiers were still in Indochina, Vietnam Veterans Against the War held a workshop on the theme, "How Much of John Wayne Is Still in Us?" Robert Jay Lifton has described how the veterans in his rap group strove against what they called "the John Wayne thing." Yet they were hard-pressed to come up with an alternative model of manhood and often reverted to John Wayne postures in their antiwar activities.[56] Some were attracted to the androgyny of the youth counterculture, others to the "victim" role cultivated by the civil rights and women's movements.[57] Americans conspicuously rewarded the passive heroism of the returning POWs, but few could name even one of the 239 soldiers who had won the Medal of Honor in Vietnam.[58]

As Lynda E. Boose has observed, the 1970s were a time when American manhood might have been "reinvented."[59] Vietnam veterans might have taken the lead in this project, had they not had so many problems of their own and so little cultural authority. When one group made the attempt, showing up in uniform to protest the Boston opening of *Rambo* as a militarist film in the John Wayne tradition, they were verbally assaulted by angry teenagers.[60] Like several other 1980s responses to the war, *Rambo* co-opted the veterans' experience while purporting to speak on their behalf. In some cases, ironically, it was those who had opposed the Vietnam War who contrived to negate its lessons for American manhood. As a result the sexes became more polarized in the 1980s than they had been in the 1960s.

IV

"I have often wondered," the journalist Susan Jacoby remarked during a 1980 symposium on the Vietnam War, "whether the millions of men my age who avoided the draft may feel 'unmanned' in a way that no woman can truly understand."[61] Soon after, as though in response to her conjecture, one of those young men in his mid-thirties published an essay in the *New York Times*, recalling how he had revived a childhood case of bronchial asthma in 1969 by inhaling canvas dust from the sewing tables of a tent factory. Michael Blumenthal, a poet and an assistant to the chairman of the National Endowment for the Humanities, suspected that he had failed more than his preinduction physical. Setting aside the question of the war's morality (a question that was seldom answered unselfishly, he says), he confessed to feeling inadequate in the company of veterans: "To put it bluntly, they have something that we haven't got. It is, to be sure, somewhat vague, but nonetheless real, and can be embraced under several headings: realism, discipline, masculinity (kind of a dirty word these days), resilience, tenacity, resourcefulness. We may have turned out to be better dancers, choreographers, and painters (though not necessarily), but I'm not at all sure that they didn't turn out to be better *men,* in the best sense of the word."[62]

Blumenthal did not invent the genre that came to be known as "Viet Guilt Chic." Fallows's "What Did You Do in the Class War, Daddy?" appeared almost six years earlier. But his essay represents a significant variation on the form. Whereas Fallows calculates the losses suffered by the working-class victims of class discrimination, Blumenthal focuses on those sustained by the beneficiaries. He and others who have written in this vein feel cheated of their manhood, not so much by their own choices as by the inequities of the draft law and the political climate of the 1960s. During the 1980s, in the throes of midlife crisis, they romanticized the Vietnam veteran in much the same way that they had once romanticized the Viet Cong. "I don't think I'll ever have what they have," Christopher Buckley said of his veteran friends, "the aura of *I have been weighed on the scales and have not been found wanting,* and my sense at this point is that I will always feel the lack of it and will try to compensate for it, sometimes in good, other times in ludicrous, ways."[63]

National Lampoon anticipated this trend and mined its ludicrous possibilities in 1978, when the magazine published a "Vietnam Combat Veterans Simulator Kit," complete with a glossary of GI slang and a generic war story that could be modified for different audiences.[64] Veterans counseling centers were not amused, however, when they had to deal with "copycat" vets, nonveterans who sought to avoid social stigma by packaging their emotional problems as post-traumatic stress. James Oliver Huberty, who killed twenty-one people at a McDonald's restaurant in San Ysidro, California, in 1984, took this to a pathological extreme. Though he was not a veteran, he wore military fatigues and declared on entering the restaurant that he had "killed many in Vietnam" and wanted to kill more.[65] In their twisted way the copycats testified to the new prestige of Vietnam veterans in the 1980s.

The veteran's image was being refurbished at a moment when many men in their thirties and forties were undergoing a crisis of masculinity. What these men needed, according to the psychotherapist Edward Tick, was a definitive rite of male passage equivalent to war. In a *New York Times Magazine* essay melodramatically entitled "Apocalypse Continued," Tick conceded that Vietnam veterans had little to feel good about, even in 1985. Yet his professional and personal experience suggested that nonveterans were no better off: "Those like me who, for one reason or another, did not serve, suffer because we chose not to perform a primary and expected rite of passage. We were never inducted, not merely into the Army, but into manhood. . . . I have had some of the usual rites—marriage, educational and professional recognition. But no matter how many passages or accomplishments I garner, I never quite feel complete."[66]

Some men sought completion in physical adventure. When one graduate of Wesleyan received a high number in the draft lottery, he went out West and became a logger to experience the "element of macho and danger" in the work.[67] Others, seeking the New Age equivalent of basic training, signed up for the men's consciousness-raising seminars that became especially popular in California. The best-known guru of the men's movement was Robert Bly, who had strongly opposed the Vietnam War. When he won the National Book Award for *The Light around the Body* (1967), he used the award ceremony as an occasion to protest the destruction of Vietnamese culture. During the 1970s Bly celebrated the flowering of feminine consciousness in conferences devoted to the "Great Mother." Around 1980 the zeitgeist again whispered in his ear. He reconciled with his father, a Minnesota farmer. Adopting the language of a folktale, he exhorted boys in their thirties and forties to steal their manhood from beneath their mothers' pillows.

Popular journalism has not treated Bly kindly. Newspaper and magazine accounts of his men's seminars have focused on their zanier features—the drums, conga lines, and neoprimitive masks.[68] The book that came out of these seminars, *Iron John* (1990), was widely parodied, notably in Joe Bob Briggs's *Iron Joe Bob* (1992). In Susan Faludi's *Backlash* (1991) Bly comes across as a rather petulant and self-absorbed person with a sinister message. According to Faludi he is teaching men "how to wrest [power] from women and how to mobilize it for men."[69] Not everyone agrees that his message is antifeminist, and of course Bly denies any such intention. But there is no denying his appeal to a segment of American males. Bill Moyers devoted a ninety-minute television special to Bly in January 1990, and *Iron John* remained on the *New York Times* bestseller list for over a year.

Bly traces the bewilderment of today's men back to the Vietnam War. The waste and violence of Vietnam, he says in *Iron John*, "made men question whether they knew what an adult male really was. If manhood meant Vietnam, did they want any part of it?"[70] Reacting against the 1950s style of masculinity and absorbing the lessons of the women's movement, these men went too far and became "soft" males. Now, Bly says, they need to get in touch with the Wild Man, the Iron John (or Hans) of a folktale collected by the brothers Grimm. The Wild Man is none other than the creature whom the New England Puritans feared and associated with the Indian. He is romanticized in *Iron John* as the primitive, instinctual being that lies at the bottom of the male psyche. He is the "deep male," the masculine essence.[71]

Can one retrieve the Wild Man without also dredging up aggressive and even violent urges? Bly finesses this question by distinguishing between the soldier and the Warrior. The former is a murderous product of the industrial revolution, motivated primarily by greed or the desire for power. The latter, who shares psychic space with the Wild Man, serves a transcendent ideal, the True King.[72] Through this dichotomy, Bly is able to repudiate John Wayne and Rambo as degraded forms of masculinity, mere soldiers, while celebrating an idealized notion of the warrior drawn from mythology and a selective reading of the Homeric poems. One gets the idea that his Warrior would never fire a shot (or throw a spear) in anger.

As long as Bly's disciples live out their warrior fantasies in closed retreats, they pose no direct threat to women or American society in general. They are a relatively harmless symptom of the "New War culture" examined by James William Gibson in *Warrior Dreams* (1994), a culture whose less benign manifestations include *Soldier of Fortune* magazine, paramilitary groups, and the movies of Arnold Schwarzenegger and Sylvester Stallone. *Iron John* nevertheless belongs to a retrograde movement that could obscure the lessons of the Vietnam War. For a more progressive treatment of sexual identity one might turn to a couple of war stories that are told at least in part by women and that focus on women's memories of the war in the late 1970s and early 1980s. Jane Fonda initiated the making of the film *Coming Home* (1978) and

Nancy Dowd wrote the original script, subsequently revised by Waldo Salt and Robert C. Jones.[73] Bobbie Ann Mason wrote the novel *In Country* (1985), also the basis for a film.

V

The musical sound track of *Coming Home* opens and closes with the Rolling Stones' "Out of Time," a song about a woman who has stepped out of a familiar social milieu and is unable to return. It applies with modification to every character in the film, but especially to Sally Hyde. Perhaps because Sally is played by Jane Fonda, *Coming Home* was widely regarded as the story of a woman who sheds her conservative upbringing and becomes an antiwar feminist. In fact one reviewer praised the film yet thought it "too ambitious for its own good" in attempting to chronicle not only Sally Hyde's love affair with Luke Martin (played by Jon Voight) but also her "political radicalization" and "feminist-styled friendship with another woman."[74]

Regarding Sally's initial conservatism there can be no doubt. Though the film is set in 1968 and conscientiously plotted against the significant events of that year (the Tet Offensive and the assassinations of Martin Luther King, Jr., and Robert Kennedy), her clothing and hairstyle belong to the Kennedy years, when patriotism was still in fashion and the feminine mystique still intact. She is upset when a friend treats the American flag and the national anthem too casually. According to her high school yearbook, the one thing she would want to have on a desert island is a husband. Years later, she has her wish: the desert island is a marine base in California and the husband is Bob Hyde (Bruce Dern), a captain who expects to be promoted to major after his tour in Vietnam.

It is appropriate that we should first see Bob as he is jogging on the base, since he regards the war as an athletic event. Back in the officers' club he confides to his wife and another couple that he feels "competitive nervousness" as he prepares to go "off to the Olympic Games, representing the United States." His combination of patriotic zeal, physical health, and marine uniform is apparently irresistible, to judge from the words another officer's wife whispers to Sally: "Bob is very sexy." Unfortunately, his sexiness doesn't manifest itself in bed, where Sally stares vacantly at the ceiling while he satisfies himself. This departure from the ideal enshrined in the feminine mystique seems not to trouble her, however. She presents Bob with a new wedding ring just before he ships out for Vietnam and tells him that she is proud of him.

Sally might eventually have shed her role as "cheery Sally, the captain's wife" regardless of what happened to Bob. But the Marine Corps inadvertently sets this process in motion when it orders him to Vietnam and banishes her from the desert island. Initially disgruntled at the policy requiring that she move out of government quarters, she comes to savor her liberation. She moves into an oceanside apartment with Vi Munson (Penelope Milford), who works in the kitchen of the base hospital to stay close to her emotionally disabled brother. She trades her conservative sedan for a black Porsche, her leisure for volunteer work in the hospital, her teased and straightened hair for "natural" curls, her dresses and pantsuits for less bourgeois attire. Knowing that Bob might regard any or all of these as mutiny, she reverts to type before meeting him for R & R in Hong Kong. Though she is falling in love with Luke, a wounded veteran who was the captain of their high school football team, she urges Bob's friend Dink Mobley (Robert Ginty) to formalize his relationship with Vi. "Like women and dogs," she says, "you have to have a license to show you're the owner."

Sally's "owner" has become moody and remote as a result of his war experience, and he disapproves of her work with the "basket cases" in the hospital. Shortly after her return from Hong Kong she initiates an affair with Luke. Though apparently emasculated by the war—he is paralyzed from the waist down—he provides her with her first satisfying sexual experience. As the day of Bob's return approaches, she faces the possibility that their marriage may belong, like the old Sally, to the past. In a poignant scene occasioned by a letter from Bob, she tells Luke that she doesn't know what will happen to them, only that she has changed. The film signals this change visually and aurally. She stands on a beach by the Pacific, dressed in a white cotton tunic and blue bell-bottom pants, holding a Frisbee and a bottle of beer. Her natural curls toss in the wind as the sound track delivers the Beatles' "Strawberry Fields Forever."

But how, precisely, has Sally changed? What does her migration from Bob to Luke say in terms of personal politics? Specifically, are the counterculture props meant to reflect counterculture attitudes toward the Vietnam War and relations between the sexes? For the purpose of discussion, we might separate the war from sexual politics, though the two are intertwined in the film.

Bob Hyde is old enough to have known the Marine Corps before Vietnam tarnished its reputation as an elite fighting unit. He associates his manliness and sex appeal with the marine uniform. "Would you have married me if I wasn't a marine?" he asks Sally on R & R. "In a second," she replies. But Bob has heard only what he expected to hear. Turning to Dink he crows, "What'd I tell ya, huh? Didn't I tell ya the uniform always used to mean something?" He and Dink then lament the recent deterioration of the corps. Bob had regarded Vietnam as an opportunity not only for promotion but also for heroism. Once in country, he learns that it is the heart of darkness rather than glory, a place where his men want to decapitate enemy corpses and place the heads on stakes to spook the VC. A freak accident further mocks his quest for heroism. On the way to the shower he stumbles and shoots himself in the calf with his M-16. He is sent home to recuperate and recommended for a medal that he knows is undeserved.

Bob's self-inflicted leg wound is apparently meant to stand for the entire American venture in Vietnam. That it is also a sexual maiming is made explicit when he confronts his wife and her lover back in California. In a final enraged assertion of masculinity he threatens them with a rifle and bayonet, calling them the names sanctioned by basic training marching songs: "Jody motherfucker" and "slope cunt." When his anger subsides, he slumps against the wall as Luke deliberately and noisily folds the bayonet and ejects the cartridges from the rifle. "I want to go out a hero," Bob tells Sally. "That way I would have done something that was mine, that I'd done." He may still be seeking a measure of heroism when we last see him. After removing his uniform and wedding ring, symbols of the two institutions that have betrayed him, he jogs with no hint of injury into the Pacific and swims to his death.

In drifting away from Bob, Sally seems to be liberating herself from American militarism and male subordination of women. If so, one wonders what she sees in Luke Martin. Luke is more deeply embittered by the war than Bob because of his paralysis and daily association with other handicapped veterans. When Vi's brother commits suicide, Luke is moved to protest the war publicly by chaining himself and his wheelchair to the entry gate of a recruit depot. He uses media attention to this episode to protest the mass suicide of Americans in Vietnam. A local high school then invites him to speak at an assembly, following a pitch by a marine recruiter. He tells the students, "When I was your age . . . I was really in good shape then, man, I was the captain of the football team and I *wanted* to be a war hero, man; I *wanted* to go out and kill for my country."

Conspicuous on the front of Luke's jacket are the words "War

Hero," a decoration he wears with some of the same sense of irony that Bob feels in wearing his Bronze Star. Like all irony, however, it affirms even as it undercuts. For Luke understands that his authority as an antiwar spokesman depends precisely on the mystique of the athlete and the soldier wounded in action. His jacket is all the more eloquent because Luke is unable to mount a real argument against the war beyond saying that war is hell and there is "not enough reason" for anyone to go to Vietnam. Pauline Kael accurately observes that the politics of the film, as expounded by Luke, are "extremely naïve, and possibly disingenuous."[75] What sounds like pacifism is actually, on the visual level, a mystification of war. In his "War Hero" jacket, Luke is more effective as a marine recruiter than his uniformed counterpart.

Perhaps it is unrealistic to expect Luke to think politically at a time when he is still coping with personal loss. One wonders, however, whether he is capable of thinking in larger terms. According to his high school yearbook, his classmates believed that the one thing he would want on his desert island is a mirror. Narcissism colors not only his view of the war but also his relationship with Sally. In the early weeks of their friendship he calls her Bender, which is both her maiden name and the key term in a crude sexual joke. When she doesn't immediately surrender to his amorous advances, he becomes peevish and sullen. Though more sensitive to her sexual needs than Bob, he is just as intent on possessing her, body and soul. He can afford to be generous to Bob on his return because he believes that he has won the prize in their contest.

Sally never ceases to be what she had been in high school and what she becomes again during a Fourth of July football game for handicapped vets: a cheerleader for the status quo. Apart from her sexual awakening, which is no challenge to the feminine mystique, she changes only in superficial ways. The "greening" of America in the 1960s is reflected in her new foliage, but never goes to the root. Since we can imagine only the most conventional future for her and Luke, the film does well to stop where it does. Indeed it should probably conclude with Bob's suicidal swim and spare us the cuteness of its final scene, which shows Sally and Vi shopping for steaks to celebrate Bob's medal. The door of the supermarket opens and they exit offscreen, leaving two words (one of them the name of the supermarket chain) etched on the screen: "Lucky Out." Lucky out for whom? For Bob, who has escaped his shame and emotional pain? For Sally, who is spared having to choose between two men? Or for Fonda and the team of screenwriters who brought their characters to this impasse?

Bobbie Ann Mason's critically acclaimed novel *In Country* (1985) likewise features a temporally dislocated young woman and veterans who have been unmanned or driven crazy by the war. The events of the novel are seen through the eyes of Samantha ("Sam") Hughes, a seventeen-year-old girl living with her veteran uncle Emmett in Kentucky. Like Chloe in *The Big Chill*, Sam is both bemused by the antics of the 1960s generation and strongly attracted to them as shapers of her identity. While her peers cruise the "mating range" between two fast-food restaurants, she becomes infatuated with an older man, a Vietnam veteran who has the advantage of resembling Bruce Springsteen. At the crucial moment, however, Tom Hudson proves to be impotent, though he tells her that the problem is psychological rather than physiological. This episode seems to epitomize—perhaps even to explain—a pattern that Sam observes in men and women of the older generation: their relationships seem always to be troubled, often by effects of the Vietnam War.

This is most obviously true of Sam's own parents, inasmuch as her father was killed in Vietnam before she was born. But it is also true of her uncle and his veteran friends. When Sam visits Emmett's girlfriend Anita in her apartment, she is struck by Anita's expectant posture: "It was as though she were sitting in a perfectly arranged setting, waiting for something to happen, like a stage set just before the curtain goes up."[76] Anita will have to wait indefinitely, it appears, since her leading man is not ready to commit himself to a life with her or anyone else. Emmett, Sam learns later, had lost most of his comrades on a patrol in Vietnam and now fears intimacy with another human being. Such fear is one of the classic symptoms of PTSD. Though some of Emmett's fellow veterans have married, none has found domestic tranquillity. One of them would rather be in Vietnam and is perpetually feuding with his wife over matters related to the war. Another, the president of the local Vietnam veterans organization, is devastated when his wife leaves him for a career in computer programming.

Speculating about the source of these tensions, Sam wonders whether men might not differ essentially from women in the value they place on human life. During an overnight campout in a swamp preserve, which she undertakes in order to experience what soldiers experienced in Vietnam, she concedes that women, too, sometimes wage war and even kill their own babies (pp. 208, 215). But she concludes that such behavior is the exception. As a rule, men kill and women do not (pp. 209–10). Otherwise, the campout proves to be a waste of time, since Emmett denies that the swamp is anything like the jungle in Vietnam (p. 220).

In the novel's concluding episode both Sam and Emmett find a measure of healing when they make a pilgrimage to the Vietnam Veterans Memorial in Washington. Will this experience enable Emmett to connect with Anita and Sam with Tom Hudson? We never know, and to that extent *In Country* declines the "lucky out," the pat epithalamic closure offered in *The Big Chill* and intimated in *Coming Home.* Yet the novel implies that neither Sam nor Anita will be quite complete until she gets her man. Sam's mother has achieved the consummation they devoutly desire. Irene Hughes, having survived her phases as war widow and antiwar activist, is now blissfully advanced in her "yuppie" phase. Her accoutrements include an IBM executive husband, a ranch home in suburban Lexington, a red Trans Am automobile, and a new baby named Heather. Sam initially regards her mother's transformation as a rejection not merely of the 1960s, to which Sam belongs in spirit, but also of herself. By the end, however, mother and daughter are reconciled and Sam plans to move in with Irene while attending college. Thus the novel reaffirms, albeit with a dose of conscious irony, a version of the feminine mystique.

Unlike Susan Fromberg Schaeffer, whose novel *Buffalo Afternoon* (1989) incorporates the perspectives of a Vietnamese girl and an American soldier, Mason wrote chiefly of what she knew at first hand. Initially she doubted whether she had the right to address the Vietnam experience at all. "What did I know?" she asked an interviewer. "I was a girl, I had never been to Vietnam. I felt intimidated writing about the subject."[77] Only after a visit to the memorial in Washington did Mason feel entitled to tell a war story simply by virtue of being an American, and even then she was reluctant to venture far from personal experience. Not only the Kentucky setting but also specific details such as Anita's sharing a bus with soldiers on their way to Vietnam and Sam's discovery of a version of her name on the memorial wall are drawn from life.[78]

Mason narrowed her range still further when she chose to tell the story from a teenager's point of view. As a result we cannot tell where she stands on a couple of key issues. Does she share Sam's belief that women are naturally nourishers of life rather than killers? Does she accept Emmett's assertion that no one can understand Vietnam without having been there? The novel lacks any mature voice to counter Sam's essentialist view of gender or her uncle's mystification of war.

Coming Home and *In Country* do not differ fundamentally, then, from Bly's *Iron John* in their treatment of war and gender. They reinforce the feminine mystique of woman as naturally domestic and nurturing and the masculine mystique of man as the warrior. Neither sex can really understand the other; indeed, each defines itself by its difference from the other. Veterans' treatments of the war are by no means free of such conventional views. Yet the more sophisticated veteran writers have tried to come up with new answers to the old questions. Below I consider three of these: Tim O'Brien, Philip Caputo, and Donald Pfarrer.

VI

O'Brien's "Sweetheart of the Song Tra Bong" first appeared in *Esquire* in 1989, then became one of the stories in *The Things They Carried* (1990). The sweetheart of the title, Mary Anne Bell, is the quintessence of American femininity as defined in 1960s mainstream culture. She is pretty, blond, blue-eyed, fair-skinned, outgoing, and just a bit flirtatious. When she arrives in Vietnam on a visit arranged by her boyfriend, Mark Fossie, she is improbably dressed in white culottes and a sexy pink sweater. She carries a suitcase and a plastic cosmetics bag. She and Fossie plan a postwar life in keeping with the feminine mystique—a "gingerbread house" in a suburb of Cleveland, three towheaded children, and a happy old age together.

Beginning with a situation similar to Sally Hyde's in *Coming Home*, "Sweetheart" represents a very different transformation of the central character. Mary Anne is daring and curious, and the lax discipline of the firebase at Song Tra Bong provides her with opportunities to learn about the Vietnamese people and the war. Initially a tourist, she becomes a nurse and eventually a soldier. These changes are reflected in her appearance. She cuts her hair short, neglects personal hygiene, wears dirty fatigues, and walks with a swagger. Her body grows harder, and her voice drops in pitch. By conventional criteria she becomes more "masculine." The masculine traits are merely symptoms, however, of her fascination with war and particularly with the jungle.

After Mary Anne goes on ambushes and then a long-range patrol with the Green Berets, described as "animals," Rat Kiley tries to distill the essence of her story: "The girl joined the zoo. One more animal—end of story" (p. 117).[79] But Rat's synopsis is wrong in two respects. First, Mary Anne does not join the zoo as an animal, male or female. When last seen by Fossie, she is wearing her pink sweater and a skirt and singing in a high-pitched voice. She appears feminine once again, except for a necklace of human tongues around her neck, presumably taken from dead enemy soldiers. The war and the jungle have brought out the killer instinct in Mary Anne rather than the Beautiful Soul; yet it is represented as a human rather than an animal impulse.

Thus far, the story resembles Conrad's *Heart of Darkness,* which O'Brien was consciously imitating.[80] But Rat's synopsis is wrong in a second respect because the story does not end with Mary Anne turning into a Kurtz. A zoo, though it contains more or less wild animals, is still a part of the *civis* or city. When Mary Anne leaves the Green Berets' compound she relinquishes all ties to civilization except for the clothing that identifies her as a woman. She no longer belongs to the army or any other social unit: "She had crossed to the other side. She was part of the land. She was wearing her culottes, her pink sweater, and a necklace of human tongues. She was dangerous. She was ready for the kill" (p. 125). The "other side" is not the VC or the NVA but the jungle, and Mary Anne is now as much a threat to the Green Berets as she had once been to the enemy.

The narrator of "Sweetheart of the Song Tra Bong" and the other stories in *The Things They Carried* is Tim O'Brien, not to be confused with Tim O'Brien the author. But most of the story is told by Rat Kiley, whose truthfulness is suspect. Since no corroborating evidence is offered, its "truth value" resides in its inherent plausibility, which in turn depends on the listener's assumptions about men and women and what they are capable of doing in extraordinary circumstances. Rat confronts this issue directly, telling his fellow soldiers that if they reject the story they do not really understand human nature or Vietnam (p. 108). Furthermore, as men, they are not ready to acknowledge that "human nature" includes women. In his own way he argues the antiessentialist position: "She was a girl, that's all. I mean, if it was a guy, everybody'd say, Hey, no big deal, he got caught up in the Nam shit, he got seduced by the Greenies. See what I mean? You got these blinders on about women. How gentle and peaceful they are. All that crap about how if we had a pussy for president there wouldn't be no more wars. Pure garbage. You got to get rid of that sexist attitude" (p. 117).

Thus "Sweetheart" challenges the more traditional gender polarity of *Coming Home* and *In Country*. It does not, however, challenge their mystification of war. On the contrary, it suggests that war is so alien, so unprecedented in ordinary human experience, that it can transform an innocent young woman into a remorseless killer almost overnight. Rat Kiley insists that Mary Anne's experience, like the soldiers', will be utterly incomprehensible to the young women back home: "Try to tell them about it, they'll just stare at you with those big round candy eyes. They won't understand zip" (p. 123).

Caputo's *Indian Country* (1987) goes a long way toward bridging the experiences of a soldier and a woman who was never in the military, much less in Vietnam. Christian Starkmann, the protagonist of the novel, defies his antiwar father by joining the army and going to Vietnam with an American Indian friend, Bonny George. In the heat of battle he calls in the wrong coordinates for an air strike and inadvertently kills his friend. Following a psychological breakdown and a discharge from the army, he moves to the part of Michigan's Upper Peninsula where he and Bonny George had fished as boys. So thoroughly has Starkmann repressed the memory of his friend's death and his complicity in it that he does not recognize it as the cause of his nightmares, flashbacks, paranoia, and other symptoms of PTSD.

Once Starkmann meets June, a waitress in Marquette, the story becomes hers almost as much as his. She may even be the hero of the novel, as Tobey C. Herzog proposes.[81] The two marry, have a daughter, and take up new careers, he as a cruiser for a timber company, she as a state social worker. On an October afternoon in 1982, nine years after their marriage, June kills a black bear while visiting one of her backwoods clients. What makes this ordinary deed extraordinary is the state of mind that June brings to it and the self-knowledge that she derives from it. When June was a girl, her mother told her a Finnish folktale in which a bear-god mated with a woman to produce a tribe of creatures who were part divine, part animal, and part human. In a fertility ritual commemorating their origin, the tribe re-created the union each year with a captured bear and a village maiden. The story stirred June's teenage imagination, prompting a nightmare in which she was chosen as the bear's mate. On waking, she felt ashamed of the pleasure mixed with her horror. Yet she recalls the dream when making love with Starkmann and again on the day of the visit to her clients, the Hermanson family.

When June first sees the bear, she associates it with the beast from her nightmare. It is reaching through the Hermansons' window to get at blueberry pies left to cool on a kitchen counter. After failing to drive it away with a skillet, she removes a hunting rifle from above the fireplace and shoots it twice. Still high on adrenaline, she approaches the dead animal and shoots it again at point-blank range. Part of her consciousness remains detached, astonished at the deed:

> She couldn't believe she was doing what she was doing; if anyone had told her she was capable of such butchery, she would have told him he was crazy. The rifle crashed again. She couldn't seem to get enough. It was so weird, but she felt somewhat the way she had when making love, those times when all her inhibitions and feminine restraints had flown and every part of her being was cast into a wonderful void; it was as if, between the transcendence of that beautiful act and the transcendence of this brutal one, there existed some bizarre connection.[82]

There is also a bizarre connection between shooting the bear and fighting a war. They are linked not only by the sexual analogy, but also by the sense of "transcendence" when social constructions of gender—"feminine restraints"—fall away. At this moment June cannot comprehend the hysteria of the Hermanson women. Like soldiers in combat, she believes that she "had done this for them" and that her violent deed is consistent with her role as a caregiver (p. 177).

The parallel between June's experience and the soldier's becomes even more explicit when the Hermanson boys appear and advise her that the bear is a pregnant sow fattening up for the winter. In effect a female "civilian," it posed no real threat to anyone. When skinned, it appears "human in its nakedness," causing June to feel as though she has committed murder (p. 183). She had thought of war as the soldier's definitive experience, corresponding to the mother's experience of childbirth, and believed neither soldier nor mother could really understand the other. When this neat dichotomy comes undone at the Hermansons', June initially clings more desperately to her "feminine" identity. "She was a good woman!" she tells herself. "A decently married, respectable woman! She kept a clean house! She had a job and children of her own!" (p. 179). But these denials fail to clear her conscience, and she feels even more guilty the following summer, when one of the Hermanson boys uses the same rifle to murder the rest of the family and commit suicide. A truly compassionate caregiver, she believes, might have prevented the tragedy.

In performing her normal duties as a social worker, June trespasses on ground that she once considered off limits to women. *Indian Coun-*

try thus goes a step beyond "Sweetheart of the Song Tra Bong" in de-
mystifying the soldier's experience as well as blurring the line between
masculine and feminine feelings and behavior. Unfortunately, the
novel's main characters are denied the insight offered to the reader. June
is so ashamed of killing the bear that she never tells her husband about
it, and he feels obliged to confess his guilt not to June but to Bonny
George's grandfather. The characters' understanding of war and gender
remains to that extent "patriarchal," though the novel's economy of
shame, guilt, and forgiveness is finally Ojibwa Indian rather than white.

Pfarrer's *Neverlight* likewise demystifies war as a distinctly masculine experience, but it allows the masculine and feminine to converge at
the novel's end. Richard Vail, the male protagonist, is a naval gunnery
officer assigned to a marine infantry unit in Vietnam. Wounded in an
ambush, he is sent home to recuperate for several idyllic weeks with his
wife, Katherine, and young daughter, Terry, on a farm in New Hampshire. During that time he decides to request reassignment to Vietnam,
though navy policy does not require this of him. The decision opens
a breach of misunderstanding between Richard and his wife that their
letters cannot fully close before he is killed in another ambush. The
final chapters of the novel record Katherine's effort to absorb this shock,
envision a future for herself and Terry, and comprehend her husband's
fatal decision.

The relationship between the Vails is intensely romantic. Their bodies are perfectly congruent in bed, a physical sympathy that has its psychic equivalent.[83] Yet they disagree strongly over the merits of war in
general and the Vietnam War in particular. Katherine regards Vietnam
as merely another move in the "monstrous game" played by politicians
who care nothing for human life. The United States has no business
interfering in a civil war, particularly on behalf of the "little military
gangsters" in South Vietnam (pp. 80–81). Even supposing there were
some good to be accomplished in Vietnam, how could it possibly offset
the loss to Richard's family if he were killed? Katherine still feels keenly
the loss of her own father in the Korean War and does not want to see
their daughter bereft in the same way.

When Katherine realizes that Richard has made up his mind to return, she wants to know why. His "You know why" throws her into a
rage; she leaves their cabin, slamming the door hard enough to break
the glass, and stomps through the woods. What grotesque variety of
machismo, she wonders, prompted his response? Once she had been

able to joke about the "Platonic Idea of Balls" that allies Richard with their male cat, whose "cruising" disrupted their domestic arrangements (p. 42). Now, glimpsing the sinister side of the male animal, she bitterly reconstructs the dialogue implicit in his reply:

> "You see, my poor little cunt, *it's not my fault*. It's the mystique of combat. How can I explain it to you?["]
>
> "Well, try, try. Maybe I could grasp one little part of it.["]
>
> "I doubt it, since you're nothing but a girl. A female. In the brief intervals between being depressed because of your period, you stupid little shit, and being nervous because you're ovulating, there's hardly any time for you to learn anything about the world, is there?["] (pp. 74–75)

Sexual difference, which normally draws the Vails closer together, here becomes a source of antagonism. Like June in *Indian Country*, Katherine counters Richard's "mystique of combat" with the mystique of motherhood: what could a man know about carrying a baby for five months, as she had, only to miscarry? Her anger cools to sarcasm by the time she returns to the cabin, and she tries once again to probe for Richard's motive. Richard doggedly resists entering into an argument, in part because he cannot fully comprehend his own reasons. He simply feels that he should return, that this is what a "good and strong" man would do.

Paradoxically, the Vails grow closer during their physical separation, both in their views of the war and in their sensitivity to the full range of "masculine" and "feminine" feelings. This rapprochement is achieved not so much through their letters, though these are frequent, lengthy, and thoughtful, as through their day-to-day experiences in rural New Hampshire and Vietnam. Their experiences are at times uncannily similar. In one chapter, Richard is mesmerized by a corpse lying against a paddy dike; in the next chapter, Katherine becomes equally fascinated with a freshly killed deer (pp. 107–8, 111–12, 123).

As a child Katherine was a daddy's girl and something of a tomboy, given to reading and unfeminine pursuits such as hunting. At fourteen she performed the quintessential male rite of passage in rural New England, killing and gutting a deer. Now, during Richard's absence, she learns more about her capacity for asceticism and sensuality as she bathes first in the snow and then in the spring sunlight. The more she grows in personal autonomy and self-awareness, the more she ponders the status of individual human beings in civilizations thought to be enlightened. She is disturbed to realize that Greek temples, roads, and walls were built of stone quarried by slaves—people who were like herself except that they never knew liberty, peace, or rest; who could not choose their asceticism as she had chosen hers. For the ancients, life itself was hardly more sacred than liberty. The Mycenaeans cast their female and defective male infants into a ravine to die. The Athenians killed all the men of Melos and enslaved their wives and children. The Romans killed all of a man's slaves when any one of them dared to kill the master.

The Vietnam War suggests to Katherine that humankind has not become more humane in the modern era. Americans were dropping napalm on the Vietnamese and speaking of "acceptable losses" of their own soldiers. Katherine recites this dreary chronicle of suffering in a letter to her husband and concludes with a question: "Dick, I only ask, is life sacred? I write this to you because you are my friend and husband and also out of fear, in a way, because, forgive me, you seem willing to kill. If you can take life, how can it be sacred?" (p. 241). Before receiving an answer to this question, Katherine is notified of Richard's death. Pfarrer is at his best in rendering the phases of her mourning, beginning with disbelief and numbness, proceeding through acceptance and emotional catharsis to resentment at being abandoned.

Ten months after Richard's death, Katherine finally musters the courage to open the package of his belongings forwarded to her as next-of-kin. In it she finds a writing tablet whose first page contains the beginning of a letter he started the day before the ambush: "Dear Kit—Yes—"(p. 284). She cannot imagine what he meant to affirm until she finds the letter in which she demanded, "Is life sacred?" Richard's reply from beyond the grave forces her to confront the contradiction in her own thinking. She realizes that she too would be willing to kill in a just war, notwithstanding her belief in the sacredness of life. For Katherine as for her husband, pacifism is an "abdication of moral responsibility" (p. 287). True, they disagreed on whether Vietnam was a just war. Where she is willing to fight only when life is threatened, he was willing to fight when freedom is threatened, as he apparently believed it was in Southeast Asia.

Richard's affirmation is hard won, for he too was oppressed by evidence to the contrary in Vietnam. On a couple of occasions he is even tempted to take his own life. Following his second suicidal fantasy, he experiences an epiphany while taking a shower. As Paul Fussell has observed, the "soldiers bathing" scene is a set piece in war literature and is often charged with homoerotic feeling.[84] In Richard's case, any erotic feeling is overshadowed by the sense of his fellow soldiers' vulnerability. Yes, he decides in response to Katherine's question, life *is* sacred (pp. 245–46). But he lacks the time and perhaps the will to re-create for her benefit the tiny point of light he glimpses in the darkness of Vietnam. When Richard dies the following morning, Pfarrer echoes with devastating irony the fatuous political and military rhetoric of the day: "There may be victory 'at the end of the tunnel' for some; perhaps only survival; there is never light" (p. 247). Yet for Katherine there is enlightenment, even though it comes too late to share with her husband.

Neverlight is politically richer than most novels and films about the Vietnam War, notwithstanding Pfarrer's belief that he had written an apolitical book.[85] Its major triumph lies in the realm of personal and sexual rather than partisan or global politics. The contrast with *Coming Home* is instructive. Pauline Kael wrote, "Jane Fonda isn't playing a character in 'Coming Home,' she's playing an abstraction—a woman being radicalized."[86] Katherine Vail is no abstraction, and she grows toward her final act of reconciliation through a lifetime of experiences, some of which trespass on the masculine side of the culturally defined gender line. The myth of the Beautiful Soul is effectively deconstructed from two directions: Katherine proceeds from her belief in the sacredness of life to its practical implications, whereas Richard proceeds from his deeds and choices to the sacredness of life as a principle. Both characters are nurturer-killers, even as both are morally conscientious persons.

One might object that O'Brien, Caputo, and Pfarrer are using their women characters, either consciously or unconsciously, to rethink masculinity. To the extent that these male writers overcome their alienation from the feminine, they risk effacing its otherness. This risk is inherent in literary and cinematic representation and is precisely the risk women were asking men to take in the 1960s and 1970s. At the same time, women were venturing into a realm shaped almost exclusively by the masculine imagination. Women veterans of the Vietnam War tell true stories that largely corroborate the fictions of male veterans.

VII

How many military women served in Vietnam cannot be easily ascertained, since their personnel records were not separated from the men's.

The Department of Defense estimates that there were about 7,500 women among the 3.14 million soldiers who went to Vietnam, whereas the Veterans Administration puts the number at 11,000. Of these, approximately 80 percent served as nurses, the majority as first or second lieutenants in the army.[87] Their story is told best in book-length memoirs, oral histories, and interviews. Though each woman's experience was unique, shaped by her personality, age, family background, education, attitudes toward the war, and place and period of service, the majority had elements in common.

Many were raised in conservative Christian (often Catholic) families and had good relationships with their fathers, who were often veterans. The women were drawn to nursing and Vietnam primarily by a desire to serve others, though the lure of adventure and romantic notions of nursing in the war zone—nurtured by World War II films and the Cherry Ames novels—also figured in their decision. They either gave little thought to the politics and morality of the war or felt that they could do good even in a bad war. On arriving in Vietnam they were struck by the smell, the heat, and the squalor of the country. They considered themselves lucky if their assigned base had latrines and showers set aside for women and the base exchange carried a supply of feminine hygiene products.

Initially the women felt compassion for the Vietnamese and some volunteered for medcaps (medical civic action programs) and work at orphanages. But after experiencing the hostility of "friendly" Vietnamese and observing their apparent lack of commitment to the anticommunist cause, many began to dislike the people and refer to them as "gooks" or "dinks." This attitude did not lessen their horror at the sufferings of innocent Vietnamese civilians who got in the way of American bombs and napalm. While treating these and American casualties, many nurses began to question the purpose of the war and to resent the American government officials and high-ranking military leaders responsible for its conduct.

Such doubts, together with the endless stream of broken bodies and minds, forced the women to build an emotional wall around themselves. They avoided learning the names of patients or anything about the patients' personal lives. Off-duty, some of them drank heavily, either alone or with the other medical personnel who distracted themselves with intense partying. Nurses who became romantically involved with doctors or helicopter pilots found that such relationships were often broken off by the war or rotation home. They learned to seek short-term emotional and physical comfort in these affairs rather than long-term commitment.

On returning to the States, military women encountered hostility in those opposed to the war and indifference in almost everyone else. The majority of Americans seemed bent on consuming goods and services or worrying about trivial matters. Their families provided a warm welcome but would listen only to the more amusing war stories. Many nurses were therefore relieved to return to duty at a stateside hospital, except that they were given far less responsibility than in Vietnam. Readjustment to stateside duty, and later civilian life, was made more difficult by the symptoms of PTSD: flashbacks, nightmares, anxiety attacks, depression, fear of intimacy, and suicidal thoughts. It was not uncommon for military women to drift from job to job and relationship to relationship without connecting their unhappiness to Vietnam.

During the 1980s, many were finally forced to deal with Vietnam by a film, a book or newspaper article about women veterans, or an event like the return of the Iranian hostages. After going through therapy, often at one of the counseling centers established by the Outreach Program in 1979, such women experienced a measure of reconciliation while visiting the Vietnam Veterans Memorial Wall or marching in one of the "welcome home" parades. Looking back on the war from the vantage point of middle age, women veterans regard it as the source of much pain but also as the most intense and meaningful part of their lives. Asked if they would do it all over again, the majority say yes.

So recounted, the story of the women's Vietnam experience resembles women's stories from other wars, such as Vera Brittain's *Testament of Youth* (1933) about World War I. It resembles even more closely the stories of many male Vietnam veterans, which should give pause to anyone who believes that the female experience of war is essentially different from the male. True, these women went to war as caregivers rather than warriors. But they shared this role with the male doctors, nurses, and medics. Furthermore, as Sara Ruddick points out, caregiving often entails some of the aggression and exercise of power we associate with the warrior role.[88] A few of the nurses' stories include moments when the women realized that they were ready to take life as well as sustain it. Lynda Van Devanter recalls wanting to avenge Viet Cong atrocities, and Saralee McGoren was so distraught at one soldier's wounds that she shouted to helicopters leaving on a mission, "Kill kill kill!"[89] Cheryl

M. Nicol had to be knocked unconscious by military police to prevent her from strangling a captured VC sniper.[90] It was many years before most of the women could express this kind of emotion, since rage is socially less acceptable in women than in men, especially if they are nurses.[91]

Rage is just one of the emotions that women shared with men in the combat zone. Klaus Theweleit, the author of *Male Fantasies,* a two-volume work that includes a study of Nazi militarism, argues that Tim O'Brien's reference to the "beauty" of an artillery barrage is characteristically male. "That sentence," Theweleit claims, "somehow marks the surface line of that abyss known as the 'gender gap.'"[92] Yet the nurses' narratives demonstrate the futility of drawing any such line. They testify to the beauty of war as spectacle, even when they know that their aesthetic pleasure is about to give way to horror in the triage and operating rooms. Winnie Smith's response to a battle scene lit by flares is typical: "It's enchantingly, disarmingly beautiful."[93] J. Glenn Gray attributes the response to a universal feeling of the sublime, speculating that in such moments the onlooker enjoys an "ecstatic" relation to a world that is outside of and more powerful than the self.[94] Any viewer of a war film, male or female, can understand this sentiment.

In one respect women's experience does differ from men's in military as well as civilian life: outside prison, men usually do not live in fear of rape. Thus the women's narratives differ from the men's in their attention to forms of harassment that could and occasionally did lead to sexual assault. Reliable statistics on the sexual harassment of military women in Vietnam are hard to come by. None of the fifty former nurses whom Elizabeth M. Norman interviewed for *Women at War* mentioned overt harassment. But she cites another study of 137 nurses in which 63 percent reported incidents ranging from pranks to threats of military discipline for refusing sex.[95] The women often felt beleaguered rather than flattered by male attention and sought privacy when off duty. They resented being treated as a sexual commodity by older male officers and sometimes cultivated a romantic relationship with one man in order to discourage the attentions of others.

The nurses' experience therefore lends some support to Susan Brownmiller's argument that rape and the fear of rape govern relations between the sexes in a war. It does not, however, support her assertion that soldiers use rape to forge a male bond, to gain entry into "the most exclusive male-only club in the world."[96] The women veterans testify repeatedly and warmly to their close emotional bond with the men, especially the enlisted corpsmen, doctors, and helicopter pilots with whom they worked every day. For many women, such camaraderie was the best part of their Vietnam experience. This kind of relationship did not discriminate on the basis of sex. Rather, according to Winnie Smith, it distinguished between those who could be trusted and those who could not:

> In war lives depend on trust. Grunts in the boonies trust everyone in a fire fight to take his fair share of risk and look after one another. In a hospital we trusted each other to take a fair share of the work and give the best care possible. Where trust is so vital, distrust is a source of loathing. We didn't trust the Vietnamese. Nor did we trust our own big brass; we felt they cared more about their careers and what fat cats in Washington thought than about what was happening to their men in the boonies.
>
> I now see that when I came home, I brought with me the sense of fair play that was a big part of our trust and a loathing for the rich and powerful who care only for themselves.[97]

Smith's notion of trust is sufficiently elastic to embrace the ordinary soldiers whom she calls her "warrior buddies" but not the war managers. Neither does it include those who stayed home, as her next sentence indicates: "But none of my friends was in the war, and none can truly understand what is happening to me."

Once an invisible minority, women veterans have become progressively more visible and influential since the late 1970s, partly with the help and encouragement of male veterans. In 1979 Bobby Muller, the founder and first president of Vietnam Veterans of America, asked Lynda Van Devanter to form a special VVA Women Veterans Project to bring the problems of women veterans to national attention. In 1987 Mary R. Stout, a former army nurse, succeeded Muller as president of the VVA. The first woman to head a major American veterans organization, she won 77 percent of delegation votes at a time when the VVA membership of thirty-five thousand included only three hundred women. Two years later she was reelected by a 72 percent majority.[98] Another army nurse-veteran, Diane Carlson Evans, chaired a drive to install Glenna Goodacre's statue of three women soldiers near the Memorial Wall, to complement Frederick Hart's statue of three infantrymen. It was dedicated on Veterans Day, 1993.

The women veterans have also become more visible in our war stories. Whereas the male-oriented television series *Tour of Duty* floun-

dered and barely lasted into a third season (1987–1990), its distaff counterpart, *China Beach*, proved more popular during its run from 1988 to
1991 and won four Emmy awards. William Broyles, Jr., its cocreator,
set out to show "the world just over the hill from combat," where men
and women were "immersed for twelve hours a day in its bloody results, a level of undiluted, industrial-strength horror that few combat
veterans witnessed."[99] Yet to the dismay of many women veterans, the
series seemed to fixate on romance and absurdity. Missing from *China
Beach*, women veterans told Elizabeth Norman, was "the daily routine
and sense of comradeship that existed among the corpsmen, nurses, and
doctors."[100]

The written narratives of military women are far more realistic. The
summary of typical experiences with which this section begins is taken
from memoirs like Lynda Van Devanter's ground-breaking *Home before
Morning* (1983), written with Christopher Morgan, and Winnie Smith's
American Daughter Gone to War (1992). Other features come from two
oral histories devoted exclusively to women who were in Vietnam,
Keith Walker's *A Piece of My Heart* (1985) and Kathryn Marshall's *In
the Combat Zone* (1987). Though few in number, these books have
shaped the way we think about Vietnam, women, and war.[101]

Susan Jeffords, a feminist critic, nevertheless argues that the oral histories "present women's narratives as if they were compensatory and
marginal, having already been excluded."[102] This is certainly the case
in Jeffords's own study of gender and the Vietnam War, which devotes
only a paragraph to the women's narratives. She relegates Van Devanter's memoir to a footnote, where it is cited along with fifteen other
titles.[103] Jeffords's treatment of the women's narratives is a throwback
to the 1970s, when feminists proceeded as though all women are white
and middle class. This changed in the mid-1980s, as they were forced
to acknowledge the perspectives of nonwhite and working-class
women. Yet some academic feminists still patronize women outside the
academy. Rather than applaud women in uniform for their achievements, they dismiss them as the instruments of patriarchy.

A more egalitarian approach would recognize the ways in which military women have challenged traditional sex roles. Though nursing was
considered a conventional career for women in the 1960s, it often radicalized those who went to Vietnam as nurses. Whether or not they had read
The Feminine Mystique, they learned its lessons. They could identify with
neither the anxious domesticity of their mothers nor the seductive helplessness of Miss America and the starlets in Bob Hope's annual Christmas

show. They also opened up military careers for the next generation of women. As the military historian Colonel Harry G. Summers, Jr., observed in 1993, "Vietnam women veterans built the foundations for the military of today, where women serve in combat divisions, in warships at sea and in the cockpits of combat aircraft."[104]

Why, then, didn't these women join the vanguard of the women's movement when they returned from Vietnam? It was probably not allegiance to patriarchy that held them back, but a sense of alienation from their nonveteran sisters. Compared to the life-and-death concerns of the combat zone, the personal politics practiced in the States often seemed trivial. "Women were burning their bras," Rose Sandecki says of this period, "and I was in Vietnam saving lives."[105] Conversely, veterans' issues appeared insignificant to leaders of the women's movement. When Van Devanter sought funding for the VVA's Women Veterans Project, she first approached an organization that she identifies only as "one of the foremost women's groups in the country."[106] She was turned down on the grounds that "women veterans were not enough of a cutting edge feminist issue." With an irony that the Playmate-feminist Gloria Steinem could appreciate fully, she received her first contribution from the Playboy Foundation.

Another kind of alienation made it difficult for the women veterans to tell their stories. On the one hand, they felt alienated by their experiences in Vietnam, and this made it harder for them to find a receptive audience. On the other hand, they also felt alienated from their experiences. Norman speculates that if the women in her study were asked to diagram their lives, they would probably draw a straight line whose beginning would stand for birth and whose end would represent the present moment. Their tour of duty in Vietnam would appear as a short line drawn above the longer lifeline. The diagram would reflect their sense that Vietnam was unique and discontinuous with the rest of their lives.[107] In the introduction to her oral history, Kathryn Marshall suggests that even this linear analogy is too neat. Speaking of Vietnam war stories in general, she says,

> They seemed deformed—fragments, images, severed pieces of plot. There was no way to order them, and trying only made the war—the world itself— recede farther and farther from me, leaving me with a weird feeling of dislocation: space would angle away, juxtapositions would become illogical, everything would seem simultaneously fixed and disturbed. After a while, the Vietnam War story became so jumbled and ambiguous it was not a narrative at all. It was a kind of nightmare geometry.[108]

In the book-length narratives of Van Devanter and Smith, this "nightmare geometry" has been largely tamed, presumably with the help of a professional writer (for *Home before Morning*) and a professional editor (for *American Daughter Gone to War*). These have the polish one expects in published war stories. They begin in medias res, then proceed more or less chronologically through the narrator's career. They incorporate other discursive forms, such as dreams and letters, for variety and ironic effect. Where the narrative is episodic in structure, the episodes are set off from one another typographically.

The oral histories are also conventionalized to some extent by the interviewer's prompts and subsequent editing of the transcript. However, one detects traces of the storytelling process in the final product. Keith Walker says that he had difficulty finding women who were willing to be interviewed. Many did not respond to his letters, others agreed to talk and changed their minds at the last minute, and a half-dozen never returned the transcripts with their approval. Avoidance and repression likewise marked the interviews he succeeded in recording on tape. Spaced periods in Walker's printed text signal the long silences during which his subjects veered toward or away from painful memories.

Once the floodgates were opened it was sometimes hard to close them. One woman returned an eighteen-page transcript of her interview with a note saying, "I feel I haven't said it, that there must be another story I have forgotten that could explain it."[109] Another recalled that she began jotting notes on a pad while watching *Friendly Fire* on television; as she wrote, the letters grew to three times their normal size and her pen began tearing the paper.[110] In such moments, the women overcame their alienation from the Vietnam experience and began to incorporate its short narrative line into the longer line of their lives. The pattern of their storytelling thus corresponds to the pattern of therapy for PTSD, wherein the stressful event is gradually assimilated into the patient's long-term sense of self.

During PTSD treatment, the therapist encourages the veteran to tell her story, then serves as the receptive audience she had not had on returning from Vietnam. Van Devanter and Smith discovered their alienation from the folks back home under similar circumstances, while showing slides to their families. "I don't think you really want to show those slides," Van Devanter's mother told her, after viewing several pictures of casualties. "Maybe it would be wise to put them away."[111] Smith began her slide show with a carefully edited commentary on the images:

"That's the Pied Piper MP guarding our villa, surrounded by the children
who played with him." I want to tell them he was shot by a sniper, but
there's a knot in my throat, and I'm afraid I'll cry.

"The old French fort in the open field across the street from Claymore
Tower, with an old man scrubbing his water buffalo in a mud puddle." I don't
mention the fire fights after dark. "And that's another old man we cared for
in a small village outside Saigon." And I tell them we took a bullet out of
his leg but not that it was an American bullet.[112]

Smith was at first puzzled by her own self-censorship. When she began
to describe her patients, however, she understood why. "Nobody wants
to hear that stuff," her mother told her. "Some things are better left
unsaid."[113]

The women in Walker's oral history, too, had gotten this message in
the past, and they showed their sense of alienation in various ways. One
woman repeatedly turned off the tape recorder; another covered her
eyes during the entire ninety minutes of the interview.[114] Another, unable to meet with Walker face-to-face, wrote a letter instead.[115] A letter
has the advantage—one shared by all written communication—of allowing the writer to imagine a sympathetic listener, someone like the
imaginary playmate of childhood soliloquies.

Male veterans of every American war, and particularly of Vietnam,
have likewise gotten the message that some war stories are better left
untold. The difference between men and women veterans is therefore
one of degree, not kind. Is patriarchy to blame for not validating the
women's experience of war as readily as the men's? If so, then ivory
tower feminism must share some of the blame, for not taking military
women as seriously as academic and professional women. What the
women veterans seek in their listeners and readers is the quality that
Smith calls trust. Since trust is born of shared experience, the women's
first audience will consist of those who have "been there" in every sense
of the phrase. As it expands to include other sympathetic listeners, we
may hear stories that equal the best men's narratives of the Vietnam
War.

VIII

Susan Faludi and others maintain that during the 1980s women suffered setbacks in politics, the workplace, and popular media as the result of a "backlash" against victories won by the women's movement in
the previous decade. Susan Jeffords believes that Vietnam War narra-

tives register the same reaction. She argues in *The Remasculinization of America* (1989) that the books and films are only nominally about the war in Vietnam. Their true subject is the war against women. The war stories represent masculinity and femininity in ways that validate patriarchy, the cultural arrangement that systematically subordinates women.

Though Jeffords's title is apparently meant to recall Ann Douglas's *Feminization of American Culture* (1977), a study of domestic ideology in the nineteenth century, her procedure owes more to Millett's *Sexual Politics*. Like Millett, Jeffords focuses chiefly on works by male writers and directors. She dwells at greatest length on the first two *Rambo* films, the two *Missing in Action* films, and *Uncommon Valor,* works that she considers typical of Vietnam War narratives and indeed of American popular culture since the 1950s. What they share is an intent, presumably on the part of men, to subjugate women, even to the extent of appropriating such womanly functions as reproduction. According to Jeffords, the Vietnam narratives deny or minimize conflicts based on race or class in order to accentuate the polarity of masculine and feminine. Taking her cue from Gerda Lerner, she argues that conflicts of race and class ultimately derive from the conflict of gender. War itself is a product of gender conflict, inasmuch as men need war to define themselves as men. "As long as there is gender," Jeffords maintains, "there will be war."[116]

Jeffords is for the most part wary of essentializing masculinity and femininity, and for that reason she distances herself from French feminists like Irigaray and Cixous. She also embraces Derrida's deconstruction of authorial presence. But having banished presence from the front door, she admits it through the back, in the form of a metaphysical category that she calls the "masculine point of view." The masculine point of view is the "disembodied voice of masculinity," the "voice through which dominance is enacted in a narrative representation."[117] It is, in other words, the voice of patriarchy hypostatized as a kind of author. Since all war stories are narrated by this voice, Jeffords claims, they are "always and already" patriarchal.

The argument of *The Remasculinization of America* might be summarized as follows. American society is patriarchal. Men and women in a patriarchal society represent gender from a masculine point of view favorable to patriarchy. Vietnam War narratives are gendered. Therefore Vietnam War narratives reinforce the patriarchal structure of American society. Considering the dreary circularity of this argument, one is not surprised that Jeffords arrives at an impasse at the end of her

study. On the one hand, she urges feminists to focus on the discourse of
warfare as "the primary vehicle for the remasculinization of American
society." On the other hand, she warns that this exercise will accomplish little as long as patriarchy remains in place. Indeed, to focus too
exclusively on a single war—Vietnam, for example—will only reinforce the patriarchal structures that caused it.[118]

If patriarchy is to be dislodged, it will require a fulcrum outside Jeffords's rather constricted world. Millett, I have noted, was far more san-
guine about the prospects for change in 1970. Her optimism can be
attributed partly to the temper of the times, when the women's movement was in the ascendant. But it also proceeded from Millett's greater
breadth of vision. She was conscious of a world beyond feminist theory
and the writings of a few "counterrevolutionary sexual politicians."
Women may have been losing the sex war in the fiction of Lawrence,
Miller, and Mailer, but they were winning in the streets and courts of law.

Historians and military strategists have frequently observed that
Vietnam was not a war of fronts. An overview of the literature and film
suggests that the war correspondingly "Vietnamized" the sex war. If
some engagements "remasculinize" American culture, others "refemi-
nize" it. Most are inconclusive. Such skirmishing in and out of our war
stories undermines the notion of patriarchy as a single, homogeneous
battlefield. Though other terms in the lexicon of gender studies have
been deconstructed, "patriarchy" has for the most part gone unchallenged. Like other signifiers, it differs not only from its presumed opposite, matriarchy, but also from itself, in an infinite series of significa-
tions. At the very least, we must acknowledge the variety of social
arrangements denoted by the same term. Patriarchy differs not only according to historical period, but also according to region, social class,
race, ethnic group, religion, economic system, and so forth. It is as
much a cultural construction as the terms "masculine" and "feminine"
and has perhaps outlived its usefulness, even as a polemical device.

Finally, we might reconsider the "sex war" as metaphor. Wars are
predicated on the notion that one party has something to gain by de-
feating another. But in the conflict between the sexes (as in the conflicts
between races and social classes) neither party wins in the long run if
either loses. This is most obvious in the realm of social policy—for example, when women's groups opposed giving an advantage to veterans
seeking civil service jobs and thereby lost veterans' support for the
Equal Rights Amendment. Conversely, both parties win when either
wins. After PTSD was recognized as a legitimate psychiatric disorder,

female victims of rape, incest, and abusive relationships benefited from therapy originally developed for Vietnam veterans.

It is in the realm of personal politics, however, that men and women may win the most by not seeking a unilateral victory. Even as Vietnam forced military women to acknowledge "masculine" rage and aggression as part of their humanity, it introduced men to a side of themselves for which there was little precedent in the John Wayne movies. One marine veteran recalled that the "female instincts" he had buried for most of his life came out on the battlefield. "If I was lifting a body," he said, "it was always done in the most gentle fashion because this bag represents somebody's son. If there were some way we could transfer that deep nurturing you feel for your buddies dying on the field of battle and point it to those on the street, what a better world it would be."[119]

CHAPTER 5

The Generation War

I

When President Nixon announced on 30 April 1970 that he had ordered American troops into Cambodia to clear out North Vietnamese
sanctuaries, he expanded the war in two directions at once. Besides taking the war into another part of Indochina, he also brought it home to
an extent that few would have thought possible. Among the college campuses that erupted in protest was Kent State University in Ohio, where,
over the course of the weekend following Nixon's announcement, students
rioted on downtown streets, burned the ROTC (Reserve Officers Training
Corps) building on campus, and defied National Guard troops sent to
disperse them. Shortly after noon on May 4 the soldiers opened fire on
the students, killing four and wounding nine.

The images that came out of Kent defied belief. In the most famous
of them, a photograph taken by John Filo, a young woman kneels beside the prone and bleeding body of Jeff Miller, her extended arms and
anguished face seeming to address a question to the guard troops and,
beyond them, to those responsible for maintaining law and order in
America: *Why?* It hardly mattered that the girl was a fourteen-year-old
runaway from Florida who neither knew Miller nor comprehended
what was happening at Kent State or in the country as a whole.[1] During
the fraction of a second it took for a camera shutter to blink her image
onto photosensitive celluloid, she expressed perfectly the shock of a generation. As Todd Gitlin observed years later, Kent State taught young

white activists nationwide the lesson that Berkeley students had learned during the People's Park controversy the previous year, namely, that their government was willing to shoot them.[2] For James Miller, like Gitlin a former member of Students for a Democratic Society, May 4 marked the end of an era. On that day, he contends, "the New Left collapsed, plummeting into cultural oblivion as if it had been some kind of political Hula-Hoop."[3]

For some, the lesson of Kent State had an even wider application. On the Ohio campus, as they saw it, a decade of simmering conflict between the younger and older generations had finally come to a boil. "Don't trust anybody over thirty," Jack Weinberg warned his fellow activists early in the 1960s, speaking from his experience as an organizer of the Congress of Racial Equality (CORE). Several years later, in response to police arrests of young demonstrators on Sunset Strip, Stephen Stills wrote one of the anthems of the turbulent decade. The lyrics of "For What It's Worth" (1966) referred ominously to a "man with a gun" who was menacing the younger generation. The identity of the gunman changed from time to time and place to place, as did that of his targets. In 1964 he was the Klansman who killed three CORE organizers in Mississippi. In the film *Easy Rider* (1969) he was the rural Southerner who blasted Billy (played by Dennis Hopper) and Captain America (Peter Fonda) off their motorcycles. During the first weekend of May in 1970 he was either a National Guardsman or one of those older citizens of Kent who, according to the novelist James Michener, "began riding around at night with shotguns, threatening to shoot on sight any young people they spotted."[4]

Like Melissa Compton (played by Susan Sarandon) in *Joe,* a film released during the summer of 1970, Kent students discovered that the man with a gun could be one's own father. Several weeks before the shootings, the Yippie leader Jerry Rubin had visited the campus. Addressing a group that included a couple of thousand students, he said, "Being young in America is illegal. We are a generation of obscenities." In the struggle with the older generation, it was kill or be killed, beginning with one's parents: "The first part of the Yippie program is to kill your parents. And I mean that quite literally, because until you're prepared to kill your parents, you're not ready to change this country. Our parents are our first oppressors."[5] Rubin's advice seemed less preposterous in the aftermath of the shootings. Of the four hundred students whom Michener interviewed for a book on the event, "a depressing number had been told by their own parents that it might have been a good thing if they had been shot."[6] Though some of these parents later backed down from this initial reaction, their children were in some cases so shocked to learn what their mothers and fathers "really thought" that they became permanently estranged from them.[7]

As Michener takes pains to show, the Kent State shootings resulted from other causes besides generational conflict. Bad blood between the town and the campus prompted some citizens of Kent to say that the guard should have shot all the students and then started in on the faculty.[8] The students' manners and mores were a constant source of irritation to the conservative townspeople, as were the radical views of some professors. To Michener and many others, however, Kent State proved that the "generation gap" was not merely a cliché of popular journalism. It was real, it was deadly, and it had something to do with Vietnam, where men with guns stalked other men with guns. "Vietnam," as Francine du Plessix Gray wrote in the *Saturday Review,* "exacerbated a new hatred of youth, as it exacerbated all divisions among us."[9] In this chapter I first separate the realities of the generation gap from the myths. Then I indicate how generational conflict played itself out in relation to Vietnam and became a theme of our war stories.

II

Before turning to stories that explore conflict between the generations, we need to reflect on the meaning of key terms and assess their usefulness. What constitutes a generation? Was the "gap" between generations—to adopt the spatial metaphor then current—any wider in the 1960s than in previous decades? What were some of the sources of generational conflict?

The term "generation" refers, first, to a biological phenomenon: within a given family, the parents belong to one generation and their children to another. When one considers the many families that make up a community or a nation, this neat generational distinction disappears since, as David Riesman points out, "people are not produced in batches, as are pancakes, but are born continuously."[10] Following World War II, however, people were produced in such concentrated numbers as virtually to constitute a "batch." The baby boom, as demographic studies show, was the work of many small families rather than fewer large ones. Mothers of the postwar period generally produced two to four children in a brief span. In contrast, during the colonial period American women averaged eight births spread over the period of their fertility.[11] Consequently, in colonial families and to a lesser extent in American families of all periods through the 1930s, the interval between parents and their youngest child was typically bridged by a graduated series of young adults and children. Thus the chronological gap was far less obvious.

Another kind of generation gap began to develop in the early 1960s, when the first baby boomers graduated from high school. These graduates, and those who followed, were far more likely than their parents to attend college, where they quickly acquired new tastes and attitudes.[12] The difference in age therefore evolved into something like a difference in social class.

When one invokes the notion of a Sixties Generation or a Vietnam Generation, however, one does not think primarily of these demographic and educational characteristics. One thinks of Freedom Summer, of the Free Speech Movement at Berkeley, of massive protests against the war, of experimentation with drugs and alternative styles of life. How representative are such images? Here the so-called Generation of 1914 provides an instructive analogy. As Robert Wohl has shown, the Generation of 1914 was not so much a chronological phenomenon as it was an idea promulgated by young intellectuals in England, Europe, and America. Those who came of age shortly before and during World War I had been schooled in generational self-awareness and fixed on the war as the experience that separated—indeed, alienated—them from their elders. Their sense of betrayal at the hands of the older generation suffuses the writings of Sassoon, Graves, Owen, Hemingway, and Remarque. Paul Bäumer seems to speak for his peers in Remarque's *All Quiet on the Western Front* when he says, "The idea of authority, which [our teachers] represented, was associated in our minds with a greater insight and a more humane wisdom. But the first death we saw shattered this belief. We had to recognize that our generation was more to be trusted than theirs."[13]

From the Generation of 1914 came, appropriately, the first sustained studies of the generation as a social force. Writers like François Mentré, José Ortega y Gasset, and Karl Mannheim took generational theory beyond crude chronological categories that divide generations into fifteen- or thirty-year units, with members behaving according to predictable patterns by age. They sought to divest the generational concept of the mythic idealism that underlies notions of national identity or the zeitgeist. They did not succeed entirely, as Wohl demonstrates in the case of the Generation of 1914. But Mannheim in particular refined genera-

tional thinking in ways that help us to understand the Vietnam Generation.

In his classic essay "The Problem of Generations" (1928), Mannheim compares the generation to a social class. Like members of a social class, members of a generation do not have to belong to a social
organization defined by age, such as the German Youth Movement; they
may not even be conscious of their position in society. By living where
they do and when, they nonetheless participate in the "common destiny" of their generation in the sense that they are preoccupied with the
same historical issues and adversaries. Since all members of a generation
do not respond to a given issue or adversary in the same way, Mannheim subdivides the generation into "generation-units" composed of individuals who share a way of organizing perceptual data, a gestalt, regardless of whether they are aware of one another. Though oriented
toward the same issue, two generation-units may directly oppose one
another.

The usefulness of Mannheim's theory emerges when it is compared
with more monolithic and deterministic accounts of generational differences. Margaret Mead, for example, delivered a series of lectures at the
American Museum of Natural History in 1969 in which she divided
cultures into three types: postfigurative, cofigurative, and prefigurative.
In the first type, children learn primarily from their forebears. In the
second, both children and adults learn from their peers. In the third,
adults also learn from children. As Mead saw it, the youth culture of
the 1960s was an instance of a cofigurative culture in the United States.
Cofigurative culture was already preparing the way, she predicted, for a
"planetary and universal" prefigurative culture.[14] Convinced that the
generation gap of the 1960s was unprecedented and irreversible, Mead
urged her audience—older people like herself, presumably—to recognize that "we have no descendants, as our children have no forebears."[15]

Mead's sense of historical determinism was shared by Leslie Fiedler
and Susan Sontag in their debate over the "mutant" counterculture of
the 1960s. Whereas Fiedler lamented the demise of political (that is,
Old Left) activism and masculine virtue, Sontag celebrated the birth of
a new and less deadly kind of personality.[16] But both erroneously conflated a particular generation-unit with the generation as a whole. The
Vietnam Generation was—and is—no more homogeneous than the
generation that came of age during the Great War. If the Generation of
1914 was the creation of a small group of intellectuals, its 1960s coun-

terpart was largely the creation of the media, which focused only on the more newsworthy generation-units, the young people who threatened to upset what Lewis S. Feuer has called the "generational equilibrium" that prevailed in America prior to the 1960s.[17]

If we accept the notion of the generation as a useful social category and further accept the proposition that there was generational disequilibrium or conflict during the 1960s, we still need to gauge the extent of the conflict and speculate about its causes. Much of the research suggests that the conflict between specific generation-units never amounted to a large-scale "generation gap" between young people of the 1960s and their parents. High school graduates who entered the workforce rather than college usually channeled generational resentment into the struggle for higher wages and better working conditions.[18] Nor, according to one study conducted at the University of California at Davis, did the majority of college students stray far from their parents' values. The study concluded that the generation gap was a myth, "a tale of children who have been seduced by alien creatures."[19]

During the 1960s Kenneth Keniston devoted books to two of the more highly visible generation-units—the culturally alienated and activist students—yet he estimated that the two groups taken together amounted to no more than 5 percent of the student population. Keniston believed that the vast majority of young people in college were better described as "interested onlookers."[20] Feuer noted that less than 3 percent of American students took part in campus demonstrations during the turbulent period from January to June 1968 and likewise concluded that "by the barometer of student activism, one might say that the generational equilibrium of American society was not basically impaired."[21]

These studies demonstrate above all the difficulty of measuring generational conflict. Some forms of conflict are more visible than others and easier to quantify. Some cannot be quantified at all in any meaningful way. For this reason the extent of a given conflict cannot be separated from its causes and effects. For the sake of discussion we might sort the causes of 1960s generational conflict into four admittedly crude categories: psychological, political, economic, and stylistic. We must remember, however, that these are rarely separable in practice and that one person's cause will be another's effect.

When Freud propounded his theory of the Oedipus complex in *The Interpretation of Dreams* (1900) and further developed it in his essay "Family Romances" (1909) and *Totem and Taboo* (1913), he provided social historians and storytellers with an influential tool, one that can still be used to explain generational conflict even when (as is usually the case today) the theory is regarded as mythology rather than science. According to Freud, in the infantile stage of sexual development the male child is libidinally attached to his mother and regards his father as a rival.[22] He wants to kill the father and replace him as his mother's lover. This desire is fraught with anxiety, for he fears that his father will punish him with castration. He may also feel guilty for wanting to kill a parent whom he admires and loves as much as he fears. The healthy male represses all memory of these murderous and incestuous feelings as he grows up to become a father and husband, but the psychoneurotic fails to develop beyond the Oedipal phase. As an adult he continues to act out his childhood desires in various phobias and compulsions.

In *Totem and Taboo* Freud speculates about how the Oedipus complex might have given rise to religion, morality, and other social structures.[23] He imagines a primal (and probably historical) episode in which a group of brothers unite to kill and devour their powerful father, who expelled them from the patriarchal horde and prevented their access to his women. Stricken by guilt at their deed even as they rejoice in their success, the brothers institute a taboo against patricide and revere the father in the form of a totemic animal. Rather than kill one another in competition over the father's women, they establish another taboo against incest with their mother or sisters. These universal prohibitions became the basis of all morality and still inform today's religious rituals. The Christian Eucharist, for example, derives from the totemic feast. Since the members of subsequent generations pass through an Oedipal phase, they have an emotional investment in the totemic system and its taboos even though they did not experience the primal event from which these evolved.

As this summary of Freud's theory suggests, he was interested primarily in male development. In late essays on the sexual development of women, he conceded that the Oedipus complex does not apply to them in the same way that it applies to men, though his qualifications did little to avert feminist criticism.[24] Freud speculated that a young girl, too, is at first sexually attached to her mother. When she realizes that she lacks the means to impregnate her mother, being already "castrated," she transfers her erotic feelings to her father and shifts from the active sexual mode to the passive. Maturity does not require of her, as it does of her brothers, so forceful an act of repression. The father is neither her first love nor an object of guilt and anxiety.

In *Growing Up Absurd* (1960), a book about the Beats of the 1950s that also spoke to the experience of many alienated youth of the 1960s, Paul Goodman traced the younger generation's disaffection to an Oedipal pattern in the family.[25] Lewis Feuer likewise used the Freudian paradigm in *The Conflict of Generations* (1969), a scholarly study of student movements throughout the world in the nineteenth and twentieth centuries. According to Feuer, a faculty member at Berkeley, the Free Speech and antiwar movements on his own campus reproduced the pattern of previous student movements in Russia, Europe, and Japan. Though the Berkeley students ostensibly protested on behalf of worthy democratic principles, Feuer maintained that unconscious motives shaped the form and direction of their protest. They sought to divest university father figures of their moral authority and gravitated toward issues where generational differences were the most pronounced, moving from free speech to civil rights to the war in Vietnam. They countered their castration anxiety with exaggerated machismo and aligned themselves with groups that they believed their fathers had oppressed historically, such as African Americans and the North Vietnamese. Especially in the later phases of the movement, they discharged the burden of patricidal guilt by self-destructive behavior, including the use of drugs.

When Feuer expressed several of these views in the *New Leader* magazine in 1964 and 1965, he outraged student leaders at Berkeley, and with good reason.[26] Thorough as he was in his historical research, he used Freud in a way that was more provocative than psychologically rigorous. Did he mean to imply that the students were all neurotics, without any legitimate basis for complaint? If so, by what mechanism had they transferred Oedipal feelings from their biological fathers to the university? Could the behavior of the women students be explained in the same way?

For psychological answers to these questions, one must turn from Feuer to Bruno Bettelheim and Christopher Lasch. Bettelheim argued that young men and women who leave home in their teens to start their own families rarely have to renegotiate the Oedipal conflict. But those who remain economically and emotionally dependent on their parents, as do many college students, will repeat the childhood Oedipal conflict. Young women will experience a parallel conflict if their "psychosocial" (as distinct from sexual) identity differs from that of their homemaker mothers.[27] Taking a different tack, Lasch argued that Oedipal tensions were greatly reduced in the 1960s by the father's withdrawal from the nuclear family into the world of work. Although the son found it easier to break away from an absent father, he found it more difficult to achieve real autonomy, which (according to Freud) must come from struggle. Even when he transferred desire from his mother to another woman, he lacked any father to replace. Consequently, says Lasch, he rejected all authority and fantasized about a "general uprising of the young."[28]

Those who trace generational conflict to political causes often begin with the politics of the family, making it difficult to distinguish between politics and psychology. Kenneth Keniston's studies of culturally alienated and activist youth are a case in point. The alienated youth, sometimes called hippies, were the spiritual descendants of the Beats of the 1950s. Profoundly pessimistic about reforming American social and political structures, they "dropped out" to cultivate subjective experience. They expressed their contempt for conventional notions of success through nonconformist dress and behavior. When Keniston investigated the family backgrounds of alienated young people, he found that they rejected their parents' social and political values, especially those of the father. When the mother's values differed from the father's, an alienated son frequently took her side against him. Thus the son's "political" behavior originated to some extent in unresolved Oedipal feelings.

What Keniston discovered when he turned his attention to activist students did not confirm Feuer's sweeping thesis about student alienation. During the summer of 1967, Keniston conducted extensive interviews with fifteen organizers of Vietnam Summer, an effort to gain broad-based support for the antiwar movement. Unlike the alienated youth, the activists believed that they could effect change within the system, so they worked together to achieve specific social, political, and ethical goals. Though they sometimes deplored their parents' tendency to pay lip service to liberal values, they strongly endorsed the values themselves, to the point of trying to put them into practice. The activists subscribed to the egalitarian ideals on which the republic was founded. During the administrations of Kennedy and Johnson, when the government itself was officially committed to liberal goals, the activists put their trust in the system. Their rhetoric, even at its angriest, was in the tradition of the Puritan jeremiad; it was an appeal to honor the old covenants.

Where Feuer saw a single category of alienated psychoneurotics, Keniston saw two distinct generation-units. Though one was still in thrall to psychological compulsions, the other had graduated to mature

political behavior. Keniston's view was confirmed by observers representing a variety of disciplines and political positions. The distinguished
Harvard psychologist Erik Erikson told J. Anthony Lukas that what we
call the generation gap "is just another way of saying that the younger
generation makes overt what is covert in the older generation; the child
expresses openly what the parent represses."[29] For Lukas, a journalist,
this insight explained the behavior of the ten young people whose case
histories he discusses in *Don't Shoot—We Are Your Children!* (1971).
The same insight informs two other books from opposite ends of the
political spectrum, Midge Decter's conservative *Liberal Parents, Radical Children* (1975) and Todd Gitlin's memoir-history, *The Sixties: Years
of Hope, Days of Rage* (1987).

None of these writers disputes another of Feuer's arguments, namely,
that economics played a significant role in setting the younger generation apart from the older. On this score they have the testimony of the
New Left activists themselves. The 1962 manifesto that came to be
known as the Port Huron Statement begins with the words, "We are
people of this generation, bred in at least modest comfort, housed now
in universities, looking uncomfortably to the world we inherit. . . . But
we are a minority—the vast majority of our people regard the temporary equilibriums of our society and world as eternally-functional parts."[30]
Thus the original members of Students for a Democratic Society acknowledged that their social and political discomfort contrasted sharply
with their economic comfort. Having the good fortune to be born in
what was then frequently called an era of "post-scarcity," they had been
raised in material prosperity and enjoyed the benefits—social and economic as well as intellectual—of a university education.

Gitlin conjectures that this affluence may well be the one unbridge-
able gap between the 1960s generation, as a generation, and their parents.[31] However similar the political values of the two generations, their
memories and experiences—and therefore what Mannheim would call
their "adversaries"—were quite dissimilar. The most significant and
widely shared adversary of the older generation, one never shared by the
younger generation as a whole, was the Great Depression. Those born
after the Depression belonged to the first American generation to enjoy,
as a kind of birthright, the stage of life that Keniston calls "youth."

Prior to the industrial revolution most people proceeded directly
from childhood to adulthood. The wealth created by industry, together
with childhood labor laws, created a new stage of development for the
offspring of the bourgeoisie. Modeled on the apprenticeship, this post-

childhood, preadult stage was named "adolescence." Then, according to Keniston, the affluence created by postindustrial society introduced another developmental phase for members of the middle class aged eighteen to twenty-six. Having weathered the storms of adolescence, these young people are psychologically adults. But they have not yet assumed the social roles of adulthood—marriage, family, and career. Middle-class youth typically spend this period seeking further education, experimenting with various lifestyles, and scrutinizing the social, economic, and political institutions that will shape the rest of their lives. This group often plays a key role in social evolution, since it has the leisure, energy, and commitment to effect change. One of the many ironies of the 1960s, explained in Oedipal terms by Feuer, is that youth used the opportunity created by material affluence to criticize affluence and identify with those who had been denied its benefits. Like the New Left mentor C. Wright Mills, they responded to conspicuous consumption with the conspicuous frugality of Levi's, work shirts, and army surplus jackets.

Keniston acknowledges that youth, defined as a stage of life between adolescence and adulthood, is a privilege of social class. Even during the 1960s boom in higher education, the majority of Americans in their late teens and early twenties could not afford the luxury of activism, alienation, or even "onlooking." They went directly from adolescence—in some cases, directly from childhood—to adult responsibilities. These offspring of the working and lower classes, together with their parents, constituted what one study calls the "real" American majority of the 1960s.[32] Generational relationships in these classes were of the kind Mead termed "postfigurative." Class conflict helps explain why 89 percent of Americans aged twenty-one to twenty-nine who were polled in 1969, shortly before the Kent State shootings, approved of college administrators taking a stronger stand against student protests.[33] Throughout the 1960s, generation-units tended to divide along the lines of social class rather than birth cohort. It was not until the mid-1970s that nonstudents registered attitudes and opinions similar to those of their peers in the colleges and universities.[34]

The fourth cause of generational conflict—style—seems at first not as significant as the psychological, political, and economic causes. Some would regard style as a consequence rather than a cause. In the early 1960s, young people deviated markedly from their parents without altering their style of dress or speech. Thus a photograph of SDS students taken a year after the Port Huron Statement shows a group of young

men and women who would not be out of place at a country club.[35] But
as the decade wore on there was less for the older generation to like
in the style of the young. Their clothes, their music, their experiments
with sex and drugs, their slovenly apartments and communes, their offensive language—these were hard to ignore. The baby boomers were so
numerous that everything they did was newsworthy, and the more deviant behavior received disproportionate attention simply because it
was new. Though parents were inclined to approve of the opinions and
activities of their own children, or at least to tolerate them, they often
disapproved of "the younger generation" as packaged by the news media.[36]

The Kent State episode illustrates what might be called the "style
gap" between the generations. By 1970 the ostensible object of the students' protest, the Vietnam War, was no longer the source of generational conflict it had been just a few years earlier. As a group, the over-
thirties had no more heart for pursuing the war than the under-thirties.
Yet in the wake of the shootings at Kent State it seemed to Michener
and his team of interviewers that everyone in the university town was
eager to vent long-standing feelings of resentment against the students.
Townspeople expressed class antipathy in letters to the local newspaper,
and one person referred approvingly to the construction workers' assault on the antiwar protesters in New York.[37] A few were understand-
ably appalled by the students' destruction of property. What most outraged the people of Kent, however, were the stylistic expressions of
cultural alienation peculiar to youth—the long hair and bizarre or un-
kempt clothing, the partying and coed living arrangements in off-cam-
pus housing. Older women seemed obsessed by the number of girls
without bras.[38] They understood intuitively what Dick Hebdige has said
of subcultural styles, that they are "*meaningful* mutations" of existing
codes, meant to irritate those who adhere to the codes.[39]

Jerry Rubin may have had all of these stylistic mutations in mind on
April 10, when he claimed in his Kent State speech that in the eyes of
the older generation he and his audience constituted "a generation of
obscenities." The implied comparison between forbidden behavior and
forbidden language is apt, for the students' manner of speaking offended the townspeople as much as their manner of dress. According to
the familiar childhood rhyme, sticks and stones hurt more than disparaging names. But at Kent State names apparently triggered the sticks
and stones. Among the minor events that escalated into tragedy was
the arrest of a student for posting a sign containing the word "mother-

fucker," whose Oedipal message is obvious. Later, when a grand jury investigated the shootings, it singled out the students' language as a provocation to violence.[40]

In the next chapter I consider obscenity as a component of the war story; here I will merely observe that obscene language carries a social and political message. Stephen Weissman, a leader of the Free Speech Movement at Berkeley, made this clear in 1965 when he exhorted students to use obscene speech as a way of identifying with the masses and rejecting middle-class liberalism.[41] At Kent State five years later, an instructor who described himself as a "libertarian communist" tutored Michener in the politics of obscenity. Madison Avenue, he explained, continually appropriates the language of the streets, forcing the disaffected young to resort to "no-retreat words." According to the instructor, the offensiveness of these words is calculated: "Young people are devising a language which older people cannot steal from them. We seek to outrage those who have been outraging us."[42]

One wonders how many of the students at Berkeley, Kent State, and elsewhere consciously used obscenity and scruffy dress to make a political statement. Most probably borrowed their style of alienation from the truly disaffected in much the same way that disaffected whites borrowed the style from racial minorities. Their offensive language and behavior were signs of group affiliation and occasional outrage rather than profound cultural or political gestures. Yet the style of the younger generation, superficial though it was, may have contributed as much to generational friction as any of the more substantive psychological, political, or economic causes. The title of David Rabe's *Sticks and Bones,* the second of his four plays about Vietnam, invites us to reflect on the connection between name-calling and physical violence, between style and the Oedipal politics of the family.[43]

III

In his introduction to *Sticks and Bones,* Rabe wonders whether the effect of his play would be different if the characters were given other names.[44] The effect would undoubtedly be different and probably less powerful. By invoking *The Adventures of Ozzie and Harriet* as his primary intertext, Rabe is able to comment on both the cultural values enshrined in the television series and the generic conventions that governed the family situation comedy of the 1950s and 1960s. Like Mailer's novel, *Sticks and Bones* attempts to answer the question "Why are we in Vietnam?" in terms other than those of foreign or domestic policy. Whereas the novel attributes American involvement to frontier mythology, the play traces it to generational conflict within the American family.

Before turning to the play, we might briefly recall the state of the American family when *The Adventures of Ozzie and Harriet* was airing on radio (1944–1952) and television (1952–1966). During these years the nuclear family again became the norm, following two decades during which economic hardship forced many to live in three-generation households.[45] Though the single-family household of the 1950s has often been described as "traditional," usually by those who espouse a return to conservative values, it was actually unprecedented in its insularity and the kind of emotional investment it required. To a greater degree than even in the nineteenth century, the American family of the 1950s was expected to be, in Christopher Lasch's phrase, a "haven in a heartless world."[46] It was supposed to supply all of the parents' and children's personal needs and satisfactions.[47]

During the period between World War II and Vietnam, prime-time television idealized and promoted this social experiment in programs like *The Adventures of Ozzie and Harriet, Father Knows Best, The Life of Riley, Leave It to Beaver,* and *My Three Sons.* Though the family situation comedy was patently unrealistic in many respects—Ozzie Nelson seemed never to have a job yet enjoyed a comfortable standard of living—it was nonetheless persuasive. Film is by nature a highly mimetic medium, an effect reinforced in the Nelsons' case by the fact that the characters were played by members of an actual family bearing the same names. Once the prime-time family was accepted as authentic, it served to reinforce social conformity.[48] A family that did not conform to the Nelson or Cleaver model was made to feel deviant.

The normative television family was white, middle-class, and suburban. It lacked any definite ethnic, religious, or regional traits. Family members were cheerfully cordial, if not physically affectionate, as reflected in the greetings that marked the entrances and exits of the Nelsons: "Hi, Mom. Hi, Pop. Hi, Rick. Hi, David. Bye, Mom. Bye, Pop," and so forth. Pop brought home the paycheck and Mom was a full-time homemaker. There were disagreements, rivalries, even fits of jealousy, but these never generated any real bitterness. Their problems usually proved to be misunderstandings that could be resolved in the twenty-two minutes of air time. The home was not a forum for political debate; in fact it seemed impervious to events in the world outside, including the Vietnam War and the Kennedy assassination. It was a place for the enjoyment and consumption of goods, not only Mom's milk and brownies but also appliances and other household products. During the years when Hotpoint was the sole sponsor of *The Adventures of Ozzie and Harriet,* much of the action was set in the kitchen, amid Hotpoint appliances. Later, Harriet sold Listerine from the kitchen, and the products of other sponsors were displayed as often as the script permitted.[49]

Few real families could measure up—or down, depending on one's point of view—to the standard set by "America's Favorite Family," not even the Nelsons themselves. Philip Bashe's recent biography of Rick Nelson, though it sets out to refurbish a reputation that was tarnished by rumors of drug use prior to his fatal plane crash, portrays what some would call the product of a dysfunctional family. Rick, who once described himself as "a greaser at heart," personified elements of the youth culture that his father was anxious to suppress on the program— juvenile delinquency, rock and roll music, and sexual promiscuity.[50] Though Ozzie successfully contained or sanitized these impulses while his family was in front of the camera, he could not prevent them from taking their course after 1966. Paradoxically, as the Nelson family became less ideal it became more representative. Interviewed for an *Esquire* article in 1971, Ozzie asked, "I think what's happened to our family in the last four or five years is the same with all other families, no?" Harriet, who had hoped to see her nuclear family grow into an extended family, was disturbed by the fissions implicit in the nuclear ideal. "There's been a whole change in the way of living," she said. "People are peeling off early, not wanting to be part of a large family unit. The whole institution seems to be in trouble. We're just as confused as everybody else. And we all used to be so sure about what we wanted, what was good. We're three separate families now. It's kind of sad."[51]

At the time of the *Esquire* interview Ozzie and Harriet were ambivalent toward the Vietnam War, David had no strong feelings about it, and Rick thought it "ridiculous."[52] Like most middle- and upper-class families of the time, they were largely insulated from the effects of the war. *Sticks and Bones* therefore begins with an unlikely premise, that David Nelson went to Vietnam as a soldier and was blinded in combat. Curiously, the war itself never becomes a political or moral issue in the play. One critic, proceeding on the assumption that *Sticks and Bones* is primarily about the war, regrets that the play is "a product of its time, perhaps even locked into its moment in the early 70s by the passage of the Vietnam war into history."[53] Actually, what Rabe said about his next play, *The Orphan,* applies to *Sticks and Bones* as well: it is "about the betrayal of the young by the old, and then the vengeance of the young on the old."[54] Vietnam is not so much the subject of the play as it is an occasion for the Nelsons to confront their basic values and motives. To the extent that their values are typical of American families of that era, and to the extent that domestic values reflected or shaped national policy, they help to account for America's conduct of the war.

Of the four causes of generational conflict previously identified, *Sticks and Bones* emphasizes the psychological. When their son is delivered like a damaged parcel to their home, Ozzie and Harriet try initially to preserve their image of themselves by ignoring David's odd behavior, glossing it over with clichés or retreating to the comforting glow of the television set. David nevertheless succeeds in penetrating the "happy family" facade and challenging the identity of each member, beginning with the patriarch. War veteran David reminds Ozzie that he sat on the sidelines during his generation's war. Ozzie tries to vindicate himself in contradictory ways. On the one hand, he claims to have experienced the equivalent of the soldier's life by working in a war industry, taking part in the male camaraderie of the factory, and getting into fights. On the other hand, he expresses revulsion at the violence of soldiering, which he equates with sadistically skinning a cat.

David calls his father's manhood into question in another way. Ozzie cherishes the memory of himself as a youthful athlete, the runner his townspeople sent for when their pride was on the line (the real Ozzie Nelson had been a quarterback at Rutgers, and his television persona occasionally sought to prove that he was as physically fit as younger men). He realizes, however, that this image precedes and is possibly at odds with his current role as husband and father. He was initiated into his present role by a mythical figure named Hank Grenweller (German for "green wave"), who personifies male potency. Having surrendered to the process by which one generation succeeds another, Ozzie clings to the belief that "Hank" is robust and healthy. When David reports that Hank is dying of a congenital illness, he forces Ozzie to confront his mortality. As Ozzie feels his life slipping through his fingers he gropes desperately for some palpable symbol of his accomplishments. He eventually settles on an inventory of his furniture and other possessions as an index of his worth.

David enlists Harriet in the project of undermining Ozzie's authority. She insists that her husband could not have beaten Hank Grenweller in a footrace and ridicules Ozzie's threat of rape. Angry at her husband because he trained David in sports and fighting and thus groomed him for war, she takes revenge by describing in detail how the aspirin he takes to relieve a headache will induce gastric bleeding. With good reason Ozzie begins to suspect malice behind her nurturing mask. "What do you give me when you give me this?" he asks, accepting a glass of juice from her (p. 110). Unable to recall anything blameworthy in his state of mind at the moment of David's conception, he blames his son's aberrations, and those of the world as a whole, on "poisonous" female organs (p. 137).

The conspiracy of mother and son against father hints at an Oedipal pattern that is made explicit in act 2, where David predicts that he will become Ozzie's father. Later in the same act, Harriet comes to David's room at night and offers to bathe him. Prior to the 1950s, there would be nothing unseemly in this gesture. But as Stephanie Coontz has remarked, all forms of intimacy became sexualized during this period, including relationships within the family.[55] Harriet's offer clearly has erotic overtones: "Take your shirt off, David. You'll feel cool. That's all we've ever wanted, your father and me—good sweet things for you and Rick—ease and lovely children, a car, a wife, a good job. Time to relax and go to church on Sundays . . . and on holidays all the children and grandchildren come together, mingling—it would be so wonderful— everyone so happy—turkey. Twinkling lights. *(She is puzzled, a little worried.)* David, are you going to take your shirt off for me?" (p. 163). Responding to his mother's subliminal message, David moves the tip of his cane along the floor, up her leg, and under her bathrobe until it is pressed firmly against her. She pulls back in revulsion, then flees the room when he begins to repeat the gesture.

David's behavior follows the pattern for sons of "absent" fathers, as described by Lasch. Though he seeks to depose his father as patriarch, he does not really want to become his mother's lover; hence he uses his cane to discourage Harriet's overtures by underscoring their Oedipal nature. David outgrew his libidinal attachment to his mother when he consummated his love with a young Vietnamese woman named Zung. How long he carried on the relationship is unknown, though the family's pastor, Father Donald, has gotten the impression from Harriet that it went on for some time. Though Rabe's Nelsons are good Catholics— unlike both the real Nelsons and their television counterparts—they are not disturbed by David's fornication.[56] They are not even upset at his sexual relations with an Asian woman, as long as he understands that she was merely a receptacle, a way to release physical tension. For Ozzie and Harriet whiteness is a "triumph" and any dilution of racial purity a form of backsliding. Father Donald regards miscegenation as a symptom of psychopathology, a rejection of one's very self. David, in contrast, associates whiteness with winter and suicide.

Considering David's alienation from his parents and white Christianity, we might wonder why he didn't bring Zung home with him and marry her in defiance. This mystery is resolved at the end of act 1, where David addresses Zung's reproachful image: "I discarded you. Forgive me. . . . Zung, there were old voices inside me I had trusted all my life as if they were my own. I didn't know I shouldn't hear them. So reasonable and calm they seemed a source of wisdom. . . . I did as they told; I did it, and now I know that I am not awake but asleep, and in my sleep . . . there is nothing" (p. 138). Though David's behavior and style align him with alienated youth through much of the play, he ultimately shares the activist's allegiance to his parents' core values, which in this case are illiberal and racist. Toward the end of act 2 David seems to have silenced the "old voices." With the image of Zung looking on, he presents himself somewhat inconsistently as both an alienated "wild wolf" among domestic dogs and as the new father of the Nelson family. But his tenure as paterfamilias is brief. Rick smashes his guitar over David's head (earlier, Ozzie had dreamed of being deposed in this fashion), and Ozzie strangles Zung. When David recovers, he helps the family tidy up the living room and passively acquiesces to their suggestion that he commit suicide by slashing his wrists with a razor. Ozzie's anxiety about death surfaces one last time, when he wishfully insists that David is "only nearly" going to die (p. 175). Otherwise, the old voices prevail and order is restored.

Ozzie's victory is not only psychological and cultural-political but also economic and stylistic. The Nelson household in the play, as in the television show, is a place where goods are sold and consumed. Rabe approximates the television medium by using a proscenium stage and a set that seems, according to one of his directions, to "belong in the gloss of an advertisement" (p. 96). As in television programming, the emotional continuity of scenes is interrupted by commercials, one for a filter cigarette, another for a spot remover. Ozzie measures his worth by the goods he has accumulated, and Harriet repeatedly translates the emotional demands of her family into hunger, which she can then satisfy with food. Whereas Rick confirms his parents' roles by acting as the ideal consumer, David rejects the "good sweet things" that constitute success in their minds—"ease and lovely children, a car, a wife, a good job" (p. 163).

David is at odds with his parents stylistically as well. He retreats from their antiseptic rooms and glib sociability to the lonely squalor of his room. When recalling his evenings with Zung, he adopts a lyrical mode of speech: "And then there was this girl . . . with hands and hair like wings. There were candles above the net of gauze under which we lay. Lizards. Cannon could be heard. A girl to weigh no more than dust" (p. 114). This kind of language is out of place in the Nelsons' suburban America, especially when used to describe someone from an alien race. Since David has occupied the high ground of lyricism, Ozzie must resort to obscenity—ordinarily the style of the younger generation—to attack him: "Who the hell you think you are? You screwed it. A yellow whore. Some yellow ass. You put in your prick and humped your ass. You screwed some yellow fucking whore!" (pp. 114-15)

It is apparently to this contrast of styles that Rabe refers in his introduction to the play, where he says, "One of the major conflicts between the characters in *Sticks and Bones* is a disagreement about the nature of the world in which they are living, or, in other words, about the kind of language that is used to define experience" (p. xx). To the extent that language and world are inseparable, names can break bones as surely as sticks and stones. For David, sleeping with Zung is poetic; for Ozzie it is obscene. Between such contrary points of view and such antipodal discourses there would appear to be no common ground. Yet David ultimately endorses the values he despises. So deeply are they ingrained in his character that he dies for them.

David's suicide is the most extreme example of behavior that would not have found a place in the family television situation comedies of the 1950s and 1960s. Throughout the play characters openly express hateful and violent feelings toward one another, then retreat behind a facade of benevolence and harmony. As David remarks, "It is only fraud that keeps us sane" (p. 134). Through its expressionistic mode, the play discloses the fraudulence or pseudomimesis of programs like *The Adventures of Ozzie and Harriet* and suggests why viewers in the 1970s were ready for situation comedies—*All in the Family,* for example— that acknowledged disharmonies in the American household. The later family programs also addressed social and political issues that could not be neatly resolved in a half hour. *Sticks and Bones* adheres to the conventions of the 1950s and 1960s even at the cost of absurdity. While

David bleeds to death surrounded by his family, Rick's guitar provides the obligatory happy ending.

In Rabe's play, as in Mailer's *Why Are We in Vietnam?*, the father ultimately wins the Oedipal struggle and sacrifices the son to his own values, which are represented as corrupt. In each case the son tries to revise those values—DJ by forging his own version of Rusty's frontier mythology, David by inverting Ozzie's myth of white superiority. Neither succeeds, and the failure is actually or potentially fatal to the son. This reversal of the Oedipal pattern entails a corresponding revision in Freud's account of totemism. It is the son rather than the patriarch who is slain and metamorphosed into a socially manageable creature, the totemic figure honored in "welcome home" parades and other public rituals. "We all agreed to have the same amnesia," Rabe observes, summing up the terms of our post-Vietnam taboo. "The vets are welcomed back, but they have to shut up."[57]

IV

Though fictional works, *Sticks and Bones* and *Why Are We in Vietnam?* dramatize a generational conflict, and in particular a father-son conflict, that smoldered in many families during the Vietnam War. As might be expected, the conflict was most pronounced in cases where the father had fought in World War II and the son refused to fight in Vietnam. This pattern pervades oral histories like Gerald R. Gioglio's *Days of Decision* (1989) and James W. Tollefson's *The Strength Not to Fight* (1993), both devoted to conscientious objectors (COs). Not all of the 172,000 young men who qualified as COs regarded their fathers' values as corrupt. Some, like Keniston's activist youth, regarded their protest as a logical extension of their fathers' beliefs. Thus one CO compared his stand to an act of moral courage performed by his father in World War II, saying, "I saw him as doing something right, something moral and ethical, despite the risk. I felt like I was taking a moral stand by choosing not to participate in the war. But he couldn't accept my choice. He could never see that I was trying to live up to his example. He never understood that he had inspired me."[58] Among the objectors were sons of the men most responsible for shaping American policy in Southeast Asia—Robert McNamara, Dean Rusk, and John Paul Vann.[59] The grandsons of two prominent army generals of World War II, S. L. A. Marshall and Lucian K. Truscott, Jr., resigned their commissions in protest against the Vietnam War.[60]

The sons who went to war in compliance with their fathers' wishes did not always grow closer to their fathers as a result. Michael Herr encountered a marine who was initially pleased to receive letters from his father expressing pride, but after eight months in country he was ready to kill his father.[61] Tobias Wolff's father likewise professed to be "damned proud" of his son's service to his country.[62] Considering the distance and strain in their relationship up to that point, Wolff might have taken some comfort in his father's words. While waiting to go over-seas, however, he had watched another father persuade his son to desert rather than sacrifice himself for the greater glory of President Johnson and General Westmoreland. Still trying to absorb this shock on his way to the airport and the plane that would take him to Vietnam, Wolff fantasized about a last-minute reprieve. He imagined the soldiers' bus being hijacked by a mysterious gang that would turn out to be their own fathers. "Crazy," Wolff says of this improbable scenario. "But not as crazy as what they actually did, which was let us go."[63]

Vietnam, Lloyd B. Lewis writes, "made a whole generation of fathers look like liars and betrayers."[64] The son's sense of betrayal could lead to patricidal rage or profound disillusion. It could also impel him, as it did so many of his generation, to replace his biological father with a more acceptable substitute. Freud suggests in "Family Romances" how a boy goes about inventing surrogates. When he becomes aware of his parents' shortcomings or begins to feel that they do not love him suf-ficiently, he concludes that he must be a stepchild or adopted. He then fantasizes about his "real," socially superior parents in ways that incor-porate a measure of verisimilitude. Once he learns about the mechanics of sexual reproduction and can no longer doubt his mother's identity, he directs all of his inventiveness toward the father, whom he now re-gards as a sexual competitor. Anticipating Keniston, Freud says that the child indirectly pays tribute to the actual father even as he rejects him, since the surrogate is based on memories of the actual father prior to his fall from grace.

As the son passes through adolescence and youth he may relinquish some of the fantasy of the family romance, but not its basic motive. Rather than fabricate a surrogate father out of whole cloth, he finds him in the public domain. Few soldiers were drawn to the left-lean-ing father figures of their peers in the antiwar movement—men such as C. Wright Mills, Paul Goodman, Herbert Marcuse, Norman O. Brown, and Timothy Leary. But they could share the admiration of the less radi-cal antiwar youth for John F. Kennedy. It is thus appropriate that Robert

Patrick should include a Vietnam veteran among the slain president's "offspring" in *Kennedy's Children* (1976). Because Kennedy died during an early stage of the war, he could stand for either the idealism that sent Americans to Vietnam or the political realism that might have brought them home sooner. Without fear of contradiction, a character in *Kennedy's Children* can assert, "If he had lived, he would have stopped the war. If he had lived, he would have solved the race problem. If he had lived, he would have found some way to bring us all together."[65]

As Patrick's play suggests, Kennedy served as a substitute father to diverse generation-units of 1960s youth who remained loyal to him after he died and elevated him to a paternal pantheon along with America's founding fathers (Washington, Jefferson, Lincoln) and frontiersmen (Boone, Crockett). What Margaret Mead said of George Washington might also be said of other historical father figures: he "does not represent the past to which one belongs by birth, but the past to which one tries to belong by effort."[66] John Hellmann has documented the protagonist's effort in several Vietnam memoirs and novels to locate a "true father" in the frontier past.[67] When students dressed up as Boone or Crockett during the Kent State demonstrations in 1970, they were implicitly contrasting these surrogate fathers with their parents and university authorities.[68]

Youth who seek a true father in history—usually as mediated by television—represent themselves as in effect members of a "third" generation. The true father stands for pristine values that the second generation, the generation of the biological parents, has betrayed and that youth want to recover. According to Werner Sollors, Americans have situated themselves in a three-generational model since Puritan times.[69] In immigrant families the third generation typically wants to recover the ethnic identity that the second generation sought to suppress in the interest of assimilation. The model oversimplifies generational change, and, as Sollors points out, the "recovered" identity is largely a fiction. But the impulse remains because the model serves both a psychological and a cultural purpose. To identify with one's grandparent is to become the parent of one's father or mother, thus fulfilling a childhood fantasy. Culturally, such identification authorizes one's jeremiads against the supposedly degenerate second generation.

These purposes may account for the prominent role played by literal as well as figurative grandparents in Vietnam War fiction and film. Taylor in *Platoon*, Joker in *The Phantom Blooper*, and Ned Charles in *Ashes and Embers* enjoy a special rapport with their grandmothers, whereas their parents are either absent or unsympathetic. In Caputo's *Indian Country,* Starkmann finds peace when he and the grandfather of his best friend mutually adopt one another. Richard Currey's novel *Fatal Light* suggests yet another reason for a Vietnam veteran to identify with his grandfather. Rather than go directly home from the war, Currey's narrator stops first at his grandfather's house in West Virginia to decompress emotionally. The novel's first section, "Mortal Places," opens with the narrator studying a photo album at his grandfather's house; the last section, "Home," closes with him about to fall asleep in the same house. What he and his grandfather share, as suggested by these activities, is an "old age" of the spirit—matched, in the grandfather's case, by an old age of the body.[70] The narrator is not yet ready to face his comparatively youthful and upbeat parents, even though his father is a war veteran and his grandfather is not.

Not every young man of the Vietnam Generation found it necessary to invent or find a surrogate father. Some sons followed the example of their veteran fathers by going to Vietnam and trying to be good soldiers themselves. Of all father-son relationships during the Vietnam era, these would seem to be the least likely to show any signs of generational conflict. However, precisely because such relationships were less polarized and more nuanced, they repay closer scrutiny. In the following section I consider how Vietnam affected two of America's most distinguished military families, the Zumwalts and the Pullers.

V

Elmo R. Zumwalt, Jr., was one of the navy's brightest stars during the Vietnam War. When he was appointed Commander of U.S. Navy Forces in Vietnam in 1968 he became, at the age of forty-seven, the youngest vice admiral in American naval history. Less than two years later he was promoted to the navy's highest position, Chief of Naval Operations. In that post he issued his famous "Z-grams" ordering a number of controversial reforms, including fuller integration of racial minorities and a more relaxed grooming code.

During his tour of duty in Vietnam, Zumwalt focused chiefly on two projects, Vietnamizing the navy—that is, turning over more of the naval operations to the South Vietnamese—and interdicting shipments of weapons from Cambodia to communist guerrillas in South Vietnam. The second of these was the mission of the "brown water" navy in which his son, Elmo R. Zumwalt III, served as a lieutenant in charge of a swift boat, a smaller and faster version of the standard river patrol boat (PBR). While patrolling the rivers and canals of South Vietnam, navy boats were easy targets for Viet Cong hidden in the dense jungle foliage. Admiral Zumwalt therefore ordered the extensive use of defoliants such as Agent Orange to protect his men. Not until years later did he realize that he had also exposed the sailors, including his son, to long-term health problems. The admiral's son died of cancer in August 1988, following years of chemotherapy and a bone marrow transplant. His grandson suffers from a severe learning disability that may have been caused by Agent Orange.

In 1985 and 1986 the Zumwalts collaborated with John Pekkanen to produce *My Father, My Son,* an oral history in which the two Zumwalts' narratives are interwoven with the testimony of family members, friends, and military colleagues. Their story is told more or less chronologically, beginning with the admiral's memories of growing up in California and ending five months after Elmo III's bone marrow transplant, when his condition seemed to be improving. Like any life narrative, this one is highly selective. The details of everyday domestic life are largely omitted, as are most details of military life. The book focuses instead on the intersections and potential conflicts between personal and professional life. Thus Lieutenant Zumwalt reports his experiences and feelings as a young officer trying to make his own way in a navy commanded by his famous father, and Admiral Zumwalt tells of conflicts between his roles as father and commander.

If there were any serious conflicts between the Zumwalts, they are largely repressed in *My Father, My Son.* Their remarkable harmony extends even to their retrospective views of the decision to use defoliants. The admiral is convinced that Agent Orange caused the ailments suffered by his son and grandson and accepts responsibility for their suffering. Yet he claims that he would still order the use of Agent Orange, even knowing its hazards, on the grounds that it reduces combat casualties. Elmo III likewise attributes his problems to the defoliant but refuses to blame his father.

As Freud tells us, hostility can take the form of jokes, including practical jokes that make a person "seem stupid by exploiting his credulity."[71] Practical jokes are so much a part of the Zumwalt story that the book's index includes an entry for them. Some of the jokes get rather rough emotionally, even allowing for the therapeutic value of humor. Shortly after the bone marrow transplant, the admiral was called away from

a business luncheon by an urgent phone call. Elmo was on the line, pro-
fessing to be "deeply distressed and hurt" because his father had gone
off to lunch while he was suffering.[72] When the conscience-stricken
father promised to come immediately to the hospital, he heard Elmo
laughing and realized that he had been fooled.

A Freudian interpretation of Elmo's joke would speculate that he resented his father's absence because it recalled the absences of his boyhood, when the admiral was often away on long cruises. Since he loved
and admired his father, he could only express his anger obliquely, in
the form of a practical joke. Elmo's reluctance to hurt his father shows
in two other ways. First, he exposed the joke by laughing before the
admiral was put to any real inconvenience. Second, he chose a mode of
communication, the private telephone call, that excluded any audience.
Freud considered a third person indispensable to the joking process because the joker usually cannot laugh at his own joke; he requires an
auditor in order to experience any personal pleasure.[73] By playing the
roles of both joker and auditor, Elmo spared his father any public humiliation. He left it up to the admiral to decide whether to tell the story
later on, and to whom. That the elder Zumwalt chose to do so in *My
Father, My Son* suggests that he did not feel seriously compromised.

Both Zumwalts attribute the son's early maturity in part to the admiral's long absences from his family. "I became a sort of third parent,"
Elmo III says of his relationship to his brother and sisters, and he later
addresses his father as a comrade-in-arms.[74] The older Zumwalt concurs, observing that their father-son relationship ended when Elmo was
still a boy. Had the book taken its title from the admiral's own description of their relationship, it would have been called "my partner, my
brother."[75] If Elmo ever aspired to supplant his father, he thoroughly
repressed the memory. Though his mother was presumably the more
"present" parent during his childhood, she is virtually absent from the
narrative. As the product of a successfully negotiated Oedipal conflict,
My Father, My Son thus reproduces textually the repression that made
it possible.

Though Pekkanen does not describe the procedure that resulted in
My Father, My Son, most of the book appears to be based on taped
interviews. The contributors seem familiar with testimony supplied by
others and often corroborate it in their own remarks. For at least some
of the interviews, the principal characters occupied the same room. The
prologue recreates an occasion when the admiral picked up his son's
story in midsentence and completed it, a gesture that typifies the book

as a whole.[76] Though one is conscious of the multiplicity of voices, one is more impressed by their univocal message. Any contention between father and son has been suppressed in the interest of a single harmonious narrative.

Superficially, the same harmony seems to reign in the lives and life stories of another famous military father and son, both named Lewis B. Puller. The father's story is told by Burke Davis in *Marine! The Life of Lt. Gen. Lewis B. (Chesty) Puller, USMC (Ret.)* (1962), a biography based on Marine Corps documents, the testimony of colleagues, friends, and family members, and extensive interviews with Chesty Puller himself. Davis's book does not pretend to be objective history. It verges on autobiography in adopting Puller's point of view and, for paragraphs at a stretch, his very language. The son tells his own story in *Fortunate Son: The Autobiography of Lewis B. Puller, Jr.* (1991), which was awarded a Pulitzer Prize in 1992. *Fortunate Son* responds not only to the flesh-and-blood Chesty Puller, whom Lewis, Jr., knew mainly after his retirement from the marines, but also to two intertexts: the Puller legend that passed orally from one generation of marines to another and Davis's written narrative.

The son owned a copy of the latter, which his father had given to him when it was published.[77] *Marine!* recounts the making of the legend against which Lewis, Jr., measured himself. When Chesty Puller came under fire for the first time while fighting rebels in Haiti, he ducked his head and was reprimanded by the former Haitian general Napoleon Lyautey, "Captain Puller, officers do not flinch under fire. They stand. The men take note of this thing. It is of first importance."[78] Puller showed that he had learned this lesson in World War II and Korea, where he led his men from the front lines rather than establish his headquarters in the rear. He frequently exposed himself to enemy fire and refused to retreat even in the face of heavy losses. Remarkably, he was wounded only once, by shrapnel from a Japanese shell on Guadalcanal. Rather than allow himself to be evacuated, he ordered the surgeons to leave a large piece of shrapnel in his thigh. There it remained for a year, during which he led the bloody assault on Peleliu.

Puller's last campaign was in Korea, where his no-retreat philosophy came into conflict with the tactics of the army leadership. After a daring and successful landing and offensive at Inchon, the First Marine Division advanced into North Korea late in 1950. The division was then ordered to retreat from the Chosin Reservoir in bitterly cold weather, with Puller's regiment serving as the rear guard. Though the regiment was often surrounded by Chinese troops during its sixty-mile march to the seaport at Hungnam, it always managed to break through and protect the division so that it could be evacuated by sea. Retreat was not Puller's style, however, and he was dismayed by how often his superiors chose to back down from a fight in Korea. He thought that their conduct of the war reflected a general decline in discipline and a failure of leadership in the American military.

When Puller retired in 1955 as a lieutenant general, he was the most decorated marine in the history of the corps. He was the subject of hundreds of stories testifying to his courage under fire, physical endurance, gung ho spirit, no-nonsense style of leadership, and salt-of-the-earth identification with the common soldier. His son absorbed the legend at the family dinner table, where it was recounted by the dozens of men who made the pilgrimage to visit Chesty Puller in retirement. At the same time, he knew his father as a gentle, loving parent who was far from indestructible. After suffering a stroke in 1954, Chesty declined steadily. In retirement he became an almost pathetic figure with little to do besides reread his collection of military histories and run errands for his wife.

The ambivalence in *Fortunate Son* proceeds from Lewis, Jr.'s, relationship to two fathers—the man for whom he felt love and compassion and the legend that he could not hope to equal, much less surpass. Lewis, Jr., glosses the story in *Marine!* at several points, such as when he explains what went through his mind as a boy of five when he learned of the retreat from Chosin and prayed the words recorded by Davis: "And dear God, please let my Father out of that rabbit trap" (p. 306).[79] But his comments typically have an ironic edge. When he killed a deer at the age of eleven, Chesty compared him favorably in *Marine!* to the young Daniel Boone (p. 376). But as Lewis, Jr., retells the story in *Fortunate Son*, he was daydreaming at his stand when a young buck practically offered itself as a sacrifice; he felt lucky to bring it down with several pellets from his shotgun.[80] In whatever sphere of action Davis represents Chesty as a hero in *Marine!*, Lewis, Jr., is sure to represent himself as an antihero in *Fortunate Son*. Thus the young Chesty comes across as a superior athlete, fighter, and outdoorsman, whereas Lewis, Jr., recounts a series of humiliations in all of these areas.

The same pattern obtains in Vietnam, where he tells of his embarrassments as a novice platoon leader. Three weeks into his command, he reports dryly, "our only confirmed kills were a pig and three bushes" (p. 86). The antiheroic mode of *Fortunate Son* begins with its title. In the John Fogerty song recorded by Creedence Clearwater Revival, the phrase "fortunate son" is used ironically; hence it befits Puller's tale of terrible misfortune. But Puller also intends the phrase to be taken straight, so it oscillates between its ironic and unironic meanings. In this respect it sets the tone of the book.

Irony is not the only way in which *Fortunate Son* plays off its intertexts. Here one needs to recall its author's dilemma. Lewis, Jr., had little aptitude for military life and would ordinarily have been disqualified from the marines for defective eyesight. He nevertheless pursued a course in which he was certain to be compared unfavorably with his father. He did so partly because he admired his father and partly because by the age of six he felt "powerless" to take another path, even though Chesty had vowed while still in Korea not to influence his son's choice of a career.[81] Whatever his original reasons for enlisting in the marines, he became his own man by repeating his father's career with significant differences. Some of these deviations made him appear the lesser man, he knew, and for these irony and self-deprecating humor are appropriate devices. But in other ways he surpassed his father, and these are best approached through a theory of storytelling that is grounded in the father-son relationship.

In a sense, as Roland Barthes observes, all narrative is Oedipal in its motivation. "If there is no longer a Father," he asks in *The Pleasure of the Text*, "why tell stories?" Storytelling, he maintains, is "always a way of searching for one's origin, speaking one's conflicts with the Law, entering into the dialectic of tenderness and hatred."[82] Beginning with much the same insight, Harold Bloom elaborates in *The Anxiety of Influence* a theory of poetic succession based on Freud's family romance. Like Freud, Bloom ignores female development, focusing exclusively on the son's relationship to the father. He argues that the ambitious young poet seeks to supplant his "father," a major literary precursor, in the father's relationship with the "mother," or muse. In his anxiety over the father's poetic authority (what Barthes calls "the Law"), the son tries to make room for his own achievement by revising—in fact, deliberately misinterpreting—the father's poems in his own work.

Bloom identifies six revisionary strategies in the "strong" poet's life cycle, though he concedes that this number is somewhat arbitrary. A given poet might pass through more phases or produce most of his work in just one or two. In his relation to his biological father, a poet may have negotiated the Oedipal phase successfully. But in his relation to his poetic father he remains "immature" and anxious or he would cease to write. The successful strong poet ends by replacing—in a sense becoming—his own poetic father. Bloom's account of the creative process has consequences for the reading and criticism of poetry, for it implies that a poem cannot be understood "in itself," as formalist criticism tries to do. Rather, each poem must be read intertextually, as the misprision of a parent poem.

Bloom is a literary critic, not a sociologist, so he does not apply his insights to generational conflict. With minor revision, however, his theory of composition might serve as a dynamic theory of adolescence and youth applicable to both sexes. Whereas Keniston's youth fall neatly into two cohorts, the alienated and the activist, Bloom's "strong" youth would pass through phases of alienation and activism. Young people would begin and end as activists, endorsing their parents' core values; between these terminals they would pass through varying degrees of alienation. This extension of Bloom's theory would also liberate the Oedipal conflict from biology, so that strong youth might contend with authorities outside the nuclear family. The social equivalent of the poetic precursor might be the university, the government, or the military. Because Bloom's scheme is meant to account for the writing of poems, it textualizes the father, or his life story, in much the same way that Clifford Geertz's theory textualizes culture. As text or narrative, the father remains present to the son or daughter in a way that he cannot always be present personally.

A text-oriented theory works best when both father and son have committed their stories to words, as is the case with the Zumwalts and the Pullers. *My Father, My Son* reproduces a dialogue between two life stories, the admiral's and the lieutenant's. Elmo III seems to have been more politically conservative than his father, more inclined to support President Nixon and his conduct of the war in Vietnam. Inasmuch as he suppresses any differences of opinion with his father, however, he is what Bloom would call a "weak" son, the weakness being in this context a defect of imagination rather than moral character. He simply cannot conceive of himself as his father's replacement. Perhaps because he faces a likely death by cancer at the end of *My Father, My Son,* he assumes that his father's narrative will encompass his own.

In contrast, Lewis B. Puller, Jr.'s, narrative is a revisionary text. Though *Fortunate Son* contains instances of all six phases described in *The Anxiety of Influence,* I will concentrate on two of the more important ones, those that Bloom calls "clinamen" and "tessera."

The Greek word "clinamen" means a swerving, and Bloom uses it to denote the strong son's revisionary movement away from his father's course, accomplished in such a way as to suggest that the father went wrong by not swerving.[83] Chesty Puller's life story reflects his single-minded dedication to the role of the warrior. He was first and foremost a fighter; in fact, one Marine Corps commandant declared that he was "the only man in any of our services who loves fighting."[84] Whereas nonwarriors prefer peace, Chesty considered himself fortunate to be living in a time when he could emulate the military heroes whom he read about and a grandfather who had fought in the Confederate cavalry. For him the warrior band was the primary social unit, and he regarded romance and domesticity as threats to its integrity. He did not marry until the age of thirty-nine, and then only after warning his fiancée that he would have to leave her side at the first beat of the martial drum.[85]

Marine! reproduces some of Chesty's letters to his wife from the front, apparently in an effort to show a complementary side of his character. If that was Davis's intention, the effect is quite the opposite. Stylistically, the letters differ so markedly from his usual manner of speech as to imply a complete disjunction of the warrior and domestic roles. Though Chesty cherished his family more as he approached the end of his career, he never revised his priorities. Taking leave of his fellow marines at a farewell party, he said, "Now, if you're Marine, you're all Marine. You'll put the Corps above your family, your country, even God and all else in some cases" (p. 371).

Lewis, Jr., spent the first years of his life in a household dominated by women and was barely out of college when he met the "raven-haired young woman" with whom he fell in love.[86] He calls himself a "fortunate young man" when recounting how Toddy agreed to marry him and thereafter represents himself as a fortunate husband as well as a fortunate son (p. 52). Lewis was not long in Vietnam before he realized that he did not want to pursue a military career. When the reality of combat became oppressive he spent hours fantasizing sexual liaisons with Toddy. After losing both legs to a booby-trapped howitzer round, he became anxious about his manhood and regarded his infant son as both a heaven-sent confirmation of his marriage and competition for his wife's attention. When he was sufficiently recovered for them to resume their sex life, he was grateful to her for helping him to feel "like a man" again (p. 185).

For Lewis, Jr., manliness was a function of private, domestic commitments rather than public service, and it expressed itself in affection rather than aggression. This departure from his father's values was no doubt partly temperamental, but it was also generational. On the one hand, Lewis, Jr., felt estranged from his college classmates by his decision to enlist in the marines. Later he felt "a generation removed" from the young people his own age who went to Woodstock or graduate school rather than Vietnam (pp. 222, 250). On the other hand, he shared the belief of many in his generation that personal relationships are more important than public responsibilities, a belief fostered by the 1950s ideals of companionate marriage and the nuclear family. What he knew about the circumstances of his father's retirement seemed to vindicate his choice. Having dedicated himself body and soul to the Marine Corps, Chesty Puller was discarded at the age of fifty-seven for reasons that were as much political as they were medical. Even before Lewis, Jr., was wounded, he was determined not to make the same mistake as his father. The son's swerve, as Bloom contends, is meant to reveal the father's flaw.

Closely allied to clinamen in Bloom's revisionary cycle, and constituting its second phase, is tessera. Bloom derives the term from the small fragment of a clay pot used as a token of identification in the ancient mystery cults. In this revision the son seeks to complete the father's work—his clay pot, so to speak—in such a way as to imply that the father did not finish the job. Retaining the father's key terms, he gives them another meaning. For the Pullers, the key terms were "retreat" and "surrender." Chesty was adamantly opposed to both and saw them as symptoms of moral and cultural failure. When ordered to join the retreat from Chosin, he was able to comply only after he had redefined the dishonorable word. "We're not retreating," he told his regiment. "We've about-faced to get at more of those bastards" (p. 6). He repeated this remark to reporters in Hungnam, saying that what looked like a retreat was actually an attack to the rear (p. 322).

Chesty's attitude toward retreat helps to explain his son's devastating guilt over the circumstances of his wounding. As Lewis, Jr., testifies in *Fortunate Son*, he was taking part in a combat assault when he spotted a squad of NVA soldiers running directly toward him. His rifle jammed after one shot, and the enemy returned fire. Turning his back on the NVA, he fled with his radio-telephone operator (RTO) down a trail toward the company command post. He had almost reached it when he tripped the booby trap that vaporized most of both legs, badly damaged both hands, and, in his words, "forever set [him] apart from the rest of humanity" (p. 157). On the medevac chopper to Danang he found the emotional pain as excruciating as the physical: "In my mind, I had spent my last healthy moments in Vietnam running from the enemy. I came to feel that I had failed to prove myself worthy of my father's name, and broken in spirit as well as body, I was going to have to run a different gauntlet" (p. 158). In the years to come he would flee the enemy over and over again in a nightmare that reminded him how he had failed to behave in a manner befitting his father's son (p. 188).

A correspondent for *Newsweek* magazine has cast doubt on Puller's account of his wounding, noting that neither the citation for his Silver Star medal nor a news dispatch filed at the time mentions any enemy soldiers or any exchange of fire before the mine exploded. The man closest to the action, Puller's RTO, likewise remembers neither the NVA nor the rifle fire. The *Newsweek* writer therefore finds it "strange and sad that [Puller] should feel the need to invent a more heroic setting for the defining moment of his life."[87] But if the enemy soldiers are Puller's invention, so is his flight, which hardly reflects credit on him. Both the heroic and the unheroic dimensions of his "defining moment" may have their basis in psychological rather than historical reality. Perhaps in the course of his long recovery he came to accept the nightmare version of events as the truer manifestation of his character.

Whatever happened to Lewis, Jr., that day in Vietnam, one thing is certain: his convalescence and rehabilitation coincided with a period when doubts about U.S. policy in Vietnam made his sacrifice seem increasingly meaningless. Following law school he ventured twice into public service, first as a member of President Ford's Clemency Board, then as an unsuccessful challenger for a seat in Congress. Neither experience encouraged him to pursue a career in government, and the latter took a heavy toll on his family life. Turning to alcohol for solace, he became an alcoholic, then a recovering alcoholic.[88] It was an Alcoholics Anonymous (AA) counselor who taught him the lesson that overturned everything he had learned from his father and the Marine Corps: "Victory is only possible through surrender" (p. 360). Serenity, he realized, lay in admitting that he had been beaten by alcohol, that he was powerless over drink and indeed over many other things, people, and places. These included Vietnam and his performance as a marine platoon leader. "I had not performed as well as my father might have," he had to admit; "but I had done the best I could, and it was time to move on to new challenges" (p. 362).

Lewis, Jr., told his AA counselor that he was planning to write an autobiography in which he would "surrender" the Vietnam War (p. 363).

Fortunate Son is in a sense his white flag, and it concludes with the words, "Often the only way to keep that which we hold most dear is to give it away" (p. 373). Like "victory through surrender," this is an AA slogan. In context it refers to the miniature military medals that Puller presented to visiting Soviet veterans of the war in Afghanistan. But it could just as well refer to the uncompromising legacy of Chesty Puller. Lewis, Jr., tried to hold on to the most precious part of his father by giving away the legend. He "completed" the legacy and in a sense re-affirmed it by redefining its key terms.

It would be gratifying to represent Lewis B. Puller, Jr., as a "strong" son analogous to Bloom's strong poet. But history added one final irony to his story. The marine lieutenant who ran—or dreamed that he ran—to avoid being shot by the North Vietnamese killed himself twenty-six years later, with a bullet to the head. When his father died in 1971, he was devastated by loss of the parent, yet hoped that he would still be able to escape the long shadow of the legend. "I wanted him back," he writes of this ambivalent moment, "and I wanted him gone" (pp. 270, 274).

In Bloom's theory of the revisionary cycle, the strong son must nego-tiate one final phase, called "apophrades," or the return of the dead. Many allow the precursor to return intact at this juncture, thereby im-poverishing themselves, but the strongest make it seem as though the precursor is merely an anticipation of themselves. The son seems then to have fathered his own father. One might account for Lewis's suicide by saying that he was unable to revise the Chesty Puller legend com-pletely, to substitute surrender and intimacy for the warrior's aggression and public leadership. Senator Bob Kerrey, who met Lewis when they were both recuperating in a navy hospital, suggested as much in a eu-logy for his friend. "I wish," he said, "your death could awaken the millions of Americans who chase their fathers' dreams, who are asleep to a life of love and personal commitment to others."[89] But there is risk in waking, too. At the time of Lewis's death, friends reported that he was having marital problems and was planning a divorce.[90] If so, he may have felt betrayed by the personal values that had sustained his swerve away from the public figure who was his father.

VI

Writing in the *New York Times* about Puller's suicide, Catherine S. Manegold observed that, of the many thousands of Vietnam veterans' deaths, some "seem larger than others, as if they could serve as obitu-aries for the war itself."[91] The suicide might be said to typify Vietnam in its wasteful, self-destructive character. If my interpretation of *Fortu-nate Son* is correct, the suicide also dramatized a feeling shared by many of the young men of Lewis, Jr.'s, generation, namely, the sense of being "secondary" or "belated" (Bloom's terms) with respect to the warrior-fathers of World War II. Some of those who did not go to Vietnam wished for a war that they could support as wholeheartedly as their fathers had supported the crusade against fascism, and some of those who went felt like losers in the company of the old crusaders.[92] Either way, they felt diminished or inadequate.

Yet there is another kind of Vietnam war story in which the son feels initially superior to his father because he has the courage either to go to Vietnam or to resist the war. Two narratives of this type, Tobias Wolff's memoir *In Pharoah's Army* (1994) and Walter Howerton's short story "The Persistence of Memory" (1991), represent dramatically different versions of the father-son relationship but engage several of the same issues. Both testify to loss, though neither could be called an "obituary for the war itself." On the contrary, they suggest that those who sur-vived the Vietnam War may live to see a peaceful resolution of the gen-eration war.

Wolff enlisted in the army not from any patriotic motive but because military service was essential to his sense of "legitimacy" as an aspiring author and human being.[93] As an apprentice writer he craved the expe-rience that had qualified Hemingway, Mailer, Irwin Shaw, James Jones, and Erich Maria Remarque as his literary heroes. His swerve toward these father figures was simultaneously a swerve away from his biologi-cal father, whose "unflinching devolution from ace pilot designer to welsher, grifter, convict" appalled him, partly because he saw so much of himself in Arthur Wolff (p. 45). "I didn't want to be like him," the son recalls. "I wanted to be a man of honor" (p. 46). Ordinarily, as Barthes suggests, the father is the Law. In Wolff's case the father was an outlaw, though this did not preclude the Oedipal "dialectic of tender-ness and hatred" of which Barthes speaks.

Wolff was pleasantly surprised to find that he had an aptitude for military life. He thrived on the physical conditioning and even acquired a bantam arrogance that passed for "command presence." These served him well in basic and airborne training and propelled him into the Spe-cial Forces, where, for the first time since enlisting, he began to feel like a fraud. A "corrosive irony" gradually insinuated itself between the sol-

dier who appeared to "know his stuff" and the young man who observed his own performance from a distance, unconvinced. It was then
that he began to lose his personal battle for honor and respectability.

Though Wolff's memoir is subtitled *Memories of the Lost War*, it
never mentions the communist victory in Vietnam. Loss is nonetheless
the book's keynote. From a biblical perspective enlistment in "pharoah's army" is bound to be a losing proposition, and Wolff records one
moral defeat after another. Even before going to Vietnam, he stonewalls
a young woman whom his best friend had gotten pregnant, finishes last
in his class at Officer Candidate School, and bungles a training jump.
Assigned as an adviser to an ARVN artillery battalion in Vietnam, he
fails to elicit respect from the troops whom he was sent to advise. Early
in his tour of duty, he loses face when he must buy a puppy in order to
rescue it from an ARVN stew pot. During a farewell dinner celebrating
the conclusion of his tour, the ARVN soldiers not only satirize his performance but also serve the puppy as a main course.

Wolff's self-esteem erodes as quickly as his "command presence."
Though he cultivated an image of himself as a sympathetic, paternal
figure in his relations with the Vietnamese, he finds himself running
over a pair of bicycles rather than risk an ambush by stopping to help
the owners disentangle them. On impulse he promises a television set
to a Vietnamese woman, then breaks the promise. He allows Vietnamese hooches to be damaged in order to score points against another officer. During the Tet Offensive of 1968 he does not question the strategy
of destroying an entire village to root out guerrillas who took refuge
there.

Wolff acknowledges that he might have come off even worse without
the help of an experienced black NCO, Sergeant Benet. In a clumsy attempt to show his appreciation, he takes Benet to a bar on Tu Do Street.
However, because the bar is located on the white side of the color line
described in Yusef Komunyakaa's poem about Tu Do Street, Benet is
made to feel thoroughly uncomfortable. When Wolff returns to the bar
later that evening to "right the wrong" suffered by his friend, he is further humiliated in his efforts to pick a fight.

More devastating than all of these failures is his confrontation with
his own loss of nerve. His courage is shaken even before he comes to
Vietnam, when he learns of the death of a good friend with whom he
had trained. It is further undermined when he realizes that he lacks the
courage to confess his own incompetence as an officer in the Special
Forces; hence what appears to be an act of bravery—accepting orders

for Vietnam—is to his mind an act of cowardice (p. 8). He is therefore secretly relieved to be given a relatively safe assignment in the Mekong Delta, though it is not without close calls. Once, when a grenade is placed in his jeep but fails to detonate, he loses control of his bowels in Benet's presence.

His most shameful defeat comes toward the end of his tour, when a Foreign Service officer, impressed by Wolff's "impersonation of a cocky young warrior" (p. 141), arranges to have him transferred to a more dangerous assignment. His bluff called, Wolff must squirm ignominiously out of the transfer. His account of this episode ends with a brilliant metonymy. First he imagines taking revenge by crushing under foot a precious Chinese bowl belonging to the Foreign Service officer. Then he protests that he could never bring himself actually to do such a thing, to "take something precious from a man—the pride of his collection, say, or his own pride," and deliberately reduce it to fragments (p. 159).

But Wolff had in fact done something similar to his father. During their last evening together before he went to Vietnam, he maliciously probed for the truth beneath his father's lies. On his return from overseas, his own pride in ruins, he feels a sense of kinship with Arthur Wolff. Rather than return at once to Washington, where most of his family and his fiancée are waiting, he dallies in San Francisco, "morally embarrassed" by the accumulation of his losses in Vietnam (p. 195). When he seeks out his father this time, he finds that they are partners in corruption. "He'd lost his claim to the high ground," Wolff recalls, "and so had I. We could take each other now without any obligation to approve or disapprove or model our virtues" (p. 198). Wolff realizes how easily their new relationship could lapse into cronyism. On one occasion he even addresses his father by a nickname, but because he is unwilling to lose the remnant of fatherly solace that Arthur Wolff represents, he quickly retreats to a more filial role.

It is on this second visit to Manhattan Beach that Wolff finally comprehends his father's attraction to *The Wind in the Willows,* which he had occasionally read to his boys. This time, as Tobias listens to his father reading the part of Toad, he realizes that Arthur *is* Toad of Toad Hall, in all his audacity, shamelessness, and incorrigibility. What is more, his father fully understands his personal complicity in the story.

During the same visit Wolff finds himself in a bar, telling a war story to his date and two male acquaintances. His account of his revenge on a know-it-all fellow officer is familiar to the reader because it is told in a previous chapter. The earlier version is tinged with Wolff's regret at his own cruelty and moral compromise, since in order to shame the officer he allows him to inflict further suffering on an already displaced group of Vietnamese. Retelling the story in the bar, Wolff fumbles for the right tone. The compassionate, regretful tone of the previous telling reflects his honest assessment of his behavior and would impress his date. But it might also be construed as phony and self-serving, "an obscene self-congratulation for the virtue required to see your mistake and own up to it" (p. 208).

Wolff doubtless faced much the same dilemma while writing *In Pharoah's Army*. On this occasion he chooses to pitch the story to one of the men at the table, a fellow veteran who serves as the "third person" of the Freudian joke. He plays up the cruelty of the revenge, going for the easy laugh and in the process disappointing his date. He does not alienate his reader, however, since the cruel version of the story is framed by the compassionate, regretful account of his fall from grace. Here, as elsewhere in his memories of the lost war, Wolff reacts to his younger self in much the same way that his father reacts to Toad's promise to reform, "shaking his head at this transparent subterfuge" (p. 202). Though Wolff undoubtedly lost much that was valuable in Vietnam, he also found something that he needed as a writer. Having sought one kind of literary authority in experience, he discovered another kind in fraud, in the subterfuge endemic to storytelling. He also found common ground with his father, whose stories he could now enjoy without having to commit himself to total belief or disbelief.

The issues of loss, authority, fraud, storytelling, and reconciliation between father and son are likewise woven together in Walter Howerton's "The Persistence of Memory." The narrator of this short story manages to reflect at some length on the significance of his name without ever mentioning it. He would prefer to have the kind of name that encourages familiarity—Jimmy, for example, or Rusty. Instead he shares his father's name, which is "long, cold, formal."[94] Like the names of the Zumwalts and the Pullers, his surname is consonant with "the prefixes and suffixes of authority." The unnamed name thus epitomizes a story that focuses on absence and the father-son relationship to the exclusion of all other social ties.

Since the narrator never recounts his life story in a systematic way, we must infer its major events, though not necessarily their chronological order, from the list his father draws up: "*MY SON: 1) College. 2) Marriage. 3) Fatherhood. 4) Deferment. 5) Divorce. 6) Insanity*" (p. 139).

The narrator never mentions his mother and says next to nothing about his marriage, offspring, or divorce. Much of what he says about his father relates to their disagreement over item four on the list, his decision to seek a deferment from the draft. The father, a veteran of World War II, assumed that his son would follow in his footsteps. Initially, the narrator admits, he requested a deferment merely to avoid conscription; later he came to oppose the war in Vietnam, though he doubts that his opposition accomplished anything.

How or when the narrator becomes "insane" in his father's eyes is left unclear, though he does allude to being hospitalized just before he takes leave of his father, perhaps forever. On this or an earlier occasion they have a physical scuffle that recalls the primal patricide of Freud's *Totem and Taboo*. Since the narrator has grown taller and heavier than his father, he has no trouble parrying the older man's raised hand. Still grasping the hand, he watches as a series of emotions register on his father's face: "Anger, confusion, fear twitched his cheeks and twisted his mouth. But he did not grow old; instead, he looked younger and I was frightened. It was the face a German infantryman might have aimed at on the beach at Anzio or in the hills near Salerno. It was not a veteran's face; it was a recruit's face. It was a foreign and familiar face. His eyes sparkled and died" (p. 147). For a moment the narrator becomes his father's enemy. He also becomes in a sense his father's father, fulfilling the childhood wish uncovered by psychoanalysis.

Yet the root of the conflict between the two men is not primarily Oedipal or even political, though they disagree about the merits of the Vietnam War and the significance of the My Lai massacre. Like Keniston's activist student, the narrator shares his father's values, including, in this case, a fascination with war. He reads everything he can about World War II and Vietnam, goes to see all the movies, studies maps and photographs—all in an effort, as he puts it, to "break the code of war" (p. 149). In sections of the narrative that alternate with his account of his relationship with his father, he demonstrates his mastery of Vietnam war stories by describing in detail what his tour of duty would have been like had he not been deferred.

He remains frustrated, however, because he lacks the key story, the one that his father refuses to tell about his experiences in World War II. The untold story constitutes the major absence in "The Persistence of Memory." It is as though a son who is "strong" in Bloom's sense of the word were trying to revise a precursor text without knowing its content. The narrator shares this frustration with his grandfather, who had

worked as a civilian welder during World War I. The veteran-father refuses to share his experience with the generations on either side of his
own, saying only that his war was unlike anything they have known
through books and movies.

Thus the major source of generational conflict in Howerton's story
is stylistic. "I didn't grow up hating war," the narrator insists; "I only
hated my father's version of it" (p. 143). The discursive forms that come
naturally to the father are the list, the proverb, and the cliché. But the
son wants stories, and he wants them so desperately that after breaking
with his father he joins a group of Vietnam veterans at a storefront
counseling center. One night he tries out a story on them, about setting
an ambush for the Viet Cong. He conjures up the face of one VC in
particular: "It was a recruit's face, I said, a foreign and familiar face. It
was a hard face to kill. . . . He raised his hand. His eyes sparkled and
died" (pp. 149–50). In the guise of a war story, the narrator recounts
the episode of his physical struggle with his father. Though it is mostly
fiction, its core of emotional truth proves so compelling that the authentic veterans gather around the copycat vet to comfort him. The narrator
feels somewhat vindicated, yet still wishes that his father had been
there. This time, presumably, he could not say, "It wasn't like that."

The narrator of "The Persistence of Memory" tells his story some
twenty years after parting from his father, and he realizes that they may
never meet again. The last two paragraphs nevertheless explore the possible grounds for reconciliation. The narrator distinguishes between
history, "what is seen," and memory, "what is said." These correspond
roughly to experience and subterfuge in Wolff's narrative. Between the
two is a space akin to the generation gap, except that it is one in which
"our chronological longings find embraces" (p. 150). Historically, father and son chose different paths when confronted with war, and their
choices led to physical separation. In the realm of history and geogra-
phy no meeting is possible, since the father still waits on a beach at
Anzio during World War II, while the son looks for him in Washington,
D.C., during the 1960s. Each remains entrenched in his defining historical moment, ironically termed the "best years of his life."

Yet in the realm of imagination the son can plausibly maintain that
he is "catching up" with his father, whether or not they actually meet.
He has, after all, told this story, which testifies to the persistence —
which is more than the mere endurance — of memory. If the war story
is a site of conflict, it can also be a site of reconciliation. "It is the
space," as Howerton writes, "in which wars end."

Whereas Wolff made peace with his father shortly after he returned from Vietnam, Howerton's narrator must postpone the armistice indefinitely. What is most remarkable about both stories, however, is that they represent the family, for several decades one of the major battlefields of the Vietnam War, as a place of reconciliation. Nor are they unique in doing so. *Reconciliation Road* (1993) is the title of John Douglas Marshall's nonfictional account of coming to terms with his father and his grandfather, the general and military historian S. L. A. Marshall. Two fine novels, Jayne Anne Phillips's *Machine Dreams* (1984) and Clyde Edgerton's *The Floatplane Notebooks* (1988), likewise represent extended families that are divided by Vietnam but prove in the end sufficiently resilient to embrace both the soldier-veteran and the antiwar activist.

Perhaps this development is not so remarkable after all. According to Freud, "the whole progress of society rests upon the opposition between generations."[95] Yet as he saw it, opposition is merely a phase through which each generation passes on its way to maturity. Beyond a certain age, only the neurotic dwells in family romances rather than confronting the actual father and making peace with him. In this respect the generation war differs from the other domestic conflicts we have considered. Like the wars between the races, the classes, and the sexes, the conflict between generations remains a permanent feature of American cultural life. But in the normal course of human growth each new generation learns to live with the older generation and eventually becomes the older generation. Mere biological progression may therefore explain the more conciliatory tone of recent Vietnam narratives. The gospel story of the Prodigal Son may yet replace Freud's family romance as the paradigm of our fin de siècle war stories.

CHAPTER 6

Toward a Politico-Poetics of the War Story

I

Since 1987 I have occasionally taught an undergraduate course in the literature of the Vietnam War, using some of the works discussed in this study. "Literary Responses to the Vietnam War" poses many of the same pedagogical challenges that I face in my other courses in modern American literature. As in the other courses, I tinker obsessively with the reading list, class format, and writing assignments so as to stimulate critical thinking and keep the devil of monotony at bay. What sets the Vietnam course apart from the others, besides its content, is the nature of my authority in the classroom. Before teaching the course, I had given little thought to this issue. I had earned a doctorate and had published books and articles in my field of study. I had the advantage of being older, not to mention grayer, than virtually all of my students, and the economics of higher education served to bolster my position. Since the students (or more typically their parents) were paying the university for informed instruction and the university was paying me to provide that instruction, I must, according to an admittedly circular logic, have known what I was talking about, even though I had never met Wallace Stevens or visited any of Faulkner's decaying mansions.

My authority in the Vietnam course is of a different kind. In addition to scholarly credentials acquired through research and publication, I have firsthand knowledge of my subject. Following graduation from college in 1968, I embarked on graduate study but was soon drafted,

inducted into the army, and sent to Vietnam. Who knows how this dis-
maying free fall might have ended? I can only say that I was relieved to
hear a parachute pop into place when the in-country orders were issued.
Though I was assigned to the notorious Americal Division, whose infantry alumni include Lieutenant William L. Calley, Jr., and the writer
Tim O'Brien, I somehow landed in the headquarters company in Chu
Lai. There I spent most of my days in a large plywood contraption that
passed for an office. At night we occasionally drew sniper fire while
taking a turn in the guard towers on the perimeter. Rockets and mortars
sometimes sent us scrambling, more asleep than awake, for the sand-
bagged bunkers. Otherwise the tropical heat and boredom were more
relentless enemies than the local Viet Cong.

   That is my war story, or the gist of it. If it lacks high drama, it is at
least representative; in Vietnam there were no fewer than six soldiers in
combat support for each one in a combat unit.[1] But because heavy combat is the norm in both popular and serious treatments of the war, the
"typical" vet is by no means typical in the public mind. To identify oneself as a Vietnam veteran can therefore be misleading, even if duly
qualified. In the classroom it has the further disadvantage of preempt-
ing discussion, since students are reluctant to challenge any experiential
knowledge that is remote from their own. Like savvy poker players,
they are wary of the professor's ace in the hole, the war story that might
trump their opinions or speculations. Rather than risk either effect, I
once taught the Vietnam course without ever mentioning my personal
involvement in the war. But this seemed disingenuous because it left the
students wondering what sort of experience shaped my judgments on
the justice of the war and other issues. In their written evaluations of
the course they said that they wanted to know "where I was coming
from."

   Where indeed? Clearly I had to find some middle ground between a
purely academic relationship to the war literature and an overly privileged and personal one. Through trial and error I hit upon the strategy
described by Barry Kroll in his thoughtful account of teaching a similar
course at Indiana University. Kroll does not allude to his own role in
the war, also in combat support, until the course is well under way. "I
preferred to wait until after the students had read a number of personal
accounts of the war," says Kroll, "so that I could explain that my status
as a veteran gave me *a* view of the war, not *the* view, and that my experience, like those we were reading about in the oral histories and memoirs, was simply another piece of a complex puzzle."[2] Once the students

have read a memoir like Caputo's *A Rumor of War* and articulated their own responses to it, they are less apt to be overawed by my experience, such as it was, or to regard my opinions as the last word in any discussion. There is nevertheless a palpable change in the atmosphere when the students realize that my investment in the subject is not purely academic. A journal entry written by one of Kroll's students could just as well have been written by one of mine: "It was very shocking to me to learn that he is a Vietnam veteran."[3]

I am not uncomfortable with authority, having exercised it—judiciously, I hope—as army sergeant, educator, and father of the two young people to whom this book is dedicated. Yet I am nearly as astonished as my students by the attention one can command with even a marginal relationship to a war that ended for most Americans nearly a quarter of a century ago. A teacher is, among other things, a storyteller. He or she plots a sequence of readings, lectures, and assignments in such a way as to make sense of a subject. Consequently, the teacher's authority is in some ways analogous to the storyteller's. But the teacher has an advantage that is usually denied the writer or filmmaker during the performance of the story, namely, physical presence before a live audience. The authority of the literary or cinematic storyteller must be encoded in the story itself or supplied in another medium—a dust jacket note, for example, or a newspaper interview.

That is my point of departure in this chapter, which is concerned with narrative authority and its encodings in the war story. Authority is a political issue, since it derives from social contracts and the distribution of power in the narrator's community, those with whom the narrator identifies or to whom the story is told. Once that entitlement or "right to tell" is embodied in a book or a film, it becomes available for formal and rhetorical analysis. The politics of a story is thus expressed as a poetics and can only be experienced that way. In the first five chapters of this study, I have examined what might be called the genealogy of our war stories—how specific cultural conflicts gave rise to stories whose form and ideology are mutually implicated.

In this chapter I set the conflicts themselves to one side in order to focus more self-consciously and systematically on the politico-poetics of the stories. My discussion is structured according to a series of basic questions: Who is entitled to tell a war story? How does he or she tell it? Why does he or she tell it? These queries do not frame a comprehensive account of the war story on the scale of Aristotle's poetics of tragedy, especially since my exhibits are drawn almost entirely from the Vietnam War and chiefly from veterans' narratives. But they afford a few toeholds, at least, on a mountain of stories that has been growing steadily since Homer entertained his contemporaries with the *Iliad* and the *Odyssey.*

II

Michael Herr's *Dispatches* opens with one of the shortest war stories ever told: "Patrol went up the mountain. One man came back. He died before he could tell us what happened."[4] To Herr, newly arrived in Vietnam, the story seemed to be missing something. When he dared to ask the storyteller what had happened to the patrol, he elicited only a scornful look in reply. "What happens" in war is presumably the concern of the neophyte. The seasoned veteran cuts directly to the outcome, which is always death. Furthermore, only the dead can tell complete war stories from firsthand experience. In a novel like *Paco's Story* the narrators might command the authority of the dead as well as the language of the living to communicate their experience. But outside fiction those who could tell us about the "end" of war, its existential truth, are unable to do so. For the Vietnam War there are over 58,000 fully qualified storytellers, none of whom will ever tell the story.

Though still alive, the soldier who relates this anecdote to Herr is more qualified than most. As a Lurp on his third tour of duty, he has already been "up the mountain" many times, returning twice as the sole survivor of his unit. Herr's experience of combat, though far less intimate, enables him to get the point of the Lurp's story after a year in country. He comes to understand "that in back of every column of print you read about Vietnam there was a dripping, laughing death-face; it hid there in the newspapers and magazines and held to your television screens for hours after the set was turned off for the night, an after-image that simply wanted to tell you at last what somehow had not been told."[5] The death-face is obscured rather than disclosed by official information sources and conventional journalism.

Those who had glimpsed the death-face in combat were often unable to articulate what they had seen. They were literally *infantry,* as speechless (to recall the root meaning of the word) as very young children. Following the siege of Hue a marine exhorted Herr to "tell it," in effect authorizing him to speak on behalf of those who could not speak for themselves.[6] Not all veterans, however, are willing to delegate this authority, and they signal their reluctance in various ways. Some, like the

Lurp, encode their experience in forms that are too cryptic for easy comprehension. Others hide the experience by placing it in plain view, on the principle of Poe's purloined letter. Thus the narrator's father in Walter Howerton's "The Persistence of Memory" uses clichés like "war is hell" and "I did what had to be done" to avoid sharing the war with his father and son. Tim O'Brien similarly reduces Vietnam to "a few stupid war stories, hackneyed and unprofound" in *Going after Cacciato*. Even the so-called lessons of the war, he continues, "were commonplace. It hurts to be shot. Dead men are heavy. Don't seek trouble, it'll find you soon enough. You hear the shot that gets you. . . .These were hard lessons, true, but they were lessons of ignorance; ignorant men, trite truths."[7]

At this level of generalization, Vietnam is "a war like any war," as both the narrator of *Cacciato* and one of the characters point out.[8] The novel thus endorses John Keegan's observation that wars differ little from one another at the level of human experience, notwithstanding changes in weapons technology.[9] But because *Cacciato* as a whole goes well beyond these commonplaces, one may suspect O'Brien of stonewalling. To tell a war story, especially a painful one, is to surrender a precious part of oneself. One has complete control over the untold story; once the story is told, it becomes partly the property of another. As Paul Ricoeur points out in *Time and Narrative,* no story is complete as configured by the writer or teller. It must also be "refigured" by a reader or listener.[10] In refiguration the reader appropriates some of the author's control over the material. The author may resent this loss of power, especially if the author anticipates a reader with different values or one who has not earned the right to such knowledge through personal sacrifice. In Mailer's *Why Are We in Vietnam?* and Heinemann's *Paco's Story,* we have seen, the narrator's hostility is part of the novel's meaning. In O'Brien's *The Things They Carried,* which I consider later in this chapter, the latent aggression of *Cacciato* takes the more overt form of an unreliable narrator.

In a review of Susan Fromberg Schaeffer's *Buffalo Afternoon* (1989), Nicholas Proffitt observes that this compelling novel announces a new era of Vietnam narratives. It suggests that the "matter" of the war has entered the public domain, becoming a common cultural property like the War of 1812 or the Civil War. One no longer needs to be a combat veteran to write fiction about combat in Vietnam. That license does not extend, however, to nonfictional combat memoirs, which we still expect to be based on firsthand experience. We may admire Schaeffer for her skill at impersonating a combat veteran, yet still pity or despise the "copycat" vets who show up at counseling centers to tell their stories. Furthermore, we expect noncombat memoirs to pay homage to the combat memoir as the norm. This often takes the form of self-deprecating humor, as in Charles Anderson's *Vietnam: The Other War* and David A. Willson's two narratives of life in the rear echelon, *REMF Diary* (1988) and *The REMF Returns* (1992).

But we would be the losers if death and near-death were the sole warrants for telling war stories. War stories would suffer from a deadly sameness, and we would be inclined to applaud the advice offered tongue-in-cheek at the beginning of *Paco's Story:* "War stories are out— one, two, three, and a heave-ho, into the lake you go with all the other alewife scuz and foamy harbor scum."[11] Fortunately, many veterans have exercised the literary realist's traditional license to tell stories about being in a particular place at a particular time, whether or not they feature murder and mayhem. The body of Vietnam war narratives published to date embraces not only the combatants' experience but also that of American doctors, nurses, missionaries, journalists, USO volunteers, entertainers, and civilian officials and workers who spent time in country. It includes stories told by Vietnamese men and women on both sides of the conflict, also by soldiers and civilians from France, England, Australia, New Zealand, Korea, Taiwan, Japan, and several other countries. If the war zone is expanded beyond Vietnam, the stories include those told by all whose lives were touched or whose imaginations were quickened by the war. It is fitting that *Dispatches*, which begins with an endorsement of the knowledge acquired "on the mountain top," should end by asserting that no one was really hors de combat during the war: "Vietnam Vietnam Vietnam, we've all been there."[12]

Herr's mountain top forms the apex of an "authority pyramid" that broadens as one descends from the few (statistically speaking) who died in combat to the many who were only metaphorically in Vietnam. In an appendix to *The Perfect War*, an analysis of American policy and military strategy in Vietnam, James William Gibson discusses another kind of authority pyramid, one that effectively inverts the one I have just described. In Gibson's pyramid those who managed the war, and who were as a rule physically remote from it, proceeded on the assumption that their knowledge was the most complete, inasmuch as all other knowledge funneled into it, usually in documentary form.[13] In this scheme of things, the manager occupies the apex and the combat soldier is demoted to a position closer to the base.

Two passages in Al Santoli's oral history *Everything We Had* offer contrasting views of the managerial pyramid. In the first, a young Hispanic platoon leader recalls a group of officers he saw in a club at the Military Assistance Command-Vietnam (MACV) headquarters near Saigon:

> They're drinking and talking about the old days, when the war was going to end real quickly and people would come out from Washington and sit on a hill and watch the war going on in the distance.
>   This was the war and these were the people who controlled the war. This was MACV. It blew me away.[14]

What "blows him away" is the disparity between his recent experience in the field and the war managers' hilltop perspective on that experience. Only months after the 1968 Tet Offensive brought the war to the threshold of the American Embassy in Saigon, they still behave as though it were a distant spectator event.

In the second passage someone closer to the top of the hill, a CIA case officer, contrasts his vantage point with that of the average infantryman: "I'm grateful that I went to Vietnam in the position I went in because I knew what was going on. I read the cables. When there was a new offensive or a new strategy, I knew what it was and I could relate it to what was happening in the village. But I knew grunts—the poor bastards jumped out of helicopters in hot LZs and didn't even know where the fuck they were except that guys were shooting at them and mortars were coming in and people were dying and screaming." As the CIA officer sees it, proximity to death confers no special authority on the "poor bastards" in the field. On the contrary, it disqualifies them as reliable sources of information. Good information comes from cool heads, is conveyed in documentary form, and can be correlated with other sources of information. The man on the hilltop, whether he is an elected political leader or one of those civilian or military technocrats whom Noam Chomsky called the "new mandarins," knows better than the man in the valley because he knows so much more and knows it dispassionately.[15]

Since the end of the Vietnam War the manager's knowledge has been reproduced, not altogether uncritically, in diplomatic and military histories, which are likewise predicated on the assumption that authority proceeds from a comprehensive review of the evidence. Official documents and memoirs produced by those in the upper echelons enjoy pride of place in these accounts, whereas lower-level personal narratives and fiction are relegated to the category that Gibson, following Foucault, calls "subjugated knowledge."[16] Diplomatic historians generally rely on managerial wisdom, whose procedures resemble their own. They tend to distrust any subjugated knowledge that does not confirm the managers' views.

The dichotomy between managerial and subjugated knowledge persists in versions of the Vietnam War that are passed on to succeeding generations. In 1987 Bill McCloud, a Vietnam veteran and junior high school teacher in Oklahoma, wrote to a group of Americans who had been involved in the war. He asked each of them a single question: "What do you think are the most important things for today's junior high students to understand about the Vietnam War?" He reproduces 128 responses, together with a brief biographical note on each respondent, in *What Should We Tell Our Children about Vietnam?* (1989). Since McCloud's contributors were being asked to speak as authorities on the war, they generally located themselves in whichever pyramid would place them closer to the apex. One can usually predict from the biographical note whether a given respondent will lay claim to managerial or subjugated knowledge. Managers like Richard Armitage, George Bush, Henry Kissinger, Harry McPherson, and Caspar W. Weinberger hold forth on such topics as global politics, the nation's true interests, and arriving at consensus in a democracy.

In contrast, the veterans and their families dwell on the human cost of war, Hollywood distortions of combat, and betrayal by their leaders. Typical of their responses are the following:

War is monotonous and boring, with a few moments of intensity. The reality is that a lot of people go to war, and some don't come back. If they do come back, they come back changed.

If I live to be one hundred years old, the memories of my brother and the horrifying reality of the Vietnam War will always be with me.

There is no way for you to fully understand Vietnam—the feel, the heat, the smell, or the incredible noise—unless you were there.

The war was a shuck, as the saying goes, and the troops in the field understood well enough that we had been "fucked"—to say it bluntly and unmistakably.

Show them the photographic footage that is real. Let them see blood and guts and vomit—and tell them, "This is war—not fun! This could be *you!*"[17]

McCloud's biographical notes, and my use of them, reflect what might be called a commonsense notion of narrative authority; that is to say, a story is deemed credible when told by someone with the right credentials. As poststructuralist critics have pointed out, this understanding of authority is predicated on a metaphysical notion of authorial presence. According to this notion, one reads a given text as though it were the direct speech of a living person.

The poststructuralist critique of presence has value as an antidote to the intentional fallacy, in which the reader labors to decipher "what the author meant" rather than the meanings encoded in the text. Yet this philosophical scruple does not prevent most of us, perverse creatures that we are, from looking beyond the work for clues to its authority. This begins with its packaging. When taking a personal narrative or a novel from the shelf, only the most committed formalist can resist a glance at the author's biographical note or photograph on the jacket. Most of us read the publisher's blurbs and testimonials and try to recall anything we know about the author from reading a review or listening to a radio interview. We ponder the dedication and acknowledgment pages. Whatever our notional commitment to the autonomy of the text, we find it hard not to be seduced by the myth of presence.

Ricoeur suggests how we might allow ourselves to be seduced yet still read with a good conscience. He observes that in their critique of presence deconstructionists restrict themselves to structural questions, ignoring the rhetorical dimension of written and spoken communication. To consider the rhetoric of a text, the means by which it persuades us of its authenticity, is not necessarily to invoke a "real author," the traditional subject of biography. Rather, it is the implied author, the author constituted in the text itself, whose authority is at stake.[18] Ricoeur's implied author has much the same textual status as the narrator of the work, though the two are not identical. For the purposes of this discussion, Ricoeur's distinction directs us to look for evidence of authority in the war stories themselves rather than pursuing elusive "real" authors into the thickets of biography. With this shift in strategy we begin to move from the question of who may tell a war story to how it is told.

III

Because I am interested mainly in war stories that embody subjugated knowledge of the Vietnam War, Gibson's managerial model may seem irrelevant to the narratives under discussion. But few war stories belong exclusively to one model or the other. We might think of the managerial and subjugated knowledge pyramids as superimposed on one another with their apexes pointing in opposite directions. So combined, they form a six-pointed star. The area formed by their overlapping shapes is the ground from which most war stories are told. Obviously, none occupies the apex of those who have experienced war to the bitter end (the dead might narrate a work like *Paco's Story,* but they are not its implied authors) and very few occupy the managerial apex at the opposite end of the figure. In the subjugated knowledge pyramid a war story commands our belief by its attention to physical detail and vernacular speech. It establishes its credibility in the managerial pyramid by using documents and presenting itself as a document.

Let us begin with physical detail as a warrant of authenticity. Since film relies more heavily than literature on a rhetoric of the image, relatively minor inaccuracies of physical detail can fatally compromise its authority. John Wayne's *Green Berets* (1968) is a notorious instance of this, with its closing image of the sun setting in the east. Viewers who had willingly suspended disbelief in its absurdities of plot and characterization were jolted awake by the reminder that these events had, after all, taken place in southern California. Though the television series *China Beach* repeatedly confronted similar problems, it benefited from the likenesses between its ostensible setting, an in-country R & R center on the South China Sea, and its shooting locations in Hawaii and California. In his low-budget film *84 Charlie MoPic* (1989), Patrick Duncan successfully disguised his California locale by cropping close. This tactic worked until the final frames, which are unfortunately intersected by a power line. When *Tour of Duty* premiered on television, it boasted extraordinary realism of setting and battle effects. Yet veterans were quick to point out that the actors carried the old-fashioned egg-shaped grenades rather than the more authentic "baseball" grenades.

The literary equivalent of the visual glitch is an error in terminology. The reader of John Crowther's *Firebase* (1975) begins to question the novel's authenticity when reading about a soldier with the rank of Spec. 3, military units designated Beta through Zoo, and an antipersonnel mine called the jumping jenny. Like previous wars, Vietnam generated its own vocabulary, an argot that combined military terms and acronyms (fire for effect, DEROS), GI slang (Charlie, frag), black vernacular (rip off, get down), and pidgin Vietnamese and French (di-di, dinkydao, boocoo, ti-ti). The play *Tracers* (1986) includes a scene in which the actors recite a litany of words and phrases peculiar to the Vietnam War, as though the language *were* the war.[19] The vocabulary of some Vietnam narratives, including the popular *Dispatches,* baffles the average reader. Most writers either translate unusual terms as they go along or provide a glossary. An author who does neither is making a political statement about the war's remoteness from civilian experience. Eventually the gap will close, as the more hermetic terms are forgotten and the more useful ones absorbed into the common parlance. Much as World War I lives on in the phrase "no man's land," Vietnam will survive in such expressions as "point man," "search and destroy," and "body count."

Perhaps more damaging to a war story's credibility than errors in terminology are lapses in idiom. Richard Currey's *Fatal Light* is proof that Vietnam fiction can be written in a highly poetic style. But a woman who served as a Red Cross worker in Vietnam characterized most war stories when she said that the terrible experiences of soldiers in the field require a "terrible" language.[20] By terrible she meant obscene. Tim O'Brien agrees, going so far as to include obscenity among the essential features of a true war story.[21] As Paul Fussell has observed, this criterion cannot be applied to war stories written before the 1960s and 1970s, when obscenity first became available to the writer.[22] Previous war narratives had to be sanitized in order to be published. Prime-time television continues to operate under the same taboo, so script writers for *Tour of Duty* had to invent a vernacular that was plausibly "down and dirty" without actually being obscene.

If today's literary storyteller enjoys greater latitude in the use of colloquial speech, he or she has a concomitant obligation to get it right. Getting it right entails more than a proliferation of words like "fucking" and "shit." Their placement is crucial. What Fussell has said about the ingenious use of "fucking" in the speech of soldiers in the Great War also applies to Vietnam.[23] The virtuoso was recognized by his skill at inserting the word in unlikely places, especially where it disrupted a conventional phrase or idiom. But there is more to artful placement than syntax, as an excerpt from Tim O'Brien's story "The Man I Killed" illustrates. Contemplating what a grenade has done to the body of a Viet Cong, a soldier says to the killer: "Oh, man, you fuckin' trashed the fucker. . . . You scrambled his sorry self, look at that, you *did,* you laid him out like Shredded fuckin' Wheat."[24] The opening clause, "you fuckin' trashed the fucker," is mildly disruptive in the way "fuckin'" comes between subject and predicate, also in the way the same word serves as adverb and noun: "fuckin' . . . fucker." With the word "scrambled" the comfortable domestic world of the breakfast table is hinted at, then juxtaposed with the world of war in O'Brien's master stroke, "Shredded fuckin' Wheat."

The same collision of disparate worlds is the point of a frequently recounted bit of Vietnam folklore: the veteran is welcomed home with a lavish meal; all goes well until the veteran asks another member of the family, usually the mother, to "please pass the fuckin' salt."[25] On the most obvious level, the joke makes fun of the veteran for a lapse into old habits. "Send guys to war," O'Brien remarks in "How to Tell a True War Story," "they come home talking dirty."[26] On a deeper level, Freud would point out, the joke is told at the family's expense. It consciously rehearses the unconscious aggression of the veteran's original slip of the tongue. The obscenity is an affront to the social milieu of "please pass"; the storyteller and his or her audience, taking the side of the veteran, enjoy the family's discomfort.

Thus the language of the war story, like the language of student protest, has a political dimension. It is "ideologically saturated," as Bakhtin says of the language of the novel. If we associate Bakhtin's "centripetal" discourse with the managerial pyramid and his "centrifugal" discourse with the subjugated knowledge pyramid, we can see what the obscenity of the war story seeks to accomplish. First, it lays claim to narrative authority. It might not be literally accurate to say, as someone has, that all war stories begin with the words "Shit, I was there!"[27] But many use obscenity to reinforce the claim to firsthand knowledge. Second, obscenity challenges any opposing claims to authority that are couched in a centripetal discourse. The most tempting target is the managerial view of the war, whose speech is characterized by euphemism, abstraction, technological jargon, circular reasoning, and willful optimism.

Official euphemism was too common in the Vietnam War and in some cases too well known—"pacification" and "friendly fire" come to mind—to require much comment here. Gibson reproduces a directive issued by MACV showing the correct and incorrect terminology for various operations. Among other things, it stipulates that American troops are never "ambushed"; they "engage the enemy on all sides," a euphemism implying that they initiated contact.[28] Along the same lines, Robert Jay Lifton observes that the names of newly developed weapons were innocuous in proportion to their deadliness.[29] Hence "Puff the Magic Dragon," the hero of a folk song by Peter, Paul, and Mary, became in Vietnam a plane armed with several Gatling guns, each capable of firing six thousand rounds per minute.

Gibson calls Vietnam a "perfect" war because it remained a self-enclosed conceptual system, largely impervious to information that did not corroborate the managers' strategy. Thomas Merton commented on the same phenomenon while the war was still in progress, adding that the perfect war had developed a correspondingly perfect language and logic. Because the managers regarded communism as a fate worse than death, villages had to be destroyed in order to save them. Vietnamese had to be killed because they were better dead than Red. Thus the discourse of the war, which Merton characterized as "narcissistic" and "managerial," reproduced the circular logic of American policy in the late 1960s. The war was "being *fought to vindicate the assumptions upon which it [was] being fought.*"[30]

The premier venue of centripetal-managerial discourse in Vietnam, the showcase of wishful thinking about the war, was the daily news briefing in Saigon, known among correspondents as the Five O'Clock Follies. Derek Maitland, an English journalist, includes an elaborate send-up of the Follies, complete with show girls, in his novel *The Only War We've Got* (1970).[31] Michael Herr adopts the more soldierly strategy of juxtaposing official speech and obscenity. In the following excerpt from *Dispatches,* I have italicized the ideologically charged phrases:

> If a commander told you he thought he had it *pretty well under control* it was like talking to a pessimist. Most would say that they either had it *wrapped up* or *wound down;* "*He's all pissed out, Charlie's all pissed out, booger's shot his whole wad,*" one of them promised me, while in Saigon it would be restructured for briefings, "*He no longer maintains in our view capability to mount, execute or sustain a serious offensive action,*" and a reporter behind me, from The New York Times no less, laughed and said, "*Mount this, Colonel.*" But in the boonies, where they were deprived of all information except what they'd gathered for themselves on either side of the treeline, they'd look around like someone was watching and say, "*I dunno, Charlie's up to something. Slick, slick, that fucker's so slick. Watch!*"[32]

At a discreet distance from the podium, official spokesmen could enlist obscenity in their own discourse. By and large, however, it remained the rhetorical weapon of the soldier in the field, to be used against the managers.

In *The Armies of the Night*, Norman Mailer draws on his memories of the army during World War II to construct an ideological defense of obscenity along Bakhtinian lines. According to Mailer, the enlisted man who calls a pompous officer a "chicken shit" strikes a blow for democracy and also witnesses to the genius of American speech, its "happy play of obscenity upon concept."[33] In his performance at the Ambassador Theater before the 1967 march on the Pentagon, as in his novel *Why Are We in Vietnam?*, Mailer set out to demolish the concepts dear to corporate and technological America. He surmised that the antiwar protesters assembled at the Ambassador, though ostensibly his allies, were ultimately loyal to the concepts behind the war. Consequently, he used the word "shit," sometimes in tandem with a contrasting expression like "bless us all," to make them squirm in their seats.

Mailer's audience may have been a surrogate target for the *New Yorker*, which, in its capacity as guardian of centripetal literary culture, had denied him the right to use the forbidden word in its pages. But the particular word he chose, and the way he used it, provides further insight into the ideology of obscene language. Negatively speaking, it assails conceptual abstraction and managerial authority. Positively, it affirms the value of basic animal functions like procreation and (in this case) the elimination of bodily waste. Shunned and euphemized in polite discourse, these take on new meaning when they might be terminated at any moment by a bullet or an exploding shell. As Paul Bäumer remarks in *All Quiet on the Western Front*, "The soldier is on friendlier terms than other men with his stomach and intestines. Three-quarters of his vocabulary is derived from these regions, and they give an intimate flavour to expressions of his greatest joy as well as of his deepest indignation. It is impossible to express oneself in any other way so clearly and pithily. Our families and our teachers will be shocked when we go home, but here it is the universal language."[34] Obscene language simultaneously punctures all pretense and endorses the pure good of organic process. As such, it is the apt medium of the war story whose authority derives from proximity to death.

Turning from the language of the war story to its use of documents and documentary form, one might begin with Ricoeur's observation that history can be distinguished from fiction by its recourse to documents.[35] Though useful as a point of departure, this distinction often breaks down in practice. Each of the authority pyramids has its own poison pill, its version of the truth sugarcoated in the discourse of the other. On the managerial side, the authors of *The Ugly American* chose to respond in kind to Greene's novel *The Quiet American.* In this way Lederer and Burdick tried to reach not only the managers of American foreign policy whom they regarded as their peers but also a large popular audience. Ultimately, however, they could not sustain Greene's confidence in the fictional medium. They appended a "Factual Epilogue" to *The Ugly American,* assuring the reader that the novel is "based on fact" and naming their sources.[36]

The reverse strategy is more common, inasmuch as the novel has always remained itself—that is, remained novel—by assimilating other genres and discourses. One would be hard-pressed to find a work of Vietnam War fiction that does not appeal to documentary evidence, though the document is usually just as fictitious as the rest of the narrative. The document may even play a central or decisive role in the story. In *Neverlight* the novel's theme is not fully worked out until Katherine Vail finds the fragmentary letter among her husband's personal effects. In *Paco's Story* we are asked to believe that Cathy's diary could, by itself, prompt Paco to leave Boone. Sam Hughes's father has no existence in *In Country* apart from his photograph, letters, and the diary that simultaneously fascinates and repels his daughter. In *Apocalypse Now* Captain Willard finally comprehends the genocidal mania in Kurtz's design when he comes upon Kurtz's typed report and the message scrawled across its cover. Even when subjugated knowledge is expressed in fiction, it often incorporates the kind of evidence valued by managers and diplomatic historians.

By lending its resources to fiction, history is repaying an old debt. As Ricoeur and Hayden White have shown, historiography traditionally relied on fictional modes of narration.[37] Mailer explores the interplay between the two in *Armies,* an early classic of the "new journalism." Since the first section of his book is "the personification of a vision," he calls it a novel; since the second section is based on research in newspaper files and other sources, he calls it a history. Forty pages into the second section, however, he concedes that these labels could just as well be reversed. The first section, to the extent that it adheres scrupulously to the facts as he remembered them, is a document; the second section, despite its use of documentary evidence, relies ultimately on intuition to make sense of the evidence.[38] Hence the book's subtitle as finally formulated: "History as a Novel, The Novel as History."

As Mailer implies, the mere inclusion of documents in a narrative matters less than the rhetorical use to which they are put. Consider the contrasting effects of John M. Del Vecchio's *13th Valley* (1982) and John Clark Pratt's *Laotian Fragments* (1974). Both are identified by their publishers and the Library of Congress as novels, and both make extensive use of documentary evidence. An author's note at the beginning of *The 13th Valley* insists that "This is a novel. The characters and their backgrounds are imaginary."[39] That obligation discharged, Del Vecchio takes extraordinary pains to establish the historical authenticity of his story. An acknowledgments page and "A Note on the Maps" tell of his personal involvement in the combat operation described, specify archival sources, and name the experts he consulted. The book reproduces official military topographic maps and, for each day of the operation, a "Significant Activities" report. A table at the end shows the number of American casualties and enemy losses, including captured weapons and rice. A glossary defines 272 unfamiliar terms, and a chronology surveys Vietnamese history from 2879 B.C. to 1975 A.D. All of this constitutes what scholars call apparatus. The novel itself contains additional documents such as a unit roster, a petition for a divorce, news clippings, popular song lyrics, a song written by an anonymous airborne bard, a medal citation, a dissertation in progress, and numerous letters.

The 13th Valley has its admirers, a couple of whom have compared it favorably to *Moby-Dick*.[40] Both works attempt an encyclopedic treatment of their subject, both manipulate a natural organism (white whale, giant teak tree) for symbolic purposes, and both use empirical fact as a springboard to metaphysical speculation. But the two are poles apart epistemologically. Del Vecchio's book is predicated on the positivist assumption that one can arrive at the truth of an event through the sheer accumulation of factual data, however embellished by the imagination. Though written in the "subjugated" medium of fiction, it sustains the managerial notion of knowledge. In Melville's novel, in contrast, Ishmael arrives at a decidedly unmanagerial conclusion when he has finished anatomizing the sperm whale: "Dissect him how I may, . . . I but go skin deep; I know him not, and never will."[41]

Though Pratt's *Laotian Fragments* resembles *The 13th Valley* in some respects, it is more Melvillean in spirit. The novel is presented as merely an edition of documents relating to Major William Blake, who served

in the Laotian theater of the war. If the major's name fails to set off
warning bells in the reader's mind, the editor's name ought to: he is York
Harding, the would-be expert on Indochina whose books lead Alden
Pyle astray in *The Quiet American*.

Harding acknowledges his debt to expert consultants—whom he cannot name because they requested anonymity—and provides a plausible
"Note on the Text." Otherwise he virtually disappears as narrator except to identify the documents, which include letters, excerpts from a
personal journal, transcribed audio tapes, teletype messages, transcripts
of Senate hearings, newspaper articles, passages from books, memo-
randa, intelligence reports, maps, an award citation, and a manuscript
poem. Though some of these "fragments" are obviously invented, others prompted the air force to classify the novel top secret for months
before it could be cleared for publication.[42] In an epilogue, Harding recounts how he obtained these materials from Blake's widow and justifies his decision to present them without interpretation: "This method
is, after all, the only objective way, even though any selection and arrangement of facts, whether in a newspaper article, a tape recording, or
a private document, inevitably mirrors someone's point of view or state
of mind. . . . For it is only, I am beginning to suspect, by admitting our
inescapable dependence on all known elements of the external world
that we are led finally to what we think we know as truth."[43]

Superficially, this passage echoes the CIA case officer's confidence in
telecables as the repository of objective truth and his belief that the man
who has all the cables has the whole truth. Considering the identities of
the novel's main character and ostensible editor, however, we have reason to ponder the clause preceding "truth" in the final sentence: "what
we think we know as." With that stroke, delivered at the very end of
the book, Pratt nudges his reader toward an abyss of indeterminacy.
We depend on "all known elements" for access to the truth, yet we
can never know them all. Any sense of wholeness, as Pratt remarked
elsewhere, is therefore an illusion.[44] Instead, the reader is invited to construct his or her own narrative, to refigure the story, from the documentary fragments supplied by the "editor." Had Pratt's novel been published after Del Vecchio's rather than before, one would be tempted to read
it as a parody of *The 13th Valley*. In the guise of centripetal discourse,
his novel challenges the very notion of a stable center.

Pratt's radical subversion of the document, and hence of the authority traditionally invested in documents, archives, and monuments, is
carried out in other Vietnam war stories, though not always intention-

ally. Oral histories, for example, have proliferated in part because they foster the illusion of telling the complete, multifaceted truth of the war without the interference of a narrator. Like the movie camera abandoned on the helicopter deck at the end of *84 Charlie MoPic,* they purport to see and record all, including the death of the camera operator. Yet the resulting jumble of discourses sometimes works at cross purposes to the historian's objective. This is most palpable in Mark Baker's *Nam,* which sets out to "bring us closer to the truth than we have come so far."[45] Unlike most oral histories, *Nam* omits even the names of contributors. Plausible as some of the voices in the book are individually, they remain as a group disembodied, anonymous, and sometimes contradictory. Baker's experiment suggests that documents—in this case edited transcripts of taped interviews—lose rhetorical force as they approach the condition of "pure" documents, lacking any trace of an author.

Ward Just noticed this phenomenon while watching news footage of Vietnam on television. "Nothing encouraged me to go on writing about the war more than watching it on television," he remarked. "What I saw on the Sony wasn't a lie, but it wasn't quite the truth, either. It took place, it seemed to me, in a demilitarized zone of the eyeballs."[46] Just, who has written both fiction and nonfiction about Vietnam, believes that "the writer comes closest to the heart of the war, its infinitely still center, when he begins to invent Vietnam." Consequently, he favors the novel as "a form whose success often varies inversely to its cargo of fact." To shift the locus of authority from the eyeballs back to the inventing mind is to enfranchise a multitude of Vietnam War storytellers, some of whom have yet to be born. Their authority derives neither from proximity to death nor from managerial access to documents. Within the ground of our superimposed pyramids, they establish their credentials in the same ways as the other storytellers, through mastery of physical detail, language, and documentary evidence. This is how they establish who they are. At the same time, they must select the mimetic and generic conventions appropriate to their stories.

IV

As Ricoeur observes, plot is the fiction at the heart of all narratives, even those purporting to be true. For Aristotle, plot is not merely a sequence of events. In a serious literary genre like tragedy it is also a form of imitation, specifically "imitation of an action which is whole, complete, and of a certain magnitude."[47] The same can be said of the war story, though this does not distinguish it from other kinds of narrative. The more distinctive features of the war story begin to emerge later, when we turn from its mimetic structure to its aims.

To say that a war story imitates an action is of course to beg the question. What sort of action does it imitate? Does the plot merely reproduce deeds and events in their chronological sequence? This notion of plot as temporal mimesis would certainly fit the many Vietnam war stories that follow a protagonist through his tour of duty or locate Vietnam in the longer span of his life. Or does plot, in keeping with another of its English meanings, reproduce the space ("plot of ground") in which the fighting takes place? If so, a Vietnam war narrative might be mapped so as to reflect the atomic structure of large bases surrounded by expanses of hostile space and the occasional friendly outpost. Or, to shift the emphasis from "action" to "imitate" in Aristotle's definition, does the plot imitate action in the sense of fitting it into a familiar narrative form—the western, romance, detective story, action thriller, science fiction tale, television sitcom, or whatever?

The short answer to these questions is: any or all of the above, depending on the particular story. More than one definition of plot may apply to a single story because, as Barthes has argued, the most realistic narrator never represents reality directly, but always as mediated by codes of representation.[48] Imitations of time and space are therefore as "intertextual" as imitations of discursive genres. One might nevertheless base a useful taxonomy of the Vietnam war story on the temporal, spatial, and generic scheme. Rather than attempt anything so comprehensive here, I will simply show how three of our most compelling Vietnam storytellers—Caputo, Herr, and O'Brien—use these mimetic devices to give form and therefore meaning to their experience. Wherever appropriate, I will indicate how other writers and filmmakers negotiate the same problems.

Caputo's *A Rumor of War* would seem to be a classic example of a story that imitates action as it unfolds in time. In the first chapter he recalls his boyhood in the suburbs of Chicago, enlistment in the marines, and military training. The remaining seventeen chapters recount, more or less in chronological order, a series of assignments leading ultimately to Vietnam and his court-martial for the murder of two Vietnamese civilians. An epilogue describes his return to Saigon in 1975 to report the collapse of the Republic of Vietnam, with a glance back at his brief involvement in the antiwar movement. One senses his earnest-

ness to put things down in the order in which they happened and his
frustration when he is unable to do so. His memory falters for the first
time when he tries to recall the early weeks of his tour: "Because of the
sporadic, confused nature of the fighting, it is impossible to give an or-
derly account of what we did. With one or two exceptions, I have only
disjointed recollections of this period, the spring of 1965. The incidents
I do remember, I remember vividly; but I can come up with no connecting thread to tie events neatly together."[49] Unable to retrieve what he
considers a legitimate plot, a "connecting thread," Caputo fills in the
gap with a series of six discrete episodes from this period. Though set
down in an apparently random order, these trace a progression from
nonvindictive to vindictive incursions into Vietnamese hamlets. Their
theme is stated in the sentence that concludes the series: "We are learning to hate" (p. 104).

Caputo returns to the vignette technique in the final chapter, this
time more artfully. He locates the series strategically between Lance Cor-
poral Crowe's account of his conversation with Le Dung, in which the
boy identifies two of his fellow villagers as Viet Cong, and his decision
to send out a patrol to kidnap the suspects. The episodes are likened to
excerpts from a film and separated by an italicized *Click!*, as though
they are still photographs. Yet these outtakes are not mere documents,
belonging to Ward Just's "demilitarized zone of the eyeballs." Rather,
they record the progressive brutalization of the marines, to the point
where an officer can kill an elderly woman without compunction. Introduced at this juncture in the narrative, they render what follows
almost inevitable. As though to underscore the maddening effects of
the war and the cloistered quality of military justice, Caputo jumps
abruptly from the discovery of Le Dung's body to the office at division
headquarters where, four months later, he is waiting to testify against
Crowe. The intervening period is eventually filled in, but not before
Caputo has made his point—that the murders are unthinkable in a
world of undisturbed sleep, regular hours, and hot meals.

I have saved for last Caputo's subtlest and most significant departure
from mere chronology, one that might be approached through Peter
Brooks's *Reading for the Plot*.[50] Like Harold Bloom, Brooks derives a
theory of reading from Freudian psychoanalysis. His model, however,
is not the Oedipus complex but the "masterplot" of organic life invoked
in *Beyond the Pleasure Principle*. According to Freud, life begins in an
erotic energy that impels the organism toward a restoration of the in-
organic state in death. Along the way, the organism changes in response

to external stimuli but strives, by however circuitous a route, to follow its own course to death. Applying Freud's masterplot to narrative, Brooks argues that stories typically begin in a state of "narrative desire" that is sometimes literally, and always figuratively, erotic. The beginning anticipates and is determined by an end, a death, that is likewise either literal or figurative. In retrospect, then, narrative resembles metaphor, in which one term is transformed into another that is the "same but different." As experienced by the reader, however, a story is a series of linked metonymies. These constitute the "dilatory space" in which narrative desire wards off premature or improper endings so as to arrive at its unique, inevitable conclusion. Desire, delay, and death correspond to the beginning, middle, and end that Aristotle considered essential to "whole" action.

"At the age of twenty-four, I was more prepared for death than I was for life." Thus Caputo opens the first chapter of *Rumor*. He goes on to develop his sense of having outlived his own life, of being older than his father. The end of his story is everywhere implicit in its beginning. Characters are already dead or maimed when first introduced, and the outcome of the war even colors his memory of a full-dress ball celebrating the birthday of the Marine Corps: "I see the hall, crowded with officers in baroque uniforms, filled with fashionably dressed women. Some are dancing; some are filing past a buffet, spearing hors d'oeuvres with toothpicks; some, holding drinks, are engaged in light conversation; all are without forebodings of what awaits them: fear, disfigurement, sudden death, the pain of long separation, widowhood. And I feel that I am looking at a period piece, a tableau of that innocent time before Vietnam" (p. 23). In this and Marian Faye Novak's similar reminiscence of the Quantico Marine Base, one encounters the essence of the Freudian masterplot: the dance of life against the backdrop of death.[51] Here the first and last terms of the story are conflated in a metaphor, the tableau of innocence viewed through the eyes of experience. The rest of *Rumor* develops the metonymies that connect the terms of the metaphor.

Narrative desire has its place along with death in Caputo's memoir. The physical excitement and anticipation of training for war become, in combat, a specifically sexual charge (pp. xv, 254, 278). The arrival of the marines in Danang triggers a mass migration of prostitutes from the south, and Caputo writes appreciatively of time spent with one of them on a Cinderella liberty early in his tour of duty. The eros of this early phase subsides as he becomes immersed in death, fulfilling his role as "officer of the dead" in his dreams as well as his waking life. By the time he comes home from Vietnam, all desire is spent and he faces the future with "an old man's conviction" that it "would hold no further surprises, good or bad" (p. 4).

So far, we have considered what Barthes would call the "proairetic code" in *Rumor*, the way its events are ordered in a narrative sequence.[52] As Brooks points out, Barthes also provides for a "hermeneutic code" that may be mounted on the proairetic code to form the plot of a story. A conspicuous feature of the detective story, the hermeneutic code is concerned with suspense, interpretation, answering questions, and discovering meaning. The hermeneutic code that shapes *Rumor* might be posed as a question: "How could I, and other patriotic, law-abiding, and even religious young Americans like me, be brought to murder innocent people in Vietnam?" After Caputo is charged with the murders, he writes a "turgid essay on front-line conditions" in response to that question, but is persuaded by his lawyer that a court-martial would concern itself only with the facts of the case, not with what Caputo knows to be the truth (pp. 310, 312). For the same reason, the space provided for "Explanatory or Extenuating Circumstances" is left blank on the investigating officer's report. As we have seen, Caputo structures this part of his story in such a way that the proairetic code (the ordering of events) serves a hermeneutic purpose (the meaning of events). One might regard the narrative as a whole as an expansion of his hermeneutic enterprise, as a belated effort to fill in the blank space on the report.

There is yet another, less obvious hermeneutic code embedded in *Rumor*. Though Caputo insists in his prologue that the book is "not a work of the imagination" (p. xx), one is nonetheless struck by its pervasive literariness, a quality that associates his story with the Great War memoirs discussed by Fussell. Its title and epigraph from the Gospel of Matthew are the first of several excerpts from the New Testament. Mottoes to the individual chapters are taken not only from the Bible but also from Hobbes, Hemingway, Howard Fast, the military strategist and historian Jomini, and an Irish ballad. Shakespeare, Siegfried Sassoon, and Wilfred Owen supply several epigraphs each. Caputo occasionally draws attention to the disparity between the world of literature and world of war, as when he surmises that Dylan Thomas would not have written "And Death Shall Have No Dominion" if he had ever been to a war (p. 233). He learns to regard a piece of ground not as landscape, in the manner of the English Romantic poets, but as terrain (p. 21). Generally, however, the literature of the past seems to anticipate his experience, especially Kipling's prescient lines, "A Fool lies here / Who tried to hustle the East" (p. 92).

Literary tradition informs *Rumor* in other ways as well. When Caputo climbs into his bunk to sleep and—wishfully, in view of his terrible night-mares—"perchance not to dream," he invites comparison with Hamlet, perhaps especially in his obsession with death (p. 295). The legacy of the English elegy, particularly Milton's *Lycidas,* Shelley's *Adonais,* and Tennyson's *In Memoriam,* shapes his response to the death of Lieutenant Walter Neville Levy, a classmate from Quantico and one of the two men to whom *Rumor* is dedicated. Like Edward King, Keats, and Arthur Hallam, Levy seemed the youthful epitome of his age. Born to privilege, including family wealth and an Ivy League education, he nevertheless had a well-developed sense of duty to his country. Killed while trying to rescue another soldier, he was truly—so it seems to Caputo as he ponders the GI slang for sudden death in Vietnam—"wasted."

Caputo's elegy for Levy follows a more prosaic reminiscence of a shared adventure at Quantico and is signaled by a shift of pronoun, from "he" to "you." "So much was lost with you," Caputo writes, sounding the "wasted" theme,

> so much talent and intelligence and decency. . . . you embodied the best that was in us. You were a part of us, and a part of us died with you, the small part that was still young, that had not yet grown cynical, grown bitter and old with death. . . . You were faithful. Your country is not. As I write this, eleven years after your death, the country for which you died wishes to forget the war in which you died. . . . It wishes to forget and it has forgotten. But there are a few of us who do remember because of the small things that made us love you—your gestures, the words you spoke, and the way you looked. We loved you for what you were and what you stood for. (pp. 212–13)

As Peter M. Sacks remarks in a study of the English elegy, the elegist frequently uses the form to exorcise self-blame by projecting it onto others.[53] This may be Caputo's case, since the amnesia of which he accuses America has a parallel in his own. The elegy is precipitated by the image of Levy whispering something in his ear. Caputo cannot recall what it was, and he is haunted by the possibility that if he could remember those words he could bring Levy back to life, at least for the reader. In part, then, the elegy—certainly this one and perhaps many others as well—is motivated by that sense of complicity known as "survivor's guilt."

In the passage just quoted, the closing distinction between what Levy was and what he stood for is a feature not only of the elegy but also of another literary type informing *Rumor*—the exemplary biography or autobiography. Plutarch's *Lives* is the classic example of the former, Augustine's *Confessions* of the latter. In such works the individual is regarded either as a model of desirable behavior or as a typical product of his age. Jimmy Carter, the most literary occupant of the Oval Office since Kennedy, seems to have placed *Rumor* in this tradition. At a White House ceremony honoring Vietnam veterans in 1979, he put aside a speech prepared by his staff and asked Caputo for permission to read from his book. In a voice suffused with emotion, he then read the passage quoted above with a variation on the final sentence: "We love you for what you were and what you stood for and we love you for what you are and what you stand for."[54]

If Levy is Caputo's paragon of American manliness, a soldier who stood for the best qualities in his generation, then Caputo himself is more typical. He had the good or bad luck to be present both at the beginning of America's large-scale commitment of troops in 1965 and at the evacuation of Saigon ten years later. He represents himself as someone who initially bought into the "missionary idealism" of the Kennedy era, then shared the disillusion of his peers to the point of joining the antiwar movement (pp. xiv, 325). Charged with the kind of crime that became synonymous with Vietnam, he understands that he is acquitted because, in the eyes of the judges presiding at the court-martial, he is not an individual but a type: "Those other officers saw in me a mirror image of themselves. I was one of them" (p. 313).

It was Caputo's special fate to be one of "them," also one of the starry-eyed children of the early 1960s, one of the angry young men and women of the Nixon years, and ultimately one of us. Caputo's standing as a representative, carefully nurtured in his narrative, helps to make *Rumor* more than the sum of its parts. Other autobiographical narratives of Vietnam that aspire to "exemplary" status are Kovic's *Born on the Fourth of July*, O'Brien's *If I Die in a Combat Zone*, Van Devanter's *Home before Morning*, and Hayslip's *When Heaven and Earth Changed Places*. Of the exemplary biographies, perhaps the most distinguished, and certainly the most ambitious, is Neil Sheehan's *A Bright Shining Lie: John Paul Vann and America in Vietnam*. The book's subtitle reflects the equation developed in the narrative; Vann is America in Vietnam, with all its faults, good intentions, and bravado. Like *Rumor,*

A Bright Shining Lie begins at the end, with Vann's funeral. The story continues beyond Vann's death in a 1972 helicopter crash and concludes, again like *Rumor,* with a brief note on the fall of Saigon. Along the way it amasses a staggering freight of material relating to Vietnamese history and culture, detailed accounts of individual battles, and portraits of many of the major and minor players in the war. Though Vann disappears from the narrative for many pages at a time, he is the connecting thread that ties it together. *A Bright Shining Lie* is what Ricoeur calls "concordant discordance" on an epic scale.

What all of these narratives share, besides their "exemplary" status, is a well-developed sense of irony. Fussell argues that irony is endemic to the war story because it is endemic to war: "Every war is ironic because every war is worse than expected. Every war constitutes an irony of situation because its means are so melodramatically disproportionate to its presumed ends."[55] Fussell invokes Northrop Frye's theory of literary modes to account for the special quality of World War I memoirs. According to Frye, literary modes follow a historical cycle, proceeding from those in which the hero's capacity to act is greater than our own (myth, romance, epic, tragedy), to those in which it is equal to our own (the eighteenth- and nineteenth-century realistic novel) and finally less than our own (the ironic works of moderns like Joyce, Kafka, and Beckett). The cycle then resumes with the "high mimetic" forms of myth, romance, epic, and tragedy.[56]

Fussell's claim that Great War autobiography signals the transition from realism and irony back to myth applies equally to the Vietnam narratives of Caputo.[57] Irony dominates *A Rumor of War* both in the part and in the whole. It is most obvious in specific anecdotes—for example, those about the colonel who orders enemy corpses to be dug up and hosed off so they can be exhibited for a visiting general, or the colonel who removes men from a bunker detail so they can finish his horseshoe pits. But it likewise suffuses Caputo's tone as he ruefully regards the antics of his younger, more innocent self. In hindsight, his capacity to act—at least to act independently and without illusion—is represented as less than our own.

Retracing Frye's cycle, Caputo moved from the ironic mode to the mythic in his novel *Indian Country,* published ten years after *Rumor.* Though his first book had begun as a novel, Caputo shifted to the memoir form when he found that he could not develop a sustained narrative about five-minute firefights. In *Indian Country* he solved the structural problem by taking the war to Michigan's Upper Peninsula and exploiting the resources of myth. The literary allusions in *Rumor* are for the most part explicit and topical. Only when the book is construed as exemplary autobiography does one think of intertexts like Augustine's *Confessions*. In contrast, *Indian Country* is a palimpsest of text and intertext. One is constantly aware of other stories that overlay the action, lending it an extra dimension of meaning and coherence.

Of all narrative patterns, the most elemental is the seasonal cycle. It is the prototype for primitive vegetation myths and rituals and contains Freud's masterplot in the way that a circle contains many arcs. *Indian Country* is divided into four books, according to the four sacred directions of Ojibwa religion. Each is in turn associated with a time of year and a time of life featured in that section of the novel. Thus east is spring and birth; west is autumn and maturity; north is winter, old age, and death; and south is summer and childhood.[58] Christian Starkmann, the protagonist, is the son of a man who personifies winter. He marries a woman named June, who longs for summer and the South.

Ancient fertility rituals mimicked the cycle of the seasons so as to ensure the return of spring and a new growing season. A god or human surrogate was drowned, buried, or dismembered in anticipation of rebirth. *Indian Country* is framed by such episodes. Early in book one, Starkmann deliberately risks his life while fishing. Dragged under by the river's current, he experiences a kind of death before being snatched back into life by his American Indian friend, Bonny George. Starkmann returns to the same river at the end of the novel to perform the ritual that finally absolves him of guilt for his role in Bonny George's death. Having forgiven himself, he throws his military uniform, with medals still attached, into the river; it briefly assumes "the appearance of a drowned man's torso," then sinks. Like a new Adam, Starkmann stands naked on the bank of the river, in a world that looks "as if it had just been created" (p. 419). At this moment his capacity to act is greater than ours, not because of personal qualities but because of his participation in the restorative power of myth.

Elsewhere in *Indian Country* one encounters a version of the myth of death and rebirth specific to Ojibwa culture. As part of his initiation into the brotherhood of priests, the candidate is symbolically killed with a white cowrie shell, then restored to new life as a man of spiritual power. Ojibwa legend and folklore supply other intertexts to the novel's plot, as do biblical, Scandinavian, and classical narratives. These frequently duplicate or echo one another. Thus the bear that mates with a maiden in Finnish folklore is associated with the bear that carries the pack of life to mankind in Ojibwa myth. The bear's pack is in turn associated with the burden of sin carried by Christian in *The Pilgrim's Progress,* and all of these are layered like acetate transparencies over the episode we have already examined, in which June kills a bear while making her rounds as a social worker.

The various intertexts develop themes central to the novel—dreaming, sin and forgiveness, apocalypse. They also converge on the theme of the son's search for a father and the father's search for a son. Throughout the novel, Starkmann seeks a replacement for the father who has disowned him. He finds that father in Wawiekumig (Louis), who is simultaneously looking for someone to replace his dead grandson, Bonny George. Their quest is posed against several mythic antecedents: the New Testament story of the Prodigal Son, an Ojibwa story about a young priest who must cross the sea to find his father, and the *Odyssey.*

The last of these recalls what James Tatum has said of the modern war story and its tellers: "As wars pass from experience into memory, those who survive them, as well as those who come long after them, shape their own discoveries of war into patterns first to be found in Homer."[59] *Indian Country* borrows several patterns from the *Odyssey* in addition to the Telemachy (Telemachos's search for his father), notably the theme of *nostos* or homecoming. Serving as epigraph to the novel is Polyphemos's prayer to Poseidon, asking that Odysseus be punished with years of wandering and return only to "find himself forgotten, unwanted, a stranger." Starkmann does come home at last—"home" is in fact the last word in the novel—but not before he has wandered both physically and mentally. He is occasionally tempted by a siren in the person of his stepdaughter Lisa, and his Penelope spends time with one real suitor, Erickson, and another man to whom Starkmann mistakenly assigns that role. The latter, Eckhardt, easily betters Starkmann in an archery contest, reversing the outcome in Homer, but he also helps the troubled veteran to understand his survivor's guilt by reading him a passage from the *Odyssey.*

What function do these intertexts, these extended narrative echoes, serve in the novel? As Brooks points out, stories always claim implicitly to be going over ground already covered, as reflected in formulaic tags like "I sing" and "I tell." This is the narrative equivalent of repetition in Freud's masterplot, in which the organism, ever the conservative, seeks to repeat the same course of life unless forced by external stimuli to take detours.[60] In *A Rumor of War* the prologue and first chapter leave no doubt in the reader's mind that the book *re*counts events that have already played themselves out; the end is told before the beginning. The intertexts of *Indian Country* serve much the same purpose, supplying "shadow endings" to Christian Starkmann's story. Not all of the endings are benign. In chapter one, for example, Bonny George quotes the witch's apocalyptic prophecy to Odin: "Axe time, sword time, ere the world falls, wind time, *wolf* time, ever shall brother his brother slay" (pp. 29–30). Starkmann seeks unconsciously to fulfill the prophecy, to repeat it, as a way of taking revenge on his father. But when he calls in the air strike that kills Bonny George, he finds that his repetition, though more horrible than any he could have imagined, does not bring repose. Instead, it precipitates twelve more years of repetition in his PTSD symptoms.

The novel therefore plots Starkmann's behavior between 1969 and 1983 against the repressed narrative of the air strike and stories that anticipate his recovery from trauma. His future life will presumably repeat the pattern of the *Odyssey,* Ojibwa initiation rituals, and the death-rebirth myths. He will be reintegrated into life and community in much the same way that his private agonies have been linked, in the telling, to a long tradition of going to war and returning home.

V

In a controversial and now classic essay entitled "Spatial Form in Modern Literature," Joseph Frank draws attention to the prominent role of myth in twentieth-century storytelling, especially in works like Joyce's *Ulysses* and Pound's *Cantos.*[61] Frank argues that myth has the effect of dehistoricizing the novel or poem. The action of a mythically structured work takes place not in linear time but in a realm akin to space. Modernist writers move further in the direction of spatial form by rearranging the temporal sequence of events, often without signaling shifts of time by such conventional devices as the flashback or the flash forward. The reader is thereby forced to suspend the particles of narrative in the "space" of consciousness until the final sentence is read and assimilated to the rest of the story.

Neither of Caputo's books is "spatial" in the manner of, say, Virginia Woolf's *Waves* or William Carlos Williams's *Paterson. A Rumor of War* conscientiously apprises the reader of every departure from strict chronological order. *Indian Country* uses myth to help relieve the pressure of historical contingency, but does so by placing the protagonist's struggle in a larger historic and prehistoric context, even though one cannot specify precisely the "time" of the *Odyssey* or the Norse and Ojibwa myths. For a war story that imitates the space of Vietnam rather than its time, we need to turn from Caputo to Michael Herr's *Dispatches*.

Herr, whose early journalism consisted of "pieces about places," admits that time posed the "biggest technical problem" he faced while reworking previously published material into the book that became *Dispatches*.[62] He solved the problem by plotting his story around a plot of ground. Space literally has the first and last words in Herr's book: "There was a map. . . . we've all been there." Proceeding from the smallest unit of narrative, a word like "there," to the larger unit of the sentence, one encounters a similar resistance to linear time. Especially in the first and last chapters of *Dispatches*, the sentences are often radically paratactic in structure. The following "sentence" has neither an explicit subject nor a main verb: "More a war movie than a Western, Nam paradigm, Vietnam, not a movie, no jive cartoon either where the characters get smacked around and electrocuted and dropped from heights, flattened out and frizzed black and broken like a dish, then up again and whole and back in the game, 'Nobody dies,' as someone said in another movie" (p. 46). These are the words of a narrator who is too breathless, too high on the adrenaline rush of war, to organize his thoughts into grammatically correct and precisely subordinated sentences. In combat things happen all at once, to the correspondent as well as the soldier, and he captures that simultaneity with an artful use of the comma splice.

Sentences like the preceding are bundled into paragraphs and the paragraphs into chapters. Because of their paratactic arrangement, it is not always obvious what links one paragraph to another. One sequence of a dozen paragraphs in the first chapter seems to deal at random with air mobility, the ghosts of the dead on helicopters, remote landing zones, a village recently hit by an air strike, flying over jungle canopy, a tense night at a remote camp, a conversation with a colonel, and a camp in the Mekong Delta (pp. 7–13). Evelyn Cobley observes that Herr usually arranges his episodes in "thematic clusters," and this proves to be the case here.[63] The theme is stated by an anonymous grunt: "Best way's to just keep moving. . . . Just keep moving, stay in motion, you know what I'm saying?" (p. 8). Herr does know, and he knows how to recreate stylistically the illusion of rapid movement by helicopter. His paragraphs are landing zones, and their discontinuity reflects the discontinuity of his experience as a correspondent. Whereas the foot soldier "keeps moving" in linear, earthbound time, the correspondent jumps spatially from one narrative to another, inserting himself vertically into linear time.

The chapters in *Dispatches* are arranged chronologically in the sense that "Breathing In" recounts scenes from the battle of Dak To in the fall of 1967, "Hell Sucks" and "Khe Sanh" report on two theaters of the Tet Offensive in early 1968, "Colleagues" mentions the May 1968 offensive, and "Breathing Out" begins with Herr's return to the States in September. But this chronology remains well in the background of Herr's narrative. The foreground is a potpourri of anecdote, observation, and portraiture loosely assembled around a theme or place. The first and last chapters, "Breathing In" and "Breathing Out," are atemporal in structure, as is "Illumination Rounds." "Hell Sucks," which deals with the Tet Offensive in Hue, and "Khe Sanh" focus on specific pieces of contested ground. "Colleagues" combines elements from all of these into a "movie" about Vietnam, the prose equivalent of a film that Herr assumes will never be made about this "awkward" war (p. 188).

These chapters are gathered into a book with an appropriately journalistic title, one that suggests brief, disconnected communications written under duress and wired to an editor for rewriting and collation with other dispatches. Herr supplies other formal analogues in the course of his story. Reflecting his fascination with the spatial dimension of the war are two maps, the old map of French Indochina he describes at the beginning of "Breathing In" and the *National Geographic* map he mentions toward the end of "Breathing Out" (pp. 3, 255). In this book of "faces and places," even the faces are often represented topographically, beginning with the Vietnamese whose expressions reveal even less than the old map of Indochina and the Lurp whose blue eyes open onto "the floor of an ocean" (pp. 3, 6, 255).

A still better analogue of the book is the collage covering one wall of a helicopter gunner's house in Cholon. Like *Dispatches* as a whole, this metonym seems at first to be composed of disconnected fragments. Images of desire (rock stars, *Playboy* photos, girls holding flowers) alternate with images of death (burning monks, Viet Cong dead, a mushroom cloud). At the end of Herr's description, however, they converge in a striking image of Freud's masterplot, "one large, long figure that began at the bottom with shiny leather boots and rouged knees and ascended in a microskirt, bare breasts, graceful shoulders and a long neck, topped by the burned, blackened face of a dead Vietnamese woman" (pp. 176–77).

The movement from the sexual excitement of combat to the esoteric knowledge of death constitutes one of the plots of *Dispatches.* A related plot traces the movement from "obscuration" to "clean information." But these progressions are foreshortened and repeated in such a way that the reader is denied the sense of *Bildung* or growth essential to the *Bildungsroman.* Not until page 22, following a series of vignettes drawn from the whole span of his tour, does Herr settle into a formula that sounds like the beginning of his story: "Day one, if anything could have penetrated that first innocence." A mere nine pages later he is on the plane back to San Francisco, conscious of having entered that "remote but accessible space where there were no ideas, no emotions, no facts, no proper language, only clean information" (p. 31). Two-thirds of the way through the book, in "Illumination Rounds," he begins all over again: "I was new, brand-new, three days in-country" (p. 167).

Herr begins in medias res not only because this has been the convention for war stories since at least the *Iliad* but also because he realizes how arbitrary, especially in the case of Vietnam, any beginning must be. It was a war that seemed to start over with each change of command and each rotation of troops. As John Paul Vann is said to have remarked, we did not have twelve years' experience in Vietnam; we had one year's experience repeated twelve times over.[64] By retracing the innocence-experience cycle several times in his personal narrative of the war, Herr carries the repetition a step further: it is as though the soldier or correspondent must lose his innocence every day of his tour.

Repetition—as opposed to growth, climax, catharsis, or a light at the end of the tunnel—informs *Dispatches* in a still more fundamental way. Like Caputo in *A Rumor of War,* Herr is consciously *re*telling his story. "This is already a long time ago," he says early in the book, "I can remember the feelings but I can't still have them" (p. 28). Consequently, the space of *Dispatches,* published nine years after Herr left Vietnam, is the metaphorical space of memory as well as the literal space represented on maps. It is the Vietnam that remains after Herr's *National Geographic* map has fallen apart along its fold lines, a country of the mind to which he and his colleagues give the name LZ Loon. The name of an actual landing zone, Loon is apotheosized to include all of "the death space and the life you found inside it" (p. 255). As such, it dissolves the boundaries between *there* and *here,* between Vietnam and the States. From the perspective of LZ Loon Herr wonders, first, whether he had ever gone to Vietnam—"There'd been nothing happening there that hadn't already existed here, coiled up and waiting, back in the World. I hadn't been anywhere" (pp. 250–51)—and then whether he had ever returned to the States—"Out on the street I couldn't tell the Vietnam veterans from the rock and roll veterans" (p. 258).

Dispatches is in some respects a traditional war story. The "Khe Sanh" chapter, in particular, is an extended meditation on what Fussell calls an "irony of situation." The irony begins with the military command's rationale for reinforcing the marine outpost and extends to such details as a shredded flak jacket on the dump, with all but the last month of its owner's tour of duty crossed out (pp. 110–11). As Herr remarks in another part of the chapter, "You always hoped that no irony would attend your passing" (p. 134). Jules Roy's *Battle of Dienbienphu* and Bernard Fall's *Hell in a Very Small Place* supply ironic intertexts for the beleaguered Khe Sanh. Elsewhere Herr finds in rock and roll lyrics—such as Stephen Stills's "For What It's Worth" and Jimi Hendrix's "Are You Experienced?"—the "ambience of mortal irony" that members of the Generation of 1914 found in the poems of Hardy.[65] As in World War I narratives, the irony frequently cycles back to myth. Herr's favorite is the frontier myth, invoked in allusions to the Puritan colonists, the Trail of Tears, Conrad's *Heart of Darkness*, the film western *Fort Apache*, and Slotkin's *Regeneration through Violence*.

The less conventional sections of *Dispatches*, those where spatial plotting replaces the temporal, can be disorienting for some readers. Herr's book may well be one of those that Kathryn Marshall had in mind when she remarked on the difference between World War II narratives and those about Vietnam. The latter failed to give her "any aesthetic pleasure, any sense of the real." "After a while," she says, "the Vietnam War story became so jumbled and ambiguous it was not a narrative at all. It was a kind of nightmare geometry. And it overwhelmed and undermined everything. There was no organizing principle, no discernible narrative line—instead there was a web of stories, each as confused as my life was."[66] Though Marshall begins by remarking on the unreality of Vietnam war stories, she ends by acknowledging their success as mimetic forms: they reflect the confusion of her life during an especially turbulent era.

VI

When Marshall goes on to say that the "nightmare geometry" of Vietnam narratives influenced her own writing, she reminds us that an author seeks to imitate not only time and space but also previous representations of time and space. Stories imitate stories as well as what we call "real life," and in that sense all are intertextual, whether the intertext is Augustine's *Confessions,* the *Odyssey,* one of the "spatial" experiments of modernism and postmodernism, or another specimen of what Barthes calls the "already written real."[67] It follows that listening, reading, and (in the case of film) viewing are likewise intertextual exercises.

Before one can identify a story's formal antecedents, one must first identify its form. The majority of Vietnam war stories adhere to the formulae of mass-market popular fiction, notably the military action thriller and the romance. Others belong to the genres of pornography and the frontier narrative, including the captivity story. R. Lanny and Victor L. Hunter's *Living Dogs and Dead Lions* represents a later evolution of the frontier story, the western. Inasmuch as the detective is a modern descendant of the western hero, the film *Apocalypse Now* appropriately combines western themes with narration (Michael Herr's contribution) that is modeled, as John Hellmann points out, on Raymond Chandler's prose.[68] Two of the books dealing with racial issues, Blyden Jackson's *Operation Burning Candle* and Walter Kempley's *Invaders,* are also, generically speaking, detective fiction. Charles Nelson's *The Boy Who Picked the Bullets Up* is an epistolary novel in the tradition of Richardson's *Pamela,* albeit with a gay protagonist. One collection of Vietnam stories, Jeanne and Jack Dann's *In the Field of Fire,* is devoted entirely to science fiction and fantasy.

Like language itself, genre amounts to an implied contract between writer and reader: the writer or filmmaker promises to deliver a certain kind of satisfaction in the story, and the reader or viewer agrees not to seek a different kind. During its three-year run (1988–1991), the television series *China Beach* provided an object lesson in generic ambiguity. Was it supposed to be serious social drama or soap opera? The script writers never quite decided, though they inclined toward the latter. A typical episode of *China Beach* would lift the veil on a troubling social issue—racial conflict, for example, or American misunderstandings of Vietnamese culture—then retreat into the clichés of daytime television drama. The series offered romantic satisfactions that were all the sweeter for being snatched from a welter of open-ended conflicts. This strategy may have offended women veterans, but it proved so effective in attracting other viewers that the less popular *Tour of Duty,* which ran concurrently and did not shy away from serious social issues, began to introduce romantic subplots into its episodes.

The reader-writer contract can be violated by either party. When Marshall complains that Vietnam narratives failed to give her pleasure, she means that she was looking for a different kind of pleasure; she wanted the stories to sound like those she had read about World War II. In Rabe's *Sticks and Bones,* it is the author who breaks the contract. Having invoked the conventions of the television situation comedy of the 1950s and 1960s, Rabe makes his point by stripping away the "sugary, sentimental veneer" of those conventions.[69]

Of all the Vietnam war stories told to date, Tim O'Brien's collection *The Things They Carried* is the most sophisticated inquiry into the reader-writer contract and the conventions of storytelling. Apart from the narrator, the book's preeminent storyteller is Rat Kiley. In "Sweetheart of the Song Tra Bong" Rat's performance is evaluated by the narrator and another member of the platoon, Mitchell Sanders. The narrator calls Rat's credibility into question even before he begins the story, remarking that Rat liked to "rev up the facts" for greater emotional impact. Yet he concedes that Rat never backed down from the details of this particular story. On the contrary, Rat invokes the ultimate claim to authority: "I *saw* it, man. I was right there."[70] His credibility is further enhanced by the narrator's description of his mood as he tells the story. Rather than consciously "performing," he appears sad, troubled, and edgy. Halfway into the story, he reviews the terms of the narrative contract by asking Mitchell Sanders whether he can guess what happened to Mary Anne Bell the night she failed to return to her boyfriend's bunk. Sanders, recalling what Rat had said previously about the Green Berets, supposes that she is with them because "That's how stories work, man" (p. 112).

As the story proceeds, however, Sanders becomes impatient with Rat on two counts. First, Rat dwells on the hermeneutic code of the story at the expense of the proairetic. "All these digressions," Sanders complains, "they just screw up your story's *sound*. Stick to what happened" (p. 117). Rat sticks more or less to what happened, the proairetic code, until he gets to the scene where he and Mary Anne's boyfriend find her in the Green Berets' hooch, wearing a necklace of human tongues. There he seems about to break off the story, having told everything he knows from personal experience. Sanders is furious:

"You can't do that."
"Do what?"
"Jesus Christ, it's against the *rules,*" Sanders said. "Against human *nature.*

This elaborate story, you can't say, Hey, by the way, I don't know the *ending.* I mean, you got certain obligations." (p. 122)

Though Rat goes on to fulfill his duties as a storyteller, he emphasizes that the ending of his story has a different warrant than its beginning. His conclusion comes from the Green Berets, mediated by another party. The powerful and probably "revved up" closing image of Mary Anne as a jungle predator therefore requires an act of faith on the part of the listener: "If you believed the Greenies . . ." (p. 125).

The dialogue between Rat and Sanders is as crucial to "Sweetheart of the Song Tra Bong" as the dialogue between Mary Anne and the jungle that we considered in chapter four because it determines the rhetorical effect of the latter. "Sweetheart" is typical of *The Things They Carried* in its self-consciousness about narrative credibility and convention. The book alternates between expounding the terms of the reader-writer contract and testing them. When both parties honor the contract, "How to Tell [i.e., narrate] a True War Story" is implicitly also "How to Tell [i.e., recognize] a True War Story."

In the piece just alluded to, Rat Kiley tries his hand at literary (as distinct from oral) narrative. When his best friend Curt Lemon is killed by a booby trap, he writes a long letter to Lemon's sister, recounting Lemon's zany exploits and telling what close friends they were. Read as a love story, Rat's intended form, the letter requires a response from Lemon's sister. She apparently reads the words but misconstrues the convention; she may even be offended by his language or the things that he says about her brother. In any case she fails to respond, and Rat disguises his hurt feelings with obscenity, calling her a "dumb cooze." Toward the end of the story, the narrator applies the same epithet to a woman who listens to his account of Rat shooting a baby water buffalo, because she too fails to recognize the love story behind the rage and gore. In desperation the narrator imagines himself retelling the story with all of the significant "facts" revised or presented as fiction. Perhaps then she will get the point.

By insisting repeatedly on the distinction between "story-truth" and "happening-truth," *The Things They Carried* undercuts the mimetic authority of mere fact and event. Like Pratt's *Laotian Fragments,* it also questions the warrant for documents of all kinds. Readers of "In the Field" are privy to several versions of the letter that Lieutenant Jimmy Cross plans to write to Kiowa's father, explaining the circumstances of Kiowa's death. Were all of them to reach written form, they would be hard to reconcile with one another. Jimmy Cross himself is unable to specify the meaning or the emotional overtones of the documents (to use the term loosely) that he receives from his girlfriend: the letters signed "Love, Martha," two photos, and the pebble sent as an ambiguous "token of her truest feelings for him" ("The Things They Carried," p. 9). When Henry Dobbins's girlfriend sends him a Dear John letter, he must quickly revise the significance of her pantyhose, which he wears around his neck as a talisman, in such a way as to preserve their magical powers ("Stockings").

The most important documents in the book are the brief essays written by the narrator, "Tim O'Brien." In some cases these are interwoven with anecdotes, as in "How to Tell a True War Story"; in other cases they occupy chapters by themselves, as in "Good Form." One is tempted to read these as nonfiction, since they resemble the sort of authorial rumination to be found in the *Paris Review* or the *New York Times Book Review*. Furthermore, the Tim O'Brien who writes them appears identical with the author of the book. He is, as he tells us several times, "forty-three years old, and a writer now." He grew up in Worthington, Minnesota, graduated from Macalester College, served as an infantryman in the I Corps region of Vietnam, and wrote the books *If I Die in a Combat Zone* and *Going after Cacciato*. Yet in other respects the "Tim O'Brien" who narrates *Things*, including the "nonfictional" parts, is a fictional creation of the author. "Tim O'Brien" has a daughter named Kathleen with whom he returned to Vietnam in the late 1980s. Tim O'Brien, we know from other sources, has no daughter; he returned to Vietnam for the first time in 1994 with a friend named Kate.[71]

O'Brien apparently had several reasons for creating a narrator in his near-likeness. He claims that by giving his own name to the narrator, he was able to tap into feelings and memories that were otherwise inaccessible.[72] He was also intrigued by the literary possibilities of reversing the procedure of "new journalists" like Norman Mailer by importing fact—that is, documentation—into fiction.[73] This strategy allows him to engage in a sometimes exasperating but ultimately productive struggle with the reader. The struggle begins even before the first story, with the disclaimer, acknowledgment, and dedication pages. It is presumably the author who writes the disclaimer ("This is a work of fiction. Except for a few details regarding the author's own life, all the incidents, names, and characters are imaginary") and the acknowledgments.[74] But if the characters are all imaginary, why is the book dedicated to a half-dozen of them? Conventionally, dedications are nonfiction and the work of the author, even when they introduce works of fiction. Here, however, the dedication is the work of the fictional narrator, "Tim O'Brien." As such, it signals our entry into a realm where narrative conventions have to be renegotiated.

This renegotiation is, on one level, the plot of *The Things They Carried*. As Brooks points out, "plot" has an insidious meaning—denoting a secret, often evil scheme—that can be an aspect of the literary meaning as well.[75] This is certainly the case in *Things*, where the narrator appears to be playing much the same kind of game with the reader that he plays with the woman in "How to Tell a True War Story." He invites an uncritical response to a story, then mockingly withdraws the grounds of that response. "How to Tell," for instance, begins with the assertion "This is true" and ends with "None of it happened" (pp. 75, 91). In "The Man I Killed" the narrator tells in great detail how he felt after killing a young Viet Cong with a grenade; he also alludes to the episode in several other stories and essay-like passages. Yet this does not prevent him from revising the story twice in "Good Form." First he says that most of the details in the first version are correct, but it was someone else who killed the young man. "But listen," he says then. "Even *that* story is made up" (p. 203). Actually, there were many dead bodies, men he had not killed and refused even to look at. Is it safe to believe this version, after being taken in by two others? One has cause to reserve judgment, especially since the chapter ends with an exchange between the narrator and his fictitious daughter.

In the context of *The Things They Carried* as a whole, "The Man I Killed" invites us to reassess not only the nature of narrative authority and the kind of truth to be found in stories but also our Aristotelian assurance that we can identify beginnings and endings. Where does "The Man I Killed" begin—on the first page of the story, or in a snatch of dialogue that appears a hundred pages earlier (p. 40)? Does it end on the last page of the story or in an allusion a hundred pages later, at the beginning of another story (p. 255)?

O'Brien mounts his most sustained assault on our conventional notions of closure in the sequence of stories dealing with Kiowa's death in a field of human waste, a paddy that the villagers use as a toilet. The first, "Speaking of Courage," is a literary exhibit, a model of the well-wrought short story typically found in classroom anthologies. Students would be cajoled or impressed into admiring the symmetries of the piece: Norman Bowker, a veteran of Vietnam, unable to tell his war story to his father, who is equally reticent about *his* war; the flares and mortars of Vietnam versus the fireworks of a small-town Fourth of July celebration; an Iowa lake with algae bloom juxtaposed against the muddy Song Tra Bong River; a drive-in intercom that sounds like a military field radio. Like Bowker's Chevy in its revolutions around the lake, the narrative traces a circle that neatly contains all of its parts.

In the very next chapter, however, the symmetry comes undone. "Tim O'Brien" tells how one letter from Bowker prompted him to write the story and how another prompted him to rewrite it in a manner more in keeping with "the full and exact truth about our night in the shit field." Bowker serves as "O'Brien's" literary conscience, playing Mitchell Sanders to his Rat Kiley. The last four sentences of "Notes" nevertheless imply that even this version of the truth is neither full nor exact: "In the interests of truth . . . I want to make it clear that Norman Bowker was in no way responsible for what happened to Kiowa. Norman did not experience a failure of nerve that night. He did not freeze up or lose the Silver Star for valor. That part of the story is my own" (p. 182). The phrase "my own" is tantalizing but ambiguous. Does it mean "something I made up" or "about me"?

Both meanings apply, as it turns out: the narrator projected onto Bowker his own feelings of complicity in Kiowa's death. As the story is revised in "In the Field," Bowker finds Kiowa's body but is not the one who allows his friend to sink beneath the ooze and suffocate. The guilty party—to use a phrase that becomes problematic in a story where everyone and no one is finally guilty—is a character described simply as "the young soldier." It was he who had turned on his flashlight just before the mortar round struck, to show Kiowa a photograph of his girlfriend. Rationally speaking, this breach of light discipline had nothing to do with Kiowa's death, since a mortar cannot be aimed so quickly or accurately. But the young soldier still feels guilty according to a *post hoc propter hoc* logic. Though he is never identified—even Lieutenant Jimmy Cross, who prides himself in treating his men as individuals, cannot remember his name—circumstantial evidence suggests that he is the narrator. The passage describing the young soldier's "tug-of-war" with Kiowa's boot duplicates the one featuring Bowker in "Speaking of Courage," and in the final chapter of *Things* the narrator says, "I watched my friend Kiowa sink into the muck along the Song Tra Bong" (pp. 193, 168, 270).

The match between the narrator and the young soldier is imperfect, since "Tim O'Brien" is represented as older and more sophisticated than the kid with a girlfriend (former girlfriend, really) named

Billie. Yet we infer that guilt motivates his return to the waste field with his daughter twenty years later, looking for "signs of forgiveness or personal grace or whatever else the land might offer" (p. 207). As told in "Field Trip," the narrator's story of his postwar adjustment differs considerably from that in "Notes." In the earlier chapter, he contrasts Bowker's anguish and aimlessness with his own graceful transition from Vietnam to Harvard and a successful career as a writer (p. 179). But in "Field Trip" he speaks of an emotional numbness and loss of direction dating from Kiowa's death (p. 210). His ritual of expiation, burying Kiowa's hatchet, does elicit the forgiveness he seeks. "In a way," he muses, "maybe, I'd gone under with Kiowa, and now after two decades I'd finally worked my way out" (p. 212).[76]

The "Speaking of Courage" sequence, like the stories linked to "The Man I Killed," forces us to confront the arbitrariness of story endings. For Aristotle a satisfactory ending is one that "follows something else but nothing follows it."[77] Though it is hard to imagine a war story in which nothing truly "follows" in the way of personal and social consequences, Aristotle praises Homer for selecting episodes from the Trojan War that could be manageably plotted. Vietnam storytellers are faced with the same problem of selecting what, in Henry James's phrase, "hangs together."[78] Even as they contrive endings, they sometimes cannot resist drawing attention to the deus ex machina. Thus Fowler, at the conclusion of Greene's *Quiet American,* is amused at Phuong's fondness for films with happy endings. At the level of action, his own story falls almost too neatly into place. What saves it (and thereby the novel) from sentimentality is his awareness of the many emotional loose ends in his life and perhaps also in Phuong's. Mason's *In Country* similarly criticizes the nostalgia for happy or socially redemptive endings, whether in movies or in real life. Sam Hughes's grandmother, for example, recalls hearing about a woman who, like herself, had lost a son in Vietnam. Ten years later the dead boy's buddy contacted the mother and initiated a relationship that "was like having a son again."[79] Here the dramatic situation ironizes the sentiment: Mamaw tells this "sweet story" (her phrase) in a restaurant while trying to decide which dessert to order.

Like Greene and Mason, O'Brien distrusts narrative closure because it violates our experience of life. In a novel published after *The Things They Carried,* entitled *In the Lake of the Woods* (1994), he offers several hypotheses regarding the disappearance of the two main characters but no definitive answers. He refuses to solve the mystery because, he asserts in a footnote, "truth won't allow it. Because there *is* no end, happy or otherwise. Nothing is fixed, nothing is solved."[80] Perhaps for that reason O'Brien takes a step beyond Greene and Mason in *Things*, showing how the "happy" or "sweet" or otherwise gratifying conclusion can be reopened at will. This strategy is especially appropriate for stories about a war whose ending is no less in doubt than its beginning. Was it over in 1973, when the last American troops were withdrawn from Vietnam? In 1975, when South Vietnam fell to the North? In 1991, when President Bush declared that the United States had "kicked the Vietnam syndrome once and for all" with its victory in the Persian Gulf? In 1995, when President Clinton extended full diplomatic recognition to the government in Hanoi? Or will the war last as long as there are people whose lives have been affected by it?

In the process of challenging narrative closure, O'Brien also invites us to examine the kind of confidence we invest in storytellers. We are at the mercy of an unreliable narrator in *The Things They Carried*, if by "unreliable" we mean a storyteller who refuses to give us a single, consistent version of events. Yet the experience of listening to "Tim O'Brien" can be productive as well as exasperating if we reflect on how his unreliability affects us.

As I suggested above, the Vietnam storyteller may be trying, at least unconsciously, to settle an old score with the reader. We recall Larry Heinemann's avowed purpose in writing novels about the war: "It's more polite than a simple fuck you."[81] At the end of the "Stepping Lightly" chapter of *If I Die in a Combat Zone*, O'Brien sarcastically invites any hawkish patriots who have picked up his memoir to take a family vacation in Vietnam, where they may still encounter some unexploded mines.[82] Unreliability is a subtler form of revenge, better suited to the reader whose sole transgression is not to have faced the same difficult choices and experiences as the author. Stepping lightly through the minefield of the text, the reader risks not mortal injury but the mocking epithet "dumb cooze." Occasionally the reader is drawn into "Tim O'Brien's" agony in *The Things They Carried*, for example when he must decide whether to evade the draft by jumping out of a boat and swimming to Canada. "Even now, as I write this," the narrator says,

> I can still feel that tightness [in my chest]. And I want you to feel it—the wind coming off the river, the waves, the silence, the wooded frontier. You're at the bow of a boat on the Rainy River. You're twenty-one years old, you're scared, and there's a hard squeezing pressure in your chest.
>
> What would you do?
>
> Would you jump? Would you feel pity for yourself? Would you think

about your family and your childhood and your dreams and all you're leaving
behind? Would it hurt? Would it feel like dying? Would you cry, as I did? (p.
59)

Here, as elsewhere, the narrator is willing to acknowledge his fear, self-
pity, and even cowardice. But he refuses to allow the reader to remain
self-righteously aloof. His unreliability is a form of guerrilla warfare
with the reader, so that his war story is also a story-at-war.

Ricoeur likewise uses the metaphor of combat, as opposed to the
"trusting voyage" of traditional storytelling, to characterize the unreliable narrator's relationship with the reader.[83] According to Ricoeur, unreliability serves an important rhetorical purpose. "The unreliable narrator," he writes, "is one element in the strategy of illusion-breaking
that illusion-making requires as its antidote." Deployed skillfully, the
device of the unreliable narrator places the reader at an ideal distance
from the text, one in which "the illusion is, by turns, irresistible and
untenable." A story that is at once irresistible and untenable conduces
not only to the reader's aesthetic gratification once the reader has acquired a taste for this kind of story, but also to his or her moral and
political education.

Though it may seem odd to speak of sustaining and even remaking
illusion, this is one of the effects of unreliable narration in *The Things
They Carried*. The book locates truth neither in empirical personal experience nor in documentation. Implicitly, it also challenges Michael
Riffaterre's notion that fictional truth is merely a function of linguistic
self-consistency or tautology.[84] The authority of *Things* derives, rather,
from the author's skill at creating powerful illusions and the reader's
willingness to suspend disbelief, if only for the duration of the story.
O'Brien supplies the reader with a field guide to the war story in "How
to Tell a True War Story," which lists the structural and linguistic qualities of the genre and supplies illustrations. But he ultimately defines the
true war story, much as Aristotle defined tragedy, according to its effect
on the listener. Whether or not it recounts historically verifiable events,
whether or not it is self-consistent, the true war story "makes the stomach believe" (p. 84). If the listener can summon the detachment to ask
whether it is really true, it is not true in a way that O'Brien considers
meaningful. But no sooner does the stomach believe than the brain is
engaged and the once irresistible story becomes untenable. In *Things* as
in every sphere of "real" life, illusions are continually being sustained
and discredited, remade and rebroken.

VII

In considering the effect of reopened stories and unreliable narration in *The Things They Carried*, we have moved beyond the question of technique, the how of the war story, to the question of purpose, the why of the war story. In this section I proceed from the storyteller's private aims to the social, political, and moral functions of the war story. This discussion, which is necessarily more suggestive than comprehensive, brings us full circle back to ideological issues explored in the first five chapters.

It also suggests some of the more distinctive features of the war story. When Michael Herr says that war stories are simply stories about people and Tim O'Brien adds that they are never really about war, they remind us that war stories are not entirely different from other stories, even in their aims.[85] Like other stories, they are told to inform, to persuade, and occasionally even to amuse. Often they are told to make money. But some purposes are more specific to the war story, and these are the ones I emphasize here.

War stories often recount events that the storyteller finds painful to remember. Few people would subject themselves to anything so unpleasant unless the narrative process offered some kind of pleasure or at least relief from pain. Such was Freud's reasoning when he considered the trauma neuroses of World War I. He speculated that war veterans and other trauma victims rehearse their painful experiences in dreams as a way of gaining mastery over them. In this respect they resemble the child whom he had observed performing imaginary rituals to "control" the departures and returns of his mother. In *Beyond the Pleasure Principle* Freud uses this preliminary insight to set up a more elaborate analysis of the ways in which the death wish collaborates with the life wish in organic and psychic life.

Recent studies of post-traumatic stress disorder and programs for treating trauma victims follow Freud's account in broad outline. In *Trauma and Recovery* (1992), Judith Lewis Herman identifies three stages of recovery to be found in most therapeutic programs for PTSD: safety, remembrance and mourning, and reconnection. In the first, the trauma victim finds a supportive social setting in which to recall the traumatic event. In the second, the victim weaves the traumatic memory into his or her personal history, then repeats the narrative until it is no longer so emotionally charged. In the third stage, the victim constructs a future with a new self, new relationships, and new beliefs.

For a theory of storytelling, Herman's second stage is the most pertinent of the three. Traumatic memories, she observes, "lack verbal narrative and context; rather, they are encoded in the form of vivid sensations and images."[86] They are not narrative but what another therapist calls "prenarrative."[87] Influenced by popular representations of trauma, PTSD victims often expect to achieve a cathartic cure when they finally overcome amnesia and confront the traumatic memory. They would find some encouragement for this view in Vietnam war fiction, where such catharsis is often the culmination of the story—the point at which Emmett decides to make his pilgrimage to the Wall in Mason's *In Country*, let us say, or Starkmann to seek Wawiekumig's forgiveness in *Indian Country*. But in real life this is only the first step on the road to recovery. The traumatic memory is often fragmentary and needs to be revised as more of the experience is recalled. It may be obsessively repeated, not only in dreams but also in waking thoughts and even behavior.[88] Ultimately, the traumatic memory must be woven into "an organized, detailed, verbal account, oriented in time and historical context" and informed by the storyteller's feelings.[89] Pain, in short, must be assimilated into the masterplot of life.

One hesitates to apply a therapeutic model to storytelling, even in the case of war stories and even when trying to specify their most intimate purpose. To do so is to suggest that a war story is the pathological symptom of a victim rather than the consciously crafted work of an artist. For this reason the veteran-poet Bruce Weigl emphatically rejects the notion that his writing is therapeutic.[90] Larry Heinemann concedes that his first attempts did serve a therapeutic purpose, but adds that by the time he wrote *Paco's Story* his work "was not catharsis in the least."[91] The narrator of *The Things They Carried* insists that therapy is not one of his motives, even though he has been talking "virtually nonstop" about the war for twenty years. Rather, he regards his writing as a way to "objectify" his experience (p. 179). This may, of course, amount to the same thing. Herman cites the "objectifications" in *Things* to illustrate her procedures, and O'Brien repays the compliment in *In the Lake of the Woods*, where he reproduces several excerpts from *Trauma and Recovery*.

Certainly there are parallels between war stories told in a therapeutic setting and those communicated in other settings and media. One oral historian has compared the process of interviewing Vietnam veterans to psychotherapy, notwithstanding their different aims. Like the therapist, the interviewer must establish a setting in which the veteran feels secure enough to tell the story.[92] If the notions of "safety" and "setting" are expanded to include sociopolitical context, we have a working model for all modes of storytelling about war. As Herman points out, trauma can be recalled only in a social milieu that affirms and protects the victim.[93] Only when America was ready to confront the repressed trauma of Vietnam could individual storytellers proceed with the work of memory, mourning, and finally reconnection.

But this is to anticipate the public purposes of the war story. Among its more private aims we might include scapegoating and self-justification. Many stories attempt to complete one or more of the following propositions: "The war was caused by—"; "We lost the war because—"; "I would have behaved better if—"; "I predicted the outcome of that policy as early as—"; "Subsequent events have vindicated my decision to—." It would be hard to find a Vietnam story that does not entail some form of apology or special pleading, especially among stories that align themselves on one side or the other of the cultural conflicts discussed in this book. Stories of wish fulfillment, such as the *Rambo* and *Missing in Action* films, play out the scenarios implicit in these accusations and regrets: "This is how it might have been, or could still be, if only—." These unproductive and potentially dangerous stories recall the fantasies of trauma victims, in which they alter the outcome of the traumatic event or take revenge on the perpetrator.[94]

Considering how painful the Vietnam era was for many who came of age then, one hesitates to include nostalgia among the motives for telling war stories. Yet many of the books and films dwell at some length and with great affection on the artifacts of the 1950s and 1960s, particularly the music. Kovic devotes most of a chapter to these in *Born on the Fourth of July* and concludes the book with memories of the hula hoop, the twist, Mickey Mantle, and Del Shannon's song "Runaway." "I remember," Kovic writes of a day when he listened carefully to the lyrics of the song, "it was a beautiful spring day and we were young back then and really alive and the air smelled fresh."[95] "Back then" was a slightly different period for each soldier in a war that stretched over a decade, but for each it acquired the pastoral glow of the summer of 1914 in Great War memoirs.[96]

For many, the age of innocence ended with direct involvement in the war. For Herr and others, however, Vietnam was the equivalent of a "happy childhood." In 1969, the year after he returned to the States and the year before his thirtieth birthday, Herr mused, "Maybe it was my twenties I was missing and not the Sixties, but I began missing them both before either had really been played out" (p. 259). Fred Reed, a marine veteran, concurs: "To many of us there, the war was the best time of our lives, almost the only time. We loved it because in those days we were alive, life was intense."[97] As members of the Vietnam generation move through middle age and beyond, they find it harder to ignore the Freudian masterplot governing their own lives. By telling war stories they scrawl a "Kilroy was here" on life. They also expand the "dilatory space" of the life narrative, constructing elaborate detours of desire even as they acknowledge the inevitable destination. Like *The Thousand and One Nights*, war stories are a desperate gambit, the organism's way of fending off premature closure.

It was death, paradoxically, that inspired the liveliness of Scheherezade's stories. They were motivated and are still haunted by the ghosts of her less successful predecessors. This suggests another purpose of the Vietnam war story: to memorialize the dead, including the storyteller's dead selves. Books such as *A Rumor of War* and *Born on the Fourth of July* do both simultaneously, though Caputo's book is chiefly an elegy for the two soldiers to whom it is dedicated and Kovic's chiefly a memorial to the "Yankee Doodle Dandy" self of his boyhood.

O'Brien gives equal weight to the two in the poignant final chapter of *The Things They Carried*. Entitled "The Lives of the Dead," it opens with a ritual in which the soldiers of Alpha Company shake hands with the corpse of an old Vietnamese man. Though the narrator refuses to take part, he cannot help thinking of a childhood friend who had died of a brain tumor. His storytelling is a less macabre way of shaking hands with a corpse. Like the soldiers, he is trying to bring the dead back to life, including his friend Linda and several of the men whom he had known in Vietnam—Kiowa, Curt Lemon, and Ted Lavender. Another casualty of the war is his "Timmy" self, the boy who was once young, happy, and convinced of his immortality. Even as he goes about "saving" these lives in his stories, he realizes that he cannot do so unassisted. Being dead, Linda tells him, is like being inside a book that no one is reading. Resurrection requires readerly assent and participation, Ricoeur's "refiguration."

Even as war stories try to forestall the end and bring the dead back to life, they implicitly acknowledge that some losses are irretrievable. In this way they carry out what Freud calls the "work of mourning." Mourning, as he uses the term, is a reaction to "the loss of a loved person, or to the loss of some abstraction which has taken the place of one, such as one's country, liberty, an ideal, and so on."[98] He distinguishes mourning from melancholia, in which the object has not actually died except as an object of love. "In mourning it is the world which has become poor and empty," whereas "in melancholia it is the ego itself."[99] The melancholic self feels impoverished because it invested libido in an object that proved itself unworthy.

Mourning and melancholia often overlap in Vietnam stories, where the loss of a particular loved one parallels or precipitates the loss of faith in a certain ideal of America. History supplied a perfect allegory of personal and cultural loss in the assassination of John F. Kennedy, which may explain why it is so often mentioned in the war literature. The *China Beach* television series similarly allegorized the 1968 Tet Offensive by killing off Cherry White (played by Nan Woods), the aptly named USO volunteer who personified the innocent America of the early 1960s. To many, the Vietnam Veterans Memorial Wall in Washington represents the convergence of mourning and melancholia. The names engraved in the polished black granite signify particular men and women, mourned by relatives and friends. The monument as a whole stands for something that was lost in the course of the war—even though, as Freud remarks of some cases of melancholia, "one cannot see clearly what it is that has been lost."[100] Confronting the wall, one sees first the names, then reflected images of the mall, then oneself as onlooker. Mourning gives way to melancholia as one plunges more deeply into the abysses of black stone.

With mourning and especially with melancholia, we move from the more private reasons for telling war stories to the more public. Jean Bethke Elshtain maintains that wars are creative as well as destructive, since they shape "the people" as a social unit. When a people make war, the war makes them. In that sense, Elshtain says, societies are "the sum total of their 'war stories.'"[101] What did Vietnam make us, to judge from our war stories? As this study indicates, the war did not make us anything we had not been before. It merely intensified the civil wars already raging in American society, some of which—the frontier and race wars, for example—have defined us as a people from the very beginning. In *The Republic* Plato calls this kind of warfare *stasis* to distinguish it from the *polemos* of war against a foreign enemy.[102] With its overtones of settled opposition and deadlock, *stasis* is an apt term for conflicts that have remained unresolved since the seventeenth century and are perhaps unresolvable.

But our war stories also suggest, by their tone as much as their content, that Vietnam made us a more skeptical people or restored us to our original skepticism. The nation's founding documents—the Declaration of Independence, the Constitution, the Bill of Rights (the Tenth Amendment in particular)—were drafted by skeptical men who sought to halt the drift of authority toward the apex of the managerial pyramid. The early 1960s was a far less skeptical era, a time when people were disposed to trust the judgment and good faith of an enlightened minority, Chomsky's "new mandarins," who derived their authority from the top of the pyramid rather than from the *Lumpen* at its base.

The war eroded our confidence in the mandarins and, by extension, in government itself. In a recent memoir of the war years, Robert S. McNamara, who served as the secretary of defense under Presidents Kennedy and Johnson, admits that the Vietnam policy of both administrations was based on mistaken assumptions about the communist threat to democracy and was conceived in profound ignorance of Vietnamese culture and politics. Though he and his associates acted in good faith at the time, they were, he believes now, "wrong, terribly wrong."[103] To judge from the public reaction to McNamara's *In Retrospect* (1995), one would think that he was revealing the nasty secrets of his stewardship for the first time. Actually, most of the information in the memoir was divulged long ago in *The Pentagon Papers* (1971), David Halberstam's *The Best and the Brightest* (1972), and testimony presented during the Westmoreland v. CBS libel suit (1982 to 1985).

The book's most significant disclosure appears almost as an afterthought, when McNamara reaffirms an article of faith that he shared with his fellow mandarin, Secretary of State Dean Rusk. Both men believed that cabinet officers are accountable only to the president, who is in turn accountable to the electorate.[104] Though McNamara and Rusk felt that President Johnson should have consulted more frequently and more candidly with the people's representatives in Congress, neither chose to criticize the president publicly or to resign in protest.[105] By McNamara's own count, over forty thousand American soldiers were killed in Vietnam following his departure from the Pentagon.[106] Yet he and Rusk remained the president's men even after retiring from public service, their misguided loyalty to one man transcending their obligation to millions of others. If the Vietnam War alienated many Americans from their political institutions and leaders, as McNamara believes that it did, then this is because government first alienated itself from the people.[107]

The last and perhaps the most important purpose of the war story is likewise related to the issue of authority. As a rule we expect people to accept responsibility for their actions and decisions to a degree commensurate with their power to act freely themselves and to influence the actions of others. In their published memoirs McNamara and Rusk belatedly claim what they take to be a just measure of blame and praise for their roles in the war—though Larry Heinemann was not alone in considering McNamara's apology "a day late and a dollar short."[108] What we might call the "responsibility pyramid" corresponds in their accounts to the managerial authority pyramid. In most of our Vietnam war stories, however, the responsibility pyramid is a mirror image of the subjugated knowledge pyramid. Those with the least political authority are held, or hold themselves, most accountable for the war.

One might approach this paradox through "just war" theory, which has been applied to Vietnam by two writers coming from different perspectives. Michael Walzer, who took part in the antiwar movement of the 1960s and early 1970s, argues in *Just and Unjust Wars* that the American war in Vietnam was unjust for two reasons. First, the United States intervened on behalf of a government that lacked popular support and was therefore illegitimate. Second, because America fought an enemy that enjoyed popular support, it was compelled to use brutal force, often against civilians.[109] William P. Mahedy, who was a Catholic chaplain in Vietnam, makes the same case for the war's injustice in *Out of the Night*, often citing Walzer with approval.[110] In assigning responsibility for the war's injustice, Walzer and Mahedy agree that blame should be proportionate to authority; thus an officer is more culpable than an enlisted man and the civilian leadership more culpable than the military, especially since the managers often subverted democratic process during the war.

Walzer and Mahedy agree, finally, that the responsible parties have not accepted their full share of blame for the Vietnam War, leaving those who were less answerable for its injustice to bear the burden of guilt. They differ, however, regarding the identity of the scapegoats. For Walzer, it is the antiwar movement that accepted responsibility for the war while it was being fought, when most Americans remained apathetic or alienated.[111] For Mahedy, it is the soldier-veteran who bore the moral brunt of the war while it was being fought and still bears it today, when most Americans try to forget about Vietnam.[112] Mahedy goes beyond Walzer in advocating a moral and even a spiritual role for the guilt-bearer. As he sees it, Vietnam is not merely a philosophical case study in unjust warfare. For those who fought the war it was a wasteland or desert experience of biblical proportions and significance, reflected in the soldiers' nihilistic refrain, "It don't mean nothin'." Mahedy believes that the experience does mean something. He urges veterans first to seek out its meaning and then to bear witness to it.

Mahedy thus concurs with Robert Jay Lifton, Shad Meshad, and others who have become disenchanted with conventional psychotherapy while counseling veterans. All agree that veterans benefited from having their symptoms identified as a stress disorder, officially recognized in the third edition of the American Psychiatric Association's *Diagnostic and Statistical Manual of Mental Disorders* (DSM-III), published in 1980. But the diagnosis had two unfortunate effects. First, as Lloyd B. Lewis points out, it served to discredit veterans as reliable witnesses. They were understood to be "possessed" by PTSD much as people were once thought to be possessed by demons.[113] Second, the diagnosis suggested a course of therapy that was calculated to eliminate symptoms rather than plumb their moral significance. Peter Marin, in an essay published the same year as DSM-III, argued that veterans were still "walking point" for their country in an alien landscape of moral guilt, a jungle that few Americans were willing to enter.[114] Instead of supporting this mission, psychotherapy was trying to neutralize it. In a follow-up essay, Marin urged therapists to treat guilt as "an appropriate if painful response to the past" rather than as a form of neurosis or pathology.[115]

Going against the grain of contemporary psychology and the prevailing American will-to-innocence, Mahedy, Lifton, and Marin sought to authorize Vietnam veterans, even to make them prophets. Veteran-prophets bear witness to several truths by means of their distress, their actions, and their stories. First and foremost, they testify that it is wrong to kill other human beings and that war is always an evil. According to just war theory, Walzer points out, soldiers are responsible, as soldiers, only for their behavior within their limited sphere of action and authority; they are not responsible for the overall justice of the war.[116] But soldiers who have killed may not find this convincing at the visceral level. A veteran in Wallace Terry's *Bloods* recalls that chaplains would try to persuade the troops that the Tenth Commandment refers not to killing but to murder. "But you knew," the veteran says, "all of that was murder anyway."[117] Anselmo, a character in Hemingway's novel *For Whom the Bell Tolls*, looks forward to a day of public penance and spiritual cleansing after the Spanish Civil War, even though he believes that he has killed in a good cause.[118] No such cleansing took place after Vietnam, and its absence is felt more profoundly than the dearth of "welcome home" parades.

Second, veteran-prophets testify to the materialism of American culture. It was not unusual for soldiers in their late teens or early twenties to reassess their spiritual and cultural values after spending a year among peasants who had few possessions to begin with and who were losing even those to the war. To someone who has been in Vietnam, Mahedy remarks, "the binges of a consumer society seem almost obscene."[119] Winnie Smith speaks disdainfully in her memoir of the American "obsession with material goods," and two fictional veterans in Schaeffer's *Buffalo Afternoon* decide that they are "not Americans"—or else qualify as some new species of American—because they no longer care about big cars and television sets.[120] To appreciate the veterans' sense of dislocation in the "land of the big PX" (post exchange), one has only to watch a Vietnam film on a major television network. There, intercut with the squalor and pain of war, are commercial images of luxury cars and hair-care products.

Third, Vietnam veterans testify to the death of God. This may seem a paradoxical message for prophets to proclaim, not to mention one that defies the conventional wisdom about atheists and foxholes. Based on years of experience counseling veterans, Mahedy nonetheless concludes that "loss of religious faith in Vietnam was the norm rather than the exception," a view supported by anecdotal and statistical evidence.[121] A former chaplain himself, he blames the military chaplaincy in part for the soldiers' disaffection, inasmuch as the priests, ministers, and rabbis lent their religious authority to the evil of war.

What these men of the cloth represented, Mahedy observes, was American civil religion rather than a genuine faith in God. Since the time of Winthrop's city upon a hill, civil religion has linked belief in God to confidence in America's special destiny. When the Puritans felt that God was allowing their enemies to win, they questioned their own fidelity to the covenant. When things went wrong in Vietnam, American soldiers questioned much more. As one of the veterans in *Bloods* remarks, "I can't really believe in God like I did because I can't really see why God would let something like this happen."[122] For Mahedy, such "atheism" is a hopeful sign, since disbelief in the American God may lead to real faith. Whether or not veterans recover their personal faith, they bear witness to the idolatry that passes for religion in America.

Peter Marin has identified a fourth prophetic message that veterans are specially equipped to deliver. He notes that psychotherapy, taking its cue from Martin Buber, has adopted the "I-thou" model of human relationships. But veterans know from experience that decisions made and actions taken within an intimate relationship can have far-reaching consequences. They are conscious of those whom Marin calls "the invisible others, the distant witnesses: those who have suffered our past acts and those who may suffer them in the future."[123] Buber's "I-thou" therefore needs to be reconfigured as "I-thou-they." When the nation's leaders and managers begin to speak of "surgical strikes" against enemy targets and represent war in the imagery of computer games, veterans can remind their country that the enemy has faces like our own.

To date, veterans have borne witness to these truths in several ways. The largest number have done so passively, by suffering the symptoms of PTSD. According to the most authoritative study of the disorder's prevalence among the 3.14 million men and women who served in Vietnam, over half (1.7 million) have suffered full or partial symptoms of PTSD at some time in their lives.[124] A much smaller number have taken action, either in domestic humanitarian programs or on missions of mercy to the people of Vietnam. A still smaller but highly influential number have assumed a role that is prophetic in the traditional sense of "speaking out" in a public forum. Veteran-prophets began to come forward while the war was still being fought, most conspicuously during the Winter Soldier Investigation organized by Vietnam Veterans Against the War early in 1971.[125] The same kind of testifying continues today in our classrooms (mine included), where consideration of the Vietnam War is often linked to ethical education. It reaches its largest audience in literature and film, where moral witness has always been a major purpose of the war story. In this respect, as Philip D. Beidler points out, our war stories differ markedly from the self-absorbed "literature of exhaustion" that was fashionable as the war was being fought.[126]

All war stories are implicitly moral, just as all are implicitly political. If veterans have been wary of overt moralizing in their stories, this may be due partly to residual hostility against the more self-righteous elements in the antiwar movement. As Charles C. Moskos has shown, many GIs in Vietnam disliked peace demonstrators not because the soldiers believed in the war themselves but because the demonstrators seemed to be attacking them personally.[127] Michael Walzer concedes in hindsight that the antiwar movement committed a tactical error when it chose to occupy the moral high ground rather than build a broad base of support.[128] Within their own area of operations, the antiwarriors were no more successful than the warriors in winning the hearts and minds of the people.

Nevertheless, some veteran storytellers have not hesitated to proclaim the injustice of the war and regret their own part in it. Among the most outspoken of these is Tim O'Brien, whose early concern for the exercise of courage in a just cause I have discussed elsewhere.[129] That concern also informs "On the Rainy River" and other stories in *The Things They Carried,* notwithstanding the narrator's assertion that a war story is never moral.[130] O'Brien's fiction since *Things* continues to demonstrate that moral seriousness is compatible with the most self-conscious experimentation. In one of the footnotes to *In the Lake of the Woods* he writes sympathetically about the anger and frustration felt by the soldiers at My Lai. Yet his aim is not to justify their behavior but to "bear witness to the mystery of evil."[131] By telling the story of John Wade, a fictional participant in the massacre, O'Brien claims that he sought to revive his own feelings of complicity in the evil, to recover the "vanished life" of the reluctant conscript who once walked the same ground as Charlie Company and shared their murderous thoughts.[132]

Not all veterans share O'Brien's conviction that Vietnam was an unjust war or that they were any less courageous than soldiers in previous wars. But whatever their beliefs, conscientious veterans hold themselves accountable for Vietnam to an extent that few managers have. This may have something to do with the kind of war it was, as well as the veterans' reception at home. In order to experience guilt, J. Glenn Gray contends, one must see oneself as an individual. Most wars disarm guilt by suppressing individuality; the soldier kills as part of a group with which he identifies completely.[133] In Vietnam, however, the system of troop rotation militated against group solidarity. The soldier arrived as an individual, was assigned to one or more units during his tour of duty, and departed as an individual. There were few in Vietnam with whom he could share the guilt for what he saw or did, and none at home.

In the introduction to this study I expressed misgivings about duplicating the ethnocentrism of our war stories by focusing on domestic conflicts. Recently, as though in response to Peter Marin's challenge, American storytellers have expanded the "I-thou" of our social contracts to include a "they." There have always been American writers who tried to imagine the experience of the Vietnamese. One thinks, for example, of nonfiction like Wendy Larsen and Tran Thi Nga's *Shallow Graves* and John Balaban's *Remembering Heaven's Face;* also of fiction like Nelson Algren's "Police and Mama-sans Get It All," Loyd Little's *Parthian Shot,* and John Sayles's "Tan." With Robert Olen Butler's *Good Scent from a Strange Mountain,* the winner of a Pulitzer Prize in 1993, an underground tradition might be said to have emerged into the full light of day. In each of the fifteen stories in Butler's collection, a Vietnamese man or woman speaks poignantly of postwar life in Louisiana. In retrospect, Oliver Stone's Vietnam film trilogy seems to have traced a paradigmatic narrative from the internecine warfare of *Platoon* to the moral pain and public testimony of *Born on the Fourth of July* to the cross-cultural empathy of *Heaven and Earth*, based on Le Ly Hayslip's memoirs. Of course the Vietnamese themselves are best qualified to tell about their experience of the war. Besides providing another perspective on the war, their stories may help us to revise our own.

VIII

The first chapter of this study is devoted to Vietnam war stories that begin either explicitly or implicitly on the American frontier. Here, by way of conclusion, we might appropriately reflect on endings. I refer not to the way in which particular authors have resolved the plots of particular stories but to the kinds of closure we envision for the Vietnam experience as a whole.

Walter Capps is one of those who find the war's "unfinished" quality disturbing, inasmuch as the unconcluded story can be revised—and therefore co-opted—by ideologically suspect storytellers. He especially deplores the "Armageddon mentality" of religious and political conservatives who seek to exorcise Vietnam in a "war to end all wars."[134] Ironically, however, he shares their desire for a definitive ending. For Capps it is precisely the inconclusiveness of the Vietnam War that constitutes its "tragedy." Vietnam, he says, was "a dramatic event with an ending that was inevitably unhappy because integral elements eluded successful resolution or closure."[135]

One might quibble with this definition of tragedy, since according to Aristotle a plot can be called tragic only if it culminates in a catharsis of pity and fear. It is therefore a genre with a decisive "finish." But whether or not our collective experience of Vietnam qualifies as tragedy in the strict sense of the word, it has doubtless remained an inconclusive cultural narrative. The war veterans, who are sometimes expected to provide a satisfactory ending, have failed to do so—at least in their oral testimony. "Before they reach conclusions," Capps observes, "they break off, as if the chronicle doesn't go anywhere, as if it involves a plot that can find no resolution, as if the telling engages a sequence of deep emotional involvement that has been interrupted or is still trying desperately to find its way."[136]

Capps is not alone in hankering for catharsis or resolution. Reflecting on a conference sponsored by the Asia Society in 1985, Timothy J. Lomperis echoed Myra MacPherson's conjecture that the veterans whom she interviewed for her book *Long Time Passing* would not recover from their psychic wounds "until a catharsis on the war is reached."[137] Noting that Vietnam continues to be invoked for contradictory purposes in contemporary politics, Lomperis goes on to say, "The Vietnam War is an historical experience that is clearly in need of some final judgments so that some resolution can be achieved. Such a resolution is not a mere academic exercise. It will determine when, if, and under what set of conditions my son and others will go to war."

Closely related to the desire for catharsis, resolution, and final judgments is the search for definitive "lessons" of the Vietnam War, as distinct from the process of "bearing witness." Necessary and admirable as this enterprise is, it often produces lessons that are so reductive as to be useless in any future crisis. Frances FitzGerald's *Fire in the Lake,* for example, is a rich and complex book about Vietnamese culture and how it was misunderstood by American policymakers. But when FitzGerald tried to distill its insights into a brief paper presented at a 1983 conference on "Lessons from a War," the results ranged from the profound to the consciously ridiculous. The lesson to be learned from President Kennedy's role in the war, she proposed with tongue in cheek, is to "beware of having too good a speechwriter—your phrases may be remembered."[138]

It is very American, somehow, to want a ten-minute summary of all we have learned from the Vietnam War—just the salient points, please. One suspects that the search for lessons is motivated in part by the desire to "put Vietnam behind us." Once the war can be fitted into a vest pocket, it need not occupy us further. This is not to say that clarity, precision, and even conciseness are qualities to be discounted in our thinking about the war. I am arguing, rather, against reductiveness, abstraction, and premature closure, especially since so many parties to the war (the Vietnamese in particular) have yet to be heard from. The Puritan in us clamors for exorcism, apocalypse, and a politics that can be chiseled on tablets of stone or crunched in a computer. Yet our long-term political and moral well-being requires a tolerance for doubt, ambiguity, and inconclusiveness.

War stories nurture such tolerance by presenting their meanings still rooted in the soil that gave them life. In this way narrative resists not only the abstraction of the overdetermined lesson but also the mystification of the underdetermined image. At the same conference addressed by FitzGerald, the journalist Phillip Knightley criticized the way his colleagues reported the war. Rather than trying to understand and explain events, they trafficked in symbols and images—a soldier setting a thatched hut on fire with a Zippo lighter, or General Loan executing a Viet Cong suspect on the street.[139] Responsible journalism, in contrast, is a form of storytelling. It seeks to locate the image or symbol in a web of human circumstance and emotion, to describe it in the "thick" manner recommended by Geertz.

Don Ringnalda has recently argued that the process of making meaning has gone too far in many of our Vietnam war stories. He maintains that the more traditional realistic narratives in particular, like Del Vecchio's *13th Valley* and James Webb's *Fields of Fire,* make sense of the war in a way that reinstates the old warrior myths. He prefers (as I do) the more experimental writings of O'Brien, Herr, Heinemann, and Pratt, which successfully "articulate the contours of *nonsense* that culminated in the war."[140] So far, so good. But in his zeal to work out a strict correspondence between military and literary strategies, between writing and fighting, Ringnalda reinstates one of the old antiwarrior myths about the Viet Cong. These he romanticizes as "postmodern" guerrillas while praising the more innovative American writers as literary Viet Cong.[141]

So we have Capps to warn us about the dangers of unfinished stories and Ringnalda to steer us clear of those that are finished before they are really begun. In their different ways, both overestimate the compulsive power of narrative and underestimate the healthy skepticism of readers in a culture at war with itself. The worst course of all, it seems to me, would be to desist from storytelling altogether. Fortunately, this is also the least likely course. America—at least the more conscious elements in the cultural entity we call America—was traumatized by Vietnam and must tell its story. Much as trauma victims learn to integrate the vivid images and sensations of traumatic memory into the life narrative, the country is gradually learning how to absorb the war into American history.

Even as our storytellers assist in this process, they are helping to make another kind of connection, the Vietnam Generation's connection with its sons and daughters. In Faulkner's *Absalom, Absalom!* a young woman receives a letter from her fiancé, a Confederate soldier, in which he recounts the last days of a dying cause. After his death she passes the letter on to an acquaintance, insisting that its contents are not especially important in themselves. What counts, she says, is the simple gesture of passing the letter "from one hand to another, one mind to another."[142] For her the tradition or "handing over" of the war story, its mere recounting in the presence of a receptive listener or reader, is itself a kind of politics. Even when the story is about loss and defeat, perhaps especially then, it can foster biological and cultural continuity.

Can we offer the next generation any lessons that will immunize them against future Vietnams? I doubt it, though for many of our writers and filmmakers this is the purpose that transcends all others. Ward Just believes that all of our Vietnam war stories convey the same message: "We must never do this again."[143] But if stories cannot prevent war (some arguably encourage it, by means of their content or style) they may help the human race to survive its prolonged and belligerent adolescence. John Keegan, for one, professes to be "impressed by the evidence that mankind, wherever it has the option, is distancing itself from the institution of warfare."[144] War, he speculates, could go the way of other cultural practices that once seemed natural and inevitable, such as slavery, infanticide, and human sacrifice.

It would be fatuous to hope that our Vietnam narratives could prevent the next war or the one after that. Word by word and image by image, however, they may add up to a significant recasting of the "rumors of war" prophecy in the Gospel of Matthew. Rather than being a sign of the last days, the prelude to apocalypse, our war stories may prove to be the means by which we postpone the end.

Notes

INTRODUCTION

1. Keegan, *History*, p. 12.
2. Gibson, *Perfect War*, p. 26.
3. Keegan also points out that "politics by other means" is a reductive paraphrase of Clausewitz (*History*, p. 3). Stressing the complementary roles of military action and diplomatic negotiation ("politics"), the classic passage in *On War* defines war as a "continuation of political intercourse, with a mixture of other means" (Clausewitz, p. 402).
4. Clausewitz, *On War*, p. 406.
5. Beidler, *American Literature*, p. 19.
6. Capps, *Unfinished War*, p. 8. The second edition of Capps's book traces the influence of the war up to about 1990.
7. Hayslip, *When Heaven*, p. xv.
8. Foucault, *Archaeology*, p. 9.
9. Linda Cropp, quoted in M. Fisher, "Jenkins," p. 3.
10. Horace Coleman, quoted in McCloud, *What Should*, p. 29.
11. The critics include Louvre and Walsh, "Preface," p. xi; Marin, "Coming," p. 43; Melling, *Vietnam in American Literature*, pp. 31, 38; Myers, *Walking Point*, p. 50. Among the author-veterans who have expressed dismay at their inability to capture the Vietnamese experience are William Broyles, Jr., William Pelfrey, John Clark Pratt, and James Webb (Lomperis, *"Reading,"* p. 63).

CHAPTER 1

1. Eastlake, *Bamboo Bed*, p. 23.
2. Summers, *Vietnam War Almanac*, p. 6.
3. Nash, *Wilderness*, p. 143.

4. In this study I refer to the indigenous people of North America as American Indians. I reserve the term "Indian" for the white European settlers' concept of the American Indian, which has been applied to the Vietnamese and others who are not American Indians.

5. Throughout this study I use the phrase "Viet Cong" for soldiers of the South Vietnam Liberation Army, the military arm of the National Liberation Front (NLF). In this regard I adopt the imprecise usage of the narratives under consideration. Though the NLF took orders from Hanoi, not all of its soldiers were communists, as the word *Cong* implies. North Vietnam's regular army, the People's Army of Vietnam, was called the North Vietnamese Army (NVA) by Americans.

6. Ricoeur, *Time*, vol. 1, pp. ix, 3-4.

7. Leed, *No Man's Land*, p. 124.

8. Caputo, *Rumor*, pp. xiv-xv.

9. Ricoeur discusses the artificially configured or fictional dimension of historiography in *Time*, vol. 1, p. 161, and vol. 3, pp. 185-86.

10. Schaeffer, *Buffalo Afternoon*, p. 19.

11. Herr, *Dispatches*, p. 49.

12. P. Miller, *American Puritans*, p. ix.

13. Bercovitch, *Puritan Origins*, p. 143.

14. Nash, *Wilderness*, pp. 10-13.

15. Ibid., pp. 24, 29.

16. Bunyan, *Pilgrim's Progress*, p. 8; R. Williams, *Key*, p. 107.

17. D. Williams, *Wilderness Lost*, pp. 14, 26.

18. Ibid., p. 58.

19. Ibid., p. 28; Nash, *Wilderness*, p. 16.

20. Bradford, "Of Plymouth," p. 17.

21. Bercovitch, *Puritan Origins*, pp. 137-38.

22. Morton, *New English*, p. 180.

23. P. Miller, *American Puritans*, p. 213.

24. D. Williams, *Wilderness Lost*, pp. 47-48.

25. Ibid., p. 63.

26. Rowlandson, "Narrative," p. 166.

27. Winthrop, "Model," p. 83.

28. Increase Mather uses the example of a man named Wakely, who was killed along with most of his family during King Philip's War, to teach this lesson in *A Brief History of the Warr with the Indians in New-England* (Slotkin and Folsom, *So Dreadfull*, p. 99).

29. Slotkin, *Regeneration*, p. 124.

30. Bercovitch, *Puritan Origins*, p. 101; Slotkin and Folsom, *So Dreadfull*, pp. 61-63.

31. Bercovitch, *Puritan Origins*, p. 141.

32. Pearce notes that Virginia abandoned its policy of peaceful coexistence with the American Indians much earlier, following an attack on white settlers in 1622 (*Savagism*, p. 7).

33. Slotkin and Folsom, *So Dreadfull*, pp. 84, 190.

34. Ibid., p. 35.

35. Bercovitch, *Puritan Origins*, p. 103.

36. Slotkin and Folsom, *So Dreadfull*, p. 373.

37. Ibid., p. 381.

38. Here I disagree with Melling, who represents Kurtz as in every respect the antithesis of those who order his assassination (*Vietnam in American Literature*, pp. 176–77).

39. Ibid., p. 22.

40. Quoted in Bugliosi, *Helter Skelter*, p. 184.

41. The more inclusive reference recalls a graffito occasionally seen in Vietnam and still printed on T-shirts available from military supply stores: "Kill them all—let God sort them out." An oft-repeated joke made the same point: How do we end the Vietnam War? Evacuate the friendlies by boat and bomb the country. Then sink the boats.

42. Marcus, "Journey," p. 54.

43. Freud derives totemic sacrifice from a primal patricide in *Totem*, pp. 141–42.

44. Marcus, "Journey," p. 54.

45. Ibid., p. 56.

46. The 70 mm version shown in some theaters likewise ended with the image of Willard's face. The credits to this version were printed on playbills and distributed to viewers (Ibid., p. 52).

47. Tomasulo, "Politics," p. 155.

48. Hellmann, *American Myth*, p. 233.

49. Quoted in Marcus, "Journey," p. 52.

50. Kermode, *Sense*, p. 8.

51. Ibid., pp. 26–27, 30.

52. Bruffee, *Elegiac Romance*, pp. 50–51.

53. Kermode, *Sense*, p. 82.

54. Slotkin, *Regeneration*, p. 145.

55. For thorough and authoritative accounts of how the middle landscape emerged as an American ideal, see H. N. Smith's *Virgin Land* and Leo Marx's *Machine*.

56. Crèvecoeur, *Letters*, pp. 60–73.

57. Jefferson, "Notes," pp. 290–91.

58. Filson, *Kentucke*, p. 49.

59. H. N. Smith, pp. 53–58. See Smith for a detailed account of the frontier hero's evolution in popular fiction.

60. Nash, *Wilderness*, p. 67.

61. H. N. Smith, pp. 250–60.

62. Norris, "Frontier," p. 1190.

63. Hellmann, *American Myth*, p. 17.

64. The jeremiad was an important rhetorical form in Puritan New England, as Bercovitch shows in *American Jeremiad*.

65. Kennedy, "Let the Word," p. 14.

66. *Pentagon Papers*, vol. 1, p. 582.

67. Martin, *Receptions*, p. 116.

68. Ward Just, for example, characterized the film as a "racist muddle" in

the *Atlantic* ("Vietnam: The Camera," p. 65). "I am puzzled and appalled," he wrote, "at the need for inventing a metaphor for the Vietnam War; I mean an invention with no basis whatever in fact." According to Pfc. Robert Garwood, who was convicted of collaborating with the enemy while a prisoner in North Vietnam, the metaphor did have some basis in fact. In a book published five years after *The Deer Hunter* was released, Garwood tells of two South Vietnamese army soldiers who were blindfolded and forced to play Russian roulette until one was killed (quoted in Groom and Spencer, *Conversations,* pp. 54–55).

69. Herr, *Dispatches,* p. 49. In the following sentences, page numbers are cited parenthetically.

70. Schroeder, *Vietnam,* p. 47.

71. Gitlin, *Sixties,* p. 400.

72. Abbey, *Desert,* p. 130.

73. Reich, *Greening,* pp. 209, 223–24, 336–37.

74. Snyder, *Earth,* pp. 103–16.

75. Snyder, *Turtle,* p. 102.

76. Reich, *Greening,* p. 192.

77. Snyder, *Earth,* p. 112.

78. Snyder, *Turtle,* p. 85.

79. Quoted in Mersmann, *Vietnam Vortex,* p. 123.

80. Bly, *Light,* p. 36.

81. McCarthy, *Hanoi,* p. 15.

82. Ibid., p. 89.

83. Sontag, *Styles,* p. 196.

84. Ibid., p. 254.

85. Nash, *Wilderness,* pp. 23, 51, 60, 65.

86. McCarthy, *Hanoi,* p. 132. For a recent defense and extenuation of the Hue massacre, see Young, who follows D. Gareth Porter in arguing that it was the work of the NLF rather than the NVA, that it was not indiscriminate, and that it was partly forced by the conditions of the NLF's retreat from Hue (pp. 217–18).

87. Snyder, *Turtle,* p. 106.

88. Quoted in Gitlin, *Sixties,* p. 184.

89. Ibid., p. 268.

90. Mailer, *Why,* pp. 1–2. Hereafter, this text is cited parenthetically.

91. Mailer, "White Negro," p. 339.

92. Schroeder believes that the boys ironically mistake America's voice for God's (*Vietnam,* p. 6). Yet it seems not to be a mistake, for the voice endorses the same lesson that they see illustrated in the natural order.

93. Beidler, *American Literature,* p. 46.

94. Mailer, *Armies,* pp. 208–9.

95. Caputo, *Rumor,* p. xviii.

96. Ibid., p. xx. Compare the similar passage in Conrad, beginning, "You can't understand. How could you?" (*Heart,* p. 122).

97. Caputo, *Rumor,* p. 309.

98. Caputo, *Indian Country,* p. 413.

99. Howes, *Voices*, pp. 124–31.

100. Ibid., pp. 51, 126, 133.

101. Ibid., p. 135.

102. Red McDaniel, quoted in ibid., p. 152.

103. Howes, *Voices*, pp. 59–60.

104. Quoted in ibid., p. 8.

105. The remains of Eleanor Vietti, a doctor working for the Christian Missionary Alliance, and Betty Ann Olsen, a nurse with the same organization, have not been recovered. The two escapees, the wife and daughter of an American contractor, were captured during the 1975 offensive and would probably have been released along with the others taken at the same time. This information is from fact sheets provided by the POW-MIA Affairs Division, Department of the Army.

106. Quoted in Howes, *Voices*, p. 140.

107. Kate Webb, a UPI journalist, was the only Australian woman to be taken captive, according to the Defense Intelligence Agency. See Newman (*Vietnam War Literature*, pp. 7, 9) for descriptions of the other *Vietnam Nurse* novels, written by Field and Roberts (both 1966). A fourth adolescent novel with the same title was published by Hawkins in 1984 (Newman, pp. 112–13).

108. *Victims*, p. 5.

109. Ibid., p. 2.

110. Herman, *Trauma*, p. 76.

111. Malek, *Viet Cong*, pp. 3–4.

112. Ibid., p. 4.

113. Grantland, *Bamboo Beast*, p. 45.

114. Slotkin, *Regeneration*, pp. 111, 129, 234.

115. Ibid., p. 132.

116. Drinnon, *Facing West*, pp. xvii–xviii.

117. Sontag, *Styles*, pp. 212–18; Howes, *Voices*, pp. 48–49.

118. Levy, "ARVN," p. 20.

119. Howes, *Voices*, p. 137.

120. Sontag, *Styles*, p. 227.

121. Fitzgerald, *Gatsby*, p. 182. Fitzgerald actually wrote "orgastic future" and told Max Perkins that "'orgastic' is the adjective for 'orgasm' and it expresses exactly the intended ecstasy" (quoted in Gross, "Back West," p. 12).

122. Heinemann, *Close Quarters*, p. 27.

123. O'Brien, *Cacciato*, p. 107.

124. Quoted in Howes, *Voices*, pp. 173, 8.

125. See, for example, Eastlake's *Bamboo Bed* (pp. 97–101), Kovic's *Born* (pp. 49–50), and O'Brien's *Cacciato* (pp. 59–60). Others books, like O'Brien's *If I Die* (p. 21), Bryan's *Friendly Fire* (pp. 17–19, 26), Webb's *Fields* (p. 33), and Hasford's *Phantom Blooper* (p. 159) make a point of telling us that the soldier grew up on land that was once American Indian country.

126. L. Jones, *Great Expectations*, pp. 50–51.

127. Michener, *Kent State*, pp. 49–50; cf. pp. 50, 68, 355, 451.

128. Herr, *Dispatches*, p. 254.

CHAPTER 2

1. Leckie, *Buffalo Soldiers*, p. 260.
2. Ibid., p. vii.
3. Foner, *Blacks*, p. 53.
4. Geertz, *Interpretation*, p. 9.
5. Ibid., pp. 10, 452.
6. J. Williams, *Captain Blackman*, p. 106.
7. Du Bois, *Souls*, p. 3.
8. For discussions of other minority responses to the war, see the essays and bibliographies in the special issue of *Vietnam Generation* edited by William M. King.
9. Foner, *Blacks*, pp. viii, 30.
10. Quoted in ibid., p. 6.
11. Ibid., pp. 15, 17, 18.
12. Ibid., p. 92.
13. Binkin and Eitelberg, *Blacks and the Military*, p. 14.
14. Foner, *Blacks*, pp. 72, 90.
15. Ibid., p. 153.
16. Glines, "Black vs. White," pp. 20–23, 26–27; Nalty, *Strength*, p. 289.
17. Foner, *Blacks*, p. 204.
18. "Birdmen," p. 37. Black soldiers so dominated the airborne ranks that they referred to whites as "foreign troops" (Johnson, "U. S. Negro," p. 16).
19. Johnson, "U. S. Negro," p. 16; Binkin and Eitelberg, *Blacks and the Military*, p. 42. Combat fatality figures vary considerably, depending on how they are computed and the source of the information. Johnson cites the Department of Defense as his authority. Binkin and Eitelberg cite a Department of the Army source for a black fatality rate of 20.1 percent in 1961 to 1966 (p. 76). Black soldiers in the other services suffered a lower death rate during the same period.
20. Johnson, "U. S. Negro," p. 16.
21. Binkin and Eitelberg, *Blacks and the Military*, p. 76.
22. "Integrated," p. 22; "Great Society," pp. 46, 48, 57; "How Negro," pp. 60–63.
23. Quoted in Shepley, "Letter," p. 11. The cover story, entitled "Democracy in the Foxhole," appears on pp. 15–19.
24. Smitherman, *Talkin*, p. 118. Like Kochman, Smitherman focuses on the rhetorical conventions of black people raised in the black community, where ethnic tradition remains strong.
25. "Democracy," p. 19.
26. Nalty, *Strength*, p. 304; Terry, "Bringing," p. 11.
27. "Democracy," pp. 15–16. For a tabulation and discussion of white and nonwhite scores on the AFQT, see Binkin and Eitelberg, *Blacks and the Military*, pp. 46–49.
28. Foner, *Blacks*, p. 202.
29. Binkin and Eitelberg, *Blacks and the Military*, p. 34.

30. McAllister, "Low-Aptitude," p. 10. At a time when the unemployment rate among low-aptitude nonveterans was 2.8 percent, the rate for Project 100,000 veterans as a whole was 10.3 percent and for black veterans 22 percent. For detailed discussions of Project 100,000, see Baskir and Strauss, *Chance*, pp. 122–31; and Hsiao, "Project," pp. 14–37.

31. Nalty, *Strength*, p. 295.

32. Foner, *Blacks*, p. 206.

33. M. King, "A Time," p. 105.

34. Ibid., p. 116.

35. Robert Williams, "USA," p. 6.

36. Halstead, *GIs*, pp. 51–52.

37. Glines, "Black vs. White," p. 20.

38. The army stockade ran about 60 percent black, whereas nonwhites accounted for 40 to 50 percent of those in the marine brig in Danang; see Addleston and Sherer, "Battleground," p. 1, and Anderson, *Vietnam*, p. 152. The high proportion of black prisoners reflects not only the level of their discontent but also the commanding officers' practice of treating their infractions of discipline more harshly.

39. Terry, "Bringing," p. 17.

40. Ibid., pp. 17–18.

41. Ho, *Ho Chi Minh*, pp. 43–51.

42. Terry, *Bloods*, pp. 137, 282.

43. Ibid., pp. 167, 212; Whitmore, *Memphis-Nam-Sweden*, p. 71. White soldiers report the same phenomenon in Helmer, *Bringing*, p. 101.

44. "Uncorrelated," no page numbers.

45. Johnson, "Negro Expatriates," p. 18.

46. Ibid.; "How Negro," p. 63.

47. Terry, *Bloods*, pp. 13, 235, 255–56.

48. Johnson, "Negro Veteran," p. 14.

49. Reginald Edwards, quoted in Terry, *Bloods*, p. 12.

50. Clarence Guthrie, quoted in Johnson, "Negro Veteran," p. 14.

51. Johnson, "Negro Veteran," p. 14.

52. Halstead, *GIs*, p. 59.

53. Quoted in H. Baker, *Journey*, p. 4.

54. Ibid., p. 31.

55. Baldwin, *Fire*, p. 141.

56. Bond, "The Roots," p. 109.

57. Taylor, "Black Consciousness," p. 20.

58. Taylor, *Vietnam*, p. 299.

59. H. Baker, *Blues*, p. 31.

60. Douglass, *Narrative*, p. 29.

61. Ibid., pp. 79–80.

62. Du Bois, *Souls*, p. 144.

63. Schroeder, *Vietnam*, p. 64.

64. Terry, *Bloods*, p. 203. Hereafter, page numbers are cited parenthetically.

65. Komunyakaa, *Dien Cai Dau*, p. 13.

66. Ellison, *Shadow*, p. 42.

67. Komunyakaa, *Dien Cai Dau,* p. 42.

68. G. Davis, *Coming,* p. 127.

69. Buder, "CORE," p. 11.

70. W. King, "'Our Men,'" pp. 115–16.

71. Komunyakaa, *Dien Cai Dau,* p. 29.

72. Komunyakaa and Matthews, "Jazz," p. 656.

73. Gotera, "Lines," p. 219; K. Jones, "Folk Idiom," p. 162.

74. Bakhtin, *Dialogic Imagination,* p. 271. The following sentences paraphrase Bakhtin's argument in "Discourse in the Novel," pp. 259–422.

75. J. Williams, *Captain Blackman,* pp. 299, 315, 230. Hereafter, this text is cited parenthetically.

76. For a version in which the monkey escapes, see Hughes and Bontemps, *Negro Folklore,* pp. 363–66.

77. Smitherman, *Talkin,* pp. 131–34. The newspaper columnist Donna Britt argues that the dirty dozens actually underscore the importance of family in black culture ("If They're Joning").

78. Here I disagree with Harris, who treats Blackman's fantasy as fact and describes him as "a self-assured revolutionary who brings America to her knees" at the end of the novel (*Connecting,* p. 41).

79. Cash, "*Captain Blackman:* An Interview," p. 87.

80. C. Williams, *Destruction,* pp. 329, 331, italics in original.

81. Ibid., p. 346.

82. Ibid., pp. 361–82.

83. Cleaver, *Soul,* p. 14.

84. Flowers, *Mojo,* pp. 122, 80. Hereafter, page numbers are cited parenthetically.

85. Hurston, "High John," p. 96.

86. Hughes and Bontemps, *Negro Folklore,* p. 184.

87. Byerman, *Fingering,* p. 6.

88. As Gates has shown, Papa LaBas can be traced back to Esu-Elegbara, the divine trickster of Yoruba mythology. Much as the Signifying Monkey is associated with black modes of rhetoric, Esu-Elegbara is associated with black modes of interpretation (*Signifying,* pp. 5, 44).

89. Hurston uses Aunt Shady Anne Sutton for this purpose in "High John" (pp. 96–97), and Hughes and Bontemps conclude a piece on hoodoo with the sentence, "That's what the old ones said in ancient times and we talk it again" (*Negro Folklore,* p. 185).

90. Gates, "African American Criticism," p. 311.

91. Ibid.

92. See H. Baker, *Blues,* pp. 88–108. Baker took the term "reconstructionists" from the title of Fisher and Stepto's *Afro-American Literature: The Reconstruction of Instruction,* to which Gates contributed an essay.

93. For a discussion of the victim-survivor mode of heroism, see Byerman, *Fingering,* p. 277.

94. Du Bois, *Gift,* p. 82.

95. Lomperis, "*Reading,*" p. 56.

96. Komunyakaa and Matthews, "Jazz," p. 646.

CHAPTER 3

1. Quoted in Naughton, "Agnew," p. 52.
2. Cook, "Hard-Hats," pp. 712–19.
3. Quoted in Perlmutter, "Heads," p. 18.
4. Quoted in Breslin, "One Way," p. 30.
5. Levison, *Working-Class Majority*, pp. 136–37, 162.
6. Quoted in Perlmutter, "Heads," p. 18.
7. Breslin, "One Way," p. 30.
8. Ibid., p. 28.
9. For an overview of opinion polls on this issue, see Levison, *Working-Class Majority*, pp. 158–60; P. and B. Sexton, *Blue Collars*, p. 245; and Hamilton, *Class*, p. 453.
10. Hahn, "Dove Sentiments," pp. 202–3.
11. Hahn, "Correlates," pp. 1186–98.
12. "Labor's New Left," p. 15.
13. Quoted in Terkel, *Working*, p. 210.
14. For a discussion of the economic impact of the war see Stevens, *Vain Hopes*.
15. Baritz, *Good Life*, p. 283.
16. Hamilton, *Class*, p. 514.
17. Fallows, "What Did," p. 7. The quotations in the next two sentences are from the same page.
18. Appy, *Working-Class War*, pp. 11–12, 58.
19. See Cohen, *Citizens*, for a discussion of the relationship between a nation's political ideology and its methods of conscription.
20. Using occupation as the chief criterion, Hamilton and Levison challenge the prevailing view that the working class had become by 1969 a minority of the American population. By counting service workers and employed wives and daughters of blue-collar workers as members of the working class, they estimated that nearly 60 percent of Americans earned their living by non-farm manual labor. See Hamilton, *Class*, pp. 152–56, and Levison, *Working-Class Majority*, pp. 22–26.
21. Baritz, noting that Americans tend to identify themselves as middle class even though they belong to the lower classes according to income or occupation, argues that "class, especially in America, is a state of mind" (*Good Life*, p. xii).
22. Badillo and Curry, "Social Incidence," p. 397; Baskir and Strauss, *Chance*, p. 9.
23. Zeitlin, Lutterman, and Russell, "Death," p. 315. The study used the Office of Economic Opportunity's scale of poverty to determine which families qualified as poor.
24. Badillo and Curry, "Social Incidence," pp. 397–406.
25. Baskir and Strauss, *Chance*, p. 9.
26. Ibid., p. 37.
27. Ibid., p. 6.

28. J. Davis and Dolbeare, *Little Groups*, pp. 57–61. Hereafter, page numbers are cited parenthetically.

29. Ladinsky, "Vietnam," p. 447.

30. Trillin, "The War," p. 60.

31. Though anyone who received a deferment was legally subject to the draft up to the age of thirty-five, no one over twenty-six was drafted during the Vietnam era (Baskir and Strauss, *Chance*, p. 29n).

32. Cited in Savage and Gabriel, "Cohesion," pp. 345, 373 n. 16.

33. Baskir and Strauss, *Chance*, p. 38.

34. Ibid., p. 39.

35. Ibid., pp. 47–48.

36. As of 1970, according to a study commissioned by the *New Republic*, more than half of the 234 draft-age sons of senators and representatives had received deferments. The sons or grandsons of only twenty-eight members of Congress had gone to Vietnam, and none was killed or listed as missing ("Long Shot," p. 11).

37. Alsop, "American Class," p. 88.

38. Fiedler, "Who," p. 41. The quotation in the next sentence is from p. 40.

39. Thomas, "Quayle," p. 21.

40. Fallows, "What Did," pp. 10, 14; Baskir and Strauss, *Chance*, pp. 6–7, 36.

41. K. Marx, *Communist Manifesto*, p. 17.

42. Leed, *No Man's Land*, p. 90.

43. K. Marx, *Economic and Philosophic Manuscripts*, pp. 106–19.

44. Terkel, *Working*, p. xi.

45. P. and B. Sexton, *Blue Collars*, p. 103.

46. Levison, *Working-Class Majority*, p. 78.

47. Quoted in Terkel, *Working*, p. 557.

48. Quoted in Lyon, "Author," p. 18.

49. Webb, *Fields*, p. 155. The "bait" analogy is pervasive. It appears in Oliver Stone's film *Platoon* and in many books, including Goff and Sanders's *Brothers*, p. 37; Santoli's *Everything*, pp. 72–73; and Hasford's *Phantom Blooper*, pp. 10, 46.

50. See, for example, Janowitz (*Professional*), Loory (*Defeated*), Savage and Gabriel ("Cohesion" and *Crisis*), Baritz (*Backfire*), and Gibson (*Perfect War*).

51. Savage and Gabriel, "Cohesion," p. 356.

52. Broyles, *Brothers*, p. 138. Caputo, also a marine platoon leader, expresses a similar sentiment in *Rumor*, p. 262.

53. Moskos, "Surviving," p. 78.

54. Regarding the younger generation's disaffection in the workplace, see Gooding, "Blue-Collar." J. Klein describes how the student counterculture trickled down to working-class youth in the late 1960s, with factory management serving as their "establishment" (*Payback*, pp. 298–99, 316).

55. Savage and Gabriel, "Cohesion," pp. 349, 359. The number of fraggings for 1969 to 1970 is taken from Pentagon testimony before a House of Representatives subcommittee.

56. Moskos, "Surviving," pp. 79–80.

57. Quoted in Santoli, *Everything*, p. 219.

58. K. Marx, *Communist Manifesto*, pp. 18–21.

59. Helmer, *Bringing*, pp. 52, 104.

60. Moskos describes the anti-ideological soldier in *American Enlisted Man*, pp. 148–52.

61. Helmer, *Bringing*, p. 238.

62. Waldman and Gover, "Employment," p. 6.

63. Michelotti and Gover, "Employment," p. 3.

64. Gover and McEaddy, "Job," p. 20.

65. Michelotti and Gover, "Employment," p. 14. Helmer cites a Bureau of the Budget survey indicating that over half of the veterans not in school or training had found the GI Bill inadequate to cover their expenses (*Bringing*, p. 224).

66. Fallows, "What Did," pp. 14–17.

67. MacPherson, *Long Time*, p. 183.

68. Sontag, *Styles*, p. 195. Hereafter, page numbers are cited parenthetically.

69. McCarthy, *Hanoi*, p. 54; subsequent citations are from this text.

70. Lynd, *Other Side*, pp. 104–109. Herbert Aptheker was with Lynd and Hayden.

71. L. Marx, "Susan Sontag's," pp. 291–314.

72. Mailer, *Armies*, p. 287. Hereafter, citations are supplied parenthetically.

73. K. Marx, *Communist Manifesto*, pp. 13–14.

74. Schroeder, *Vietnam*, p. 154.

75. Quoted in Corliss, "*Platoon*," pp. 56, 57.

76. Stone, Address, p. 252.

77. Quoted in Perry, "First," pp. 17, 19.

78. Koehler, Letter, p. 7.

79. Quoted in McGilligan, "Point Man," p. 16.

80. Stone, "One," p. 5.

81. McGilligan, "Point Man," p. 16; M. Norman, "*Platoon*," p. 18.

82. Baird, *Ishmael*, pp. 16, 29.

83. Quoted in Blauner, "Coming," p. 64.

84. Ibid.

85. Stone, "One," p. 10.

86. Quoted in McGilligan, "Point Man," p. 16.

87. Stone, *Oliver Stone's* Platoon, p. 21. Hereafter, the screenplay will be cited parenthetically.

88. Stone, Address, p. 250.

89. Ibid.

90. Among those who make this argument are Auster and Quart (*How*, p. 136), Desser ("'Charlie,'" p. 88), Dittmar and Michaud ("America's Vietnam," p. 9), Haines ("'They Were Called,'" pp. 92–94), Kinney ("*Gardens*," pp. 163–64), M. Klein ("Historical Memory," pp. 25, 28–29), Martin (*Receptions*, p. 129), D. Miller ("Primetime," pp. 182–83), and T. Williams ("Narrative," p. 118).

91. Haines, "'They Were Called,'" pp. 81–82, 94; Kinney, "*Gardens*," pp. 153–54; D. Miller, "Primetime," pp. 186–87.

92. Dittmar and Michaud, "America's Vietnam," p. 14.

93. Jameson, *Political Unconscious*, p. 142.

94. Quoted in McGilligan, "Point Man," p. 60.

95. Stone, "One," p. 8. The quotations in the rest of this paragraph are from p. 9.

96. Frye, *Anatomy*, p. 33.

97. Stone, "One," p. 9.

98. Ibid., p. 7.

99. Ibid., p. 9.

100. Frye, *Anatomy*, pp. 186–87.

101. Ibid., pp. 107, 162.

102. Ibid., p. 193.

103. Helmer, *Bringing*, p. 199.

104. Adams, "Platoon," p. 385.

105. Corliss, "Platoon," p. 61.

106. Bruffee, *Elegiac Romance*, p. 50.

107. Ibid., p. 209.

108. Ibid., pp. 221–22.

109. Perry, "First," p. 16.

110. Frye, *Anatomy*, pp. 154, 197.

111. Jameson, *Political Unconscious*, p. 141.

112. Chase, *American Novel*, p. 2.

113. Jameson, *Political Unconscious*, p. 104.

114. Ibid., p. 132.

115. Blauner, "Coming," p. 62.

116. Jameson, *Political Unconscious*, p. 144.

117. Ibid., p. 80.

118. Quoted in Lyon, "Author," p. 15.

119. Quoted in ibid., p. 18.

120. Geng, "Capable," p. 111.

121. Schroeder, *Vietnam*, pp. 152–53.

122. Heinemann, *Close Quarters*, p. 265.

123. Towers, "All-American," p. 26.

124. There is also a Texas Lunch in *Close Quarters*, located in Springfield, Kentucky (Heinemann, p. 306). Kentucky would of course be an appropriate location for a town named Boone.

125. Heinemann, *Paco's Story*, p. 116. Hereafter, page numbers are cited parenthetically.

126. In a review of the novel, Nicosia places the descriptions of Paco's dishwashing and Gallagher's father in the mock-epic tradition; thus the bus driver's nightly ritual "reads like Achilles taking off his armor" ("War Story," p. 7). If so, it also suggests the difference between Stone and Heinemann, between epic heroism and its deflation.

127. Quoted in Lyon, "Author," p. 18.

128. Jesse may be based on veterans whom Heinemann interviewed while studying the "tripwire veterans" of Washington's Olympic Peninsula. Jesse's remark that he is "a fully stamped, qualified *slab* animal—successful species—

who made it out of their fucking lab" (*Paco's Story*, pp. 155–56) is taken almost verbatim from an interview quoted in Heinemann's "'Just Don't Fit,'" p. 62.

129. As originally published in *TriQuarterly,* "The First Clean Fact" is narrated by a single ghost. His voice became the voice of all the company's dead when Heinemann revised the story as the first chapter of his novel.

130. Heinemann, Interview, 1990.

131. Towers, "All-American," p. 26.

132. Schroeder, *Vietnam,* p. 159.

133. Jameson, *Political Unconscious,* p. 297.

134. Barthes, "From Work."

135. Montrose cautions against the error of aestheticizing culture in "New Historicisms," p. 401.

136. Frye, *Anatomy,* pp. 38–39.

137. Jameson, *Political Unconscious,* p. 291.

CHAPTER 4

1. It was the literature of Hemingway's war that established the convention of the emasculated veteran, as Gilbert notes ("Soldier's Heart," p. 198).

2. D. Smith, "Dating," pp. 321–35. Like most researchers, Smith sees little change in nonmarital sexual activity between the 1920s and the 1960s.

3. The Kinsey study is cited in O'Neill, *Coming Apart,* p. 300n.

4. Chafe, *Unfinished Journey,* p. 437. See also L. Jones, *Great Expectations,* pp. 205–207.

5. Friedan, *Feminine Mystique,* pp. 16, 150, 162–63, 385, 386.

6. Ibid., p. 46. Gubar has shown that the image of woman was already thoroughly eroticized in World War II propaganda generated by both the Axis and the Allies ("'This Is My Rifle'").

7. Friedan, *Feminine Mystique,* pp. 258–81.

8. In *Second Stage* Friedan recommends that the women's movement address the issues of home and family in response to the emptiness many women feel while pursuing careers exclusively.

9. Eleanor Smeal, then president of NOW, emphasized other obstacles to ratification in a speech delivered several days before the extension expired. She attributed the defeat of the ERA to the opposition of the Republican party, corporations that benefit from discrimination on the basis of sex, and defection within the ranks of the Democratic party (quoted in M. Hunter, "Leaders Concede," p. 19).

10. Cited in MacPherson, *Long Time,* p. 560.

11. D. Phillips, "The Case," p. 357. Two women filed individual suits against the U.S. Air Force in 1971 and 1972; otherwise, according to Phillips, no discrimination suits were filed against the armed services in any of the federal district courts during the Vietnam War.

12. Van Breems, "Feminists," p. 12.

13. Friedan, *Second Stage,* pp. 23, 164.

14. Gitlin, *Sixties,* p. 365.

15. Evans, *Personal Politics,* p. 116.

16. See, for example, the SNCC position paper and "Sex and Caste: A Kind of Memo," both drafted by Hayden and King and reprinted in ibid., pp. 233–38.

17. Mailer, *Armies*, p. 288.

18. Ibid., pp. 307–308.

19. O'Neill, *Coming Apart*, pp. 195–97; Evans, *Personal Politics*, p. 150.

20. Quoted in Gitlin, *Sixties*, p. 337.

21. Quoted in Evans, *Personal Politics*, pp. 240–41.

22. Millett, *Sexual Politics*, p. 25.

23. Ibid., p. 233.

24. Ibid., p. 362.

25. Sontag, *Styles*, p. 273.

26. Ibid., pp. 199–202.

27. Van Breems, "Feminists," p. 12.

28. Elshtain, *Women*, pp. 140–49, 163–93.

29. Beauvoir, *Second Sex*, p. 267.

30. Raymond Williams, *Marxism*, pp. 167–69.

31. Ruddick, *Maternal Thinking*, pp. xi, 151–56.

32. Van Devanter, *Home*, p. 68.

33. Mead, *Culture*, p. 31.

34. I understand that much of the sexism has been eliminated from military vocabulary and training in the past two decades. What I say here applies to the Vietnam era and before.

35. O'Brien, *If I Die*, p. 52.

36. Caputo, *Rumor*, p. 10.

37. Hasford, *Short-Timers*, p. 13.

38. O'Brien, *If I Die*, p. 69.

39. Ibid., pp. 41–42.

40. Ellmann, *Thinking*, p. 6.

41. Caputo, *Rumor*, p. 254.

42. Herr, *Dispatches*, pp. 20, 144.

43. *Pentagon Papers*, vol. 3, p. 354.

44. Quoted in Gibson, *Perfect War*, p. 435.

45. Rusk, *As I Saw It*, p. 499.

46. Gibson, *Perfect War*, p. 11.

47. In the version that I heard, the razor blades were mounted in a cardboard or plastic tube with the cutting edges facing inward; the tube could then be inserted in the vagina without injury to the woman. For a discussion of the folklore on this subject, see Gulzow and Mitchell, "'Vagina Dentata.'"

48. O'Brien, *If I Die*, p. 110.

49. Brownmiller, *Against*, pp. 98–101.

50. Brownmiller identifies her sources as the news correspondent Dan Rather and two soldiers (ibid., pp. 92n, 105, 107).

51. Ibid., p. 33.

52. Duras, *The War*, pp. 116–41.

53. Leepson, "Norman," p. 29.

54. Cox, Letter, p. 5.

55. Allusions to John Wayne abound in the war fiction and nonfiction. Kovic, for example, mentions Wayne in the epigraph of *Born* and a half-dozen times thereafter (pp. 11, 54-55, 74, 86, 112, 171).

56. Lifton, *Home*, pp. 94, 238-39, 251-56.

57. Regarding the victim role in these movements, see Evans, *Personal Politics*, pp. 41-42, 127-28; and Gottlieb, *Do You*, pp. 64-65. For Friedan, the tendency to identify with the victims rather than the "spirited heroines" portrayed in women's magazines was a disturbing symptom of the feminine mystique (*Feminine Mystique*, pp. 52-53).

58. Stanton lists the U.S. Army recipients of the medal, 155 of them, in *Vietnam Order*, pp. 350-52.

59. Boose, "Techno-Muscularity," p. 72.

60. Ibid., p. 81.

61. Jacoby, "Women," p. 199.

62. Blumenthal, "Of Arms," p. 23.

63. Buckley, "Viet Guilt," p. 72.

64. T. Carroll and O'Rourke, "Born."

65. Cummings, "Neighbors," sec. B, p. 5.

66. Tick, "Apocalypse," p. 60.

67. MacPherson, *Long Time*, p. 176.

68. See J. Carroll, "Father Figure," for example, and Chapple, "In Search."

69. Faludi, *Backlash*, p. 310.

70. Bly, *Iron John*, p. 2.

71. Ibid., p. 6.

72. Ibid., pp. 150-51, 227.

73. Marin reports that Dowd was "outraged" by the revisions in her script ("Coming," p. 46). If so, more of the responsibility for the finished product belongs to Fonda and her director, Hal Ashby.

74. Rich, "The Dark," p. 68.

75. Kael, "Mythologizing," p. 119.

76. Mason, *In Country*, p. 62. Hereafter, page numbers are cited parenthetically.

77. Schroeder, *Vietnam*, p. 168. The information in the following sentence is from pp. 169-70.

78. Mason, Interview, p. 7; and "*In Country*: A Film Guide."

79. O'Brien, *Things*, p. 103. Hereafter, this text is cited parenthetically.

80. O'Brien, Interview (1990).

81. Herzog, *Vietnam War Stories*, p. 180.

82. Caputo, *Indian Country*, p. 177. Hereafter, page numbers are cited parenthetically.

83. Pfarrer, *Neverlight*, p. 251. Hereafter, page numbers are cited parenthetically.

84. Fussell, *Great War*, pp. 299-309.

85. Pfarrer, Interview, p. 1.

86. Kael, "Mythologizing," p. 119.

87. K. Marshall, *Combat Zone*, p. 4.

88. Ruddick, "Notes," pp. 118-22.

89. Van Devanter, *Home,* pp. 151, 157; McGoren, quoted in K. Marshall, *Combat Zone,* p. 250.

90. K. Walker, *A Piece,* p. 358.

91. Van Devanter and Lily Adams comment on the importance of expressing rage in PTSD therapy in Palmer, "The Nurses," p. 42.

92. Theweleit, "The Bomb's Womb," p. 312. He refers to a passage in O'Brien's *Things,* p. 87.

93. W. Smith, *American Daughter,* p. 147.

94. J. Gray, *Warriors,* pp. 33–36.

95. Paul, "Wounded," p. 574; cited in E. Norman, *Women,* p. 71.

96. Brownmiller, *Against,* p. 32.

97. W. Smith, *American Daughter,* pp. 305–306.

98. "Convention Report," p. 17.

99. Broyles, "Vietnam," p. 85.

100. Quoted in Leepson, "Up," p. 21.

101. There is also a considerable body of literature written about Vietnam by nonveteran women. D. Butler lists 781 items published between 1954 and 1987 (*American Women*).

102. Jeffords, *Remasculinization,* p. 49.

103. Ibid., p. 188 n. 14.

104. Summers, Editorial, p. 6.

105. Quoted in K. Walker, *A Piece,* p. 17.

106. Van Devanter, *Home,* p. 345.

107. E. Norman, *Women,* p. 155.

108. K. Marshall, *Combat Zone,* p. 14.

109. Quoted in K. Walker, *A Piece,* p. 120.

110. Ibid., p. 106.

111. Van Devanter, *Home,* p. 259.

112. W. Smith, *American Daughter,* p. 250.

113. Ibid., p. 251.

114. K. Walker, *A Piece,* pp. 34, 94.

115. Ibid., pp. 229–32.

116. Jeffords, *Remasculinization,* p. 73.

117. Ibid., p. xiii.

118. Ibid., p. 186.

119. Edward Robinson, quoted in Benshoof-Holler, "Posttraumatic," p. 44.

CHAPTER 5

1. Michener, *Kent State,* pp. 545–54.

2. Gitlin, *Sixties,* p. 414.

3. J. Miller, *"Democracy,"* p. 311.

4. Michener, *Kent State,* p. vii.

5. Quoted in ibid., p. 179.

6. Ibid., p. 453.

7. Ibid., p. 455.

8. Ibid., p. 447.

9. F. Gray, "Slum," p. 77.

10. Riesman, *Abundance*, p. 309.

11. L. Jones, *Great Expectations*, pp. 12, 32.

12. Ibid., p. 94.

13. Remarque, *All Quiet*, p. 16.

14. Mead, *Culture*, p. 50.

15. Ibid., p. 61.

16. Sontag responds to Fiedler's "The New Mutants" in "What's Happening in America" (*Styles*, pp. 193–204).

17. Feuer, *Conflict*, p. 318.

18. Ibid., pp. 31–32.

19. Coopersmith et al., *The Myth*, p. 278.

20. Keniston, *Young Radicals*, p. 298.

21. Feuer, *Conflict*, p. 491.

22. The summary in this paragraph is based on chapter five of Freud's *Interpretation*, "The Material and Sources of Dreams."

23. The summary in this paragraph is based primarily on chapter four of Freud's *Totem*, "The Return of Totemism in Childhood."

24. See Freud, "Female Sexuality" (1931) and "Femininity" (1933).

25. Goodman, *Growing*, p. 123.

26. See Feuer, "Rebellion" and "Pornopolitics." Feuer describes the student response to these essays in *Conflict*, pp. 455, 471.

27. Bettelheim, "Problem," pp. 69–70, 72–73.

28. Lasch, *Haven*, pp. 123–25.

29. Quoted in Lukas, *Don't Shoot*, p. 446.

30. Quoted in J. Miller, "*Democracy*," pp. 329–30.

31. Gitlin, *Sixties*, p. 17.

32. Scammon and Wattenberg, *Real Majority*.

33. Gallup poll cited in Coopersmith et al., *The Myth*, p. 321.

34. Ibid., p. 341.

35. Reproduced in J. Miller, "*Democracy*," following p. 208.

36. Coopersmith et al., *The Myth*, pp. 90, 317–18.

37. Michener, *Kent State*, p. 441.

38. Ibid., p. 451.

39. Hebdige, *Subculture*, p. 131.

40. Michener, *Kent State*, pp. 241–42.

41. Feuer, *Conflict*, p. 455.

42. Quoted in Michener, *Kent State*, p. 243.

43. Rabe meant *The Orphan* to be one of his Vietnam plays, along with *Sticks, The Basic Training of Pavlo Hummel,* and *Streamers* (*Vietnam Plays, Volume Two*, p. 190).

44. Rabe, *Vietnam Plays, Volume One*, p. xxiv. Hereafter, page numbers are cited parenthetically. In the original production of *Sticks* at Villanova University, the characters were named Ozzie, Ginger, David, and Richie (Kolin, *David Rabe*, p. 30).

45. Coontz, *Way*, pp. 13–14.

46. Lasch, *Haven*, pp. 6–7.

47. Coontz, *Way*, p. 27.

48. Halberstam, *Fifties*, p. 509.

49. E. Taylor, *Prime-Time*, p. 20; Coontz, *Way*, p. 175; Bashe, *Teenage Idol*, p. 38n.

50. Davidson, "Happy," p. 161.

51. Quoted in ibid., p. 97.

52. Ibid., pp. 99, 166.

53. Cooper, "David Rabe's," p. 614.

54. Quoted in Kolin, *David Rabe*, pp. 54–55.

55. Coontz, *Way*, p. 195.

56. Ozzie Nelson was an atheist; Harriet, though religious, did not believe in formal religion (Davidson, "Happy," p. 157).

57. Schroeder, *Vietnam*, p. 208.

58. Quoted in Tollefson, *Strength*, p. 30.

59. For Craig McNamara's antiwar sentiments, see Shapley, *Promise*, pp. 380–81, 408, 482–83; for Richard Rusk's, see D. Rusk, *As I Saw It*, pp. 419–20; for Jesse Vann's, see Sheehan, *Bright*, pp. 27–31.

60. John Douglas Marshall tells his story in *Reconciliation*, comparing it with that of Lucian K. Truscott IV on pp. 42–46.

61. Herr, *Dispatches*, p. 29. Steve Metcalfe's play *Strange Snow* (1982), on which the film *Jacknife* (1989) is based, portrays a fictional veteran who likewise blames his father for the illusions that prompted him to enlist in the army. He feels cheated when his father dies during his tour of duty because he is thereby prevented from taking revenge.

62. Wolff, *Pharoah's Army*, p. 109.

63. Ibid., p. 128.

64. Lewis, *Tainted War*, p. 50.

65. Patrick, *Kennedy's Children*, p. 28.

66. Mead, *And Keep*, p. 49.

67. Hellmann, *American Myth*, pp. 99–137.

68. Michener, *Kent State*, pp. 49–50; cf. pp. 50, 68, 355, 451.

69. Sollors, *Beyond Ethnicity*, p. 212.

70. Currey, *Fatal Light*, pp. 184–85.

71. Freud, *Jokes*, p. 199.

72. Zumwalt, *My Father*, p. 206.

73. Freud, *Jokes*, p. 155.

74. Zumwalt, *My Father*, pp. 23, 212.

75. Ibid., p. 196.

76. Ibid., p. 3.

77. Puller, *Fortunate Son*, p. 55.

78. B. Davis, *Marine!*, p. 36. Hereafter, page numbers are cited parenthetically except where ambiguity might result.

79. Compare Puller, *Fortunate Son*, p. 4.

80. Ibid., p. 23. Hereafter, page numbers are cited parenthetically except where ambiguity might result.

81. Ibid., p. 5; B. Davis, *Marine!*, p. 331.

82. Barthes, *Pleasure*, p. 47.

83. Bloom, *Anxiety,* p. 85.

84. B. Davis, *Marine!,* p. 4.

85. Ibid., p. 91.

86. Puller, *Fortunate Son,* p. 33.

87. Adler, "Death," p. 44.

88. This humiliation may qualify as the phase called "kenosis," or "self-emptying," that follows "tessera" in Bloom's revisionary cycle.

89. Kerrey, "For Lew," p. 13.

90. Adler, "Death," p. 44; Manegold, "Suicide," p. 8.

91. Manegold, "Suicide," p. 8.

92. Baskir and Strauss, *Chance,* p. 248. Rather than join traditional veterans organizations like the American Legion and Veterans of Foreign Wars, where they did not feel welcome, some Vietnam veterans formed their own groups, the largest being Vietnam Veterans of America.

93. Wolff, *Pharoah's Army,* p. 44. Hereafter, page numbers are cited parenthetically.

94. Howerton, "Persistence," p. 140. Hereafter, page numbers are cited parenthetically.

95. Freud, "Family Romances," p. 237.

CHAPTER 6

1. Anderson estimates that there were six or eight soldiers in support for each one in combat (*Vietnam,* p. 2). Gibson puts the ratio at ten to one (*Perfect War,* p. 189), Emerson at twenty to one (*Winners,* p. 10).

2. Kroll, *Teaching,* p. 32.

3. Quoted in ibid., p. 33.

4. Herr, *Dispatches,* p. 6.

5. Ibid., p. 218.

6. Ibid., p. 207.

7. O'Brien, *Cacciato,* p. 338.

8. Ibid., pp. 338, 237.

9. Keegan, *Face,* pp. 297–98.

10. Ricoeur, *Time,* vol. 3, pp. 3, 159. As Barthes points out in *S/Z,* some works demand more active refiguration than others, and he calls these "writerly" texts (p. 4).

11. Heinemann, *Paco's Story,* p. 3.

12. Herr, *Dispatches,* p. 260.

13. Gibson, *Perfect War,* pp. 464–65.

14. Quoted in Santoli, *Everything,* p. 129. The quotation in the following paragraph is from p. 177.

15. Chomsky, *American Power,* p. 27.

16. Gibson, *Perfect War,* p. 462.

17. These passages are drawn from McCloud, *What Should,* pp. 32, 38, 48, 58, and 64.

18. Ricoeur, *Time,* vol. 3, p. 160.

19. DiFusco et al., *Tracers,* pp. 10–11.

20. Cindy Randolph, quoted in K. Marshall, *Combat Zone,* p. 234.

21. O'Brien, *Things,* p. 77.

22. Fussell, *Great War,* p. 334.

23. Ibid., p. 179.

24. O'Brien, *Things,* p. 140.

25. The story is told, for example, in Van Devanter, *Home,* p. 256, and *Hamburger Hill.*

26. O'Brien, *Things,* p. 77.

27. Lydia Fish, quoted in Lomperis, *"Reading,"* p. 41.

28. Gibson, *Perfect War,* p. 188.

29. Lifton, *Home,* p. 353.

30. Merton, "War," pp. 114–15 (Merton's italics).

31. Maitland, *Only War,* pp. 173f.

32. Herr, *Dispatches,* p. 47. In the original, *The New York Times* is italicized, as is the word "so" in the sentence beginning "Slick."

33. Mailer, *Armies,* p. 61.

34. Remarque, *All Quiet,* p. 13.

35. Ricoeur, *Time,* vol. 3, p. 142.

36. Lederer, *Ugly,* p. 229.

37. Ricoeur, *Time,* vol. 1, p. 161 and vol. 3, pp. 185–86; White, *Tropics,* pp. 121–34.

38. Mailer, *Armies,* p. 284.

39. Del Vecchio, *13th Valley,* n. p.

40. Plummer, *"Moby Dick,"* p. 71; and Myers, *Walking Point,* pp. 56–69.

41. Melville, *Moby-Dick,* p. 318.

42. Lomperis, *"Reading,"* pp. 90–91.

43. Pratt, *Laotian Fragments,* p. 240.

44. Quoted in Lomperis, *"Reading,"* p. 90.

45. M. Baker, *Nam,* p. xvi.

46. Just, "Vietnam—Fiction," p. 202. The quotations in the following sentences are from pp. 199 and 203.

47. Aristotle, *Poetics,* p. 15.

48. Barthes, *S/Z,* pp. 80, 167.

49. Caputo, *Rumor,* p. 90. Hereafter, page numbers are cited parenthetically.

50. The summary in this paragraph is from chapters two and four of Brooks's *Reading.*

51. Novak, *Lonely Girls,* p. 152. Here the intertextual connection is easy to trace, since Novak speaks of her indebtedness to *Rumor* and to Caputo personally on pp. 271–72.

52. Barthes defines the five codes of the story in *S/Z,* pp. 18–20.

53. Sacks, *English Elegy,* p. 22.

54. Figley, "Postscript," p. 366.

55. Fussell, *Great War,* p. 7.

56. Frye, *Anatomy,* pp. 33–67.

57. Fussell, *Great War,* p. 312.

58. Caputo, *Indian Country,* p. 153. Hereafter, page numbers are cited parenthetically.

59. Tatum, "The *Iliad,*" p. 16. Shay's *Achilles* is a book-length elaboration of this insight, with special attention to Homer's depiction of combat stress.

60. Brooks, *Reading,* pp. 97, 102.

61. For further discussion of spatial form, together with a retrospective essay by Frank, see Smitten and Daghistany, *Spatial Form.*

62. Schroeder, *Vietnam,* pp. 34, 41–42.

63. Cobley, "Narrating," p. 110.

64. Quoted in Lewy, *America,* p. 118.

65. Fussell, *Great War,* p. 4.

66. K. Marshall, *Combat Zone,* p. 14.

67. Barthes, *S/Z,* p. 167.

68. Hellmann, *American Myth,* p. 191.

69. Rabe, *Vietnam Plays, Volume Two,* p. 193.

70. O'Brien, *Things,* p. 102. Hereafter, page numbers are cited parenthetically.

71. Schumacher, "Writing," p. 36; O'Brien, "Vietnam in Me" and Interview (1994).

72. O'Brien, Interview (1990); also Schumacher, "Writing," p. 38.

73. Schumacher, "Writing," p. 38.

74. In the paperback edition of O'Brien's *Things,* the disclaimer appears in much reduced type on the copyright page.

75. Brooks, *Reading,* p. 12.

76. The author Tim O'Brien experienced a similar serenity in 1994, when he revisited a rice paddy where his unit had to probe for one of its dead following a two-hour battle ("Vietnam in Me," pp. 56–57; Interview [1994]). Life in this case imitated art.

77. Aristotle, *Poetics,* p. 16. Aristotle's comment on Homer, cited in the next sentence, appears on p. 50.

78. James, *Theory,* p. 200.

79. Mason, *In Country,* p. 14.

80. O'Brien, *Lake,* p. 304.

81. Schroeder, *Vietnam,* p. 159.

82. O'Brien, *If I Die,* p. 130.

83. Ricoeur, *Time,* vol. 3, p. 164. The quotations in the following sentences are from pp. 169–70.

84. Riffaterre, *Fictional Truth,* pp. 7–8.

85. Herr, *Dispatches,* p. 245; O'Brien, *Things,* p. 91.

86. Herman, *Trauma,* p. 38.

87. Richard Mollica, quoted in ibid., p. 175.

88. Ibid., pp. 39, 179–80.

89. Ibid., p. 177.

90. Schroeder, *Vietnam,* p. 182.

91. Ibid., p. 147.

92. C. Smith, "Oral History," pp. 17–19.

93. Herman, *Trauma*, p. 9.

94. Ibid., pp. 39, 189.

95. Kovic, *Born*, p. 224. Hasford's *Phantom Blooper* contains a similarly nostalgic passage (p. 51).

96. See Fussell's discussion of the summer of 1914 in *Great War*, pp. 23–24.

97. Reed, "A Veteran Writes," p. 44.

98. Freud, "Mourning," p. 243.

99. Ibid., p. 246.

100. Ibid., p. 245.

101. Elshtain, *Women*, p. 166.

102. Plato, *Republic* V.470b (pp. 98–101).

103. McNamara, *In Retrospect*, p. xvi.

104. Ibid., p. 314; cf. Rusk, *As I Saw It*, pp. 515–17.

105. McNamara and Rusk both disagreed with Johnson on such matters as the bombing of targets in Hanoi. McNamara, however, was more at odds with the president's conduct of the war and therefore had more cause to resign. He chose not to do so, even "silently" in the manner of Dean Acheson and Cyrus Vance, because he believed that he could still influence the president's decisions (*In Retrospect*, p. 314). Rusk, though he understood that resignation was an option (*As I Saw It*, p. 517), apparently believed in the basic aims of the war until his death.

106. McNamara, *In Retrospect*, p. 321.

107. Ibid., pp. xv-xvi.

108. Heinemann, Letter, p. 18.

109. Walzer, *Just War*, pp. 98–100, 195–96.

110. Mahedy, *Out*, pp. 91–97.

111. Walzer, *Just War*, p. 303.

112. Mahedy, *Out*, pp. 39–40.

113. Lewis, *Tainted War*, pp. 164–65.

114. Marin, "Coming," p. 52.

115. Marin, "Living," p. 71.

116. Walzer, *Just War*, p. 304.

117. Haywood T. Kirkland, quoted in Terry, *Bloods*, p. 91.

118. Hemingway, *For Whom*, p. 196.

119. Mahedy, *Out*, p. 50.

120. W. Smith, *American Daughter*, p. 308; Schaeffer, *Buffalo Afternoon*, p. 535.

121. Mahedy, *Out*, p. 111. Writer-veterans who spoke at the Asia Society conference in 1985 generally professed to be agnostics, with Kovic asserting flatly that Vietnam had killed God (Lomperis, *"Reading,"* p. 52). In one systematic study, 17 percent of Vietnam veterans reported no religious preference, as compared with 8 percent of the general population (Kulka et al., *Trauma*, p. 29).

122. Harold Bryant, quoted in Terry, *Bloods*, p. 30.

123. Marin, "Living," p. 80.

124. Kulka et al., *Trauma*, p. 53.

125. Excerpts from their testimony are reprinted in *Winter Soldier*.

126. Beidler, *Re-Writing,* p. 2.

127. Moskos, "Vietnam: Why," pp. 234–36.

128. Walzer, *Just War,* p. 303.

129. Bates, "Tim O'Brien's Myth."

130. O'Brien, *Things,* p. 76.

131. O'Brien, *Lake,* p. 203.

132. Ibid., p. 301.

133. J. Gray, *Warriors,* pp. 174–77.

134. Capps, *Unfinished War,* pp. 118, 137.

135. Ibid., p. 16.

136. Ibid., p. 78.

137. Lomperis, *"Reading,"* p. 113. The quotation in the next sentence is from the same page.

138. Frances FitzGerald, "How Does," p. 302.

139. Knightley, "Role," p. 108.

140. Ringnalda, *Fighting,* p. ix.

141. Ibid., pp. 11, 35–36.

142. Faulkner, *Absalom,* p. 101.

143. Just, "Vietnam—Fiction," p. 204.

144. Keegan, *History,* p. 59.

Works Cited

Abbey, Edward. *Desert Solitaire: A Season in the Wilderness.* New York: McGraw, 1968.

Adams, William. "*Platoon:* Of Heroes and Demons." Review of *Platoon,* dir. Oliver Stone. *Dissent* Summer 1987: 383–86.

Addlestone, David F., and Susan Sherer. "Battleground: Race in Vietnam." *Civil Liberties* 298 (1973): 1–2.

Adler, Jerry, with Eleanor Clift. "Death of a 'Fortunate Son.'" *Newsweek* 23 May 1994: 44.

Algren, Nelson. "Police and Mama-Sans Get It All." *The Last Carousel.* New York: Putnam, 1973. 144–50.

Alsop, Stewart. "The American Class System." *Newsweek* 29 June 1970: 88.

Anderegg, Michael, ed. *Inventing Vietnam: The War in Film and Television.* Philadelphia: Temple UP, 1991.

Anderson, Charles R. *Vietnam: The Other War.* Novato, Calif.: Presidio, 1982.

The Anderson Platoon. Dir. Pierre Schoendoerffer. CBS, 4 July 1967. Videocassette. Bridgestone, 1989.

Apocalypse Now. Dir. Francis Ford Coppola. United Artists, 1979. Videocassette. Paramount, 1987.

Appy, Christian G. *Working-Class War: American Combat Soldiers and Vietnam.* Chapel Hill: U of North Carolina P, 1993.

Aristotle. *The Poetics of Aristotle.* Trans. Preston H. Epps. Chapel Hill: U of North Carolina P, 1970.

Ashes and Embers. Dir. Haile Gerima. Mypheduh, 1982.

Auster, Albert, and Leonard Quart. *How the War Was Remembered: Hollywood and Vietnam.* New York: Praeger, 1988.

Badillo, Gilbert, and G. David Curry. "The Social Incidence of Vietnam Casualties: Social Class or Race?" *Armed Forces and Society* 2 (1976): 397–406.

Baird, James. *Ishmael.* Baltimore: Johns Hopkins UP, 1956.

Baker, Houston A., Jr. *Blues, Ideology, and Afro-American Literature: A Vernacular Theory.* Chicago: U of Chicago P, 1984.

———. *The Journey Back: Issues in Black Literature and Criticism.* Chicago: U of Chicago P, 1980.

Baker, Mark. *Nam: The Vietnam War in the Words of the Men and Women Who Fought There.* 1981. New York: Berkley, 1983.

Bakhtin, M. M. *The Dialogic Imagination: Four Essays.* Ed. Michael Holquist. Trans. Caryl Emerson and Michael Holquist. Austin: U of Texas P, 1981.

Balaban, John. *Remembering Heaven's Face: A Moral Witness in Vietnam.* New York: Poseidon, 1991.

Baldwin, James. *The Fire Next Time.* 1963. New York: Dell, 1964.

Baraka, Amiri. "Last Day of the American Empire (Including Some Instructions for Black People)." *Home: Social Essays.* New York: Morrow, 1966. 189–209.

Barbarella. Dir. Roger Vadim. Paramount, 1968.

Baritz, Loren. *Backfire: A History of How American Culture Led Us into Vietnam and Made Us Fight the Way We Did.* New York: Morrow, 1985.

———. *The Good Life: The Meaning of Success for the American Middle Class.* New York: Knopf, 1989.

Barthes, Roland. "From Work to Text." *Textual Strategies: Perspectives in Post-Structuralist Criticism.* Ed. Josué V. Harari. Ithaca: Cornell UP, 1979. 73–81.

———. *The Pleasure of the Text.* 1973. Trans. Richard Miller. New York: Hill and Wang, 1975.

———. *S/Z.* 1970. Trans. Richard Miller. New York: Hill and Wang, 1974.

Bashe, Philip. *Teenage Idol, Travelin' Man: The Complete Biography of Rick Nelson.* New York: Hyperion, 1992.

Baskir, Lawrence M., and William A. Strauss. *Chance and Circumstance: The Draft, the War, and the Vietnam Generation.* New York: Knopf, 1978.

Bates, Milton J. "Tim O'Brien's Myth of Courage." *Modern Fiction Studies* 33 (1987): 263–79.

Beauvoir, Simone de. *The Second Sex.* 1949. Trans. H. M. Parshley. New York: Knopf, 1952.

Beidler, Philip D. *American Literature and the Experience of Vietnam.* Athens, Ga.: U of Georgia P, 1982.

———. *Re-Writing America: Vietnam Authors in Their Generation.* Athens, Ga.: U of Georgia P, 1991.

Benshoof-Holler, Margaret. "Posttraumatic Stress Disorder." *Vietnam* Dec. 1993: 38–44.

Bercovitch, Sacvan. *The American Jeremiad.* Madison: U of Wisconsin P, 1978.

———. *The Puritan Origins of the American Self.* New Haven: Yale UP, 1975.

Bettelheim, Bruno. "The Problem of Generations." *Youth: Change and Challenge.* Ed. Erik H. Erikson. New York: Basic, 1963. 64–92.

The Big Chill. Dir. Lawrence Kasdan. Columbia, 1983.

Binkin, Martin, and Mark J. Eitelberg, with Alvin J. Schexnider and Marvin M. Smith. *Blacks and the Military.* Washington: Brookings Institution, 1982.

"Birdmen with Black Rifles: Screaming Eagle Paratroopers." *Ebony* Oct. 1966: 37–42.

Blauner, Peter. "Coming Home: Director Oliver Stone Relives His Vietnam Nightmare in *Platoon*." Review of *Platoon*, dir. Oliver Stone. *New York* 8 Dec. 1986: 60–76.

Bloom, Harold. *The Anxiety of Influence: A Theory of Poetry*. New York: Oxford UP, 1975.

Blumenthal, Michael. "Of Arms and Men." *New York Times* 11 Jan. 1981, sec. 4: 23.

Bly, Robert. *Iron John: A Book About Men*. Reading, Mass.: Addison-Wesley, 1990.

——. *The Light around the Body*. New York: Harper, 1967.

Bond, Julian. "The Roots of Racism and War." C. Taylor 107–13.

Boose, Lynda E. "Techno-Muscularity and the 'Boy Eternal': From the Quagmire to the Gulf." Cooke 67–106.

Bradford, William. "Of Plymouth Plantation." P. Miller 5–20.

Breslin, Jimmy. "One Way to End the War." *New York* 22 June 1970: 26–30.

——. *Table Money*. New York: Ticknor and Fields, 1986.

Briggs, Joe Bob. *Iron Joe Bob*. New York: Grove-Atlantic, 1992.

Britt, Donna. "If They're Joning Your Mama, It's Just for Fun." *Milwaukee Journal* 14 Nov. 1993, sec. J: 5.

Brittain, Vera. *Testament of Youth: An Autobiographical Study of the Years 1900–1925*. New York: Macmillan, 1933.

Brooks, Peter. *Reading for the Plot: Design and Intention in Narrative*. New York: Knopf, 1984.

Brown, Dee. *Bury My Heart at Wounded Knee: An Indian History of the American West*. 1971. New York: Bantam, 1972.

Brown, Larry. *Dirty Work*. Chapel Hill: Algonquin, 1989.

Brownmiller, Susan. *Against Our Will: Men, Women, and Rape*. New York: Simon, 1975.

Broyles, William, Jr. *Brothers in Arms: A Journey from War to Peace*. New York: Knopf, 1986.

——. "Vietnam: How the War Became the Movie." *Smart* July-Aug. 1990: 85+.

Bruffee, Kenneth A. *Elegiac Romance: Cultural Change and Loss of the Hero in Modern Fiction*. Ithaca: Cornell UP, 1983.

Bryan, C. D. B. *Friendly Fire*. New York: Putnam, 1976.

Buckley, Christopher. "Viet Guilt." *Esquire* Sept. 1983: 68–72.

Buder, Leonard. "CORE 'River Rats' Stress Militancy." *New York Times* 14 Mar. 1964: 11.

Bugliosi, Vincent, and Curt Gentry. *Helter Skelter: The True Story of the Manson Murders*. New York: Norton, 1974.

Bunyan, John. *The Pilgrim's Progress*. 1678, 1684. Oxford: Oxford UP, 1984.

Butler, Deborah A. *American Women Writers on Vietnam: Unheard Voices*. New York: Garland, 1990.

Butler, Robert Olen. *A Good Scent from a Strange Mountain*. New York: Holt, 1992.

Byerman, Keith E. *Fingering the Jagged Grain: Tradition and Form in Recent Black Fiction*. Athens, Ga.: U of Georgia P, 1985.

Canby, Vincent. "The Vietnam War in Stone's *Platoon*." Review of *Platoon*, dir. Oliver Stone. *New York Times* 19 Dec. 1986, sec. C: 12.

Capps, Walter H. *The Unfinished War: Vietnam and the American Conscience.* 2nd ed. Boston: Beacon, 1990.

Caputo, Philip. *Indian Country.* 1987. New York: Harper Perennial, 1991.

———. *A Rumor of War.* 1977. New York: Ballantine, 1978.

Cardullo, Bert. "Viet Nam Revisited." Review of *Platoon*, dir. Oliver Stone. *Hudson Review* 40 (1987): 458–64.

Carn, John. *Shaw's Nam.* Indianapolis: Benjamin Books, 1984. Rpt. as *Vietnam Blues.* Los Angeles: Holloway, 1988.

Carroll, Jerry. "Father Figure to the New, New Man." *San Francisco Chronicle* 19 Mar. 1986: 36+.

Carroll, Tod, and P. J. O'Rourke. "Born Again on the Fourth of July: Vietnam Combat Veterans Simulator Kit." *National Lampoon* July 1978: 65+.

Cash, Earl A. "*Captain Blackman*: An Interview with John A. Williams." *Black World* June 1973: 51+.

Casualties of War. Dir. Brian De Palma. Columbia, 1989.

Chafe, William H. *The Unfinished Journey: America Since World War II.* New York: Oxford UP, 1986.

Chapple, Steve. "In Search of the Beast Within." *San Francisco Examiner* 11 Jan. 1987, *Image* magazine: 12+.

Chase, Richard. *The American Novel and Its Tradition.* 1957. Baltimore: Johns Hopkins UP, 1980.

China Beach. Created by William Broyles, Jr., and John Sacret Young. ABC. 26 Apr. 1988–22 July 1991.

Chomsky, Noam. *American Power and the New Mandarins.* New York: Pantheon, 1969.

Clausewitz, Carl von. *On War.* 1832. Ed. Anatol Rapoport. Trans. J. J. Graham. New York: Penguin, 1982.

Cleaver, Eldridge. *Soul on Ice.* New York: Delta-Dell, 1968.

Cobley, Evelyn. "Narrating the Facts of War: New Journalism in Herr's *Dispatches* and Documentary Realism in First World War Novels." *Journal of Narrative Technique* 16 (1986): 97–116.

Cohen, Eliot A. *Citizens and Soldiers: The Dilemmas of Military Service.* Ithaca: Cornell UP, 1985.

Coming Home. Dir. Hal Ashby. United Artists, 1978.

Condon, Richard. *The Manchurian Candidate.* New York: McGraw, 1959.

Conrad, Joseph. *Heart of Darkness* and *The Secret Sharer.* New York: Signet-NAL, 1950.

"Convention Report." *VVA Veteran* Sept.-Oct. 1989: 17.

Cook, Fred J. "Hard-Hats: The Rampaging Patriots." *Nation* 15 June 1970: 712–19.

Cooke, Miriam, and Angela Woollacott, eds. *Gendering War Talk.* Princeton: Princeton UP, 1993.

Coontz, Stephanie. *The Way We Never Were: American Families and the Nostalgia Trap.* New York: Basic, 1992.

Cooper, Pamela. "David Rabe's *Sticks and Bones:* The Adventures of Ozzie and Harriet." *Modern Drama* 29 (1986): 613–25.

Coopersmith, Stanley, Mary Regan, and Lois Dick. *The Myth of the Generation Gap.* San Francisco: Albion, 1975.

Corliss, Richard. "*Platoon:* Viet Nam As It Really Was." Review of *Platoon,* dir. Oliver Stone. *Time* 26 Jan. 1987: 54–61.

Cox, Paul. Letter to the editor. *VVA Veteran* Feb. 1990: 5.

Crèvecoeur, Hector St. John de. *Letters from an American Farmer* and *Sketches of Eighteenth-Century America.* New York: Signet-NAL, 1963.

Crowther, John. *Firebase.* London: Constable, 1975.

Cummings, Judith. "Neighbors Term Mass Slayer a Quiet but Hotheaded Loner." *New York Times* 20 July 1984, sec. A:1+.

Currey, Richard. *Fatal Light.* 1988. New York: Penguin, 1989.

Dann, Jeanne Van Buren, and Jack Dann, eds. *In the Field of Fire.* New York: TOR, 1987.

Davidson, Sara. "Happy, Happy, Happy Nelsons." *Esquire* June 1971: 97+.

Davis, Burke. *Marine! The Life of Lt. Gen. Lewis B. (Chesty) Puller, USMC (Ret.).* Boston: Little, 1962.

Davis, George. *Coming Home.* 1971. Washington: Howard UP, 1984.

Davis, James W., Jr., and Kenneth M. Dolbeare. *Little Groups of Neighbors: The Selective Service System.* Chicago: Markham, 1968.

Decter, Midge. *Liberal Parents, Radical Children.* New York: Coward, McCann, 1975.

The Deer Hunter. Dir. Michael Cimino. EMI/Columbia/Warner, 1978.

Del Vecchio, John M. *The 13th Valley.* 1982. New York: Bantam, 1983.

"Democracy in the Foxhole." *Time* 26 May 1967: 15–19.

Desser, David. "'Charlie Don't Surf': Race and Culture in the Vietnam War Films." Anderegg 81–102.

Diagnostic and Statistical Manual of Mental Disorders. 3rd ed. Washington: American Psychiatric Association, 1980.

DiFusco, John, et al. *Tracers.* New York: Hill and Wang, 1986.

Dittmar, Linda, and Gene Michaud. "America's Vietnam War Films: Marching toward Denial." Dittmar and Michaud 1–15.

———, eds. *From Hanoi to Hollywood: The Vietnam War in American Film.* New Brunswick: Rutgers UP, 1990.

Douglas, Ann. *The Feminization of American Culture.* New York: Knopf, 1977.

Douglass, Frederick. *The Narrative and Selected Writings.* Ed. Michael Meyer. New York: Modern Library, 1984.

Drinnon, Richard. *Facing West: The Metaphysics of Indian-Hating and Empire-Building.* New York: Meridian-NAL, 1980.

Du Bois, W. E. B. *The Gift of Black Folk: The Negroes in the Making of America.* Boston: Stratford, 1924.

———. *The Souls of Black Folk.* 1903. New York: Dodd, 1979.

Duras, Marguerite. *The War: A Memoir.* 1985. Trans. Barbara Bray. New York: Pantheon, 1986.

Durden, Charles. *No Bugles, No Drums.* New York: Viking, 1976.

Eastlake, William. *The Bamboo Bed.* New York: Simon, 1969.

Easy Rider. Dir. Dennis Hopper. Pando-Raybert/Columbia, 1969.

Edgerton, Clyde. *The Floatplane Notebooks.* 1988. New York: Ballantine, 1989.

84 Charlie MoPic. Dir. Patrick Duncan. New Century/Vista, 1989.

Eliade, Mircea. *The Myth of the Eternal Return.* 1949. Trans. Willard R. Trask. New York: Pantheon, 1954.

Elliott, Ellen. *Vietnam Nurse.* New York: Arcadia, 1968.

Ellison, Ralph. *Shadow and Act.* New York: Random, 1964.

Ellmann, Mary. *Thinking about Women.* New York: Harcourt, 1968.

Elshtain, Jean Bethke. *Women and War.* New York: Basic, 1987.

Emerson, Gloria. *Winners and Losers: Battles, Retreats, Gains, Losses, and Ruins from the Vietnam War.* New York: Random, 1976.

Evans, Sara. *Personal Politics: The Roots of Women's Liberation in the Civil Rights Movement and the New Left.* New York: Knopf, 1979.

Fallows, James. "What Did You Do in the Class War, Daddy?" *Washington Monthly* Oct. 1975: 5–19.

Faludi, Susan. *Backlash: The Undeclared War against American Women.* New York: Crown, 1991.

Faulkner, William. *Absalom, Absalom!* 1936. New York: Vintage-Random, 1990.

———. *Go Down, Moses.* 1942. New York: Vintage-Random, 1973.

Feuer, Lewis S. *The Conflict of Generations: The Character and Significance of Student Movements.* New York: Basic, 1969.

———. "Pornopolitics and the University." *New Leader* 12 Apr. 1965: 14–19.

———. "Rebellion at Berkeley." *New Leader* 21 Dec. 1964: 3–12.

Fiedler, Leslie. "The New Mutants." *Unfinished Business.* New York: Stein and Day, 1972. 187–208.

———. "Who Really Died in Vietnam?" *Saturday Review* 18 Nov. 1972: 40–43.

Field, Della. *Vietnam Nurse.* New York: Avon, 1966.

Figley, Charles R. "A Postscript: Welcoming Home the Strangers." Figley and Leventman 363–67.

Figley, Charles R., and Seymour Leventman, eds. *Strangers at Home: Vietnam Veterans Since the War.* New York: Brunner/Mazel, 1990.

Filson, John. *The Discovery, Settlement, and Present State of Kentucke.* 1784. Rpt. as *The Discovery and Settlement of Kentucke.* Ann Arbor: University Microfilms, 1966.

Fisher, Dexter, and Robert B. Stepto, eds. *Afro-American Literature: The Reconstruction of Instruction.* New York: MLA, 1979.

Fisher, Marc. "Jenkins Reaffirmed as D.C. School Chief." *Washington Post* 14 June 1988, sec. B: 1+.

Fitzgerald, F. Scott. *The Great Gatsby.* New York: Scribner's, 1925.

FitzGerald, Frances. *Fire in the Lake: The Vietnamese and the Americans in Vietnam.* 1972. New York: Vintage-Random, 1973.

———. "How Does America Avoid Future Vietnams?" Salisbury 300–305.

Flowers, A. R. *De Mojo Blues.* New York: Dutton, 1985.

Foner, Jack D. *Blacks and the Military in American History.* New York: Praeger, 1974.

Foucault, Michel. *The Archaeology of Knowledge.* 1969. Trans. A. M. Sheridan Smith. New York: Pantheon, 1972.

Frank, Joseph. "Spatial Form in Modern Literature." *The Idea of Spatial Form.* New Brunswick: Rutgers UP, 1991. 5–66.

Frazer, Sir James George. *The Golden Bough: A Study in Magic and Religion.* 3rd ed. 12 vols. New York: Macmillan, 1935.

Freud, Sigmund. *Beyond the Pleasure Principle.* 1920. *Standard Edition* vol. 18: 7–64.

———. "Family Romances." 1909. *Standard Edition* vol. 9: 237–41.

———. "Female Sexuality." 1931. *Standard Edition* vol. 21: 228–29.

———. "Femininity." 1933. *Standard Edition* vol. 22: 112–35.

———. *The Interpretation of Dreams.* 1900. *Standard Edition* vols. 4–5: 1–621.

———. *Jokes and Their Relation to the Unconscious.* 1905. *Standard Edition* vol. 8: 9–236.

———. "Mourning and Melancholia." 1917. *Standard Edition* vol. 14: 243–58.

———. *The Standard Edition of the Complete Psychological Works.* Trans. James Strachey et al. 24 vols. London: Hogarth, 1953–1974.

———. *Totem and Taboo: Some Points of Agreement between the Mental Lives of Savages and Neurotics.* 1913. *Standard Edition* vol. 13: 1–161.

Friedan, Betty. *The Feminine Mystique.* New York: Norton, 1963.

———. *The Second Stage.* Rev. ed. New York: Summit, 1986.

Frye, Northrop. *Anatomy of Criticism: Four Essays.* 1957. New York: Atheneum, 1967.

Full Metal Jacket. Dir. Stanley Kubrick. Warner, 1987.

Fussell, Paul. *The Great War and Modern Memory.* New York: Oxford UP, 1975.

Gaines, Ernest J. *The Autobiography of Miss Jane Pittman.* New York: Dial, 1971.

Gates, Henry Louis, Jr. "African American Criticism." Greenblatt and Gunn 303–19.

———. *The Signifying Monkey: A Theory of Afro-American Literary Criticism.* New York: Oxford UP, 1988.

Geertz, Clifford. *The Interpretation of Cultures.* New York: Basic, 1973.

Geng, Veronica. "Capable of Anything." Review of *Paco's Story,* by Larry Heinemann. *New Yorker* 11 May 1987: 111–14.

Gibson, James William. *The Perfect War: Technowar in Vietnam.* Boston: Atlantic, 1986.

———. *Warrior Dreams: Paramilitary Culture in Post-Vietnam America.* New York: Hill and Wang, 1994.

Gilbert, Sandra M. "Soldier's Heart: Literary Men, Literary Women, and the Great War." Higonnet 197–226.

Gioglio, Jerry. *Days of Decision: An Oral History of Conscientious Objectors in the Military during the Vietnam War.* Trenton, NJ: Broken Rifle, 1989.

Gitlin, Todd. *The Sixties: Years of Hope, Days of Rage.* New York: Bantam, 1987.

Glines, C. V. "Black vs. White." *Armed Forces Management* 16 (June 1970): 20+.

Goff, Stanley, and Robert Sanders, with Clark Smith. *Brothers: Black Soldiers in the Nam.* 1982. New York: Berkley, 1985.

Gooding, Judson. "Blue-Collar Blues on the Assembly Line." *Fortune* July 1970: 69+.

Goodman, Paul. *Growing Up Absurd: Problems of Youth in the Organized System.* New York: Random, 1960.

Gotera, Vicente F. "'Lines of Tempered Steel': An Interview with Yusef Komunyakaa." *Callaloo* 13 (1990): 215–29.

Gottlieb, Annie. *Do You Believe in Magic? The Second Coming of the Sixties Generation.* New York: Times, 1987.

Gover, Kathryn R., and Beverly J. McEaddy. "Job Situation of Vietnam-Era Veterans." *Monthly Labor Review* 97.8 (1974): 17–26.

Grantland, Scott. *The Bamboo Beast.* [Glendale, Calif.]: Pompeii, 1968.

Gray, Francine du Plessix. "Slum Landlords in Eden." *Saturday Review* 18 Nov. 1972: 73–78.

Gray, J. Glenn. *The Warriors: Reflections on Men in Battle.* 1959. New York: Harper, 1967.

"The Great Society in Uniform." *Newsweek* 22 Aug. 1966: 46+.

The Green Berets. Dir. John Wayne. Batjac/Warner, 1968.

Greenblatt, Stephen, and Giles Gunn, eds. *Redrawing the Boundaries: The Transformation of English and American Literary Studies.* New York: MLA, 1992.

Greene, Graham. *The Quiet American.* 1955. New York: Penguin, 1980.

Groom, Winston, and Duncan Spencer. *Conversations with the Enemy: The Story of PFC Robert Garwood.* New York: Putnam, 1983.

Gross, Barry. "Back West: Time and Place in *The Great Gatsby.*" *Western American Literature* 8 (1973): 3–13.

Gubar, Susan. "'This Is My Rifle, This Is My Gun': World War II and the Blitz on Women." Higonnet 227–59.

Gulzow, Monte, and Carol Mitchell. "'Vagina Dentata' and 'Incurable Venereal Disease': Legends from the Viet Nam War." *Western Folklore* 39 (1980): 306–16.

Hahn, Harlan. "Correlates of Public Sentiments about War: Local Referenda on the Vietnam Issue." *American Political Science Review* Dec. 1970: 1186–98.

———. "Dove Sentiments among Blue-Collar Workers." *Dissent* May–June 1970: 202–205.

Haines, Harry W. "'They Were Called and They Went': The Political Rehabilitation of the Vietnam Veteran." Dittmar and Michaud 81–97.

Halberstam, David. *The Best and the Brightest.* New York: Random, 1972.

———. *The Fifties.* New York: Villard/Random, 1993.

Halstead, Fred. *GIs Speak Out against the War: The Case of the Fort Jackson Eight.* New York: Pathfinder, 1970.

Hamburger Hill. Dir. John Irvin. Paramount, 1987.

Hamilton, Richard F. *Class and Politics in the United States*. New York: John Wiley, 1972.

The Hanoi Hilton. Dir. Lionel Chetwynd. Cannon, 1987.

Harris, Norman. *Connecting Times: The Sixties in Afro-American Fiction*. Jackson: UP of Mississippi, 1988.

Hasford, Gustav. *The Phantom Blooper*. New York: Bantam, 1990.

———. *The Short-Timers*. 1979. New York: Bantam, 1980.

Hawkins, Evelyn. *Vietnam Nurse*. New York: Zebra, 1984.

Hayslip, Le Ly. *When Heaven and Earth Changed Places*. 1989. New York: Plume-Penguin, 1990.

Hearts of Darkness: A Filmmaker's Apocalypse. Dir. Fax Bahr and George Hickenlooper. Triton, 1991.

Hebdige, Dick. *Subculture: The Meaning of Style*. London: Methuen, 1979.

Heinemann, Larry. *Close Quarters*. 1977. New York: Fawcett, n.d.

———. "The First Clean Fact." *TriQuarterly* 45 (1979): 178–88.

———. Interview. Lannan Literary Videos, no. 20. Videocassette. Lannan Foundation, 1990.

———. "'Just Don't Fit.'" *Harper's* Apr. 1985: 55–63.

———. Letter to the editor. *New York Times* 26 Apr. 1995, sec A: 18.

———. *Paco's Story*. 1986. New York: Penguin, 1987.

Hellmann, John. *American Myth and the Legacy of Vietnam*. New York: Columbia UP, 1986.

Helmer, John. *Bringing the War Home: The American Soldier in Vietnam and After*. New York: Free Press, 1974.

Hemingway, Ernest. *For Whom the Bell Tolls*. New York: Scribner's, 1940.

Herman, Judith Lewis. *Trauma and Recovery*. New York: Basic, 1992.

Herr, Michael. *Dispatches*. 1977. New York: Vintage-Random, 1991.

Herzog, Tobey C. *Vietnam War Stories: Innocence Lost*. London: Routledge, 1992.

Higonnet, Margaret Randolph, et al., eds. *Behind the Lines: Gender and the Two World Wars*. New Haven: Yale UP, 1987.

Ho Chi Minh. *Ho Chi Minh on Revolution: Selected Writings, 1920–66*. Ed. Bernard B. Fall. New York: Praeger, 1967.

Howerton, Walter. "The Persistence of Memory." *Writing Fiction: A Guide to Narrative Craft*. Ed. Janet Burroway. 2nd ed. Boston: Little, 1991. 135–50.

Howes, Craig. *Voices of the Vietnam POWs: Witnesses to Their Fight*. New York: Oxford UP, 1993.

"How Negro Americans Perform in Vietnam." *U.S. News and World Report* 15 Aug. 1966: 60–63.

Hsiao, Lisa. "Project 100,000: The Great Society's Answer to Military Manpower Needs in Vietnam." W. King 14–37.

Hubbell, John G. *P.O.W.: A Definitive History of the American Prisoner-of-War Experience in Vietnam, 1964–1973*. New York: Reader's Digest, 1976.

Hughes, Langston, and Arna Bontemps, eds. *The Book of Negro Folklore*. New York: Dodd, 1958.

Hunter, Marjorie. "Leaders Concede Loss on Equal Rights." *New York Times* 25 June 1982, sec. A: 1+.

Hunter, R. Lanny, and Victor L. Hunter. *Living Dogs and Dead Lions.* New York: Viking, 1986.

Hurston, Zora Neale. "High John de Conquer." Hughes and Bontemps 93–102.

———. *Their Eyes Were Watching God.* 1937. New York: Harper, 1990.

In Country. Dir. Norman Jewison. Warner, 1989.

"*In Country*: A Film Guide." Ed. Frederic and Mary Ann Brussat. New York: Cultural Information Service, 1989.

"The Integrated Society." *Time* 23 Dec. 1966: 22.

Jackknife. Dir. David Jones. Cineplex, 1989.

Jackson, Blyden. *Operation Burning Candle.* New York: Third Press, 1973.

Jacoby, Susan. "Women and the War." *The Wounded Generation: America after Vietnam.* Ed. A. D. Horne. Englewood Cliffs: Prentice, 1981. 193–204.

James, Henry. *Theory of Fiction: Henry James.* Ed. James E. Miller, Jr. Lincoln: U of Nebraska P, 1972.

Jameson, Fredric. *The Political Unconscious: Narrative as a Socially Symbolic Act.* Ithaca: Cornell UP, 1981.

Janowitz, Morris. *The Professional Soldier.* New York: Free Press, 1971.

Jefferson, Thomas. "Notes on the State of Virginia." *Writings.* New York: Library of America, 1984. 123–325.

Jeffords, Susan. *The Remasculinization of America: Gender and the Vietnam War.* Bloomington: Indiana UP, 1989.

Joe. Dir. John G. Avildsen. Cannon, 1970.

Johnson, Thomas A. "Negro Expatriates Finding Wide Opportunity in Asia." *New York Times* 30 Apr. 1968: 1+.

———. "Negro Veteran Is Confused and Bitter." *New York Times* 29 July 1968: 1+.

———. "The U.S. Negro in Vietnam." *New York Times* 29 Apr. 1968: 1+.

Jones, Kirkland C. "Folk Idiom in the Literary Expression of Two African American Authors: Rita Dove and Yusef Komunyakaa." *Language and Literature in the African American Imagination.* Ed. Carol Aisha Blackshire-Belay. Westport, Conn.: Greenwood, 1992. 149–65.

Jones, Landon Y. *Great Expectations: America and the Baby Boom Generation.* New York: Coward, 1980.

Just, Ward. "Vietnam: The Camera Lies." *Atlantic* Dec. 1979: 63–65.

——— "Vietnam—Fiction and Fact." *The Writer in Our World: A Symposium Sponsored by* TriQuarterly *Magazine.* Ed. Reginald Gibbons. Boston: Atlantic, 1986. 199–204.

Kael, Pauline. "Mythologizing the Sixties." Review of *Coming Home,* dir. Hal Ashby. *New Yorker* 20 Feb. 1978: 119–21.

———. Review of *Platoon,* dir. Oliver Stone. *New Yorker* 12 Jan. 1987: 94–96.

Keegan, John. *The Face of Battle.* New York: Viking, 1976.

———. *A History of Warfare.* London: Hutchinson, 1993.

Kempley, Walter. *The Invaders.* New York: Saturday Review/Dutton, 1976.

Keniston, Kenneth. *The Uncommitted: Alienated Youth in American Society.* New York: Harcourt, 1965.

———. *Young Radicals: Notes on Committed Youth*. New York: Harcourt, 1968.

Kennedy, John F. *"Let the Word Go Forth": The Speeches, Statements, and Writings of John F. Kennedy*. Ed. Theodore C. Sorensen. New York: Delacorte, 1988.

Kermode, Frank. *The Sense of an Ending: Studies in the Theory of Fiction*. New York: Oxford UP, 1967.

Kerrey, Bob. "For Lew." *New Republic* 6 June 1994: 12–13.

King, Martin Luther, Jr. "A Time to Break Silence." *Freedomways* 7 (1967): 103–17.

King, William M. "'Our Men in Vietnam': Black Media as a Source of the Afro-American Experience in Southeast Asia." W. King 94–117.

———, ed. *A White Man's War: Race Issues and Vietnam*. Special issue of *Vietnam Generation*, 1.2 (1989).

Kinney, Judy Lee. "*Gardens of Stone, Platoon,* and *Hamburger Hill:* Ritual and Remembrance." Anderegg 153–65.

Klein, Joe. *Payback*. 1984. New York: Ballantine, 1985.

Klein, Michael. "Historical Memory, Film, and the Vietnam Era." Dittmar and Michaud 19–40.

Knightley, Phillip. "The Role of Journalists in Vietnam: A Feature Writer's Perspective." Salisbury 106–109.

Kochman, Thomas. *Black and White Styles in Conflict*. Chicago: U of Chicago P, 1981.

Koehler, Dennis P. Letter to the editor. *VVA Veteran* May 1987: 7.

Kolin, Philip C. *David Rabe: A Stage History and a Primary and Secondary Bibliography*. New York: Garland, 1988.

Kolodny, Annette. *The Lay of the Land: Metaphor as Experience and History in American Life and Letters*. Chapel Hill: U of North Carolina P, 1975.

Komunyakaa, Yusef. *Dien Cai Dau*. Middletown, Conn.: Wesleyan UP, 1988.

Komunyakaa, Yusef, and William Matthews. "Jazz and Poetry: A Conversation." Mod. Robert Kelly. *Georgia Review* 46 (1992): 645–61.

Kopit, Arthur. *Indians*. New York: Hill and Wang, 1969.

Kovic, Ron. *Born on the Fourth of July*. 1976. New York: Pocket, 1977.

Kroll, Barry M. *Teaching Hearts and Minds: College Students Reflect on the Vietnam War in Literature*. Carbondale: Southern Illinois UP, 1992.

Kulka, Richard A., et al. *Trauma and the Vietnam War Generation: Report of Findings from the National Vietnam Veterans Readjustment Study*. New York: Brunner/Mazel, 1990.

"Labor's New Left Launches an Attack." *Business Week* 1 July 1972: 15.

Ladinsky, Jack. "Vietnam, the Veterans, and the Veterans Administration." *Armed Forces and Society* 2 (1976): 435–67.

Lang, Daniel. *Casualties of War*. New York: McGraw, 1969.

Larsen, Wendy, and Tran Thi Nga. *Shallow Graves: Two Women and Vietnam*. New York: Harper, 1986.

Lasch, Christopher. *Haven in a Heartless World: The Family Besieged*. New York: Basic, 1977.

Leckie, William H. *The Buffalo Soldiers: A Narrative of the Negro Cavalry in the West.* Norman: U of Oklahoma P, 1967.

Lederer, William J., and Eugene Burdick. *The Ugly American.* 1958. New York: Ballantine-Fawcett, 1983.

Leed, Eric J. *No Man's Land: Combat and Identity in World War I.* Cambridge: Cambridge UP, 1979.

Leepson, Marc. "Norman vs Brian: De Palma KO'd." Review of *In Country,* dir. Norman Jewison, and *Casualties of War,* dir. Brian De Palma. *VVA Veteran* Sept.-Oct. 1989: 29.

———. "Up in Arms over China Beach." *VVA Veteran* July 1989: 21.

Levison, Andrew. *The Working-Class Majority.* 1974. New York: Penguin, 1975.

Levy, Charles J. "ARVN as Faggots: Inverted Warfare in Vietnam." *transaction* 8.12 (1971): 18-27.

Lewis, Lloyd B. *The Tainted War: Culture and Identity in Vietnam War Narratives.* Westport, Conn.: Greenwood, 1985.

Lewy, Guenter. *America in Vietnam.* New York: Oxford UP, 1978.

Lifton, Robert Jay. *Home from the War: Vietnam Veterans: Neither Victims nor Executioners.* New York: Simon, 1973.

Linn, Edward, and Jack Pearl. *Masque of Honor.* New York: Norton, 1969.

Little Big Man. Dir. Arthur Penn. National General, 1970.

Little, Loyd. *Parthian Shot.* New York: Viking, 1975.

Lomperis, Timothy J. *"Reading the Wind": The Literature of the Vietnam War.* Durham, N.C.: Duke UP, 1987.

"Long Shot." *New Republic* 21 Feb. 1970: 11.

Loory, Stuart H. *Defeated: Inside America's Military Machine.* New York: Random, 1973.

Louvre, Alf, and Jeffrey Walsh, eds. "Preface." *Tell Me Lies about Vietnam: Cultural Battles for the Meaning of the War.* Milton Keynes, England: Open UP, 1988. xi-xii.

Lukas, J. Anthony. *Don't Shoot—We Are Your Children!* New York: Random, 1971.

Lynd, Staughton, and Thomas Hayden. *The Other Side.* New York: NAL, 1966.

Lyon, Jeff. "Author 1st Class." *Chicago Tribune* 7 Feb. 1988, sec. 10: 10+.

MacPherson, Myra. *Long Time Passing: Vietnam and the Haunted Generation.* 1984. New York: Signet-NAL, 1985.

Mahedy, William P. *Out of the Night: The Spiritual Journey of Vietnam Veterans.* 1986. New York: Ballantine, 1988.

Mailer, Norman. *The Armies of the Night: History as a Novel, the Novel as History.* New York: Signet-NAL, 1968.

———. "The White Negro: Superficial Reflections on the Hipster." *Advertisements for Myself.* New York: Putnam, 1959. 337-58.

———. *Why Are We in Vietnam?* 1967. New York: Holt, 1982.

Maitland, Derek. *The Only War We've Got.* New York: Morrow, 1970.

Malek, Parma. *Viet Cong Defilers.* Chatsworth, Calif.: Stag, 1976.

Manegold, Catherine S. "Suicide of a Veteran, Amid Pain and Fame." *New York Times* 14 May 1994: 8.

Mannheim, Karl. "The Problem of Generations." *The New Pilgrims: Youth Protest in Transition*. Ed. Philip G. Altbach and Robert S. Laufer. New York: McKay, [1972]. 99–138.

Marcus, Greil. "Journey Up the River: An Interview with Francis Coppola." *Rolling Stone* 1 Nov. 1979: 51–57.

Marin, Peter. "Coming to Terms with Vietnam." *Harper's* Dec. 1980: 41–56.

——. "Living in Moral Pain." *Psychology Today* Nov. 1981: 68+.

Marshall, John Douglas. *Reconciliation Road: A Family Odyssey of War and Honor*. Syracuse: Syracuse UP, 1993.

Marshall, Kathryn. *In the Combat Zone: An Oral History of American Women in Vietnam, 1966–1975*. Boston: Little, 1987.

Martin, Andrew. *Receptions of War: Vietnam in American Culture*. Norman: U of Oklahoma P, 1993.

Marx, Karl, and Friedrich Engels. *The Communist Manifesto*. 1848. Ed. Samuel H. Beer. New York: Appleton, 1955.

——. *Economic and Philosophic Manuscripts of 1844*. Ed. Dirk J. Struik. Trans. Martin Milligan. New York: International, 1964.

Marx, Leo. *The Machine in the Garden: Technology and the Pastoral Ideal in America*. 1964. New York: Oxford UP, 1972.

——. "Susan Sontag's 'New Left Pastoral': Notes on Revolutionary Pastoralism." *Literature in Revolution*. Ed. George Abbott White and Charles Newman. New York: Holt, 1972. Rpt. in *The Pilot and the Passenger: Essays on Literature, Technology, and Culture in the United States*. New York: Oxford UP, 1988. 291–314.

Mason, Bobbie Ann. *In Country*. 1985. New York: Harper, 1986.

——. Interview. *New York Times Book Review* 15 Sept. 1985: 7.

McAllister, Bill. "Low-Aptitude Veterans Gain Little in Military, Study Finds." *Washington Post* 24 Feb. 1990: 1+.

McCarthy, Mary. *Hanoi*. New York: Harcourt, 1968.

McCloud, Bill. *What Should We Tell Our Children about Vietnam?* Norman: U of Oklahoma P, 1989.

McGilligan, Pat. "Point Man." *Film Comment* Jan.–Feb. 1987: 11+.

McNamara, Robert S., with Brian VanDeMark. *In Retrospect: The Tragedy and Lessons of Vietnam*. New York: Times/Random, 1995.

Mead, Margaret. *And Keep Your Powder Dry*. New York: Morrow, 1942.

——. *Culture and Commitment: A Study of the Generation Gap*. Garden City: American Museum of Natural History/Doubleday, 1970.

Melling, Philip H. *Vietnam in American Literature*. Boston: Twayne, 1990.

Melville, Herman. *Moby-Dick*. 1851. Ed. Harrison Hayford and Hershel Parker. New York: Norton, 1967.

Mersmann, James F. *Out of the Vietnam Vortex: A Study of Poets and Poetry against the War*. Lawrence: UP of Kansas, 1974.

Merton, Thomas. "War and the Crisis of Language." *The Critique of War: Contemporary Philosophical Explorations*. Ed. Robert Ginsberg. Chicago: Regnery, 1969. 99–119.

Metcalfe, Steve. "Strange Snow." *Coming to Terms: American Plays and the Vietnam War*. New York: Theatre Communications Group, 1985. 276–312.

Michelotti, Kopp, and Kathryn R. Gover. "The Employment Situation of Vietnam Era Veterans." *Monthly Labor Review* 95.12 (1972): 7–15.

Michener, James A. *Kent State: What Happened and Why.* New York: Random/Reader's Digest, 1971.

Miller, Daniel. "Primetime Television's Tour of Duty." Anderegg 166–89.

Miller, James. *"Democracy Is in the Streets": From Port Huron to the Siege of Chicago.* New York: Simon, 1987.

Miller, Perry. *The New England Mind: From Colony to Province.* 1953. Boston: Beacon, 1961.

———. *The New England Mind: The Seventeenth Century.* 1939. Boston: Beacon, 1961.

———, ed. *The American Puritans: Their Prose and Poetry.* Garden City: Anchor-Doubleday, 1956.

Millett, Kate. *Sexual Politics.* Garden City: Doubleday, 1970.

Missing in Action. Dir. Joseph Zito. Cannon, 1984.

Moi, Toril. *Sexual/Textual Politics: Feminist Literary Theory.* London: Methuen, 1985.

Molloy, Tom. *The Green Line.* Charlestown, Mass.: Charles River, 1982.

Montrose, Louis. "New Historicisms." Greenblatt and Gunn 392–418.

Morton, Thomas. *New English Canaan.* 1637. Ed. Charles Francis Adams, Jr. 1883. Burt Franklin Research and Source Works Series, No. 131. New York: Burt Franklin, 1967.

Moskos, Charles C., Jr. *The American Enlisted Man: The Rank and File in Today's Military.* New York: Russell Sage, 1970.

———. "Surviving the War in Vietnam." Figley and Leventman 71–85.

———. "Vietnam: Why Men Fight." *The Anti-American Generation.* Ed. Edgar Z. Friedenberg. N.p.: Transaction, 1971. 217–37.

Myers, Thomas. *Walking Point: American Narratives of Vietnam.* New York: Oxford UP, 1988.

Nalty, Bernard C. *Strength for the Fight: A History of Black Americans in the Military.* New York: Free Press, 1986.

Nash, Roderick. *Wilderness and the American Mind.* 3rd ed. New Haven: Yale UP, 1982.

Naughton, James M. "Agnew, in Delaware, Criticizes 'Elitism.'" *New York Times* 15 Oct. 1970: 52.

Nelson, Charles. *The Boy Who Picked the Bullets Up.* New York: Morrow, 1981.

Newman, John, with Ann Hilfinger. *Vietnam War Literature: An Annotated Bibliography of Imaginative Works about Americans Fighting in Vietnam.* 2nd ed. Metuchen, N.J.: Scarecrow, 1988.

Nicosia, Gerald. "A War Story That Tells the Truth." Review of *Paco's Story,* by Larry Heinemann. *Chicago Tribune* 23 Nov. 1986, sec. 14: 6–7.

The Night of the Hunter. Dir. Charles Laughton. United Artists, 1955.

Norman, Elizabeth M. *Women at War: The Story of Fifty Military Nurses Who Served in Vietnam.* Philadelphia: U of Pennsylvania P, 1990.

Norman, Michael. "*Platoon* Grapples with Vietnam." Review of *Platoon,* dir. Oliver Stone. *New York Times* 21 Dec. 1986, sec. 2: 17–18.

Norris, Frank. "The Frontier Gone at Last." *Novels and Essays*. New York: Library of America, 1986. 1183–90.

Novak, Marian Faye. *Lonely Girls with Burning Eyes: A Wife Recalls Her Husband's Journey Home from Vietnam*. New York: Little, 1991.

O'Brien, Tim. *Going after Cacciato*. 1978. New York: Laurel-Dell, 1987.

———. *If I Die in a Combat Zone*. 1973. New York: Laurel-Dell, 1979.

———. Interview with Terry Gross. *Fresh Air*. National Public Radio. WUWM, Milwaukee. 21 Aug. 1990.

———. Interview with Terry Gross. *Fresh Air*. National Public Radio. WUWM, Milwaukee. 2 Nov. 1994.

———. *In the Lake of the Woods*. Boston: Houghton/Seymour Lawrence, 1994.

———. *The Things They Carried*. Boston: Houghton/Seymour Lawrence, 1990.

———. "The Vietnam in Me." *New York Times Magazine* 2 Oct. 1994: 48–57.

O'Neill, William L. *Coming Apart: An Informal History of America in the 1960s*. New York: Quadrangle/Times, 1971.

Palmer, Laura. "The Nurses of Vietnam, Still Wounded." *New York Times Magazine* 7 Nov. 1993: 36+.

Parks, David. *G.I. Diary*. New York: Harper, 1968.

Patrick, Robert. *Kennedy's Children*. New York: Random, 1976.

Paul, Elizabeth A. "Wounded Healers: A Summary of the Vietnam Nurses Veterans Project." *Military Medicine* 150 (1985): 571–76.

Pearce, Roy Harvey. *Savagism and Civilization: A Study of the Indian and the American Mind*. 1965. Baltimore: Johns Hopkins UP, 1967.

The Pentagon Papers: The Defense Department History of United States Decisionmaking on Vietnam. Senator Gravel ed. 5 vols. Boston: Beacon, 1971.

Perlmutter, Emanuel. "Head of Building Trades Unions Here Says Response Favors Friday's Action." *New York Times* 12 May 1970: 18.

Perry, Mark. "First, They Have to Find You: The Return of Oliver Stone's Platoon." *VVA Veteran* Sept. 1987: 15–21.

Pfarrer, Donald. Interview. *Milwaukee Journal* 6 June 1982, entertainment sec.: 1+.

———. *Neverlight*. 1982. New York: Laurel-Dell, 1984.

Phillips, Dean K. "The Case for Veterans' Preference." Figley and Leventman 343–62.

Phillips, Jayne Anne. *Machine Dreams*. 1984. New York: Pocket, 1985.

Plato. *Republic 5*. Trans. S. Halliwell. Warminster: Aris and Phillips, 1993.

Plummer, William. "*Moby Dick* in Vietnam." Review of *The 13th Valley*, by John M. Del Vecchio. *Newsweek* 26 July 1982: 71.

Pratt, John Clark. *The Laotian Fragments*. 1974. New York: Avon, 1985.

Proffitt, Nicholas. "Pete Bravado's War and Peace." Review of *Buffalo Afternoon*, by Susan Fromberg Schaeffer. *New York Times Book Review* 21 May 1989: 7.

Pruitt, James N. *Striker One Down*. New York: TOR/Tom Doherty, 1987.

Puller, Lewis B., Jr. *Fortunate Son: The Autobiography of Lewis B. Puller, Jr.* New York: Grove Weidenfeld, 1991.

Rabe, David. *The Vietnam Plays, Volume One: The Basic Training of Pavlo Hummel, Sticks and Bones.* New York: Grove, 1993.

———. *The Vietnam Plays, Volume Two: Streamers, The Orphan.* New York: Grove, 1993.

Rafferty, Terrence. Review of *Platoon,* dir. Oliver Stone. *Nation* 17 Jan. 1987: 54–56.

Rambo: First Blood Part Two. Dir. George P. Cosmatos. Tri-Star, 1985.

Reed, Fred. "A Veteran Writes." *Harper's* Dec. 1980: 42–45.

Reich, Charles A. *The Greening of America: How the Youth Revolution Is Trying to Make America Livable.* New York: Random, 1970.

Remarque, Erich Maria. *All Quiet on the Western Front.* 1928. Trans. A. W. Wheen. New York: Fawcett, 1982.

The Return of the Secaucus Seven. Dir. John Sayles. Salsipuedes/Libra, 1980.

Rich, Frank. "The Dark at the End of the Tunnel." Review of *Coming Home,* dir. Hal Ashby. *Time* 20 Feb. 1978: 68.

Ricoeur, Paul. *Time and Narrative.* 3 vols. Vols. 1–2 trans. Kathleen McLaughlin and David Pellauer; vol. 3 trans. Kathleen Blamey and David Pellauer. Chicago: U of Chicago P, 1984–1988.

Riesman, David. *Abundance for What? and Other Essays.* Garden City: Doubleday, 1964.

———. *The Lonely Crowd: A Study of the Changing American Character.* New Haven: Yale UP, 1950.

Riffaterre, Michael. *Fictional Truth.* Baltimore: Johns Hopkins UP, 1990.

Ringnalda, Don. *Fighting and Writing the Vietnam War.* Jackson: UP of Mississippi, 1994.

Roberts, Suzanne. *Vietnam Nurse.* New York: Ace, 1966.

Rowlandson, Mary. "Narrative of the Captivity of Mrs. Mary Rowlandson." *Narratives of the Indian Wars, 1675–1699.* Ed. Charles H. Lincoln. New York: Scribner's, 1913. 107–67.

Ruddick, Sara. *Maternal Thinking: Toward a Politics of Peace.* Boston: Beacon, 1989.

———. "Notes toward a Feminist Peace Politics." Cooke 109–27.

Rusk, Dean, and Richard Rusk. *As I Saw It.* New York: Norton, 1990.

Sacks, Peter M. *The English Elegy: Studies in the Genre from Spenser to Yeats.* Baltimore: Johns Hopkins UP, 1985.

Sakai, Joe. *Sex Slaves of the Viet Cong.* [New York: Star Distributors], n.d.

Salisbury, Harrison E., ed. *Vietnam Reconsidered: Lessons from a War.* New York: Harper, 1984.

The Sands of Iwo Jima. Dir. Allan Dwan. Republic, 1949.

Santoli, Al. *Everything We Had: An Oral History of the Vietnam War by Thirty-Three American Soldiers Who Fought It.* 1981. New York: Ballantine, 1982.

Savage, Paul L., and Richard A. Gabriel. "Cohesion and Disintegration in the American Army: An Alternative Perspective." *Armed Forces and Society* 2 (1976): 340–76.

———. *Crisis in Command: Mismanagement in the Army.* New York: Hill and Wang, 1978.

Sayles, John. "Tan." *Soldiers and Civilians: Americans at War and at Home*. Ed. Tom Jenks. New York: Bantam, 1986. 107–125.

Scammon, Richard M., and Ben J. Wattenberg. *The Real Majority: An Extraordinary Examination of the American Electorate*. New York: Coward-McCann, 1970.

Schaeffer, Susan Fromberg. *Buffalo Afternoon*. New York: Knopf, 1989.

Schroeder, Eric James. *Vietnam, We've All Been There: Interviews with American Writers*. Westport, Conn.: Praeger, 1992.

Schumacher, Michael. "Writing Stories from Life." *Writer's Digest* Apr. 1991: 34–39.

Severo, Richard, and Lewis Milford. *The Wages of War: When America's Soldiers Came Home—From Valley Forge to Vietnam*. New York: Simon, 1989.

Sexton, Patricia, and Brendan Sexton. *Blue Collars and Hard-Hats: The Working Class and the Future of American Politics*. New York: Random, 1971.

Shapley, Deborah. *Promise and Power: The Life and Times of Robert McNamara*. Boston: Little, 1993.

Shay, Jonathan. *Achilles in Vietnam: Combat Trauma and the Undoing of Character*. New York: Atheneum, 1994.

Sheehan, Neil. *A Bright Shining Lie: John Paul Vann and America in Vietnam*. New York: Random, 1988.

Shepley, James R. "A Letter from the Publisher." *Time* 26 May 1967: 11.

Slotkin, Richard. *Regeneration through Violence: The Mythology of the American Frontier, 1600–1860*. Middletown, Conn.: Wesleyan UP, 1973.

Slotkin, Richard, and James K. Folsom, eds. *So Dreadfull a Judgment: Puritan Responses to King Philip's War, 1676–1677*. Middletown, Conn.: Wesleyan UP, 1978.

Smith, Clark. "Oral History as 'Therapy': Combatants' Accounts of the Vietnam War." Figley and Leventman 9–34.

Smith, Daniel Scott. "The Dating of the American Sexual Revolution: Evidence and Interpretation." *The American Family in Social-Historical Perspective*. Ed. Michael Gordon. New York: St. Martin's, 1973. 321–35.

Smith, Henry Nash. *Virgin Land: The American West as Symbol and Myth*. Rev. ed. Cambridge: Harvard UP, 1970.

Smith, Winnie. *American Daughter Gone to War: On the Front Lines with an Army Nurse in Vietnam*. New York: Morrow, 1992.

Smitherman, Geneva. *Talkin and Testifyin: The Language of Black America*. Boston: Houghton, 1977.

Smitten, Jeffrey R., and Ann Daghistany, eds. *Spatial Form in Narrative*. Ithaca: Cornell UP, 1981.

Snyder, Gary. *Earth House Hold: Technical Notes and Queries to Fellow Dharma Revolutionaries*. New York: New Directions, 1969.

———. *Turtle Island*. New York: New Directions, 1974.

Soldier Blue. Dir. Ralph Nelson. Avco-Embassy, 1970.

Sollors, Werner. *Beyond Ethnicity: Consent and Descent in American Culture*. New York: Oxford UP, 1986.

Sontag, Susan. *Styles of Radical Will.* 1969. New York: Farrar, 1987.

Stanton, Shelby L. *Vietnam Order of Battle.* New York: Galahad, 1987.

Stevens, Robert Warren. *Vain Hopes, Grim Realities: The Economic Conse-quences of the Vietnam War.* New York: Watts-New Viewpoints, 1976.

Stockdale, James B. *A Vietnam Experience: Ten Years of Reflection.* Stanford: Hoover, 1984.

Stone, Oliver. Address to the National Press Club. National Public Radio. 7 Apr. 1987. Rpt. as the Afterword to *Oliver Stone's* Platoon *and* Salvador, 249–54.

——. *Oliver Stone's* Platoon *and* Salvador: *The Original Screenplays.* New York: Random, 1987.

——. "One from the Heart." *American Film* Jan.-Feb. 1987: 17+. Rpt. as the Foreword to *Oliver Stone's* Platoon *and* Salvador, 5–12.

——, dir. *Born on the Fourth of July.* Universal, 1989.

——, dir. *Heaven and Earth.* Warner, 1993.

——, dir. *Platoon.* Orion, 1986. Videocassette. Home Box Office, 1988.

——, dir. *Wall Street.* Twentieth-Century Fox, 1987.

Summers, Harry G., Jr. Editorial. *Vietnam* Dec. 1993: 6.

——. *Vietnam War Almanac.* New York: Facts on File, 1985.

Tatum, James. "The *Iliad* and Memories of War." *Yale Review* 76.1 (1986): 15–31.

Taxi Driver. Dir. Martin Scorsese. Columbia, 1976.

Taylor, Clyde. "Black Consciousness in the Vietnam Years." C. Taylor 7–20.

——, ed. *Vietnam and Black America: An Anthology of Protest and Resis-tance.* Garden City: Anchor-Doubleday, 1973.

Taylor, Ella. *Prime-Time Families: Television Culture in Postwar America.* Berkeley: U of California P, 1989.

Terkel, Studs. *Working: People Talk about What They Do All Day and How They Feel about What They Do.* New York: Pantheon, 1974.

Terry, Wallace. *Bloods: An Oral History of the Vietnam War by Black Veterans.* 1984. New York: Ballantine, 1985.

——. "Bringing the War Home." *Black Scholar* 2.3 (1970): 6–18.

Theweleit, Klaus. "The Bomb's Womb and the Genders of War (War Goes on Preventing Women from Becoming the Mothers of Invention)." Cooke 283–315.

Thomas, Cal. "Quayle Not Alone in Avoiding Vietnam Service." *Milwaukee Journal* 25 Aug. 1988, sec. A: 21.

Tick, Edward. "Apocalypse Continued." *New York Times Magazine* 13 Jan. 1985: 60.

Tollefson, James W. *The Strength Not to Fight: An Oral History of Conscien-tious Objectors of the Vietnam War.* Boston: Little, 1993.

Tomasulo, Frank P. "The Politics of Ambivalence: *Apocalypse Now* as Prowar and Antiwar Film." Dittmar and Michaud 145–58.

Top Gun. Dir. Tony Scott. Paramount, 1986.

Tour of Duty. Created by L. Travis Clark and Steve Duncan. CBS, 24 Sept. 1987–25 Aug. 1990.

Towers, Robert. "All-American Novels." Review of *Paco's Story,* by Larry Heinemann; *That Night,* by Alice McDermott; and *Cigarettes,* by Harry Mathews. *New York Review of Books* 21 Jan. 1988: 26–27.

Trillin, Calvin. "The War in Kansas." *New Yorker* 22 Apr. 1967: 56–145.

Uncommon Valor. Dir. Ted Kotcheff. Paramount, 1983.

"Uncorrelated Information Relating to Missing Americans in Southeast Asia." Department of Defense, vol. XV. 15 Dec. 1978.

"The Unquiet Earth." Writ. Alan Brennert. *China Beach.* Dir. Michael Rhodes. Prod. Mimi Leder. ABC. WISN, Milwaukee. 20 Sept. 1989.

Updike, John. *Rabbit Redux.* New York: Knopf, 1971.

Van Breems, Arlene. "Feminists Zero In on Volunteerism." *Los Angeles Times* 7 Sept. 1971, sec. 4: 1+.

Van Devanter, Lynda, with Christopher Morgan. *Home before Morning: The Story of an Army Nurse in Vietnam.* 1983. New York: Warner, 1984.

Victims of the Cong. New York: Star Distributors, n.d.

Viet Cong Rape Compound. New York: Star Distributors, 1982.

"The Vote Is In." *VVA Veteran* Aug. 1987: 9–11.

Waldman, Elizabeth, and Kathryn R. Gover. "Employment Situation of Vietnam Era Veterans." *Monthly Labor Review* 94.9 (1971): 3–11.

Walker, Alice. *Meridian.* New York: Harcourt, 1976.

Walker, Keith. *A Piece of My Heart: The Stories of Twenty-Six American Women Who Served in Vietnam.* 1985. New York: Ballantine, 1987.

Walzer, Michael. *Just and Unjust Wars: A Moral Argument with Historical Illustrations.* 2nd ed. New York: Basic, 1992.

Webb, James. *Fields of Fire.* 1978. New York: Bantam, 1979.

Weston, Jessie L. *From Ritual to Romance.* 1920. New York: Peter Smith, 1941.

White, Hayden. *Tropics of Discourse: Essays in Cultural Criticism.* Baltimore: Johns Hopkins UP, 1978.

Whitmore, Terry, with Richard Weber. *Memphis-Nam-Sweden: The Autobiography of a Black American Exile.* Garden City: Doubleday, 1971.

Whyte, William H. Jr. *The Organization Man.* New York: Simon, 1956.

Williams, Chancellor. *The Destruction of Black Civilization: Great Issues of a Race from 4500 B.C to 2000 A.D.* Rev. ed. Chicago: Third World, 1974.

Williams, David R. *Wilderness Lost: The Religious Origins of the American Mind.* Selinsgrove, Pa.: Susquehanna UP, 1987.

Williams, John A. *Captain Blackman.* 1972. New York: Thunder's Mouth, 1988.

Williams, Raymond. *Marxism and Literature.* Oxford: Oxford UP, 1977.

Williams, Robert F. "USA: The Potential of a Minority Revolution." *Crusader* 5.4 (1964): 1–7.

Williams, Roger. *A Key into the Language of America.* 1643. Ed. R. C. Alston. English Linguistics, 1500–1800: A Collection of Facsimile Reprints, No. 299. Menston, England: Scolar Press, 1971.

Williams, Tony. "Narrative Patterns and Mythic Trajectories in Mid-1980s Vietnam Movies." Anderegg 114–39.

Willson, David A. *REMF Diary.* Seattle: Black Heron, 1988.

———. *The REMF Returns.* Seattle: Black Heron, 1992.

The Winter Soldier Investigation: An Inquiry into American War Crimes. Boston: Beacon, 1972.

Winthrop, John. "A Model of Christian Charity." P. Miller 79–84.

Wohl, Robert. *The Generation of 1914.* Cambridge: Harvard UP, 1979.

Wolff, Tobias. *In Pharoah's Army: Memories of the Lost War.* New York: Knopf, 1994.

Young, Marilyn B. *The Vietnam Wars, 1945–1990.* New York: Harper, 1991.

Zeitlin, M., K. G. Lutterman, and J. W. Russell. "Death In Vietnam: Class, Poverty, and the Risks of War." *Politics and Society* 3 (1973): 313–28.

Zumwalt, Elmo, Jr., and Elmo Zumwalt III, with John Pekkanen. *My Father, My Son.* New York: Macmillan, 1986.

Index

Text:	10/13 Sabon
Display:	Sabon
Compositor:	J. Jarrett Engineering, Inc.
Printer and Binder:	Haddon Craftsmen, Inc.